The Oxfam Gender Training Manual

Suzanne Williams
with Janet Seed
and Adelina Mwau

With contributions from Oxfam staff and others

Oxfam
(UK and Ireland)

Published by Oxfam UK and Ireland 1994

Reprinted by Oxfam GB, 1998, 1999

ISBN 0 85598 267 5

A catalogue record for this publication is available from the British Library.

Available from the following agents:
USA: Stylus Publishing LLC, PO Box 605, Herndon, VA 20172-0605, USA
tel: +1 (0)703 661 1581; fax: + 1(0)703 661 1547; email: styluspub@aol.com
Canada: Fernwood Books Ltd, PO Box 9409, Stn. 'A', Halifax, N.S. B3K 5S3, Canada
tel: +1 (0)902 422 3302; fax: +1 (0)902 422 3179; e-mail: fernwood@istar.ca
India: Maya Publishers Pvt Ltd, 113-B, Shapur Jat, New Delhi-110049, India
tel: +91 (0)11 649 4850; fax: +91 (0)11 649 1039; email: surit@del2.vsnl.net.in
K Krishnamurthy, 23 Thanikachalan Road, Madras 600017, India
tel: +91 (0)44 434 4519; fax: +91 (0)44 434 2009; email: ksm@md2.vsnl.net.in
South Africa, Zimbabwe, Botswana, Lesotho, Namibia, Swaziland: David Philip Publishers, PO Box 23408, Claremont 7735, South Africa
tel: +27 (0)21 64 4136; fax: +27(0)21 64 3358; email: dppsales@iafrica.com
Tanzania: Mkuki na Nyota Publishers, PO Box 4246, Dar es Salaam, Tanzania
tel/fax: +255 (0)51 180479, email: mkuki@ud.co.tz
Australia: Bush Books, PO Box 1958, Gosford, NSW 2250, Australia
tel: +61 (0)2 043 233 274; fax: +61 (0)2 092 122 468, email: bushbook@ozemail.com.au

For the rest of the world, contact Oxfam Publishing, 274 Banbury Road, Oxford OX2 7DZ, UK.
tel + 44 (0)1865 311311; fax + 44 (0)1865 313925; email publish@oxfam.org.uk

Published by Oxfam GB, 274 Banbury Road, Oxford OX2 7DZ, UK

Designed and typeset by Oxfam Design Department OX1428/PK/94
Printed by Information Press Ltd.
Set in Times 12 pt

Oxfam GB is registered as a charity (no. 202918) and is a member of Oxfam International.

Contents

C.11 Strategies for change 557

C.12 Evaluations 589

Resources

Acknowledgements

This manual is the result of the work of gender trainers all over the world, over many years. The majority of the activities presented here have been used by Oxfam trainers in workshops and training courses in Africa, Asia, Latin America and the Middle East, or in courses run in the UK for Oxfam staff. Many of these activies were developed by Oxfam staff; many more have been used and adapted by so many trainers over the years that it is impossible to trace their original sources. However, wherever we have been able to identify the source, we have always cited it. Thanks are due to gender trainers who sent us activities specifically for this Manual: they are Carola Carbojal, Sheelu Francis, Michelle Friedman, Irene Guijt and Alice Welbourn.

Thanks are also due to those who read and commented on the early drafts — Judy El-Bushra, Sheelu Francis, Michelle Friedman, Irene Guijt, Naila Kabeer, Itziar Lozano, Nicky May, Eugenia Piza-Lopez, Janet Sly and especially Bridget Walker. We are grateful for the feedback from Irungu Houghton, Wanjiku Mukabi Kabira, Wambui Kimathi, Masheti Masinjila, Anne Obura and Dutea Onyango, who attended a three-day readers' workshop on the Manual in Kenya.

Betty Hawkins keyed in all the material (more than once). Many thanks to her for this arduous task, and also to Rebecca Dale and Charlotte Higgins for their help.

Suzanne Williams researched, collated, wrote, and edited the Manual, with the help of Janet Seed, who contributed material, advised on the Facilitator's notes, and wrote sections B and C9. Adelina Mwau contributed material and ideas, and convened the Kenya readers' workshop.

This book has drawn on the work of gender trainers, and writers on gender issues, from all over the world. Wherever possible, the source is given for each activity and handout, unless the material was provided by one of the authors, or by Oxfam. Oxfam is grateful to the following individuals and organisations for permission to use published material: Aga Khan Foundation Canada; Mary Anderson; Michelle Friedman; Sara Hlupekile Longwe; Liz Mackenzie and CACE Publications, University of the Western Cape; Mambo Press, Zimbabwe; Caroline O N Moser; Margaret Murray; New Internationalist Magazine; Dave Richards; Alice Welbourn; Whyld Publishing Co-op; Zed Books. We have been unable to trace the sources and copyright holders for some of the material included. We would be glad to hear from anyone whose material has not been fully acknowledged, so that any omissions can be corrected should the book be reprinted.

Oxfam is grateful to Swiss Development Co-operation (SDC) for their generous contribution towards the cost of producing and distributing this manual.

Foreword

'At this training we have learnt that women are all the same: they fight for survival, and do not wait for a man to bring food.'

'We have shared freely and learnt from each other, building sisterhood. I know now that as a woman I have no country, no tribe; my tribe, my country, is the whole world.'

'Nobody can stop me using what I have learnt at this workshop.'

The voices are those of participants at gender training sessions in Kenya and Tanzania. They show the potential of gender training to transform people's perceptions of themselves and their communities. The Oxfam Gender Training Manual represents the experience of Oxfam (United Kingdom and Ireland) of using gender training in the implementation of gender policy, enabling women to end their vulnerability, assert their power, and effect positive change.

Oxfam's Gender and Development Unit (GADU) was set up in 1985 to address a growing concern that many development initiatives, far from benefiting women, were actually marginalising them and rendering them powerless. Since the early days of GADU's existence, gender training has been a key strategy, used to sensitise Oxfam staff and partners to gender issues, and to learn from our grassroots experience.

Throughout the world, women's marginalisation is justified on the grounds of culture and tradition. Current global political and economic trends are worsening women's poverty and vulnerability. In 1992, Oxfam ratified an organisational gender policy, formalising its commitment to positive action to promote the full participation and empowerment of women in existing and future programmes, and to ensure that development benefits both women and men equally.

Trainers from within GADU and outside Oxfam have conducted workshops and training sessions with our partner organisations, and women at grassroots level, in order to ensure that women's voices are heard, and Oxfam can respond to their needs.

Together with planning, monitoring and evaluation, and recruitment, gender training is a tool in the process of implementing gender-fair development, rather than an end in itself. Rather than promoting a mechanical implementation of gender equitable development, gender training aims to develop thought and action in a transformational manner, enabling participants to explore the issues, understand the dynamics of their societies and apply the concept of gender analysis to everyday development practice.

Gender training seeks to stimulate recognition and respect for women's own knowledge, leading to increased awareness and ability to address gender inequity. It is concerned, not with others, but with us ourselves, our work and our organisations. As such, it is a two-way process where facilitators and participants share knowledge and learn together.

Gender training differs from other forms of training in several important ways. First, it challenges the beliefs of both participants and trainers, consciously and unconsciously. Gender training forces everyone involved to examine themselves and their relationships with others. Once it is initiated at a training session, the process of gender sensitisation continues in daily life.

Conducting gender training requires a wide range of skills: knowledge of development, and of the theory of gender analysis; interpersonal skills; commitment to multiculturalism; and respect for the views of others. Trainers are often required to deal with resistance: they need to accept that for some, working towards gender equity is not, and will never be, a priority. A good gender trainer will be passionate about the work, and committed to enabling women to determine their own destiny, through supporting the personal development of both women and men, and recognising that men can and should play an active role in this transformation.

This Manual is the result of an interactive learning process between Oxfam's Gender Team, field staff, and women's resource centres. The training methods featured here have been developed in a co-operative and collective manner. Wherever possible, acknowledgement has been given in the Manual of the origin of each exercise; however, with many, tracing this origin has not been possible. As feminist historians have proved over the past decades, the contribution of women, especially poor women from the South, has often been ignored and their creativity appropriated by louder voices in the North. Oxfam respects these facts, and acknowledges the valuable work of those whose names are not known.

In the Gender Team, training work has been mostly carried out by Eugenia Piza Lopez, Jan Seed, and Bridget Walker, with the support of Oxfam's field staff, including Adelina Mwau, Vishalakshi Padmanabhan, Galuh Wandita, Lot Felizco, Sonia Vasquez, Assitan Coulibaly, and Mariam Dem. Suzanne Williams, who has extensive experience in gender and development work, and a close association with the Gender Team, was asked to help us to put together a training resource. A debt of gratitude is owed to her and to Jan Seed and Adelina Mwau, for their roles in the development of the Manual. In this process, they have drawn upon the richness of Oxfam's experience of working with trainers from all over the world.

Finally, thanks are due to the pioneering work of those who have developed theoretical frameworks which enable practitioners to understand gender and development theory. These include Caroline Moser, Sara Hlupekile Longwe, Maxine Molyneaux and Naila Kabeer. Thanks to them, we are able to assess and challenge their thinking, and our own practice.

Eugenia Piza Lopez
Gender Team Leader
Oxfam UK/I

Preface

In recent years Oxfam has made a firm commitment to address gender inequality and the impoverishment of women in all its development and relief work, and to seek models and methods which respond to women's specific needs as well as those they share with men. This is a task which provides a continuous challenge. The field of gender analysis is constantly developing, and Oxfam's contribution to this field is part of a learning process which we share with our counterpart organisations all over the world.

In the spirit of this mutual learning about gender, we have put together a training manual which draws on our experience over the years, and the work of many colleagues in the North and the South. The conceptual framework is based on the work of many writers and practitioners in the field of gender and development, and on the work of Oxfam's Gender and Development Team. Within this framework, we have put together a large number of participatory activities which have been tested in gender workshops and training courses all over the world — most have been used by Oxfam trainers for training field staff and men and women from amongst our counterparts in development. They have been gathered from a variety of sources and reflect the experiences and approaches of women from different cultural, economic and national backgrounds.

This manual is designed for the use of staff of non-governmental organisations (NGOs) who have some experience in running workshops or training courses, and for experienced gender trainers. Its aim is to provide practical tools for the training of development workers who are in a position to influence the planning and implementation of development and relief programmes at different levels. While the manual offers an introduction to the basic concepts used in gender analysis and how to apply them to practical work, the activities are not intended for awareness-raising for grassroots groups.

We hope this will be a special contribution to the field of gender training. There has been a strong demand from the NGO sector for training materials of this kind. When Oxfam's Gender and Development Unit (now the Gender Team) was established in 1985, training in gender awareness was the first and most urgent demand from the field offices for its services. Over the past seven years Oxfam trainers have carried out gender training in Latin America, Asia, and Africa, as well as with staff in the UK headquarters through regularly-programmed Gender and Development and Gender and Communications courses. The demand is still growing, from within and outside Oxfam. We trust that this manual will be a helpful response to what is an encouraging growth of awareness in the NGO sector of the central importance of gender analysis in development and relief work.

A distinctive feature of this manual is that it combines self-awareness work, through activities which address women's and men's self-awareness and gender awareness, with training in methods of gender analysis. We believe that self-awareness in relation to gender is central to training development and relief agency staff in the use of analytical tools. Awareness training addresses attitudes, perceptions and beliefs; unless people are sensitive to gender inequalities, gender analysis training is unlikely in the long run to change planning and practice in development and relief agencies' work. We believe that unless people's emotions are touched, and their practices in their personal lives are brought into the discussion, there is a risk that gender awareness will remain merely an intellectual construct, and will be limited in its power to bring about meaningful social change.

We have produced this manual in a format to facilitate reproduction of the activities, handouts and other material. Please use it in this way, but always cite the source clearly: **The Oxfam Gender Training Manual,** whenever you copy parts of the manual.

Finally, as we are engaged in a process of constant renewal of our ideas and revitalisation of our experience, we would welcome hearing from you, as users, with your feedback on the manual, as well as your discoveries and new insights in the field of gender training.

Suzanne Williams
Oxford, September1994

A.1 A guide to this manual

Welcome to this Manual! Before you take the plunge into it, here are a few notes to help you find your way around it.

Basic Structure

The Manual begins with information and ideas for you, the trainer/facilitator. The **Introductory Section A2** offers a brief summary of the **Key concepts** related to Gender and Gender and Development for your reference throughout the course; **Section B** presents detailed **Facilitator's guidelines** with the principles behind gender training, and steps to follow when planning and carrying out a workshop.

Section C is organised like a training course or workshop. The topic sections are roughly in the order they should be used, but we have not set them out as a pre-designed course. By selecting the topics you need, you should be able to run a range of different courses appropriate to the needs of your group, from a day-long gender analysis workshop for NGO emergency staff to a two-week course for project workers on gender awareness, analysis and planning. **Section C**. flows like this:

Sections C.1 and C.2 start the group off, and begin to look at participants' views about development (**Introductions** and **Expectations; Sharing work experience** and **Consensus on development**). Any course you run will need to start off with some of these activities.

Section C.3 contains a number of activities on **Gender awareness** and **Self-awareness for women and men.** Some of these are for women or men only, other are for mixed groups. The women- or men-only ones could also be used with mixed groups; this depends on your particular group, its needs, and its level of awareness, its capacity to take risks. You will be the best judge of this!

Because we believe that in gender training you should not separate self-awareness from analysis, we suggest you always include some of the activities in **Section C.3**. How deep you want to go will depend on how much time you have; but don't leave it out altogether.

Sections C.4, C.5 and C.6. begin to move into gender analysis and more in-depth exploration of concepts and ideas about development and relief work. **Gender roles and needs** are followed by suggested factual inputs on **Women in the world**, and work on **Gender and development**, including wrong assumptions about women and development, the concepts of participation and empowerment, and their application to development and relief work.

The roles and needs activities are essential for laying the foundations for gender analysis, particularly the Moser method, which is taught in detail in **Section C.7, Gender-sensitive appraisal and planning**. Wrong assumptions should always be counteracted by facts about women.

Section C.7 includes activities on a range of different gender frameworks of analysis used by Oxfam (**Moser, Harvard, UNHCR, CVA, Longwe, Munroe**) and a number of **Case study** activities. Some of the case studies are linked to the frameworks, others are presented with questions to bring out particular issues. This section also contains a set of guidelines for preparing and writing your own case studies.

This section must be preceded by activities from the sections outlined above, unless you are working with a group already very well-versed in gender analysis, who need only a follow-up or more advanced training.

Section C.8, Gender and global issues uses the analysis and awareness learned in the workshop to look at particular issues from a gender perspective: these include conflict, environmental issues, economic crisis, and culture. Many of these activities require a great deal of preparation from you, the facilitators, and from the participants, as they are most effective when using case studies drawn from your own, or the group's, experience.

Section C.9 follows the global perspective with a much closer focus on how to set about **working with women and men** in NGOs, in villages and communities. Having learned gender analysis, how do you build it into your practice?

Section C.10 on Gender and communications, which is about making and using images and text to communicate gender-sensitive messages, could itself form the core of a specific workshop, but is presented here as an element of any gender training.

Section C.11 looks at **Strategies for change:** planning and implementing work on gender. This is a critical section, and a gender training workshop must always finish up with participants formulating some concrete plans for using the insights and skills they have learned in their development and relief practice.

Section C.12 concludes the workshop with activities designed for participants and facilitators to **evaluate** what has and has not been learned. This will help you in your future planning as a facilitator, and also gives participants some yardstick for their own progress, and future training needs.

Some hints and warnings!

❑ Always read the *Facilitator's Notes* on each activity before you select it. Some of them need preparation of several months ahead — to prepare case studies, for example — and some need setting up visits to villages or local NGOs. Some are suitable for only women, some for only men, some for groups with little understanding of gender, some with an advanced understanding of gender. The *Facilitator's Notes* will always indicate how the activity has been used, or should be used, and often has suggestions of ways you could adapt the it for your specific purposes, so that you can use some of your own creative skill!

❑ At the beginning of each section, you will find a list of the activities in it, with the accompanying **Handouts**, and the timing for the activities. These are approximate, giving you a guide so you can plan your workshop. All the activities and handouts are listed in the Contents List, and a short topic index at the back of the Manual gives you a quick guide into the way subjects are covered, and where to find them.

❑ It is tempting to pick out activities because they look attractive — don't do it that way! Work out your aims and objectives, identify the needs of your group, plan the workshop **then** choose activities which meet your requirements.

❑ The Handouts are designed to be easy to photocopy. We have tried to keep the explanatory or analytical sections at the beginning of the Manual short, and put lots of information into the Handouts, so that participants will be able to take this information home with them. Because of this, some handouts are rather long, but you can adapt them as you need to.

❑ We have used the word 'flipchart' to describe the large sheets of blank paper, used in training sessions, which are bound together into a pad, and sometimes used on a flipchart-stand. These are not always available, so any large sheets of paper, such as newsprint, can be used instead. Similarly, we have used 'marker pens' to describe the large, often felt-tipped, pens commonly used by trainers; but other writing implements can be used where these are not available.

A.2 Key concepts

Gender

The key to understanding how development and relief work affects men, women, girls, and boys is grasping the concept of **gender**.

What is gender? The word was used by Ann Oakley and others in the 1970s to describe those characteristics of men and women which are **socially** determined, in contrast to those which are **biologically** determined. This distinction between gender and sex has very important implications, which are elaborated throughout this manual.

> *Essentially, the distinction between sex and gender is made to emphasise that everything women and men do, and everything expected of them, with the exception of their sexually distinct functions (childbearing and breastfeeding; impregnation) can change, and does change, over time and according to changing and varied social and cultural factors.*

The term **gender** can meet with resistance, amongst both native English speakers and speakers of other languages. Language and culture shape each other, and it says much about our deeply based cultural assumptions that a term to describe the possibility of change and variety in men and women's roles has been introduced so recently! But while the term itself may sound alien to many people, the concept resonates powerfully with the lived experience of both women and men. It is this concept that is important, and the early sections of this manual offer ways of making it real through experiential learning. (see **Section C3 Building Gender Awareness**).

> *A working definition of gender: people are born female or male, but learn to be girls and boys who grow into women and men. They are taught what the appropriate behaviour and attitudes, roles and activities are for them, and how they should relate to other people. This learned behaviour is what makes up gender identity, and determines gender roles.*

❑ **Gender is a dynamic concept:** gender roles for women and men vary greatly from one culture to another, and from one social group to another within the same culture. Race, class, economic circumstances, age — all of these influence what is considered appropriate for women and men. Furthermore, as culture is dynamic, and socio-economic conditions change over time, so gender patterns change with them. Sudden crises, like war or famine, can radically and rapidly change what men and women do — although sometimes (as women ex-combatants in liberation struggles have found) after the crisis the old attitudes may return. But sometimes the changes have a permanent impact.

❑ **Gender helps us to understand other differences:** understanding gender differentiation and gender discrimination helps us to understand differentiation and discrimination on other grounds. Different roles and characteristics are assigned to people not only on the basis of their gender, but of their race, caste, class, ethnic background and age. Our social analysis becomes finer, our social interventions more finely tuned, when we are aware of all the complex ways in which society slots people into different categories and roles, and of the ways these roles can be the basis of both cooperation and conflict. For neither women nor men form a homogeneous group in any society. Women may come into conflict with each other because of racial difference, or women of different nationalities or class groups may find solidarity in their gender identity.

Aspects of gender differentiation

The social construction of differentiated gender roles has profound implications for women and men:

❑ **In relation to work**: both women and men have roles in the spheres of production (of goods and services) and public life, from the community to the governmental level. However, the tasks associated with the reproduction of society (ensuring basic needs at family and household level are met, homes and children are maintained and cared for) fall almost entirely on women's shoulders. One of the results of this is that, the world over, women have longer working days than men.

Another key issue is the way work is valued. For all its enormous importance, reproductive work is undervalued — its lack of value is expressed by the failure to recognise that it is 'real' work. Women who labour in the home commonly say 'oh, I don't work', because their work is not recognised and remunerated. In the UK, for example, if the reproductive (or domestic) work of women were valued at current market rates, women would earn in the region of £12,000 to £15,000 a year for it.

The productive work of women is often seen as an extension of their reproductive work — and likewise undervalued. While men's agricultural work is often cultivating cash crops, for example, women's food production for family consumption is unpaid and taken for granted. Women, effectively, pay themselves, through self-provisioning. But their work is often not considered, by themselves as well as by others, to be 'real work'. (See **Handouts 21**and **22**: Mr Moyo goes to the Doctor and The Lie of the Land)

In the public sphere, at all levels, with a few notable exceptions, it is men who hold the high-status positions and have decision-making power: women tend to fill the roles of support persons and organisers. While men's work in this sphere is highly rewarded, women's work is often under-valued.

The inequalities in gender roles, and the resulting different needs of women and men, is explored in **Section C.4: Gender Roles and Needs**.

❑ **In relation to sharing the world's resources and benefits**: gender inequality is very evident. The often-quoted UN statistics still hold true:

- *women perform 2/3 of the world's work;*
- *women earn 1/10 of the world's income;*
- *women are 2/3 of the world's illiterates;*
- *women own less than 1/100 of the world's property*.

Access to resources and benefits, and control over them is allocated according to gender, in both obvious and quite subtle ways. In some societies, for example, women may not own land, and their access to it for growing food may depend on a male relative or husband. In other cases, there may be no explicit reason why women should not attend, say, literacy classes — but their access will be limited by their workload, and lack of extra hours or energy to take advantage of so-called equal opportunities. The notions of unequal access and control come up throughout this manual, and are more closely defined in **Section C.7: Gender-sensitive Appraisal and Planning.**

❑ **In relation to human rights:** the world over, women are denied their human rights. Gender differentiation is about inequality and about power relations between men and women. Half the world's people is subordinate to the other half, in thousands of different ways, because of the sex they are born with. Despite international human rights law which guarantees all people equal rights, irrespective of sex, race, caste and so on, women are denied equal rights with men to land, to property, to mobility, to education, to employment opportunities, to shelter, to food, to worship, and over the lives of their children. Women are denied the right even to manage, control and care for the health of their own bodies, and their reproductive functions. In many cultures women's bodies are ritually maimed and mutilated, and women are routinely beaten and even murdered in the name of cultural tradition, despite the fact that international human rights law prohibits cultural practices which are damaging to women. Violence against women is an abuse of human rights.

❑ **In relation to culture and religion**: women face the same discrimination as they do in other spheres, and both religion and culture are sources of gender oppression and inequality. While religions may teach equality between people, in practice women usually have a subordinate role and may be excluded altogether from the religious hierarchy. Different interpretations of religious texts, and different religious traditions within the Christian church, for example, have different implications for women. Religion nevertheless holds out the promise of equality and justice, and this is why despite its role as a powerful form of male control over the lives of women, it continues to be a source of hope and support to many women. There are many culturally-sanctioned practices — such as genital mutilation, and preferential feeding of boys — which damage women and make their lives more difficult and painful. Culture, however, like religion, can also be the source of cohesion and solidarity amongst women, and amongst women and men. Cultural aspects of gender come up throughout the manual, and some specific issues are discussed in activities in **Section C.8 Gender and Global Issues.**

Gender oppression takes a multitude of forms, and is an added dimension to oppression based on race, ethnic identity, class and caste. Its forms also vary with these factors, and we should never make assumptions about forms of gender oppression in cultures or social groups we do not fully understand. However, it is universal that women's experience of male domination is felt by them in every sphere of life — in political office, in the courts and judicial system, in the marketplace, in the classroom, in the clinic, in the trade union, in the community organisation, in the household, and in the bedroom.

On the road to social equity, gender is the last barrier, because it involves transformation of attitudes and practice in all societies, for all people: it touches all of us, all the way to our most intimate relationships. For this reason it arouses very strong feelings among both women and men, and these feelings are often brought out by gender awareness training. Section C.3: Building Gender Awareness, and Section C.9: Working with Women and Men, raise some of these issues.

Gender and development analysis

Development approaches

Gender and Development (GAD), and Women in Development (WID) are often used interchangeably, and programming with a gender focus is often thought to mean supporting more projects for women. It is important to remember that while these terms only incorporate 'development' they apply equally to relief in emergencies.

The WID approach usually seeks to integrate women into development by making more resources available to women, in an effort to increase women's efficiency in their existing roles. Very often, this approach has increased women's workloads, reinforced inequalities, and widened the gap between men and women.

The GAD approach seeks to base interventions on the analysis of men's and women's roles and needs in an effort to empower women to improve their position relative to men in ways which will benefit and transform society as a whole. GAD is thus driven by a powerful motivation — to work for equity and respect for human rights for all people. These approaches are presented in **Section C.6: Gender and Development**, which also explores the issues of women's empowerment and participation in development and relief in emergencies.

Gender awareness

Gender cannot simply be 'stitched on' to existing development models, nor added into development and relief programmes as an extra component. Gender awareness is not a separate or additional issue to be addressed; it is a way of seeing, a perspective, a set of insights which informs our understanding of people and society. As we have seen, gender is at the heart of human identity and all human attitudes, beliefs and actions. We take it for granted. Yet when we begin to look into it, and question our assumptions, we find that the world looks different.

Gender awareness means looking with new eyes, in a way which is constantly open to learning more. Looking into development and relief work with these new eyes reveals what is now well- documented in countless examples from all over the world: that women's needs, as distinct from men's, have been invisible in most agency planning until very recently, with the result that many development and relief programmes have not only failed to bring any improvements to women's lives, but have made them worse. It was this realisation which led to the closer examination of the impact of development on women, and to the beginnings of GADt analysis.

GAD analysis and planning

GAD analysis challenges development models which measure benefits in purely economic terms, and which are based, one way or another, on the old 'trickle-down' theory. This theory proposed that benefits fed into the top of social structures (like the household or family) or community organisations would 'trickle down' to everyone belonging to them. However, this has been shown over and over again not to work, because the relationships within communities and the household are not egalitarian, but based on complex systems governed by power and status.

Thus we cannot assume that 'community development' will benefit all the people within the community; within this social group there are always differences in power, determined by gender, class, caste, race, or religion, and combinations of all of these factors. Within the household, the favoured social unit of development and relief interventions, women do not have the same rights as men, and benefits at the household level are seldom shared equally between males and females. **(See Section C.2 Consensus on Development)**

Neither can we assume that emergency relief, delivered to people in extreme circumstances, will benefit women, men, and children equally. In refugee camps, for example, where women and children are usually the majority of the population, distribution of food is often controlled by men and is seldom allocated equitably between the sexes. Patterns of unequal resource distribution between women and men at community or household level are likely to persist even where these social units have been severely disrupted by conflict or by natural disasters.

The analytical tools of gender and development disaggregate, or take apart, these familiar conceptual units such as the community, the household, the family, and look at the relations and distribution of resources within them. 'Gender-disaggregated data' is information collected in a way which distinguishes between the different activities, aspirations, needs, and interests of women and men.

GAD tools and frameworks of analysis form the basis for gender-sensitive project appraisal and planning from a gender perspective. The activities which present them, and practical ways of using them, are to be found in **Section C.6 Gender and Development,** and **Section C.7 Gender-sensitive Appraisal and Planning.**

GAD tools of analysis and analytical frameworks

The gender division of labour

This refers to the different kinds of work done by men and women (**see above: Section 2.1. Gender**) and the different value ascribed to the work. The gender division of labour varies from one society and culture to another, and within them; it also changes with external circumstances and over time. Analysing the gender division of labour in any group can clarify the interdependence and cooperation, on one hand, and the inequalities and conflicts, on the other, in the work relationships of women and men. It is the understanding of these relationships which is fundamental for planning: we have to know how our support will affect the work done by women and by men, and how our interventions affect the relationships between women and men, and the way female and male tasks are related to each other.

Women's 'triple role'

This is a way of classifying the kind of work done by women.. As discussed above, it usually refers to reproductive, productive and community work. Women have a 'triple role', because it is predominantly women who carry out reproductive work. In this manual we take 'community work' to include all activity in the public sphere, from organising festivals and caring for the sick, to lobbying authorities for services, forming a trade union, or holding political office. It can be useful to distinguish between two forms of community role, referred to by Moser[2] as the community managing, and the community politics role. **(See Section C.4, Gender Roles and Needs)** The way these forms of work are valued affects the way women and men set priorities when it comes to planning programmes or projects. Childcare provision, for example, is not likely to be a priority for men in project planning: but it can make or break women's chances of taking advantage of development opportunities.

'Practical' and 'strategic' needs

The distinction between practical and strategic needs[3] and the analysis of women's triple role are part of what is called gender planning. **(See Section C.7: Gender-sensitive Appraisal and Planning)** This is a framework for gender analysis and planning developed by Moser, based on the distinction by Molyneux between women's and men's practical and strategic gender interests. In this manual we use notions of both needs and interests. For further discussion of these **see Section C.7.**

It is useful to think about this distinction in relation to the **condition** of women — the immediate, material circumstances in which they live — and their **position** in society relative to men, which is the way gender determines power, status, and control over decisions and resources.

Practical needs are related to the **condition** of women and their present workloads and responsibilities. They refer to, for example, the need for a clean and nearby water supply, stoves for more efficient cooking, credit schemes or seeds. These needs can be addressed by practical and short-term development interventions, but are in themselves unlikely to change unequal aspects of gender relations. Also, if practical needs are not seen within the context of strategic interests, addressing them in isolation can actually worsen women's situation in the long run.

Strategic needs arise from the analysis of women's subordination to men, and are related to changing women's **position**. These needs may include equal access to decision-making power, getting rid of institutionalised discrimination in the areas of labour, land ownership, and education, measures to eradicate male violence against women, and shared responsibility with men for child-rearing. It is critical that women themselves identify what the strategic issues and paths of action are for them. Response to practical needs, however, may be an important entry point into work with women, and needs to be done in a strategic way. For example, distributing food relief aid through women supports them in their customary authority over food, and also gives them a measure of control over its allocation. Addressing the strategic needs of women requires long-term planning, and changes in the attitudes of men. The issue of men's practical and strategic needs and interests raises a number of complex questions in relation to gender inequalities and power: these are discussed in **Section C.7.**

While these two categories of needs are a useful analytical tool, in practice they often overlap. For example, women's felt and immediate need for basic numeracy and literacy skills in order to operate in the local market may bring the longer-term strategic advantage of enabling them to participate more effectively in community organisations or training courses. On the other hand, there are dangers in supporting projects which address practical needs — say, for income — in ways which do not take strategic needs into account. Thus projects which support income-generating activities without components for training in accounting skills, management of organisations, and control over primary resources, may reinforce existing gender inequalities, and rob women of control over the benefits of the project.

The Harvard Analytical Framework: Access and Control

Analysing the gender division of labour and roles of women and men begins to give us insights into the power relationships within society and what they are built on. Power is vested in control over resources, such as land, equipment, other assets or labour, and over benefits, such as cash, or political prestige. Women may have *access* to some of these resources, such as land, but if they lack *control* over land they will be unable to assert their priorities for its use, and their access to the benefits of land cultivation will be restricted. Because women generally work longer hours than men, they have less access than men to one of the most precious resources: time. This in turn restricts women's access to social resources and benefits such as schools and training, which could open up new life-chances and income-earning opportunities.

The Harvard Analytical Framework[4] **(See Section C.7)** charts profiles of women's and men's activities, access to and control over resources and benefits, and the external factors (political, environmental, economic, cultural) which influence these profiles. This enables us to analyse the different ways in which these factors influence women and men at many different levels, and to look at other differentiating characteristics such as age, culture and class.

The People-oriented Analytical Framework

This is based on the Harvard Framework and was devised as a practical planning tool for refugee workers. While any tool or framework for gender analysis can be used in emergency relief work, the People-oriented Framework highlights concerns which are particularly acute for refugees: dramatic change in people's roles and resources, and issues related to legal and social protection. The theme of loss is central to this analysis.

Capacities and Vulnerabilities Analysis (CVA)

CVA emerged from the International Relief/Development Project coordinated at Harvard in the late 1980s, in which over 50 European and US NGOs collaborated. It can be applied to relief or development work, and points to their interconnectedness. It distinguishes between short-term, immediate needs of women and men in crisis, and their long-term vulnerabilities, which precede crisis, make them susceptible to it, and affect their capacity to respond to it. The CVA[5] framework stresses that it is people's capacities in emergencies which should be the focus of interventions: these capacities can be social, organisational, or resource-based, and strengthening them offers people the best chance of recovering from disaster. The framework allows for disaggregation by gender and other social factors, and can be used at any stage of the project or programme cycle.

Checklists

There is now a wide range of gender tools of analysis and planning, and gender analysis frameworks. In this manual we present only those which we have used, or which have been used by our contributors. A checklist of questions or criteria with which to measure women's development is a useful tool at both the appraisal and planning stage: indicators can then be based on these criteria to evaluate the success of development or relief programmes. A number of checklists are presented in **Section C.7**, with Activity 54 Checklists, which aims to enable participants to use them, or devise their own.

Tools of appraisal

Appraisal tools, such as Rapid Rural Appraisal (RRA) and Participatory Rural Appraisal (PRA), as well as others with more emphasis on participative learning, such as Participatory Learning Methods (PALM) or Participatory Assessment, Monitoring and Evaluation (PAME), have been developed with the assumption that because they use participatory methods, they will elicit information from women equally with men. Whether this is the case will depend on the social and cultural factors governing gender relations in any given area or social group, and the extent to which women are able to respond without fear. For these appraisal tools to be gender-sensitive, they have to be used by gender-aware practitioners, and be based on some pre-existing understanding of local determinants of gender relations. **Section C.7** presents some of the participatory tools of appraisal which can be used in gender analysis.

Participatory training

Training is a planned process designed to expand or refine skills and knowledge, and to examine attitudes, ideas and behaviour with a view to modifying them. It covers a wide range of learning, from technical skills, such as weaving or computer operation, to more complex sets of ideas which can challenge commonly and strongly held values and beliefs. Training is often short-term and intensive, as it is seen as complementary to broader education. It is usually targeted quite specifically to particular skills, people, or institutional needs.

The term — and even the concept of — training is sometimes seen as problematic. Some people in India have commented that it has militaristic connotations, and is thus particularly inappropriate for gender training. While we use this term in the manual, we are sensitive to the fact that all forms of education must be responsive to cultural and social differences and be adaptive and flexible.

A participatory approach to training

This approach is based on the belief that people learn more effectively when their own capacity and knowledge is valued, and when they are able to share and analyse their experiences in a safe collective environment. In the preparation of the training and throughout its process, the content should match people's needs and be appropriate to their life and work. The role of the trainer is to facilitate the process of learning, rather than to teach. This form of training owes much to the ideas of the Brazilian educator Paulo Freire[6]:

- Education based on the 'banking' approach, which aims to deposit information into passive pupils, is disempowering and oppressing; to be liberating, education should pose problems to people and provide frameworks for their active participation in solving them.
- Education must be based on people's needs and life experience.
- The educative process is one of exchange and dialogue, of reflection and action.

Experiential learning

People learn most effectively when they are active participants in the process. The activities in this manual use a variety of different techniques, exercises, and games to involve people in analysis and reflection about their experience. The activities present theories and frameworks of analysis to assist people in this process, and to lead them towards planning for action based on what they have learned. Experiential learning within a group means that people have the opportunity to share knowledge and problems with others and work together to find solutions. This also means that the building of group trust right at the beginning of any training which uses the experiential method, is crucial to its success.

The role of the facilitator is to help participants get as much as possible out of the activities and make sure that the key concepts and ideas are communicated and understood. She or he should also be ready to adapt the programme in response to needs and ideas which come up in the course of the training. This is further discussed in **Section B: Facilitator's guidelines.**

A word of warning about training

Training is a tool, a means to achieve certain objectives but not an end in itself. Problems or shortcomings will not be resolved by simply throwing training at them. For training to be worth doing and fulfil its objectives, it has to be part of a strategy within a structure which supports it. There have to be established policy, procedures and practice which take up the results of training. Otherwise, the danger is that training can be used by institutions as an excuse not to do anything else!

Endnotes

1 Ann Oakley, *Sex, Gender and Society*, first published in 1972 by Temple-Smith, London.

2 Caroline Moser defined the triple role of women as reproductive, productive, and community managing. Later in *Gender Planning and Development Theory Practice and Training*, published by Routledge, London, 1993, she distinguishes community management from community politics. These are examined in more detail in **Section C.4 Gender Roles and Needs**.

3 The distinction between women's practical and strategic interests was first defined by Maxine Molyneux in Molyneux M (1985) 'Mobilisation without emancipation? Women's interests, state and revolution in Nicaragua', *Feminist Studies*, 11 (2), and later developed into the notion of practical and strategic needs by Caroline Moser in 'Gender planning in the Third World: meeting practical and strategic gender needs', *World Development* 17; 11, 1989. See also *Changing Perceptions: Writings on Gender and Development*, ed. Wallace and March, Oxfam, Oxford, 1991.

4 This is outlined in Overholt, Anderson, Cloud and Austin (eds), *A Case Book: Gender Roles in Development Projects*, Kumarian Press, 1985.

5 The CVA framework of analysis is described in Anderson and Woodrow (1989) *Rising from the Ashes*, Westview Press/UNESCO.

6 Paulo Freire, in *Pedagogy of the Oppressed (1972, Penguin Books)*, states of the teacher-student relationship: 'problem-posing education, breaking the vertical patterns characteristic of banking education, can fulfil its function of being the practice of freedom only if it can overcome the contradiction [in the student-teacher relationship]. [Teacher and student] become jointly responsible for a process in which all grow.'

B Facilitator's guidelines

These guidelines are for you, the facilitator/trainer. Please read them **before** selecting the activities. Even if you are an experienced facilitator, there are particular issues to consider in planning gender training with this Manual. If you lack experience, read these guidelines carefully and plan your first workshops with experienced co-facilitators.

We have divided this section into three parts: **Key issues**, **The seven steps of planning,** and **Running the training.**

Key issues

What is gender training?

Gender training is a development intervention which aims to change awareness, knowledge, skills, and behaviour in relation to gender. It differs from training in some other subjects in that it touches on personal and political issues, even where this is not deliberately planned.

The term 'gender training' covers a variety of methods and approaches. These range from feminist-oriented workshops using techniques such as songs, games and discussions to raise awareness with grassroots women, to more formalised training in gender-aware project design for male or mixed groups of decision-makers in governments, multi-lateral agencies or NGOs.

In practice, there is not usually a clear-cut division between these approaches, and much gender training contains elements of both. Although the approaches seem to be different, they can both be seen to follow the development education principle of starting from people's own experience, whether it be the daily work of looking after the family or dealing with project documents.

Oxfam's experience, which is reflected in the content of this Manual, suggests that gender training works best if there is a strong element of awareness-raising as well as skills-building. Otherwise, there is a danger that techniques will be learnt, but prejudicial attitudes will still remain; or that awareness will be raised but work practices will not change. The exact balance of the two elements will depend on the particular training needs and characteristics of the groups, such as, job requirements, sex, and educational level.

Why gender training?

Gender training is becoming increasingly popular with many institutions, as a way to improve the quality of relief and development work. The negative effects of ignoring gender issues are now widely acknowledged. For example, projects may fail because women's key roles and contributions to the economy have been overlooked; women's workload may be increased as a result of development interventions and income-generating or credit schemes may fail to affect women's access to cash, because their husbands control the money. In addition, development agencies' commitment to social justice requires them to consider how power relations between men and women can become more balanced.

However, there is a difference between acknowledging the importance of gender issues, and being able to put this into practice. Most people working for development agencies do not intentionally discriminate against, or intend to disadvantage, women, yet that is what may happen if they do not have the necessary awareness and skills. *It is not enough to have good intentions.*

It has been shown that gender training *does* make a significant difference, but it is not a cure for all problems — changes in policy, procedures and staffing also need to be considered as alternatives or additions to training. Before deciding whether gender training is the right course of action, these key questions need to be asked:

- What is the problem?
- Is training (part of) the solution?
- How will training best be achieved?
- What is the desired outcome of the training?
- How will you know if success is realised?

It must be made clear what training can and cannot achieve — to avoid over-high expectations, inappropriate selection of trainees, and inappropriate content.

Preparation for success

The success of gender training in practice depends to a large extent on external factors — including attitudes and priorities of those in power within organisations, and pre-existing power struggles.

Training should be part of an overall strategy, leading to the desired change. This will involve development and implementation of an institutional gender policy, and changes to working procedures and practices, such as the ways in which projects and programmes are planned and monitored. It may involve changes of personnel, or changes in responsibilities of existing personnel.

Gender training is more likely to be successful if some preparatory work is done before the first workshop or training course is even planned. Poats and Russo[1] have found that training can serve as an extremely effective mechanism to integrate perspectives and gender analysis into the operations of a variety of institutions. They identify a number of key organisational issues which need to be addressed if gender training is to be successful.

1 There must be an explicit mandate for gender training from the top of the organisation, which must be clearly articulated to all the divisions of the institution as being relevant to them, not just the gender workers. This includes training the heads of the institution.

2 Training is a process and requires sufficient time for effectiveness. A series of

training courses may be the most effective system, with time to incorporate what has been learned into work practices.

3 Gender training must be managed and supported by strong,qualified professionals whose experience is respected within the organisation.

4 Someone, preferably full-time, from within the institution should have responsibility for training. External consultants may be used to do the training, but they need to work with someone from within the institution to co-ordinate logistics, and provide information on organisational culture, procedures, and participants, to the trainers.

5 Training is more effective and efficient when the same team, or at least members of that team, conducts the training over the initial training period when gender analysis is being introduced to the institution.

6 Training of trainers (TOT) is a critical element for achieving long-term integration of gender issues and analysis in an institution. TOT courses can be conducted either within or outside the institution.

7 Budgeting for a training programme must be comprehensive. Trainers require adequate resources and support personnel. Trainers need to give full attention to the process of training and thus need proper administrative and logistical support to enable them to do this. This should be budgeted for.

9 There is no single training strategy that will fit all institutions. Each training strategy, and each training workshop, must take into account the nature of the particular organisation and the social and political context in which it works.

10 Finally, it is important that the gender training programme is supported and not contradicted by other training in the organisation. This may mean making changes to courses on other topics, sometimes by including specific sessions on gender.

Organisational resistance to gender training

Ways of avoiding dealing with gender issues have been well-documented. Gender training may be defined as divisive or disruptive; there may be a refusal to frame a policy on gender, or to change existing discriminatory practices. The issues are similar to those involved in the introduction of anti-racism training in an organisation, and considerable work may need to go on before the topic of training is even mentioned. Care should be taken that attending a gender training is not seen as implying that the person is sexist or unaware of gender issues. Oxfam's experience, if anything, implies the opposite: people who already have some awareness of gender issues are more likely to take part in gender training.

The seven steps of planning

It is essential that any training should be well planned. *Every training course needs preparation time.* This should normally be between three and eight days for each day's training. You may reduced this to a minimum of one day's preparation for one day's training if the same team are conducting the same training with different groups, but you should still allow time for adapting materials and structures to the specific context and needs of the participants.

The methods and the content, often the first to be considered, should be chosen only after full consideration of the aims and objectives of the training, and the learning needs of the target group. One way to ensure that all aspects have been considered is to check the seven steps of planning:[2] **Why? Who? When? Where? What for? What? How?** The steps are best done roughly in this order, but some steps will also need to be considered together.

1 Why?: the aims and objectives of the training

The aims are over-riding, general, guiding, long-term, and open statements of intent, but they must be clear and explicit (e.g. to increase gender awareness, to improve quality of life for women in the project). Objectives must be specific, measurable, achievable, relevant and time-bound (e.g. by the end of the training all staff will be able to analyse projects using the Moser framework; the level of participation of women in the management committees will have risen by at least 10 per cent).

The aims and objectives need to be realistic in terms of what training can achieve, and what other changes are needed to support the aims. One way of deriving objectives is through learning-needs analysis (see point 5).

It is wise to begin to think about how the training will be evaluated, at this stage, because the achievements of training should always be measured against its aims and objectives.

2 Who?

a. The learning group

This has to be considered together with **1 The Aims and Objectives of the Training**, and **5 Learning-needs Analysis**. Selection of participants is crucial to a successful training course or programme. Who should attend, who they represent, and how they will be encouraged to attend is one of the most important steps in the whole training strategy.

Training is easier if the group is as homogenous as possible, but in some cases, a group will require training together in order to build collective responsibility and unity. In this case the training should be designed to take into account the very different abilities, needs, responses, and receptivity of people with different abilities and experiences. As in any other project, disaggregated data should be obtained about the different roles and needs of men and women, and how these may be affected by age, class and ethnicity.

As much as possible should be found out about the group so that the training matches the needs of its members. The composition of the group will affect the group dynamics, and you will need to consider whether you want to specify an equal balance of men and women, or managers and junior staff, in order to avoid a minority feeling isolated and intimidated.

In some cases it will be useful to have separate courses for men and women or for other groups where there are large differences between learners in existing knowledge, status, literacy levels or confidence to speak in groups. Women often have difficulty speaking in groups, particularly large groups, and particularly if there are many men, and the discussion is academic or technical. Men, however, may have greater difficulty in small groups, discussing themselves and their feelings — or even in seeing these as valid subjects for discussion. We have indicated in the trainer's notes whether an activity is suitable or not for particular groups. In other cases, it may be desirable to split the group up into separate-sex groups for certain activities. (See **Section C.3 Gender Awareness and Self-awareness**)

Existing skills, interests and capabilities — such as language and literacy levels of both women and men — need to be assessed. Other factors you should consider are: experience in development, and in emergency work, levels of experience in the organisation, job role, responsibility and status, region or country learners come from. It is also important to find out people's previous levels of knowledge on gender issues and any previous relevant training or experience.

Generally people learn best in small groups, particularly where they are asked to participate. Groups of 10-20 are ideal. Larger groups require more trainers and more complex planning.

Learning theory shows that there is an optimum level of stimulation for learning to take place. Where the subject is contentious, as gender training may be, this can produce anxiety, defensiveness or hostility. This type of 'stimulation' can be so high that it can block effective learning. It may be important to do preliminary work with the group or the group's representatives, to listen to them and understand their concerns and fears, in order to pitch the training at the right level. The **Expectations** activity is useful here, but pre-session discussions can do a lot to allay anxiety, and to clarify what the session will cover and what it will not.

Women and men may have very different expectations of the training. Some men may reluctantly accept the need for training as a requirement of the organisation, but find the idea anxiety-provoking. For some women it may be the culmination of several years of internal lobbying — so they will have high, and perhaps unrealistic, hopes. Some people, particularly men, with some understanding of gender may expect a 'recipe book', rather than expecting to change their perceptions and attitudes, and their approach to development work in fundamental ways.

These pre-training discussions are also a time for establishing learning needs and contracts (see point 5.). If it is impossible to meet participants before the training, for example, where people are coming from different countries, this information has to be obtained indirectly through representatives from the area, and directly through letters and pre-course questionnaires. (See questionnaire with **Activity 6 Expectations, Hopes and Fears**).

b. The trainers

Ideally, there should be at least two facilitators or trainers. Where this proves to be impossible, try to get at least one resource person from within the organisation to help you to plan. Your co-facilitators could be involved at various stages – joining in the basic needs assessment and planning, or just being brought in to run certain sessions. However, in all cases share some of the planning with co-facilitators.

Two or more facilitators are useful because:

- Facilitating gender training can be extremely challenging and tiring.
- Co-facilitators can give each other support, and also provide a useful check on a facilitator being drawn into colluding with prejudicial sentiments.
- Having one male and one female facilitator helps the group dynamics, particularly in mixed groups, and stops gender being seen as only a women's issue.
- It is important for at least one trainer to come from the same area and ethnic group as the majority of the participants. This will provide relevant local knowledge, and help to counter racism, especially in workshops for Southern offices of Northern-based NGOs.
- Having at least one facilitator with knowledge of local languages enables small-group discussion to be held in people's first language. This may be particularly important to prevent women or the less educated from being disadvantaged in discussions.

You need to consider all the above points when choosing your co-facilitator(s).

Facilitators need to work together as a team, and to be seen to be doing so, because:

- The reactions of the participants will vary according to their perceptions of the facilitators in terms or their sex, ethnicity, age, class and many other factors.
- The group may cast them in different roles, for example 'expert'/'non-expert', 'one of us'/ 'outsider',and try to play one off against the other.
- The same message will be interpreted differently depending on who it comes from.

In order to work effectively as a team, and so that your training is not undermined by your co-facilitator, you should:

- Discuss your training styles and methods, and also specific issues likely to arise from the issues in the manual.

- Make sure that you agree on the basics about gender.
- Discuss strengths and weaknesses and use these constructively as a basis for planning.
- Agree fees, responsibilities, and time required for planning and training.
- Make arrangements in good time — good gender trainers tend to have full diaries.

During the planning time, co-facilitators should spend time getting to know each other. During workshops, one person should be responsible for each session. Facilitators should not interrupt each other, but invite comments at the end. Each should ask the other for support, and be prepared to give it. It may be useful to use some of the listening activities (see **Section C.9 Working with Women and Men**) every day as part of your preparation.

After the workshop, review the event, and what each facilitator felt went well and why. Examine what each facilitator found easy, difficult, and valuable about working with the other person. Explore any changes each facilitator would like to make if running the workshop again.

Facilitators should have a questioning openness of attitude and a commitment to social justice. Although gender is the focus of the training it should take place within the general context of challenging prejudice, discrimination and oppression at all levels and in all areas. The facilitators need to look at their own lives and be aware of their own culture, prejudices, and assumptions, including assumptions about participants. You need to work through some of these issues before starting to run workshops. In participatory learning, facilitators need to be prepared to listen and learn as well as to lead and teach.

You need to have some knowledge and understanding about gender, and must read and understand all the hand-outs and work through all the case studies before using them.

c.Facilitation skills

It is assumed that people using this manual will have some experience of facilitating groups and/or running training workshops. There are many good guides to the general principles of participative training (see **Resources section**), which will not be considered here.

You do not need formal educational qualifications; they could be a barrier if participants are alienated by the implied superiority of the trainer. The credibility of the facilitators is important, and this will depend on the composition of the learner group.

Facilitators need good listening skills, an understanding of group dynamics, and to be able to encourage mutual respect and understanding between themselves and the group (see also section on running sessions, below). The behaviour and language of the facilitator, both in and out of the training sessions, should always be congruent with the aims, values and principles of participative development. For example, facilitators should be very careful not to discriminate, deliberately or unwittingly, against people with disabilities, illiterate people, or any other group. Once again the facilitator needs to examine her or his own prejudices and assumptions.

d. Other support

You need to consider administrative and logistical support. This is particularly important when planning the report of the workshop. It is much easier to write up the report while you are running the training than to try to get it done later. You may also want someone to take photographs for the report. If possible, have a non-facilitator in charge of all practical arrangements including venue, accommodation, refreshments, transport, childcare facilities, translators, access, and special needs. Some tasks may be carried out by some of the participants, for example, liaison with the staff of the venue, time-keeping, security. This will encourage a sense of responsibility in the group and enable the facilitators to give full attention to the task of training. Participants may also be asked to lead sessions. In these cases you should be clear about what you expect of them, and whether they are part of the facilitation team planning the whole event, or just leading specific sessions. Outside resource-people may also be asked to come and give inputs and lead discussions on particular topics. This can give fresh perspectives, but such people need to be fully briefed on the aims and objectives of the workshop and the expectations of their sessions. The same issues also need to be considered when arranging for support-people to be co-facilitators.

e. Core group

Oxfam has often run training workshops using a 'core group' to help to plan and run the event. The core group includes the facilitators plus key participants or organiser(s) from the host team or organisation. People are chosen for their skills, knowledge, and experience to make the workshop more relevant to the participant group and the local context. One or two participants may also be asked to join the core group to assist with monitoring and re-planning, once the workshop is under way. It is best not to have more than three to five people on a core group, and to be clear about group members' roles and responsibilities. The core group should be led by a team leader who has an overview of the whole process.

3 When?

You may want to consider a variety of methods: training workshops, evening classes, phased training, or on-the-job training. Choose the type of training which best suits the group, and their needs. In setting the dates for the workshops or training courses, consider the other plans and responsibilities which women and men have at different times of the year (such as work schedules, daily and seasonal routines, participation in religious festivals). In deciding times for classes, remember women's and men's different situations (such as busy times, family responsibilities, social constraints on women going out at night). Obtaining this information will in itself be an exercise in obtaining gender-disaggregated data.

Allow enough time for the facilitation team or core group to meet and plan the training in detail. A **minimum** would be one day's planning for one day's training, if the facilitators are experienced, have done some pre-planning and have full administrative back up. Include extra time for study visits, writing or adapting materials, testing out materials. Plan for at least one day's rest between planning and training — otherwise you will be exhausted before you start. In calculating the amount of time you need for the actual training, remember to allow time for rest, exercise, socialising, visits to projects or groups, and any personal study. Participants must be committed to attending all sessions, so to avoid disrupting the training, you may need to include free time, for example, for shopping or sightseeing.

4 Where?

You will need to consider the availability, convenience and cost of the venue. You also need to check whether the place is accessible to all those who wish to come. You need to consider: safety, access for people with disabilities, access by public transport, ability to cater for special dietary needs or other special needs. Special thought needs to be given to women with young children otherwise they may be excluded indirectly. A 'creche' or accommodation for their 'nanny' or person looking after the child needs to be provided and budgeted for.

Consider the possible disadvantages of having training workshops in cities; participants may be intimidated or distracted. Residential courses often allow for a more intense experience, where participants can give their full attention to the topic, but some people may find them more difficult to attend. You may want to hold the training near a place that is suitable for a study visit, such as a particular project location.

5 What for?: learning-needs analysis

You need to identify the learning needs of the group, so that you can set specific objectives for the training, as well as general aims (see point **1 Why? Aims and Objectives**). It may be that the learning needs of a group are too diverse to be covered in one training.

For employees of a hierarchical organisation, learning needs are best identified by collaboration between the trainer, the learner, and the manager (the 'three-cornered contract'). Then consider whether these needs can be met by training, and what other support or changes need to take place. Also consider the levels of responsibility and authority of the participants — do they have the power to effect change? Do they have the authority to implement action plans? If not, how much support do they have from their manager and the rest of the organisation? By considering these questions, there is a better chance that the participants will be able to put what they have learned into practice. You also need to consider what the learning needs might be for the future, for example if the job changes, or someone is moved to a new job.

Learning needs are identified by looking at the gap between what someone already knows, and what they need to know. This can be done by:

• asking people about their successes, difficulties and what else they need to know; about the key gender issues for them, and how gender affects their work. This can be done by sending a pre-course questionnaire (see **Activity 8 Expectations, Hopes and Fears**).

- observing people's activities, skills, confidence and competencies;
- studying results of surveys, job descriptions, project documents, minutes of meetings and financial records.

It is important that you gather information about learning needs in good time, particularly if you are using external facilitators or planning a workshop outside your home area.

The objectives of the training course should be based on the learning needs of the particular group. Each separate activity should also have its own clear objectives. Think about how you will evaluate whether the objectives have been met.

6 What? Content

The course content consists of the topic areas, based on the objectives derived from the learning needs of the participant group. It can include:

- awareness (e.g. understanding gender and awareness of stereotypes)
- knowledge (e.g. about various forms of discrimination against women)
- skills (e.g. in analysing projects from a gender perspective)
- behaviour (e.g. changes in the way of working with mixed groups).

It is important to include gender awareness at a personal as well as a theoretical level in every training, to provide a firm basis for skill acquisition and behaviour change. Without this there may be a danger that development workers see gender as a dispensable issue outside themselves and their concerns. It is also important to include analysis and planning skills as well as awareness-raising, so that the training has real impact.

Put the content in a logical order, and always start with introductions and activities to encourage trust and cohesion within the group, and end with practical forward planning and evaluation of the course. Calculate the approximate times needed, and you have your draft programme.

Some examples:

A one-day training programme for UK-based staff

a.m.
- Introduction and expectations
- Gender awareness
- Women in the world

p.m.
- Gender and development approaches
- Facts about men and women in the world
- Understanding gender issues (case study)
- Action plan and evaluation

A three-day training course for development workers

This workshop was first held in East Africa, and has since been repeated many times in different places, with some adaptations. It was for a group who had various levels of knowledge about gender and aimed to introduce the Moser method of project analysis.

Day 1

a.m.
- Introductions and expectations
- Sharing country programmes
- Gender awareness

p.m.
- Gender awareness (cont.)
- Women in the world

Day 2

a.m.
- Gender roles and needs
- Gender and development

p.m.
- Project appraisal

Day 3

a.m.
- Project appraisal (cont.)
- Summary of workshop

p.m.
- Strategies for change
- Evaluation and close

A follow-up workshop for emergencies workers who have previously participated in basic gender training

a.m.
- Introductions & expectations
- Difference between emergency and development work
- Learning to listen

p.m.
- Working with women
- Surveying needs
- Assessing community perspectives
- Action plan
- Evaluation and close

7 How? : Training Methods

Whichever type of training you use, whether workshops or evening classes, participatory methods are the most appropriate for adult learning, and for development work. They are the most effective and enjoyable. Participatory training is characterised by a respect for the participants, who are active in their own and others' learning.

Once you have decided on a workshop, and worked through the first six steps of planning, you are at last ready to choose the activities! Activities must not be picked at random, but with a purpose. Within participatory training, there are a number of different methods and techniques which should be chosen to meet the specific objectives and content of the training sessions. Learning skills is best done through practice; games and songs are most useful for awareness-raising; while factual information can be given through videos, quizzes and lectures. All these aspects are inter-related, and different methods can be used for many different purposes.

Training techniques can be described as either 'open' or 'closed'. The 'open' techniques stimulate creativity, raise awareness, and do not have a pre-set outcome. Examples of these are: **brainstorm** (where all contributions are written up on a newsprint without questioning), t**elling a story based on pictures, designing a poster or project**. The 'closed' techniques are useful where there is a pre-set outcome, and can be used to learn facts or methods of analysis or to practise skills. Examples of these are the **Moser and Harvard analytical frameworks**. Both open and closed techniques can be participative and may use similar materials.. Training techniques can also be classified into: **Creative/Investigative** (e.g. PRA,Listening Survey); **Analysis** (case study, project analysis); **Planning** (Action Plans); and **Informative** (presentation, factual quiz). It is best to use a variety of these methods, and to enable the group to go through a process of learning, discovering, and creating new solutions to problems.

Individuals have different learning styles, and this should be catered for. In places where education is based on the 'banking' model, participatory methods may seem not only unfamiliar but also threatening or time-wasting. Some of the frameworks for analysis which require people to fill in boxes will feel uncomfortable to those more used to descriptive reporting.

Men and women often have different learning styles. Many women find it easier to talk in pairs or smaller groups and in single-sex groups — and these activities should be included. Men may have more difficulty in discussing personal feelings in groups, and may deride such discussion as 'gossip'. In these situations, you will need to go slowly, with respect for the participants. Accept people's comments without defensiveness — no method is perfect. Through mutual trust, you will enable people to learn from a variety of methods. A mix of different methods within any one training event is best, and keeps people's interest. Try and use people's knowledge and creativity to come up with ideas that are particularly relevant for them.

Case-study methods have been very successfully used as a part or even the main method of gender training (Poats and Russo, op.cit.). We have found them very useful towards the end of a course, as a way of using the awareness, knowledge and skills that have been built up on the course. They provide opportunities to apply theory and analysis to real situations, and thus are best if they reflect the experience of participants.

Role-plays, drawing, songs and games are excellent methods which do not rely on written materials. However, they need to be handled with caution for some highly-educated groups, who may sometimes feel they are not being treated with sufficient dignity in these activities. As trust and respect builds up in the group, you may find that you are able to introduce them. In mixed groups it is important to choose games which are seen as culturally acceptable interactions for men and women.

You will also need to give inputs or presentations. They should be clear and brief, especially where the training is not in the first language of some participants. Recommendations from learning theory about presentations include:

- Limit any segment of speaking to a maximum of 20 minutes — after that people will not be able to concentrate.

- Condense what you want to say to the bare essentials that people absolutely have to know (for example, 'the five key points', 'the four guiding principles'). You can expand or give brief illustrations of other points, but people must go away remembering the main points

- Use visual aids to back up what you are saying (acetate, flipchart, newsprint, or handout).

Prepare your materials well in advance. You will need:

- flip chart, newsprint or other very large sheets of paper

- felt tip (marker) pens

- 'Blu-tack', masking tape etc. to stick papers to wall.

- Handouts: make sure these are chosen, written, or adapted in good time and that you have more than enough for all participants and facilitators. If you have written new materials such as case studies, work through them to make sure they are clear and contain enough relevant information.

- small sheets of paper or index cards for individual work.

You may also need:

- overhead projector and acetates, video and VCR, slides and slide projector. These will make your training more interesting but are not indispensable. If you use any of them, do make certain you know how to use them and that they are in proper working order. Have a trial run to check.

- other materials specific to the activity, e.g. props for role-play, photos. These are indicated on each activity.

Use activities which fit the educational abilities of the group and their level of knowledge about gender — they should be easily understood by all. You may need to adapt some of the materials to make them relevant to your particular group or context. If materials designed for one context are used without thought in another, misunderstandings may occur, learning may not take place, and participants may feel misunderstood or undervalued. The activities in this manual have been field-tested, often in a variety of countries, but you do need to check if the situation described in, for example, the case study or role-play really does occur in the experience of your participants.

You also need to **read the activities carefully** and plan accordingly. Some of the activities require preparation months ahead, for example, case studies for some analytical frameworks (Activity 47), sharing country information (Activity 39). Some depend on having done other activities previously (for example, activities to teach the Moser method: 36, 38, and 47). Some are alternatives and you will need to choose the most appropriate. Remember that training is a process, and the activities should have a coherent order. Later activities should build on earlier ones.

You need to pace the course content to suit your participants, and to stimulate and sustain motivation and interest. This is best done by varying the type and length of activity, the size of group, and the skills and involvement each activity requires. Where an activity demands intense concentration, you can start with a brief energiser or game. Keep the length of sessions to not more than two hours and include enough refreshment and exercise breaks. Consider the time of day; for example, try not to plan theoretical inputs immediately after a heavy lunch as you may find people falling asleep! Include space for enjoyment and local cultural activities such as songs and dances.

In this manual, we have included a variety of training methods, but please do not choose an activity because of the method. **Choose it because it will meet your specific objectives for that session, and will be suitable for the group**. If necessary, adapt the activity that meets your objectives. For example, an activity which asks people to write lists, such as the stereotypes activity 25, can be adapted so that people draw or act out the stereotypes, rather than write them down. Simple case-studies can be turned into a drama, if you feel the group would understand it better if it were acted out rather than read.

For further details of how to choose activities see **Section A1 A Guide to This Manual.**

Example of training programme: choosing the activities

Once you have the content worked out, you can fill in the particular activities which you will use, taking into account all the above points. Overleaf is the programme used for an East Africa three-day training, based on the outline programme given above.

This was quite a tight programme, and in some cases we over-ran on time, and changed the programme slightly. We could have done with more time. In designing a programme you need to include enough flexibility to make changes if necessary. There is no point in just going ahead with activities if the group has not understood the previous session.

Programme for a three-day Workshop

Day One

9.00	Introduction to the Workshop
9.15	Getting to know each other
10.15	Expectations
11.00	Refreshment break
11.15	Sharing work experience
12.30	Roles and Activities Quiz
1.00	Lunch
2.00	What is Gender?
2.30	Myths and Effects (Part 1)
3.15	Refreshment break
3.30	Myths and Effects (Part 2)
5.00	Finish and Monitoring Groups
	Evening Video: Promised the Earth

Day Two

8.30	Introduction to the day
8.40	Myths about Gender and Development
9.10	The 24-hour day
10.30	Refreshment break
10.45	Women's Roles and Needs
11.30	Statements about Gender and Development

1.00	Lunch
2.00	Policies and Approaches to Women and Development
2.30	Case Studies — Analysis of Projects
3.45	Refreshment break
4.00	Visit to Game Park
6.00	Case Studies — Discussion
	Monitoring Groups

Evening videos: 'Man-made Famine', 'The Voice of African Women'

Day Three

9.00	Introduction to the day
9.05	Mwea Case Study: Part 1
9.45	Mwea Case Study: Part 2
10.15	Discussion of Case Study
11.00	Refreshment break
11.15	Video: 'Lost Harvest'
11.45	Discussion
12.00	Summary of workshop
12.15	Sharing of positive ideas and experiences from own programme
1.00	Lunch
2.00	Identification and achievement of goals in relation to gender
3.30	Refreshment break
3.45	Action Plans
4.45	Evaluation
5.00	Close

Running sessions

The role of the facilitator

Once the workshop starts, you are responsible as facilitator for ensuring that the group accomplishes the tasks set, and maintains itself as a group.

Task: This might include setting clear programme objectives, providing clear introductions and instructions to participants, providing materials, keeping to the time schedule, summing up and concluding.

Maintenance: This might include observing and listening. to be aware of the way individuals are reacting in the group, and of group dynamics; enabling each person to feel accepted as part of the group, and able to participate equally; enabling participants to listen and learn from each other; drawing common threads and pointing out differences of opinion. You also need to be aware of possible difficulties, such as 'scape-goating' of individuals, or individual members dominating the group, and be able to deal with them constructively.

Group dynamics

There are trainer's notes for the individual activities in this manual. In addition there are some aspects of group dynamics which may be particularly relevant to gender training. Some of these are shared with anti-racism training or any other training which challenges prejudice (see *Missing Links* training pack listed in resources section) and some are specific to gender training.

Encouraging balanced participation

People learn better and feel better if they are in a group with balanced participation. As a facilitator you need to be very aware who is speaking and who is not. For those people who find it difficult to speak out in a group, the facilitator can:

- build confidence and trust within the group by working in small groups, and using introductory activities;
- make explicit the principles of participatory training and help the group to establish relevant ground rules (this may include telling the group that men usually talk more than women in groups and as this is gender training you would like to encourage more equal participation);
- make everyone feel valued and that their experiences are relevant;
- draw people out by using specific questions or rounds;
- do a round of 'something I've been wanting to say all morning';
- divide into separate-sex groups, if the women are being quieter than the men.

However, people should not be forced to participate in a certain activity if they really do not want to.

Some individuals speak too much and dominate the group. In these cases the facilitator can:

- use the 'talking stick', 'conch shell' or other object, which is passed around the group in turn, and people only speak when they hold the object; no interruptions are allowed;
- divide people into small groups, with the quiet ones together and the talkative ones together;
- speak privately to the individual concerned;
- asking the dominant individual to present a topic, which others then discuss;
- introduce a rule that no-one speaks twice before everyone has spoken once.

Another possibility is to bring the issue of unequal participation to the group for open discussion This may be a more risky option, but could be worth trying if the men are speaking more than the women and you have enough time to work through the issue. You would need to split the group into small groups to discuss it first. You need to be aware that both men's and women's perceptions of how much men speak is likely to be less than how much they actually speak.

Dealing with resistance and hostility

It is important for people to feel accepted for who they are, and to feel able to express their thoughts and feelings. However, it must be clear that the training is challenging the oppression of women. There is a fine line between making a friendly, welcoming, accepting and open climate for discussion, and allowing prejudiced remarks to pass by unchallenged. Where the group is participating well, such remarks may be challenged by other group members; the expectation that this sort of challenge is acceptable may be explicitly encouraged in the ground-rules. You, as facilitator, have to decide how much to support, challenge or ignore what the participants say. If you challenge too much, especially at the beginning, participants may feel they have to say the 'correct' thing and will thus express opinions they feel that they *ought* to hold rather than giving a true account of their feelings.

Learning will be hindered if people hide what they really think and feel, so allow people to express their opinions. Challenges should come in the form of generalised summing up (such as 'it was said that', 'some people feel that') and questions, rather than direct personal attack. People do not learn well when they are being attacked. Challenging may be interpreted differently by men and women; for example, men may be more used to debate, confrontational speeches, and challenges, and may not be aware of the impact these have on others. Challenges will also be interpreted differently according to who makes the challenge — eg a challenge by a man may be taken better by the group than the same challenge by a woman. Other factors are also important, such as the status and role of the challenger, and the context. Despite these difficulties, it is important to challenge — do not avoid challenges in order to have an easy time. Facilitators should show their own commitment and knowledge. This is particularly important for male facilitators.

Despite the most skilled facilitating, gender issues can be controversial and some people may feel uncomfortable, threatened or defensive. Your aim should be to keep such discomfort or disturbance to a level where it promotes the impetus for change, rather than being counter-productive.

For the facilitator to face a certain level of resistance and to handle it well may be helpful to participants, as they may face similar resistance when they try to share their learning about gender and women's empowerment.

A frequent occurrence in gender training and anti-racism training is denial of or diversion from, the facts and the implications of oppression. Some examples of this are:

- Using untypical societies or projects as examples (especially in Activity36 The 24- hour Day; or project analysis activities) to imply that women have more power than they do. This can be avoided to some extent by not allowing people to pick their own favourite projects for analysis. If they do, then it can be pointed out that this type of project is the exception rather than the rule — which will be supported by the results of the other small groups' analysis.

• Challenging any statistics which are presented, on the basis of their method of collection or categorisation, as not showing the true picture, and refusing to believe that things are as bad for women as the statistics show. People are especially likely to challenge statistics from their own programmes, countries or localities. Statistics can never be totally accurate, and questioning them is valid. For example, the way in which the information about 'work' is collected for calculating the Gross National Product (GNP) of countries ignores much of women's work. (See Activity 40 Facts about men and women) However, this questioning can sometimes be a way of challenging the facilitator and literally refusing to face facts. In such a case it is useful to point out that although there might be slight inaccuracies, the overall picture obtained from many countries is the same: women do more work and have less money and power than men. One way of overcoming the challenge of 'biased' statistics is for participants to gather this information themselves in preparation for the workshop.

• Focusing on the oppressor group, in this case, men. Although most development work and training is targeted at men, people often overlook this and object to what they feel is too much attention being paid to women.

It is very useful to consider implications of male gender roles for men, and to discuss the benefits to men of having more equitable gender relations, and we have included some adaptations to activities to allow this. However, this should not be permitted to detract from women's experience of injustice and oppression.

The facilitators need to be aware of, and make clear to the group the following:

• When women are habitually ignored, any consideration of them can appear excessive. An example of this is research which showed that when men judge that they have spoken equally with women in a group, women judge them to have spoken more. In reality the men spoke more than either the women or the men estimated.

• Both men and women are damaged by sex-role stereotyping: for example, men have to hide their tears, and women have to hide their anger. However, worldwide, in general, men have more power and wealth and less work than women. Individual men may not mistreat women, yet they benefit from the system which oppresses women (patriarchy).

Personal issues

Some men do not have much experience of relating to women outside their families or partnerships, or as work colleagues except in a subordinate or support role. This will affect the way in which they relate to women participants in the group. Be aware of the gender dynamics, but do not be intimidated by them.

In discussion of injustice such as gender oppression, it is possible that participants will raise very personal issues, including domestic violence and sexual abuse. They may express anger, hurt or guilt. Whilst these activities have been carefully designed not to raise overwhelming feelings, facilitators should be aware of the possibility of strong feelings being expressed and be able to accept these without panicking. This is much easier if the facilitators have already thought through and discussed these issues themselves. Also, check the trainer's notes for each activity. Do not do an activity which is potentially very controversial or threatening if there is no feeling of trust within the group.

Be aware of the feelings and experiences that participants may not be able to raise, either because of the strong feelings mentioned above, but also because of embarrassment; for example, discussing the needs of menstruating women for appropriate supplies and underwear in a refugee camp.

Monitoring and evaluation

Monitoring and evaluation of training is essential, and need to be considered right at the beginning, together with the aims and objectives of the training. Before you do a monitoring or evaluation activity, explain to the participants what you are doing and why.

Monitoring should be done throughout the course to assess both task and maintenance functions of the group, as well as practical details. For courses that last more than one day, it is useful for small groups to meet at the end of each day to discuss the day's activities and report back to the facilitators. This enables you to assess levels of learning and keep the course pitched at the right level, and it allows participants some control over the process. It can also alert you to any difficulties in group dynamics, and help you to make changes to the programme if needed.

A variation on this, which is particularly useful for larger groups, is for the group to elect representatives for liaison with the facilitation team. People discuss their complaints and comments about the course and the facilities with these representatives, who pass them on to the facilitators.

A technique that we have found particularly useful for ensuring that individual learning takes place, and individual's questions are answered is **'The Fridge'**. Participants are encouraged to raise questions that are puzzling them. If it is not appropriate to answer immediately (perhaps because the preliminary work has not yet been done with the group), the question is written on a newsprint (which can be designed like a fridge). Later, at an appropriate time, the question is brought 'out of the fridge' and answered. This can also serve as a useful indicator and reminder to the facilitators as to the concerns of the group.

A method that is useful for longer courses is the learning record. Individuals write their own learning goals for the course. These may be discussed with their manager before they come on the course, and may be raised in the pre-course questionnaire and the Expectations activity 6. The learning record is their record of what they have learned during the day, with particular reference to their learning goals. This is a more individualised method, but can be combined with the use of monitoring groups.

A round of 'what I have learned today ' is a quick method of monitoring and evaluating the day's programme. Other questions can be added, such as 'what I still feel unsure about', 'what I still want to get out of the course', or 'how I am going to put it into practice '. Rounds can also be useful at the start of the day to find out how people are feeling, and enable them to raise any questions they have from the previous day.

Verbal evaluations can also be supplemented by written evaluation sheets (see **C.12 Evaluation**). These should be filled in and handed to you before the end of the training. They measure the opinions of the participants about how useful, interesting, and enjoyable the course was, but may fail to find out how the course affects participants' work or life subsequently. Follow-up visits or questionnaires some time after the course may offer some useful information here. This also illustrates the benefits of a phased training programme, where periods of training alternate with periods of practice in the real situation.

Written 'tests' can be given at the beginning and end of the course to evaluate changes in knowledge, skills and attitudes. The questions chosen should reflect the specific objectives of the course. However, some groups might not find them acceptable because they may seem like an exam paper. One can lessen this by allowing each person to score their own evaluation sheets, and then write a summary of his or her changes.

Another method which can be used to look at the long-term effectiveness of the training related to the overall aims, rather than specific session objectives, is analysis of behaviour and documents before and after the course, to look for specific changes in, for example, the amount of data collected separately of males and females in baseline surveys; the number of project documents identifying the implications for women and men separately; or the number of women involved in decision making in projects.

In these cases, other factors besides the training would also have to be considered, such as changes in staff or organisational changes in policy, procedures and workingpractices; the effect of other meetings, conferences, visits and discussions on gender issues within and outside the organisation; and wider political and social changes. These other factors may be harder to document.

Reports

Always try to write up the report during the course of the training. Reports of training events can serve a number of purposes:

- a reminder for the participants about what they learned, and what they decided to do as a result, and a document for the follow-up;

- information for the participants and their managers to assess the extent to which learning needs were met, and consider future training requirements;

- information for other team members who were unable to attend the training;

- information for people in other organisations or regions who are considering organising gender training;

• details of activities, which can then be adapted and used by participants in training sessions they run for their own groups;

• details of any recommendations, plans or strategies to be implemented.

A report usually contains two elements: the process (activities) and the content. List the activities you have used in the order you used them, and choose a format which makes them easy to follow, and easy for others to use. You can use the layout of the activities in this manual as a model, always including objectives, method, materials, timings, and trainer's notes.

The content comes from the prepared inputs and handouts, the newsprints that have been written on during the training, and notes taken in each session. You will need to arrange for one or two 'scribes' per session who will take notes and then produce a written report. It may be useful to give guidelines for writing the reports (i.e. reports should include key points of the discussions, research findings, recommendations, and action plans).

Follow-up

Training is not an end in itself; it should have some connection with and impact on the lives of the participants. If the training is being carried out within an organisation, it should be supported by other efforts in relation to policy and practice. Examples of specific changes are: altering the project application documents to include specific questions on gender related to the method of analysis learned in the gender training; using concepts from the gender training in documents and training in other areas; support from the manager to follow-up on the objectives as previously discussed in the three-cornered contract and the learning record.

You need to consider the impact of gender training on participants' lives and perhaps allow time for discussion of this within the workshop. There may be fears about conflict arising from working on gender issues. Whilst some of these may be groundless (for example, that families will be broken up if women start talking about gender issues), others may reflect reality (for example, resistance shown to women's groups by community organisations, sabotaging of women's groups by individual men, hostility towards individual women from their male partner).

Empowerment and change are often seen as threatening and thus it is not at all surprising for ideas about gender to be met with fear, resistance or hostility. However, there are ways of reducing resistance (see Activity 93 Maseno West case study) and people can share experiences at a follow-up workshop.

Phased training is a good method of ensuring the relevance of the training. Here, training workshops are interspersed with periods of working in the field, trying to put what has been learnt into practice. Even where phased training has not been planned, follow-up sessions or workshops are useful for sharing the successes and difficulties of putting the learning into practice, and moving forward. For example, a workshop on gender awareness and project appraisal may be followed by one on strategies for working with women and men in an area of conflict. Training should be sensitive to changing needs.

If possible, help participants to set up support networks for themselves with other participants, especially if they work with or near each other. Consider also how you will get support for yourselves as trainers — celebrate your successes and learn from your mistakes. Good luck!

Endnotes

1 Poats S V and Russo S L Training in WID *Gender Analysis in Agricultural Development: A review of experiences and lessons learned*, prepared for the Women in Agricultural Productin and Rural Development Service of the FAO, Florida, USA, 1989. (Available from GADU, Oxfam UKI.)

2 The 'Seven Steps of Planining' are adapted from Vella J, *Learning to Teach: Training of Trainers for Community Development*, Save the Children Fund and OEF International, Washington, USA.

C.1 Training techniques, icebreakers and energisers

This section is complementary to **Section B: Trainer's Guidelines** and provides a short description of the training techniques used in this Manual, as well as some extra games, energisers, and icebreakers to be used whenever appropriate throughout the training.

Training techniques

• **Introductions and 'icebreakers'**: these are short activities designed for the beginning of the workshop, or of each day in a long workshop, to help people relax, get to know each other, and gain confidence to speak in front of the group. They should encourage participation and mutual support among the women and men at the workshop, and thus shouldn't demand deep personal disclosures or actions which could make people feel ill at ease. Most trainers have a number of these that they have tried and tested; you will probably have your favourites. In this Manual we present a few which also begin to introduce the idea of gender, to start people thinking about it in a non-threatening way.

It is important to select the icebreakers most suited to your group. This is likely to vary according to how well the participants know each other, their cultural backgrounds, their gender and so on. There is a list of icebreakers below.

• **Brainstorming**: the aim of brainstorming is to collect from the workshop participants as many ideas as possible on a specific topic within a given time, in an uninhibited way. Once you have presented the topic to the group, invite them to call out ideas, comments, phrases or words connected to it. Write all contributions on a newsprint or flipchart as they come up, without comment or question. Participants should not comment on each other's suggestions. People should feel that what they say is not evaluated or judged. The list of ideas is then used as the basis for further work, which may involve discussion of them and categorising them, rejecting some, prioritising others, and so on. A brainstorm can be a good way of starting off an activity on a new topic.

Variations on brainstorming include **'webs'** or **'balloons'**. Here the trigger word is written in a 'balloon' in the centre of the page. As the individual or group comes up with connected ideas, these are written on the page, showing the connections. A related activity for individuals is **'free writing'**. Here individuals write non-stop for a very short period (three to five minutes) and not longer. As in all these methods, the aim is to encourage free-flow of ideas and feeling without censorship.

• **Group discussion**: this is a very common method which can be combined with other methods in one activity. Discussion in a large group is useful for learning from the experiences of all the members of the group and allowing participants to draw conclusions from activities. Facilitators may need to encourage equal participation, and discussion between participants.

Most of the activities in this Manual require the participants to be divided into smaller groups of three to six people for discussion or to complete a task. Often a spokesperson from the smaller group will report back to the full group, for further discussion. People can find it easier to share experiences in pairs or small groups, and to relate the subject under discussion to their own lives. In gender training, strong emotions are often aroused by examining relations between women and men, and sharing experiences in small groups is a less threatening way of doing this.

Speaking in a smaller group also enables less confident people to participate more fully in the workshop, and to build up confidence for speaking in the plenary sessions.

Certain activities also require splitting the participants into single-sex groups. When you do this, it is important to follow up such an activity with one which brings the group together again.

There are a number of ways of working with small groups, depending on the training. You may, for example, wish to establish 'home groups' or groups whose membership does not change through the training — although people may be split differently on other occasions. Home groups enable participants to build up trust and solidarity with one another. Or you may wish to make sure that people mix thoroughly by being in different groups in every activity. It is best if you, the facilitator, divide the participants into groups, through counting or some other method.

• **Buzz groups**: participants form pairs or threes to quickly discuss ('buzz') some aspect of what the speaker has been saying. It helps to break up the monotony of input and is a good way to get discussion going in a large group. Buzz groups can report back to the large group, or 'snowball' by each buzz group talking to another pair, and then the four talking to another four, until the group is back together.

• **Role plays**: role plays or simulation games imitate reality by assigning roles to participants and giving them a situation to act out. Each person in a role play needs to have a clear idea of the role they have been assigned, and the objectives of the role play should be well-defined. The aim of a role play is to make attitudes, situations and experiences come to life in a dramatic and enjoyable way: they aim to help people learn through experiencing and feeling. They can also be used to practise skills e.g. of raising gender issues. They can be based on real-life cases, or carefully designed to bring out certain roles and attitudes. In some cases, the participants may bring their own situations to be acted out. In gender training, role plays can be a very effective way of enabling men to experience what it is like to feel powerless or invisible in a situation (when they play a woman) and to put women in touch with their own feelings about their gender roles.

Role Play is a fairly 'open' technique, allowing the situation to develop once people have their character roles and the basic setting established. The examples in this manual are more structured with specific learning objectives. We have found that role plays often cause anxiety amongst participants, particularly British ones. If there is anxiety, it can be lessened by not using the words 'role-play' but 'drama' or 'acting out a situation'. They should be used after group trust has built. It is very important to allow sufficient time after role-plays for a thorough de-brief (for each player to say how they felt in role), de-role (for each player to come out of their role and realise that they are themselves), and for summarising the lessons learned. Otherwise there is a danger that participants may be carrying on inappropriate feelings and thoughts.

- **Codes**: a code also sets up a situation, but is a more 'closed' technique than role play in that the result is pre-determined. The key issue, or generative theme is 'encoded' into something which is presented to the group to generate discussion. (See *Training for Transformation*, in Resources Section, for a full description of this method.) A code can be anything from a picture, story, tableau or drama in which an issue is encoded. A drama is always scripted, so that the players perform a stylised act rather than develop it as they go along as in a role play. The code is then interpreted and discussed by the group: it is a technique for generating discussion, which may be based on some key questions linked to the code. (See Activity13 The Liberator)

- **Statement ranking**: this Manual uses a number of activities based on choosing or ranking a list of statements on a certain topic. These are designed to be controversial and to stimulate thought and discussion. In the activities we have used we have drawn up a list of statements, but many trainers may have their own and prefer to use them. The statements should be carefully chosen in accordance with the objectives of the activity. Participants are asked to rank the statements according to how much they agree or disagree with them.

- **Sentence completion**: this allows people to work on their own to express ideas and later discuss these with others. It is a more open activity than statement ranking, because each person has to come up with her or his own statements rather than choosing existing ones.

- **Questionnaires**: these are usually used to test knowledge, but can examine attitudes too.

- **Case studies**: these may be based on real cases or be designed as hypothetical situations but based on real issues. They provide the material on which participants practise using the analytical tools they have learned. They also stimulate participants' critical faculties by presenting successes and failures in development and relief work. Case studies should always be carefully designed with specific objectives in mind, and tailored to fit the concepts or problems they are intended to address. Case studies need careful preparation and testing out. (See Activity 56, Handout 59 Designing case studies.)

• **Guided fantasy or visualisations**: the facilitator reads out a prepared fantasy, or one can be developed by the group. It can be used for private reflection or shared with the group. It is useful to start with general relaxation to enable individuals to let go and free their imaginations.

• **Creative work**: this includes collage, drawing, painting, modelling, composing songs, poems, stories, or plays. These can be done individually or as a group effort to enable expression of issues in a different way. It is important to stress that these activities are a vehicle for ideas, not a test of people's talent or drawing ability.

• **'Starters'**: these are objects, photographs, cartoons, drawings or newspaper articles which may be provided by the facilitator or by each participant. The aim is to provide a focus for discussion. The facilitator should make sure the starter or the questions about it are related to the content of the workshop (e.g. ask participants to choose an object which represents their life as a woman).

• **Debates**: these can help to clarify thinking on controversial issues, and allow different perspectives to be seen. There are a number of different variations of debates e.g. goldfish bowldebate, TV debate.

• **Rounds**: a round is an exercise in which each participant has the opportunity to say something quickly, in turn, in answer to a question or to report an opinion or feeling. Rounds are a useful quick monitoring exercise to give a sense of individual and group mood and learning. It is particularly useful if you have very uneven participation in the group. However, some people may not want to reveal their true thoughts on certain topics to the group. In this case you can use **index cards** or slips of paper, and ask each person to write a question or opinion on a card. The cards are then collected in, shuffled, and each person takes one card, which they read out. Thus everyone's feelings are obtained, anonymously. This is also known as the 'Ballot Box'.

• **Games and energisers**: these are useful for breaking up monotony, raising energy levels and letting people enjoy themselves. They can also raise sensitive topics in a lighthearted way.

• **Study visit**: this can be particularly useful in a long training course, to break up the routine, and to enable people to put theory into practice. Study visits require a lot of careful preparation by the core group to set them up before the training. A briefing session is necessary, so that participants know why they are going and what questions they will be researching on the visit; also a de-briefing session after the visit, so that full use can be made of the learning.

Icebreakers

Greeting

Explain or ask how people in different countries greet each other. Then ask participants to pick a pre-prepared slip from a hat or basket, on each of which will be written one of the following:

Place hands together and bow (India)
Kiss on both cheeks (France)
Rub noses (Iceland)
Hug warmly (Russia)
Slap on each hand and bump each hip (some parts of Southern Africa)

Ask the participants to move around the room greeting each other in the way indicated on their slip.

Your own space

Ask each person to find a space where they do not touch anyone else. Then ask them to close their eyes and do anything they wish to do within their own space (eg. jump, dance, exercise etc.) Then ask them to hug themselves and generally feel and touch themselves. Ask them to move again within their own space, and them ask them to describe quickly how they feel about themselves (relaxed, tense, good, bad etc.)

Wallpaper

Ask participants to draw a picture of themselves doing something they enjoy doing. After 10 or 15 minutes ask each one to show and explain their picture. Afterwards each person signs their picture and puts it up on the wall. As some people feel very anxious about drawing, only do this with a group of people who will be able to do it without anxiety.

Beautiful Bee

'I'm Bee and I'm beautiful'... Each person says their name and a positive word to describe themselves (no putdowns allowed!) and goes on to introduce the preceding members of the group: 'I'm Lynne and I'm lovely... this is Sue and she's super... William and he's wonderful... Cathy and she's courageous...'. A variation on this is for people to say their name and one thing about themselves (not necessarily starting with the same letter): 'I'm Cathy, I have three children'. In the same way they introduce the preceding members: 'I am Thandi and I like working in groups, this is Cathy, she has three children', and so on.

What I do

This is useful near the beginning to help get to know each other in a fun way.

Each person briefly shows in mime something that they do. This does not have to be something to do with their work — in fact it is better if it is something that is unknown by most of the participants. The second person does the previous person's action and then their own. The third person does the first, second and third actions until the last person does the actions for all the group. This can be made more fun by also including a sound (not words) to go with the mime.

Energisers

Energisers can be used at any time in the training when energy or attention is flagging: after lunch or a session on theory. They can also be used to encourage group feeling — which is useful at the beginning of the training, after separate sessions for men and women, or where there have been sharp differences of opinion. They are also great fun. Here are some suggestions — choose only the ones which are culturally appropriate for the group, add your own, and also ask your group if they have any games or songs — this also encourages the feeling of group participation. (Further ideas for energisers can be found in books listed in the **Resources section.**) Each takes about 10-15 minutes, depending on group size. Facilitators should join in too — you also need to be revived at times!

Opening the day

Stand in a circle. Each person takes a turn to make a sound and a gesture to show how he or she is feeling. This is a good one to do at the start of a day, for people to express their feelings. A variation is for people to imitate the sounds and actions of others.

Untangling

Ask the group to stand in a circle, and close their eyes, until you tell them to open them again. Move slowly towards each other stretching out your hands until each person is holding some-one else's hand in each of their hands. Check to make sure that everyone is holding only one hand in each hand. Then all open your eyes.

You will find the group is in a tangled knot. Then, with eyes open, but still holding hands, try and untangle yourselves until you are standing in a circle again holding hands.

All change

Take away one of the chairs, or mats so that there is enough room for all except one person to sit down. The standing person calls out all people who have a certain characteristic eg 'all people wearing something blue' or 'all people who have an E in their name'. Those people then stand up and rush to find another seat. The person who is the caller also rushes to try and find a seat. One person fails to get a seat, and then they go into the centre. If the person calls 'all change', then everyone has to stand up and run to get a seat.

This game can be used just to get people moving, but it can also be used to build awareness and provide information on a topic: you could ask for people who are parents, grandparents, daughters, brothers, managers, heads of household, etc. An alternative, non-threatening way to play the game is to allocate names of fruit or vegetables to people; the caller then calls out these names, and those people run to get a new seat.

Be aware with this game that there may be certain areas that people do not feel comfortable to share in such a public way. Also be aware that some people may not be able to run. In this case it is possible to have other people act as 'runners' for them.

Word and deed

The first person in the circle does one action, while describing another. For example, she says 'I'm cooking' while pretending to type. The second person then acts out the thing that the first person says she was doing, while saying she's doing something else: 'I'm scratching my nose' while pretending to cook. This then continues round the circle. This one is hilarious — but it's not for people who want to remain dignified at all costs!

Tropical rainforest

Standing in a circle, the facilitator starts rubbing her hands together and the next person copies, then the next all the way round. Then the facilitator changes to snapping her fingers, and everyone gradually changes over... then she starts slapping her hands on her thighs ... then stamping her feet ... then repeats the sounds in reverse until everyone is silent again. It sounds like a rainstorm in a forest, starting quietly, building up and gradually dying away again. It is important that each person copies the actions of the person to the right of them, not the facilitator; and that the facilitator waits until everyone is doing the action before changing to a new one.

C.2 Getting started

The activities in this section are divided into four groups:

- **Introductions**
- **Expectations**
- **Sharing work experience**
- **Consensus on development**

We have given a number of activities for each group so that you can choose those most appropriate to your needs and the needs of the group and the objectives of the workshop. However, as we have stressed in **Section B Training guidelines**, it is very important to use the activities in a certain order. Introductions, Expectations and Ground Rules should all be at the beginning of the workshop.

Introductions

This set of activities is most important for helping participants to get to know each other, build up trust, and set up a safe and positive environment for the duration of the workshop. They are intended for use at the very beginning. How many of these you choose to do depends on a number of factors, such as:

- how well the participants know each other, and in what context (work or personal lives);

- how long or short the workshop will be (even a very short training should not leave these out altogether);

- what the main purpose of the workshop is, and the extent to which you think tackling gender issues is going to challenge the participants and arouse strong feelings.

Expectations

This set of activities are designed to give participants a space to talk in the group about their hopes and fears for the workshop, to suggest adaptations and to agree collectively on ground rules for the course of the workshop. This is the point at which you, the facilitators, need to be clear about which expectations can or cannot be met, and how much flexibility you can have in the programme. This will depend on the kind of group, the objectives of the workshop, and the time you have available.

Sharing work experience

This activity starts off the discussion about gender in relation to the concrete work experiences of the participants. This will help you to discover participants' different perceptions of what gender means and how they approach it in their work. It is important to keep a good note of the issues that come up in discussion, as you may wish to refer back to these in the course of the training. This will help participants to keep their own experience in the forefront as they learn new tools of analysis and deepen their understanding of gender.

Consensus on development

The activities in this section begin to explore participants' ideas about development, and enable them to share and discuss them. They aim to help the group come to a common understanding of what is meant by development in the context of the workshop, and the different kinds of work the participants do. The activity on development for women, for men, and for the community lays the foundation for thinking about gender roles, and for bringing out the importance of disaggregating data and concepts such as 'the community'. It is important that these activities come in the first part of the workshop, before gender and gender roles are analysed more directly.

C.2 Activities

Time: 30 mins

Meaning of names

Objectives

1 To introduce the participants to each other;

2 To establish trust and respect;

3 To bring out people's different personal and cultural backgrounds.

Method

1 Use flipchart pinned up, or on the floor.

2 Ask each participant to write their name on the flipchart and explain the meanings and associations of their name. Include your name(s).

(20 mins)

3 Sum up with a short discussion about particular cultural and gender issues brought out by the origins of the names, and how people feel about their names.

(10 mins)

Materials

Flipchart, pens.

Facilitator's Notes

The name can be either the whole name or the name they wish to be known by in the workshop, depending on time. Be aware of the implications in many cultures of given names, reflecting race or caste differences.

In most cultures, female names are different from male names. Even where the name sounds the same, it usually has male and female spellings. The meaning of the name is often very important. For example, in a workshop with pastoral women in Kenya, each woman explained the meaning of her name, and why she was so named. Some names referred to what the mother was doing up until the time her child was born, some referred to women's roles or their work, or to their relationship with a male relative.

Recent research has shown that the name we are given can affect our later behaviour — female students with names rated as more 'feminine' were found to behave in more stereotypically feminine ways.

Time: 50 mins

Admiring the opposite sex

Objectives

1 To draw out stereotyping as well as positive untypical roles.

2 To help participants to start thinking about male/female relations, early in the training.

Method

1 Ask the participants to pair up (women/men).

2 Ask each participant to think of a person of the opposite sex whom they admire.

3 Ask them to share with their partners the qualities they admire in their chosen person.

4 Individuals then report back to the group the qualities their partner had described.

5 Write down the qualities on a flipchart under Male and Female headings.

(20 mins)

6 Go through all the qualities both for men and women. Bring out any stereotypes of women and men and discuss these with the group.

(30 mins)

Materials

Flipchart, pens

Facilitator's Notes

1 Asking participants to think of a member of the opposite sex who is distant from them may be less threatening: eg a famous woman or man.

2 In workshops in Kenya, Tanzania, and Zimbabwe this activity has been used early in the training course. It helps to break the ice and to build a non-threatening atmosphere to get the group talking about men and women and thinking about gender.

3 There are two potentially opposite outcomes of this activity. Gender stereotyping may result from it, but overlap of stereotypes in itself helps to challenge them. It is also possible that participants may describe qualities in the opposite sex precisely because they don't often find them. For example, one group of women admired gentleness in men — because it was a rare quality.

Time: 1 hr

Sharing our experiences of gender

Objectives

1 To explore gender relations in participants' own lives and workplaces.

2 To give them an opportunity to talk about themselves and how they feel.

Method

1 Divide the group into four single-sex groups of three to six people. Ask each group to discuss these questions:
  a. How does my gender affect my life and work?
  b. What changes would help me make use of my full potential?

(45 mins)

2 Combine a group of men with a group of women to make two mixed groups. Ask the men and women to share with each other the experiences and comments from the first discussion groups.

(45 mins)

Facilitator's Notes

1 This activity is best used with people who are familiar with the concept of gender and have thought about it in relation to their lives. It would not be suitable for groups who are very new to the idea. The adaptation described below can be used in any group.

2 ***Adaptation****: If the group is small, and time permits, participants can be asked to take a few minutes to write on a piece of paper*

a. Two things they like to do that are considered typical for their gender.

b. Two things they hate doing that are typical for their gender.

c. Two things they like doing that are considered non-traditional for their gender.

d. Two things they really wish they could do that are non-traditional.

If the participants know each other a little (as in an internal workshop), they can be asked to make one of these comments an absolute lie, and the rest of the group has to guess what the lie is. This exercise takes about half-an-hour for a group of 12.

(Adaptation from: ***Two Halves make a Whole: Balancing Gender Relations in Development****), (CICC, MATCH and AQOCI, Ottawa 1991)*

Time: 45 mins — 1 hr

Who am I: where do I come from?

Objectives

1 To help participants to get to know each other.

2 To start the process of thinking about oppression.

3 To make the group a safe place for people to be who they are.

Method

1 Give a brief input on the importance of listening for participative learning, and how to do it. Explain the objectives of the exercise, and what will happen. Explain that participants will report back on themselves, not on others.

(5 mins)

2 Ask the participants to find a partner that they would like to talk to but who they do not know very well. In pairs each one speaks for five minutes about who they are, in terms of the groups they belong to and where they come from — sex, race, class, religion, caste, parents, area or region of birth, and any other important factors. The other person listens attentively and does not interrupt. After five minutes they swap and the other person talks.

(10 mins)

3 In the large group, ask each participant to share the key facts about who they are and where they come from. Explain that in society certain groups are discriminated against and oppressed. This can make people from these groups feel inferior, insecure, or resentful. In groups who are fighting oppression, eg in development circles, there may be a tendency for people in the privileged or oppressor groups to feel guilty or ashamed. It is crucial to make clear that this training is one small step to fighting oppression, and in this all people are equally welcome and accepted for who they are. Allow time for group reaction/discussion.

(30-40 mins +)

Facilitator's Notes

1 It is important that the facilitators spend time together doing this exercise for themselves, and reflecting on how they feel about it during the preparation for the training.

2 This activity may feel rather risky if the group is used to pretending that there are no differences between people, or that differences do not matter. Thus, it should not be the very first activity that is done with a group. However, it is useful to have it near the beginning so that safety and real sharing can be established.

3 See ***Section 9 Activitiy 75*** *and* ***Handout 90*** *for guidelines on good listening. The important thing here is that the listener is totally accepting of whatever the talker says, does not interrupt, and only if the talker dries up, can prompt on the key questions.*

4 This activity also gives additional information to the facilitators about the composition of the group, and what some of the dynamics might be. Be particularly aware of people in a minority and what support they might need to feel safe in the group — ask them privately, outside the session.

5 Feelings will come up in this activity! Be prepared for them, and encourage the participants to be prepared for them. You may need to allow extra time for this activity, depending on what comes up.

Time: 1–1½hrs

Life story

Objectives

1 For participants to get to know each other in a deeper way.

2 To start to think about gender issues.

3 To create mutual understanding.

Method

1 Ask participants to form groups of three or four with others that they don't know well.

(5 mins)

2 Join a small group yourself — if there is more than one facilitator, they should join different groups.

3 Ask the people in each group to share the story of their lives, particularly focusing on when they first became aware of gender issues.

(60 mins)

4 In the large group, ask each person to say one point that they found important

(25 mins)

Materials

Flipchart and pens (if doing adaptation).

Facilitator's Notes

1 ***Adaptation****: People can represent their life story graphically using coloured pens and flipchart. Allow about 15 minutes for each drawing, before sharing in small groups. The life story can be represented as a river, going back to the source (early years with the families), and going through the different times in their life, representing calm and troubled waters, and major influences (tributaries).*

2 This can be a very deep sharing exercise or a more superficial one. It can increase self-awareness, and build up trust. It can provide the opportunity for people to have some hurts in their lives respectfully listened to. Listening to others' stories can make us more aware and sensitive to their needs and hurts. In this way we can build up trust, understanding and respect in the group. However, because in sharing personal stories people make themselves vulnerable, it may be wise not to use this exercise where there are deep tensions or extreme lack of trust in the group. Especially in a gender training, the facilitators should also be ready for the possibility of a female participant disclosing sexual or physical attacks by men.

3. When Oxfam used this activity with development staff in East Africa, some common points to emerge were:

- *the important role women have had in all our lives, for example, our mothers;*
- *changes in development thinking over the years; only recently has gender become an issue;*
- *women working in a men's world — building up strength and solidarity*
- *disruptive effect of field work on family life.*

Time: 1 hr

Expectations, hopes and fears

Objectives

1 To allow participants to express any feelings which could prevent them from participating fully.

2 To enable the facilitators to adapt the programme if necessary.

3 To enable participants to be clear about the programme so that they do not have unrealistic expectations.

4 To encourage a feeling of participation and solidarity and reduce potential hostility or fear.

5 To arrange reporting of the training.

Method

1 **Preparation**: send out pre-course questionnaires (**Handout 1**) which should be returned at least two weeks before the workshop starts.

2 Before the session starts prepare flipchart, listing responses to 'what are the main issues concerning gender as they relate to your work', (see pre-course questionnaire) and 'What do you hope to get out of the training'.

3 Put up the flipchart, explaining that you have tried to design the training around these issues. *(5 mins)*

4 Ask participants to form groups of three or four and discuss their expectations of the workshop, listing them on paper. *Explain that participants do not have to agree*. Expectations should be listed under the following headings:
a. Hopes: what they hope to get out of the workshop. The groups can amend or add to hopes expressed in the pre-course questionnaires.
b. Fears: what they hope will not happen, or they fear may happen. Encourage participants to share their fears openly.
c. Contributions: Each person brings some special experience (e.g. of being discriminated against because of gender, or race), certain skills (e.g. listening skills), and aptitudes (e.g. a willingness to learn and change). Give these

examples to the group and encourage everyone to identify their own contribution to the process of learning.

(30 mins)

5 Put the lists up on the wall and ask them to report back — first each group's hopes, then each group's fears, then their contributions.

6 Go through these expectations and explain any which may not be met, and why, in each case.

(30 mins)

7 Go through the programme if this has not been done. Explain how much flexibility there can and cannot be in timing of sessions and meals and breaks.

(10 mins)

8 Arrange reporting and monitoring groups for the end of the day.

(15 mins)

Monitoring groups should be small and remain the same throughout. Explain that the groups will discuss and report back to you on:

a. Is it appropriate, relevant, comprehensive, pace too fast or too slow?

b. Process: how are the group dynamics, is everyone getting a chance to contribute?

c. Practical details: such as food and accommodation.

Alternatively, if the group is large, you may ask the participants to choose a monitoring team and a practical administration team who will channel information to you.

9 It is very useful to have a report of the workshop or course. Discuss with the group if and why a report should be produced, who it is for, and who will prepare it. (See **Section B: Facilitator's Guidelines**)

Materials

Flipchart and pens

Facilitator's Notes

1 It is important not to give out the programme before you do this activity, or people's expectations may be influenced by what is on the programme.

2 This session is followed by one on ground rules.

3 ***Adaptation****: if there is very limited time, such as half a day, and the group is committed to gender training, it is possible to have a shorter round of 'What I expect from today'. Invite people to mention hopes, fears and contributions. Explain which expectations will and will not be met, and why.*

Handout 1 *Activity 6*

Pre-course questionnaire

1. Name:

2. Address & Tel. No.

3. Job

4. Have you attended any other Gender Training courses? YES/NO
   (Please give brief details)

5. Have you attended any training courses of any kind?

6. What do you hope to get out of the training?

7. What are the main gender issues related to your work? (Briefly, please!)

8. Do you have any requirements to enable you to participate fully in the training?

   a. Special diet (vegan, vegetarian)

   b. Facilities (wheelchair access, provision of signers)

   c. Help with childcare

   d Other — please give details

9. Have you any materials (slides, photos, videos, case studies) you would like to bring? Describe briefly.

10. Please add any other information or comments you feel are relevant.

Time: 15 mins

Ground rules

Objectives

1 To arrive at common norms of behaviour during the course of the workshop.

Method

1 Explain to the participants the need for having a set of rules for behaviour.

(5 mins)

2 Ask the group for suggestions for rules the group should adhere to, and make it clear that the rules should be agreed upon by the group.

(10 mins)

3 Write the agreed ground rules on flipchart.

Materials

Flipchart, pens

Facilitator's Notes

1. A sample of some common Ground Rules:

Everyone should keep to the timings.
No smoking in the workshop room.
Do not interrupt while others are speaking.
Everyone should try to listen as well as speak.
Maintain confidentiality of what is shared — no gossiping.
Show respect to others, and others' experiences.
Do not make personal attacks.

2 The facilitator, as a member of the group, can also suggest ground rules if others do not come up with them. You should also include rules that are rules of the centre or venue.

Time: 20 mins

Introduction to the workshop

Objectives

1 To welcome everybody.

2 To introduce the workshop programme, discuss timing of meals and breaks and check that practical details such as accommodation and participants' special needs are attended to.

3 To prepare participants by giving a summary of the purpose of the workshop or course.

Method

1 Ask everyone to introduce themselves to the group, stating who they are, where they come from, and the kind of work they do. Include yourself in this.

(10 mins)

2 Give the proposed timing of sessions, meals and breaks and make sure that this is acceptable to participants.

(5 mins)

3 Go through the objectives of the workshop, which you have previously written up on a flipchart.

(5 mins)

Materials

Flipchart, pens.

Facilitator's Notes

1 If the participants are not used to speaking in a large group, you can adapt this activity. If one or more of the previous introductory activities have been used, omit step 1 of the method.

2 ***Adaptation****: Suggest participants pair up with people they don't know. Ask each pair to spend five minutes talking about who they are, where they come from and the work they do. Ask each person to introduce their partner to the group.*

4 This activity can be used if time is short, but should not be done before the Expectations, Hopes and Fears Activity 6. You could expand step 2 of the method to include one or more elements of the introductory activities in this section.

Time: 1 hr

Objectives jigsaw

Objectives

1 To show the objectives of the workshop and the importance of co-operation to achieve those objectives.

Method

1 **Preparation**: Before the workshop, design a black and white picture representing the group or the subject of the workshop. Overwrite the picture with sentences describing the objectives of the workshop. Then divide the picture into three sections, all meeting at one point, and colour each section a different colour.

Cut out ten pieces, three of one colour only, and one which has all three colours on it. Put the pieces into envelopes according to colour (e.g. a red envelope, blue, yellow — with the pieces of that colour in it) and add the multi-coloured piece to one of the envelopes.

2 Divide the participants into three groups.

3 Give each group one envelope of pieces and explain that the point of the game is for each group to finish their puzzle — do not explain that the three puzzles are interlinked.

(15 mins)

4 If, after 15 minutes, the groups have not realised the three puzzles make a whole puzzle, interrupt the groups and ask the groups to come together to make the whole Jigsaw

(15 mins)

5 Ask the group to discuss the following questions:
a..What did you feel when you were working in your group?
b. How did you help your group to accomplish the task?
c. How did you hinder your group in accomplishing the task?
d. What did you learn from this activity about co-operation?(30 mins)

Facilitator's Notes

1 The basis of this game is that people have to come together to finish the puzzle. They may not finish the puzzle in the time available — which happened when this activity was done in a Kenya workshop. The reaction of some participants was that the activity had not 'worked' because the puzzle was not finished.

2 There can be negative reactions to this game because participants are not given all the information — they can feel tricked. However, it raised important points:

- *that everyone should be involved in planning, and know what goals and objectives are being set;*

- *that sometimes a group does what an outsider wants them to do, rather than what they want to do;*

- *a group can be led into actions without knowing why.*

Time: 1 -2 hrs

Sharing work experience

Objectives

1 To enable participants to work together and consider gender issues in their work.

2 To enable participants to understand gender issues in other people's work.

3 To find out what kinds of groups and activities people work with.

Method

1 Two months before the training, write to all the participants and ask them to prepare a short presentation of 10-15 minutes on gender in their work. This should be based on a pre-course questionnaire (**Handout 2**). If participants come in groups from country offices, or agencies, there should be one presentation per group.

2 The evening before the session, ask participants to write very brief answers on flipchart to the questions on the questionnaire.

3 At the session, ask participants to present their report for 10-15 minutes. If the group includes people who work together in teams, the teams may present a joint report through one of the members.

4 Sum up, asking participants to note any common issues in the presentations.

Materials

Handout 2
Flipchart, pens

Facilitator's Notes

1 The questionnaire included is an example of one which has been used for a training of international NGOs, and would not be suitable for other groups. The questionnaire must be relevant to the participant group, and to the purpose of the training. It is a good idea to test out a sample questionnaire before you use it in training to check that the questions are readily understood, and provide the information you require; and then revise it where necessary. For example, if your questions ask about 'gender strategy' do all the participants have the same understanding of that term? How do you make it clear that gender issues affect all projects, not just women-only ones? If you ask about women only, will you risk alienating some people? Be aware of people's sensitivities. The aim is not to make people feel defensive about their work, but to encourage honest reflection and sharing.

2 If possible have a break after this exercise and encourage people to discuss and question each other about common points of interest. Alternatively, you can arrange this formally by putting people into small groups with people they don't work with.

3 The material that people bring with them can be used later in the workshop as case material for programme analysis and planning. If the information is detailed enough, it can be used to raise questions related to gender roles and needs.

4 If this activity is done after a full discussion on gender, and participants have the opportunity to make revisions in the light of what they have learned it can help to prevent a feeling that the presentations are a kind of test.

Handout 2 *Activity 10*

Pre-course questionnaire

1. How many projects are there in your programme?

2. What are the main sectors you work in?

3. How many are women-only? i.e. designed for and run by women.

4. How many are men-only?

5. How many are designed for men and women together?

6. How many projects have some component addressed specifically to women?

7. What sort of activities are done with women?

8. What are the objectives of work with women?

9. In the mixed projects how are the women involved? i.e. what proportion of the people who attend meetings are women, do women speak in meetings, do they hold decision-making posts, do they contribute their labour, how do they benefit?

10. Do you have any strategy or policy for working with women?

11. What achievements and constraints have you experienced in your work with women?

Time: 2 hrs

What is development

Objectives

1 To reach a common understanding of what we mean by development and the way we are promoting development in our work.

Method

Part 1

1 **Preparation**: before the session select and pin up or spread on tables about 50 photos showing a wide range of images which could be linked to development.

2 Divide the group into threes. Ask each trio to select from photos: two showing what development is and two showing what development is not.
(10 mins)

3 Ask a spokesperson from each trio to explain to the whole group why they selected their photos.
(3 mins per trio)

Make notes on flipchart of the main points.

4 Draw out common themes to help the group to reach a consensus on development.
(20 mins)

Part 2

1 Divide the group into teams, based on country of origin, organisation or kind of work. Ask each team to discuss the following questions:
a. How are we working to promote development in relation to our definition?
b. What are the obstacles we face in promoting development?
c. How are we working with women? *(40 mins)*

2 Ask a spokesperson from each team to report back to the whole group.
(10 mins per team)

Materials

Flipchart, pens, about 50 photos

Facilitator's Notes

1 Ask if there was broad agreement between people as to what development was — were there differences according to sex, or for other reasons? (See also notes for following **Activity 12, Community Development.***)*

2 As a variation to coming up with a common statement about development, you could ask participants to agree on a symbolic representation of development, or a picture, or some other graphic way of expressing it.

3 If you plan to do the activity on Community Development (Activity 12), or you have used photographs already, you could ask the participants to draw what to them would represent development. Emphasise that it is not the drawing itself that is important, but what it expresses.

4 ***Adaptation*** *This activity can also be used as a shorter, simpler* ***Ice-breaker****. Participants each choose a picture they find striking and discuss it in groups of four. Each group reports back to the plenary on whatever they have noticed in particular about women and men.*

Time: 1 hr

Community development

Objectives

1 To create a common understanding of :
development for women
development for men
development for the community.

2 To explore the meaning of the word 'community'.

Method

1 **Preparation**: before the session spread out a number of photographs of development projects and everyday life.

2 Divide participants into three groups — A, B and C.
Each person in Group A is asked to choose a picture which represents community development to them.
Each person in Group B is asked to choose a picture which represents development for men to them.
Each person in Group C is asked to choose a picture which represents development for women to them.

3 Ask all participants to look at pictures that are spread on the table, in silence, and make a first and second choice. After ten minutes ask them to pick their pictures. If their first choice is taken, they pick up their second choice.

(10 mins)

4 Ask each group to discuss and write down all the aspects of development portrayed by the pictures they have picked.

(20 mins)

5 In the plenary share what development is for women and for men, and what community development is. Focus on development as a process of men and women improving their lives, and raise the question of the meaning of community.

(30 mins)

Materials

Flipchart, pens
Photographs portraying aspects of development work

Facilitator's Notes

1 It is better if each group does not know the task of the other groups. One way to ensure this is to give each group an envelope containing a card indicating what they are to find pictures about (one card would say 'development for women', another 'development for men', and the other 'development for the community').

2 In summing up note that we do have different images of what constitutes development for men, for women, and for the community, and ask for the possible reasons for this. It is essential to have sufficient a wide range of pictures so that there is adequate choice; you do not want people to say that they only chose those images because the ones they wanted were already taken by the other groups.

An example, at a workshop with project partners in Kenya.

Development for men: concrete projects, with practical results, technical projects, designed by outside experts, men's involvement in development as policy makers and supervisors.

Development for women: the provision of basic needs and services for the family; balance between development of structures and of people, equal control over decision making.

Development for the community: all members involved at all levels of decision making, mobilising available resources to meet their basic needs.

All groups mentioned the issue of the importance of change in attitudes, and the difficulty of doing this and of measuring it. However, the purpose of change in attitudes is to change the situation, and this can be measured.

3 This activity should focus on understanding the concept of community, and community development. It should lead to disaggregating the notion of 'community' as a unit used in development planning, and looking at all the different interests within it: women and men, young and old, able-bodied and disabled people, richer and poorer, and between people of different race, caste or ethnic groups.

Time: 1 hr

The liberator

Objectives

1 To analyse the process of development and to identify its impact on women.

2 To find out what this process has given to women both positively and negatively.

3 To examine how development has continued to perpetuate the traditional role of women.

Method

1 Identify seven participants who are willing to act in front of the group.

2 One women should be in traditional dress with one leg tied to a rock by a chain. As the acting begins this woman should be sitting down by herself, looking helpless.

3 The other people involved should each have one of the following items:
a. Identity card
b. Bible
c. A book and pen
d. Money
e. Flag
f. Needle and thread

4 Each person comes, in turn, to the woman who is sitting on the floor with her leg tied. She wakes up as each person comes close, smiles, and receives the present. She tries to look around, cut her chains, but all in vain. She drops the present and goes back to her previous position. The same procedure is followed for all the presents.

After she receives all the presents she returns to her original posture. The play ends here. There should be music playing in the background. It goes loud as she receives each of the presents but fades as she returns to her previous position.

(30 mins)

5 After the play discuss the following questions:
a. What did you see happening?
b. Who did the woman in the traditional dress represent?
c. Who did the people bringing presents represent? What did the chain represent?
d. What similarities can we see between the play and real life?
e. What kind of woman is produced by the situation?
f. How do programmes we run for women change the situation of women? How do they reinforce the traditional role of women?

(30 mins)

Materials

Chain
Music
Identity card
Bible
Book
Pen
Flag
Money
Needle and thread

Facilitator's Notes

1 The items used in this activity are symbols for different kinds of interventions: political, religious, educational, nationalistic, income-generating.
2 This activity could be adapted for specific cultural or political situations by introducing other symnbols and roles; in an emergency workshop, for example, food or second-hand clothes.
3 This is a good activity to get participants thinking about different kinds of intervention, and to prepare the gound for later work on women's roles and needs. This could also be used after a disucssion of roles and needs (see activities in Section C4) to bring upl in a light and graphic way, the ways that interventions can fail to address women's strategic gender needs.
4 This method uses a 'code' (see C1 Taining techniques.)

(Source: Hope and Timmel (1984) Training for Transformation: A Handbook for Community Workers, Mambo Press, Zimbabwe.)

C.3 Gender awareness and self-awareness

This section is in two parts:
- Building gender awareness
- Self-awareness for women and men

In this section we provide a number of awareness-raising activities for use with different kinds of groups. Please use those most suited for the level of gender awareness of your group, and to the kind of group you are training. It is, however, essential that any gender training course includes at least one of the gender-awareness activities in this section, so that the group has a shared understanding of gender before going on to gender analysis.

Building gender awareness

The activities in the first part introduce the concept of gender, explore participants' emotions and ideas about gender relations, and begin to look at gender and development. Some of the activities are very basic, suitable for groups who are new to gender analysis and who have had no or very little exposure to gender training (e.g. The gender game, **Activity 16**. Others assume a familiarity with the concept (e.g. What is gender?, **Activity17**). Some activities are controversial and should only be used after the first, basic activities or with groups who are familiar and comfortable with the basic construct of gender. Many of these activities throw up strong emotions, whether people are new to them or not, and facilitators should be prepared for this!

Before going through this section, we advise that you read through **Section A.2 Key Concepts** to refresh your memory if you haven't done very much gender training, or you have not done it recently. The activities are suitable for mixed-sex groups.

Self-awareness for women and men

The activities in the second part are all potentially highly-emotional sessions. Activities such as Millie's mother's red dress **Activity 23** and Violence against women **Activity 31** are likely to touch some women very deeply. You should ensure that the feeling and atmosphere in the group are sufficiently supportive for women to be able to express their feelings without fear. The activities are for women-only or men-only. However, if you want to try them with a mixed group — and this could be very powerful and an important learning experience — it may work best to run the sessions concurrently with women-only and men-only groups, and then bring them together at the end for discussion.

C.3 Activities

Time: 30-40 mins

Choosing the sex of your child

Objectives

1 To bring out participants' assumptions about female and male children.

2 To examine how true and deep-rooted these assumptions are.

Method

1 Tell the participants this story:

A couple are struggling to conceive a child. They go to a diviner who tells them they will have a child, but only after they have decided which sex they want it to be.

2 Give each participant a piece of paper and ask them to imagine being in this situation. Ask them to write down the sex they would choose for their child.

3 Ask participants also to write down their reasons for choosing the sex. Give them a few minutes, and collect the papers. Put the result on a flipchart: 'Number of those who chose girls' and 'Number of those who chose boys', and list the reasons.

(10 mins)

4 Discuss with participants:
a. Numbers of boys and girls.
b. Reasons for choosing the sex they chose.
c. The effect of assumptions like:
Boys will continue the kin.
Boys will take care of parents during old age.
Boys will remain with parents, girls will get married.
Boys will inherit, girls will not.
d. Discuss implications of how male and female children are socialised and treated, to prepare them for the roles they play in society.

(20-30 mins)

Facilitator's Notes

1 This activity was used with grassroots women and men in Kenya and it was quite revealing. The discussion took several directions. Almost all participants chose boys. Family planning became the centre of the discussion because women and men continue having children in order to have a boy. The whole question of who determines the sex of the child (biologically) was addressed.

2 It raised the question of how the community looks at a woman with only girl children and the implications of succession and inheritance differences for boys and girls.

3 The activity can provoke a great many issues. It is a good introduction to looking at socialisation processes and conceptualising gender roles and the relationship between men and women.

4 If the group is made up of people of different cultures, you may need to look at very different assumptions made about girls and boys, and discuss these differences between one culture and another.

Time: 40 mins

'My organisation is a male/female organisation'

Objectives

1 To allow participants to discover some of the contradictions and complexities in the structure of their organisation.

2 To allow participants to practice putting forward their point of view and hearing the opposing points of view.

3 To raise the energy level and to get everybody involved.

Method

1 Explain the activity and divide the group into two teams. One team has to hold the view that 'My organisation is a male organisation'. The other team has to hold the view that 'My organisation is a female organisation'. Give each team ten minutes to prepare their arguments. Tell the teams to consider staff, volunteers, and the programme, and look at issues of position, power and status in the hierarchy. Meanwhile, arrange two chairs in the centre of the room facing each other. (This is a 'gold-fish bowl' debate.)

(15 mins)

2 Each team chooses one representative to start the debate, sitting on the chairs. When the person on the chair has made their point, or when another member of their team feels they want to take over, the team member taps the person sitting on the chair on the shoulder. The team member then takes their place and the debate continues. This changing over of places must be done quickly in order to keep the discussion lively. A number of people should have the chance to put forward their views.

(15 mins)

3 At the end of the debate, discuss with the participants how they found the exercise, and whether any new information came out. Ask them how easy or difficult it was to think up arguments to support their position, and to rebut the arguments that the other team were putting forward. *(10 mins)*

4 At the end of the discussion bring out the key points about the organisation and hand out relevant documents, such as Equal Opportunities statements or policy documents.

Materials

Handouts: The organisation's Equal Opportunities Policy Statement, or Gender Policy.

Facilitator's Notes

1 What is interesting about this debate is that it can bring out facts about the organisation which are true of the society in which we live.

2 The terms 'male' and 'female' rather than 'gender-aware' are used deliberately to enable people to look at all aspects of the organisation.

3 The exercise is an open one to encourage debate, but you should make sure that certain key points are covered. In many organisations, women are working voluntarily or in lower-paid positions than men. Many development agencies claim to target the 'poorest of the poor' and much research shows that on average women are poorer than men, so could be classified as the 'poorest of the poor'. Yet in many organisations the top positions are held by men, and many of the development programmes involve men more than women. This is unlikely to be because of a specific strategy to exclude women, but, because all organisations are operating within a context where women are excluded and discriminated against, this will happen unless there are specific steps to redress the balance. Even where there are women in some of the top jobs in an organisation, it does not necessarily follow that programmes will be gender-aware. Yet it seems unlikely that a gender-aware programme can emerge from an organisation which is itself very gender-imbalanced.

4 The activity described here is for a training where all the participants belong to, or are connected with, the same organisation. If people are from different organisations, you could simply get people into small groups to discuss this question, and list up the arguments for their organisations being a 'male' or a 'female' organisation, to look at any similarities and differences.

Time: 30 mins

The gender game

Objectives

1 To introduce the term 'gender' to a group unfamiliar with the concept.

Method

1 Ask the group if they understand the difference between 'gender' and 'sex'.

2 Explain the difference quickly and simply. *(5 mins)*

3 Hand out sheets of paper to the participants and ask them to write the numbers 1 to 10 in a list on the paper.

4 Read out the numbered list of statements on **Handout 3** and ask participants to write 'G' against those they think refer to gender, and 'S' to those they think refer to sex.

(5 mins)

5 Distribute **Handout 3** and discuss the answers with the whole group. Focus on these questions and key ideas:

a. Did any statements surprise you?
b. Do the statements indicate that gender is inborn or learned?
c. Gender roles vary greatly in different societies, cultures and historical periods.
d. Age, race and class are also major factors which determine our gender roles.
e. Women in every country experience both power and oppression differently.

(20 mins)

Materials

Paper, pens and **Handout 3**.

Facilitator's Notes

1 This is an activity to be used with participants who have very little, or no, understanding of gender, or who feel that they need to go back to basics to be sure of their grasp of gender.

2 ***Adaptation****: The group can be split into small groups of four or five to discuss their classification of the statements.*

(Source: ***Class, Gender and Race Inequality and the Media in an International Context****, Focus for Change, 1992)*

Statements about men and women

1 Women give birth to babies, men don't. (S)

2 Little girls are gentle, boys are tough. (G)

3 In one case, when a child brought up as a girl learned that he was actually a boy, his school marks improved dramatically. (G)

4 Amongst Indian agricultural workers, women are paid 40-60 per cent of the male wage. (G)

5 Women can breastfeed babies, men can bottlefeed babies. (S)

6 Most building-site workers in Britain are men. (G)

7 In Ancient Egypt men stayed at home and did weaving. Women handled family business. Women inherited property and men did not. (G)

8 Men's voices break at puberty, women's do not. (S)

9 In one study of 224 cultures, there were 5 in which men did all the cooking, and 36 in which women did all the housebuilding. (G)

10 According to UN statistics, women do 67 per cent of the world's work, yet their earnings for it amount to only 10 per cent of the world's income. (G)

Time: 30-90 mins

What is gender?

Objectives

1 To allow each person to air their views on gender.

2 To encourage active listening to build up trust.

3 To arrive at a common understanding of the term 'gender'.

4 To start making the links between gender and development (optional).

Method

1 In pairs, discuss 'What is gender?' It is important that ideas are generated. Pairs should not be aiming to come up with a complete definition.

(5-10 mins)

Additional option: Why are development NGOs interested in gender?

2 In large group, 'brainstorm' answers and write all answers on a flipchart.

(5-10 mins)

3 Arrive at common understanding of the meaning of the concept of gender, including the key points of socialised, culturally-specific roles for men and women.

(20mins-1hr)

4 **Optional**: Lead discussion on the relevance of gender to development NGOs.

5 Give out **Handout 4 or 5** at end of session or end of day.

NB: The timings for this exercise will vary considerably depending on many factors such as language, how often participants have discussed this before, and how many different views come up.

Materials

Flipchart
Handout 4 and 5

Facilitator's Notes

1 It is important to allow participants to express their discomfort with the word 'gender'. Many people feel it is an English word which is untranslatable. It may be worth pointing out that the use of the word gender, as distinct from sex, is relatively recent, and thus is a new concept for all. It is also important to point out that one does not need to have been using the word gender to have been aware of and working on the roles and relationships between men and women as a development issue. Participants could be asked, at some point in the training, to discuss what words they use to explain these issues to grassroots groups.

2 From the brainstorm, you should bring out the key points:

a. Gender is different from sex: it is not biologically determined.
b. It varies from culture to culture, and with the economic, social and political context.
c. It varies over time.
d. We learn gender roles: this implies that they can change.
e. People who act outside their gender roles may face disapproval.
f. It is important to consider gender relationships.

3 In answer to the second optional question, be prepared to let people discuss such answers as 'development NGOs are not really concerned about gender', or 'are only concerned because it is fashionable'. Point to the need to consider gender in order to enable development for both men and women.

4 ***Adaptation****: An additional stage can be added in which two or three volunteers take the flipcharts and try and come up with a one or two-line definition of gender. This is then presented to the group for discussion. Definitions produced by other workshops or other people can be included for discussion to show similarities (and differences); but care should be taken not to confuse people.*

5 This activity, or one similar to it, must be used at the start of every training, to ensure that people have a common understanding of the basic concepts. The time taken can be reduced if people have previously done gender training.

6 This activity is very useful for people who have done some work with gender, but has not proved helpful in workshops with people who are new to the concept.

7 We have included two handouts, one giving a historical perspective and more detail, and a shorter, simpler one, which also introduces some of the analytical concepts to be addressed later in the workshop. Use the one most appropriate for your group.

Why gender is a development issue

The issues concerning women and their part (or not) in the development process have been increasingly examined over the years. However, the ways of addressing these issues have varied as understanding of women's position in development, and of gender roles themselves, has grown. Although the principle of equality of men and women was recognised in both the UN Charter in 1945 and the UN Declaration of Human Rights in 1948, the majority of development planners and workers did not fully address women's position in the development process. Several researchers have shown that development planners worked on the assumption that what would benefit one section of society (men) would trickle down to the other (women).

The ways of defining women's position in development has changed through the years:

In the 1950s and 1960s, women's issues in development were subsumed under the question of human rights, and women were viewed as objects to protect or make recommendations for but not necessarily to consult. UN Conventions of particular concern to women included:

1949 Convention for the Suppression of Traffic in Persons and the Exploitation of the Prostitution of Others

1951 Equal Remuneration for Men and Women Workers for Work of Equal Value

1952 Convention on the Political Rights of Women

In the 1970s, although women were still not necessarily consulted, their key position in the development process became more widely recognised. This was especially so in connection with population and food issues. Women were viewed as useful resources to be integrated into the development process, thus rendering the particular projects more efficient and more successful:

'These are the women (the more than 500 million women illiterates) upon whom the success of our population policies, our food programmes and our total development efforts ultimately rely. The success of these policies depends, in other words, on those who are least equipped to carry them out.' (Helvi Sipila, *The Times*, 23.4.75)

In 1972 it was decided to declare 1975 'International Women's Year', which led into the UN Decade for Women.

In the 1980s there has been a growing trend towards seeing women as agents and beneficiaries in all sectors and at all levels of the development process. It is partly through an understanding of gender roles that this trend has emerged.

In 1985 the UN decade culminated in a conference in Nairobi which, after a period of intensive discussions involving women from all over the world, resulted in the adoption of the 'Forward-Looking Strategies'.

The Forward-Looking Strategies took the main themes of the Decade for Women (equality, development and peace, with the sub-themes health, education and employment), and set out the obstacles facing women in each of these areas; proposed general strategies for overcoming them, and made recommendations to governments and other bodies for creating greater opportunities for equality for women at all levels.

What is gender?

The conceptual distinction between sex and gender developed by Anne Oakley is a useful analytical tool to clarify ideas and has now been almost universally taken up. According to this distinction sex is connected with biology, whereas the gender identity of men and women in any given society is socially and psychologically (and that means also historically and culturally) determined.

Biological and physical conditions (chromosomes, external and internal genitalia, hormonal states and secondary sex characteristics), lead to the determination of male or female sex. To determine gender, however, social and cultural perceptions of masculine and feminine traits and roles must be taken into account.

Gender is learnt through a process of socialisation and through the culture of the particular society concerned. In many cultures boys are encouraged in the acts considered to display male traits (and girls vice versa) through the toys given to children (guns for boys, dolls for girls), the kind of discipline meted out, the jobs or careers to which they might aspire, and the portrayal of men and women in the media. Children learn their gender from birth. They learn how they should behave in order to be perceived by others, and themselves, as either masculine or feminine. Throughout their life this is reinforced by parents, teachers, peers, their culture and society.

Every society uses biological sex as one criterion for describing gender but, beyond that simple starting point, no two cultures would completely agree on what distinguishes one gender from another. Therefore there is considerable variation in gender roles between cultures.

Division of labour in society

The division of labour between the sexes is best explained by gender but, because reproduction is based on a universal biological difference between the male and female sex, societies use this as a basis for allotting other tasks. These tasks are allotted according to convenience and precedents in the particular culture, and determine masculine and feminine roles.

'Professor George Murdock has surveyed the data for 224 societies (mostly preliterate) and shows that the tendency to segregate economic activities in one way or another according to sex is strong. Taking a list of 46 different activities, he suggests that some are more often masculine than feminine, and vice versa. For example, lumbering is an exclusively masculine activity in 104 of his societies and exclusively feminine in 6: cooking is exclusively feminine in 158 and exclusively masculine in 5. Hunting, fishing, weapon making, boat building and mining tend to be masculine, while grinding grain and carrying water tend to be feminine. Activities that are less consistently allocated to one sex include preparing the soil, planting, tending and harvesting the crops, 'burden bearing' and body mutilation.' (Oakley 1972, p.128)

Even in child-rearing men play a substantial role in some societies:

'The Arapesh, for example, consider that the business of bearing and rearing a child belongs to father and mother equally, and equally disqualifies them for other roles. Men as well as women 'make' and 'have' babies, and the verb 'to bear a child' is used indiscriminately of either a man or a woman. Child-bearing is believed to be as debilitating for the man as it is for the woman. The father goes to bed and is described as 'having a baby' when the child is born.... The Trobriand Islanders are renowned for their ignorance of the father's biological role in reproduction, but they stress the need for the father to share with the mother all tasks involved in bringing up children.' (Oakley 1972, p.134-135)

We see, then, that tasks and the division of labour do not relate to the sex of the individuals concerned, and so are not common to one sex from one culture to another, but are culture specific. Thus gender is culture specific.

Gender not only varies from one culture to another but it also varies within cultures over time; culture is not static but evolves. As societies become more complex, the roles played by men and women are not only determined by culture but by socio-political and economic factors.

Why is gender a development issue?

The roles that women play are different in any given society, and their situation is determined by the legislation, religious norms, economic status or class, cultural values, ethnicity and types of productive activity of their country, community and household. Women are usually responsible for domestic work; the care of children, family health, cooking and providing food and other household services. In most societies they also play a major role in the productive activities of the family; in farming, paid domestic labour, services, industries and income-generating activities. In some societies they also have clear community roles.

In each of these areas — reproduction, production and the community — women have often been adversely affected by the development process. There is a wide gap between women's high, yet unrecognised, economic participation and their low political and social power, and development strategies have usually taken the needs of the most vocal and politically active as their starting point. To understand gender the activities of men and women need to be addressed separately. The reproductive, productive and social or community roles women are playing must be looked at as well as the roles played economically and socially by men. By examining men's and women's roles a greater understanding of their needs and involvement in power and decision-making around specific tasks and issues will be reached.

Historically, development workers have used notions of gender imported from the North. The majority of projects were — and still are — based on the false assumption that the nuclear household supported by a non-productive wife dependent upon a male head, is universal. This is not the pattern for many cultures. In *The Family Among the Australian Aborigines*, Malinowski wrote:

> 'A very important point is that the woman's share in labour was of much more vital importance to the maintenance of the household than the man's work ... even the food supply contributed by the women was far more important than the man's share ... food collected by women was the staple food of the natives ... economically [the family] is entirely dependent upon women's work.' (Malinowski 1963 as cited in Oakley 1972, p.139)

Studies of women's roles in agriculture from a sample of African peoples living in Senegal, Gambia, Uganda and Kenya show that women contribute between 60 per cent and 80 per cent of the total agricultural work done.

How to approach gender in development

It is of vital importance in development work not to use imported notions of gender, nor regard 'the community' and 'the household' as the basic units. One must go beyond the household and break it down into its component parts. By assessing and understanding the gender roles in a given society the specific needs of women (and men) can be ascertained and addressed within projects (Moser and Levy 1986).

The primary practical requirement for incorporating a gender analysis into development is to consult with and listen to women so that their roles and resulting needs are better understood. How the issues of gender are actually addressed depends upon the policy direction envisaged. One approach is to design projects and programmes to make life 'easier' for women and help them in their given gender tasks. For example, an agricultural project could include provision of support for female agricultural tasks, as well as those carried out by men. Women's needs for better equipment, improved seeds, and advice would be taken into consideration. In health projects, the particular concerns of the women would be elicited from them and their priorities addressed in the project. On the domestic front, projects could aim to alleviate the drudgery and heavy physical demands of women's work by providing more efficient grinders or stoves, or improving women's access to water. Whether working with women alone or within the community as a whole the primary objective would be to enable women to perform their existing roles better.

An alternative but complementary approach is to challenge the *status quo* or address the perceived inequalities between men and women. This could involve, for example, working for change in laws that discriminated against women; increasing women's access to land; giving women decision-making power within projects, etc. The aim is social change and the empowerment of women. For agencies such as Oxfam, which espouse social change, justice, and empowerment in their rhetoric, meeting women's needs for more radical change should be within the adopted policy approach to gender.

Why is it that addressing gender inequalities is taboo and yet tackling inequalities in terms of wealth and class is not? It is often argued that by addressing gender the traditions or culture of a society are being tampered with. This is not necessarily the case and the attitudes to gender may be no more 'traditional' than attitudes to class or power. When the traditions and cultural attitudes to gender are clarified, then the actual gender relations can be assessed and addressed within a programme or project. Development is a process that should involve all members of a society to the same extent, according to their individual needs.

Source: Based on 'Why gender is a development issue', by April Brett in *Changing Perceptions*, Oxfam

Unpacking gender

Gender is an old word which has taken on a new meaning. It is a 'portmanteau' word, containing a set of inter-related ideas. Because this use of the word is new, a kind of shorthand, it is difficult to translate. The friend of an Oxfam worker in Ethiopia was both curious and amazed that Oxfam appeared to be spending three days 'discussing sex'. In fact, the workshop in Addis Ababa examined the distinction between sex and gender. Understanding this difference, and the concept of gender, is essential to our understanding of how development processes affect men and women, girls, and boys, in different ways.

Sex is a fact of human biology; we are born male or female; it is men who impregnate, and women who conceive, give birth, and breastfeed the human baby. On this biological difference we construct an edifice of social attitudes and assumptions, behaviours and activities: these are our gender roles and identities. Questioning them may feel threatening, attacking the very foundations of our understanding of ourselves, our personal and social relations, our culture and traditions.

Yet is important to understand how we learn to be boys and girls, to become women and men; how we define masculine and feminine behaviour; how we are taught activities regarded as appropriate for our sex, and the way in which we should relate to one another. What we learn depends on the society into which we are born, and our position within it, our relative poverty or wealth, and our ethnic group For unlike sex, gender roles are variable. In some societies women are farmers, own oxen, plough their own fields; in others this is 'against God and nature'; in yet other instances where war, migration, or other factors have left many women entirely responsible for their households, custom has been modified to enable them to have the means of production to provide for their families. So, gender roles are not only different but also change over time.

Gender analysis looks not only at roles and activities but also at relationships. It asks not only who does what, but also who makes the decisions, and who derives the benefit, who uses resources such as land, or credit, and who controls these resources; and what other factors influence relationships, such as laws about property rights and inheritance.

This reveals that women and men, because of their different gender roles and responsibilities, have different experiences and needs. Both men and women play a role in the sphere of productive work and community life, but women's contribution may be less formal. While men's agricultural work may result in a cash income, women may be producing food for family consumption, and the cash value remains hidden. In community life, men generally have the role of public representation;

women's role of organisation may be crucial, but less visible, particularly to outsiders. Underlying both productive work and community life is the work of biological and social reproduction. This is the foundation of human society: the care of children and family, the maintenance of the household, collecting water, and fuel, preparing, processing and cooking food, keeping people and home clean and healthy. These tasks can be arduous and time-consuming — and taken for granted. Generally they fall to women. The result has been that this work is not valued and is not included in development planning, often with disastrous consequences. For example, failure to take into account both women's role as the mangers of water, and also the many and varied tasks of their working day, has resulted in water supply projects which may be technically sound but are socially inefficient; providing water at too great a distance, at the wrong time of day for women, who already have to juggle a series of different activities to meet their practical needs.

Development programmes which have not been gender-aware have not only not benefited women; sometimes they have further disadvantaged them, adding to their workload and failing to recognise their roles in reproductive work and community life.

Gender analysis reveals the roles and relationships of women and men in society and the inequalities in those relationships. The much quoted UN statistics remain as true today as they were when they were formulated over a decade ago:

- women perform two-thirds of the world's work
- women earn one-tenth of the world's income
- women are two-thirds of the world's illiterates
- women own less than one-hundredth of the world's property.

Work on gender issues brings women out of the background and into sharp focus. We can classify women's situation in two main ways:

- the **social condition** of women: the material conditions they face of poverty, heavy workloads, poor health care, etc. and
- the **social position** of women: the social, political, economic and cultural position of women relative to men in the same group.

Development interventions designed to alleviate women's condition can be said to be responding to their practical needs. But it is also necessary to respond to the social position of women, to address their strategic needs, and overcome problems which stem from their subordinate position in society.

How do we address these needs? It is a basic principle of community development that people themselves should participate in making the decisions which affect their lives. This means that women as well as men must be consulted, and that men as well as women must tackle gender inequality. In western Kenya, a group of men and women have been working together to reduce the problems of poverty and increase agricultural production. People say that not only are they materially better-off as a result, but that the quality of community life and relationships has improved. The women value the fact that there is less drunkenness and beating; the young people feel more able to have a dialogue with their elders; men say they have discovered that the sky does not fall down if they share women's work. Gender has become a shorthand for relationships of mutual respect, a step perhaps on the path to a more just world.

Time: 50 mins

A baby is born

Objectives

1 To introduce gender as a source of social differentiation in relation to other factors such as ethnicity, class, caste, disability.

2 To introduce gender in a non-threatening manner to groups which may be resistant.

3 To explain how gender cuts across many other areas of social differentiation.

Method

1 **Preparation**: Before the session prepare 30 cards each with an opposite (eg rich/poor, boy/girl, dominant ethnic majority/marginalised ethnic minority, member of dominant religious group/member of marginalised religious group; labourer/land holder; child of single mother/child with mother and father; physically or mentally disabled child/child without any disability).

Prepare flipchart or two flipcharts, one for 'successful child' and one for a 'less successful child' and place them on a wall next to each other.

2 Introduce and explain the session to participants:
- Ask participants to sit in a circle.
- Ask the group to imagine that they are about to become a mother or father of a child and they wish for this child the best opportunities and options for the future.

(5 mins)

3 Distribute two randomly chosen cards to each participant. *(2 mins)*

4 Then explain to the participants that his or her child will have more or less chances of 'success' depending on many social, cultural and personal issues.

(2 mins)

5 Ask the first participant to bring his or her first card and place it on either of the charts and to explain to the group why s/he has chosen the 'successful' or 'less successful' chart. A short discussion could take place if generated spontaneously by the group.

(3 mins)

6 Then ask whoever has the opposite card to come forward and place iton the other chart. Ask the participant to explain why she believes that her card is the opposite one. Repeat the process until all cards are finished.

(30 mins)

7 Sum up the session highlighting:

a. Gender is one of many forms of social differentiation and thus needs to be understood in social contexts and not in a social vacuum;

b. In most societies gender differentiation means that girls have less chance of success (however that culture defines success);

c. Although gender is one form of social differentiation it is also affected by other aspects of social identity such as age, class or caste.

(5 mins)

Materials

Cards with social opposites
Flipchart

Facilitator's Notes

1 This session is a good way to initiate a discussion of gender in social structures and institutions. You, as trainers, need to be fully aware of and informed about the main issues.

2 Because social differentiation is culture-specific, opposites need to be designed according to the background of the group.

3 With mixed nationalities it is more difficult to make generalisations and thus the activity may lose its sharpness. You may wish to experiment with difficult categories.

4 It is important for the success of this activity that the facilitator actively promotes discussion.

Time: 30 mins

Gender circles

Objectives

1 To allow participants to move around.

2 To help participants recall their emotions and ideas about gender.

Method

1 Ask participants to form two concentric circles, facing each other, and move around in opposite directions.

2 After a few seconds, ask them to stop, and pair up with the person standing opposite them from the other circle.

3 Read out a statement about gender and ask the participants to react to it, talking about it in their pairs for about one minute each.

4 Ask them to move around again and repeat the exercise until they have talked about all the statements. *(20 mins)*

5 Ask participants to form a large group again, and comment on the exercise. *(10 mins)*

Materials

A list of statements participants may commonly hear. Examples of such statements are:

1 Men and women can never be equal because they are biologically different.
2 Gender is just another word for women.
3 Women should be employed in NGOs because they are more efficient.
4 The word gender is not translatable and therefore not relevant in the field.
5 All this talk about gender brings conflict to the family.
6 My organisation talks a lot about gender but it is not reflected in the structure.
7 Work on gender should always respect people's social and cultural context.

Facilitator's Notes

1 This exercise is not very suitable if space is very limited as it may be rather difficult to hear conversation. You could use music, stopping the music when you want the participants to share views.

2 ***Adaptation****: an alternative version is 'gender walkabout', where participants walk freely about the room and at the agreed signal stop and talk to whoever is nearest. In this case, stress that people should walk in different directions, not just stay close to their friends, since one of the aims of this exercise is to hear different people's opinions.*

3 The statements should be chosen to be relevant to the group, possibly statements that you have heard in the past from the participants or people with whom they work. The statements should be those which will generate some discussion, although at this stage it may be better to avoid issues over which there is a lot of conflict, or personal issues.

4 It is possible to use words rather than statements for people to talk about. An example from a recent workshop in South Africa used the words: powerless, tradition, white men, middle-class, rural, ethnicity, sex, domination, mother, affirmative action.

5 This exercise can be used for many different purposes, depending on the words chosen and the discussion afterwards. It is an 'open' exercise i.e. one which has no right or wrong answers but which encourages exploration and sharing of ideas. The method can be used, with appropriate words or phrases to introduce any new subjects.

Time: 1-1 ¼hrs

Choose your spot

Objectives

1 To get people moving around.

2 To start discussion about key topics.

3 To show up differences of opinion within the group.

Method

1 **Preparation**: On five sheets of flipchart draw the five faces below:

Pin the sheets up on the walls around the room.

2 Explain to the participants that the faces represent the options: strongly agree, agree, neutral, disagree, strongly disagree; and that when each statement is read out they should choose the face which most closely represents their feelings.

3 Ask all participants to stand in the centre of the room as you read each statement, and then go and stand beside the face that represents how much they agree or disagree with the statement. After they have discussed each statement in their groups, they should choose a spokesperson to share key ideas from the group with everyone in the room.

(5 mins)

4 Read the statements one by one, allowing about eight minutes for discussion and reporting back on each one.

(60-70 mins)

Materials

List of statements

1 The most important goal of women's development is for women to attain economic autonomy.

2 Integrating women in development is important because it increases the efficiency of the project.

3 We should not support the development of an autonomous women's movement because it is divisive.

4 Domestic violence is a development issue that NGOs ought to address.

5 Supporting the development of traditional women's skills (sewing, cooking, etc) is an effective strategy for empowering women.

6 Relations between men and women in the family and the community are cultural; foreign agencies should not challenge it.

7 It is for women to decide about their own fertility and reproduction.

8 We should target our development aid to the family. This is the best way to ensure that the benefits reach all members.

Facilitator's Notes

1 Different statements can be included, or replace the examples given above, according to the nature of your group.

2 This is an effective activity for bringing out strong views, and provoking open discussion. Allow plenty of time for discussion, and emphasise that there are no right or wrong answers — it is all open to debate.

Time: 50 mins

The two baskets

Objectives

1 To create a space where participants can air their fears and difficulties about addressing gender issues.

2 To identify early in the workshop possible problems or issues that need to be tackled.

Method

1 **Preparation**: place two baskets in a room with a gap of two to three metres between each one.

2 Explain the objectives of the session. *(5 mins)*

3 Ask participants to stand in a circle and to imagine that in this session thinking of gender will be like moving house: they will leave behind in the rubbish basket all the negative feelings they have about tackling gender issues and bring with them to the new house all the useful positive ideas.

(5 mins)

4 Give each participant two papers. Ask them to write one thing they bring (a positive feeling they have about tackling gender issues) and one thing they leave behind (a negative feeling they have about tackling gender issues) on each piece of paper.

(5 mins)

5 Ask each participant to put in the rubbish basket their negative paper and share the contents with the group explaining what it is and why they feel that way. Then they put their paper with positive feelings in the positive basket to take with them to their new home.

(25 mins)

6 While participants play the game, write down key words emerging from participants' explanations on a flipchart.

7 Sum up the session highlighting the positive and negative feelings the group has to gender and explaining how some issues will be addressed during the workshop.

(10 mins)

Materials

A new, colourful basket
An old, worn-out, ugly basket

Facilitator's Notes

This activity may be used to end a day or session, as it offers participants the chance to leave behind certain beliefs or ideas which may hold them back, and take with them those which may enhance their experience of the workshop.

Time: About 1 hour

World upside down

Objective

1 To create an imaginary situation through which people can experience the way that beliefs about women and limitations on women's roles can affect their lives.

Method

1 Ask participants to get comfortable. Tell them you are going to read them a story about an imaginary world, and that they may like to close their eyes and focus on the story. You may wish to have two readers alternating sections of the story.*(3 mins)*

2 Read the following story in a clear, soothing voice.

Have you ever been bothered by the way the word 'man' is used to include all people? Does it bother you, for instance, that when people refer to 'the rights of all men', they really mean the rights of men and women, or the rights of all people?

Imagine a world that is similar to our own, but slightly different. In this imaginary world, 'woman' is the term that refers to all people. That is, when we use the word 'woman', we mean everyone.

Close your eyes and imagine that when you read the daily newspaper or listen to the radio, what you see or hear about are women politicians, women trade union leaders, women directors of large companies. Imagine a world in which most books, plays, films, poems and songs have women as their heroes. Imagine that women are the people you learn about when you study the great scientists, historians, journalists, revolutionaries. Imagine that it is women who will be making major decisions about the future in this different world.

Recall that everything you have ever read in your life uses only female pronouns — 'she', 'her' — meaning both boys and girls, both women and men. Recall that you have no men representing you in government. All decisions are made by women.

Men, whose natural roles are as husband and father, find fulfilment in nurturing children and making the home a refuge for the family. This is only natural to balance the role of the woman, who devotes her entire body to the human race during pregnancy, and who devotes her emotional and intellectual powers to ensuring the progress and survival of the planet throughout her life.

Imagine further now, about the biological explanations for women as the leader and power-centre. A woman's body, after all, represents perfection in design. Even female genitals, for instance, are compact and internal, protected by our bodies. Male genitals are exposed, so that he must be protected from outside attack to assure the perpetuation of the race. His vulnerability clearly requires sheltering. Thus, by nature, males are more passive and timid, and have a desire to be protectively engulfed by the compact, powerful bodies of women.

In the world that we are imagining, girls are raised as free and self-confident beings. They play, they run, climb trees, take risks with the encouragement of all adults around them. The family puts a priority on the physical and intellectual development of girls, since they are the ones who will ultimately be responsible for the future of our society.

Boys, on the other hand, are raised to be timid and obedient. They are encouraged to play quiet games in the home which will prepare them for their life as caretakers of the family. From an early age, they are expected to help their fathers. They learn to look up to women, to try to please and care for them. They are taught to become the mirror in which the strength of women can be reflected.

Now remember back to the birth of your first child, if you have children. In your last month of pregnancy, your husband waits with anxiety, wondering what the sex of the child will be. Your first child is a boy. Your husband sits by your side holding this newborn, already instinctively caring for and protecting it. There are tears in your husband's eyes and you know that at the same time that he is filled with joy at your son's birth, he is also looking forward to having another, hoping for the birth of the girl child that will carry on the family name.

(15 mins)

3 Small group discussion. Ask people to number off into five groups to talk about the feelings they had as they listened to the story. Were they angry, amused or confused? Did any part of the story make them laugh?

(10 mins)

4 Large group discussion.

a. Ask them how the imaginary world compares to the world in which we live. Is it a complete role reversal? If you put the word 'man' in each place that 'woman' was mentioned, would you have an accurate description of the world in which we live? Why or why not?

b. Would people like to live in the world described in thestory? What would be wrong with this world? What would be right with it? Would we, as women, want to have the type of power that men currently have? If we did, would we use it in similar ways?

c. End the discussion by talking about what an ideal world would be like.

(40 mins)

(Source: *On Our Feet:Taking Steps to Challenge Women's Oppression*, CACE, UWC, South Africa.)

Facilitator's Notes

This activity can be used for either a women-only or mixed group. It is written up here for women, and would require a slight adaptation of the final paragraph of the story to make it suitable for men and women, and an additional question to ask men how they feel about taking on women's roles.

Time: 1 hr

Millie's mother's red dress

Objectives

1 To create an awareness for individual women that change begins with themselves.

2 To reflect on women's stories to draw out individual experiences.

3 To bring out through the stories or experiences that gender roles are socially, historically, and culturally constructed and can change.

Method

Preparation
Try to obtain a red dress and have this hanging up in the room so participants can see it.

1 Ask two participants to read out **Millie's Mother's Red Dress (Handout 6)** , standing in front of the dress.

(5 mins)

2 Give participants copies of the story to read on their own.

(10 mins)

3 Discuss the following questions:
   a. How does the story make you feel?
   b. Does the story reflect the reality of women today in our society? Is it like your life? The life of your mother?
   c. What factors influence women so that they give, sacrifice and deny themselves?
   d. Should the situation be changed? What can women and men do to change the situation?

(45 mins)

Materials

A red dress
Handout 6

Facilitator's Notes

1 Adapt the questions in this activity to the needs of the group and the level of sharing amongst participants.

2 This story can arouse many strong emotions, as women relate it to their own socialisation process. Draw out issues such as women sacrificing themselves and allowing men to be selfish; raise the question of how women and men reinforce social roles for girls very early in life, allowing boys to grow up believing girls are there to serve them.

3 You can choose other stories relevant to the group. If it is a long story, have different women reading sections. Or have the group act the story — this makes a powerful impact.

4 This is an activity for women only.

5 When this activity was used in Kenya it became a reference point for the women, to use in challenging the attitude within themselves, that they exist for the sake of others.

A reading for two women

It hung there in the closet
While she was dying, Mother's red dress,
Like a gash in the row
Of dark, old clothes
She had worn away her life in.
They had called me home,
And I knew when I saw her
She wasn't going to last.

When I saw the dress, I said,
'Why Mother — how beautiful!
I've never seen it on you.'

'I've never worn it,
Sit down, Millie — I'd like to undo
A lesson or two before I go, if I can.'

I sat by her bed.
And she sighed a bigger breath
Than I thought she could hold.

'Now that I'll soon be gone,
I can see some things
Oh, I taught you good — but
I taught you wrong.'

'Mother, whatever do you mean?'

'Well — I always thought
That a good woman never takes her turn,
That she's just for doing for somebody else.
Do here, do there, always keep
Everybody else's wants tended and make sure
Yours are at the bottom of the heap.
Maybe someday you'll get to them,
But of course you never do.
My life was like that — doing for your dad,
Doing for the boys, for your sisters, for you.'

'You did — everything a mother could.'

'Oh, Millie, Millie, it was no good -
For you — for him. Don't you see?
I did you the worst of wrongs.
I asked nothing — for me!

'Your father in the other room,
All stirred up and staring at the walls —
When the doctor told him, he took
It bad — came to my bed and all but shook
The life right out of me. 'You can't die,

Handout

Do you hear? What'll become of me?
What'll become of me?'
It'll be hard, all right, when I go.
He can't even find the frying pan, you know.
'And you children.
I was a free ride for everybody, everywhere.
I was the first one up and the last one down
Seven days out of the week.

'I looked at how some of your brothers treat their wives now,
And it makes me sick, 'cause it was me
That taught it to them. And they learned
They learned that a woman doesn't
Even exist except to give.
Why, every penny that I could save
Went for your clothes, or your books,
Even when it wasn't necessary.
Can't even remember once when I took
Myself downtown to buy something beautiful -
For me.

'Except last year when I got that red dress.
I found I had twenty dollars
That wasn't especially spoke for.
I was on my way to pay it extra on the washer.
But somehow — I came home with this big box.
Your father really gave it to me then.
"Where you going to wear a thing like that to —
Soap opera or something?"
And he was right, I guess.
I've never, except in the store,
Put on that dress.

'Oh, Millie — I always thought if you take
Nothing for yourself in this world,
You'd have it all in the next somehow.
I don't believe that anymore.
I think the Lord want us to have something -
Here — and now.
'And I'm telling you, Millie, if some miracle could get me off this bed, you could
look
For a different mother, 'cause I would be one.
Oh, I passed up my turn so long
I would hardly know how to take it.
But I'd learn, Millie.
I would learn!'

It hung there in the closet
While she was dying, Mother's red dress,
Like a gash in the row
Of dark, old clothes
She had worn away her life in.

Her last words to me were these:
'Do me the honor, Millie,
Of not following in my footsteps.
Promise me that.'
I promised.
She caught her breath
then Mother took her turn
In death.

(Source: Adapted from 'Millie's mother's red dress' by Anita Canfield *Self Esteen for the Latter-Day Saint Women)*

Time: 30 mins

A Hindu story — Radha

Objectives

1 To help women reflect on and relate their experiences by discussing Radha's story.

2 To raise awareness of different cultural rituals that are used to perpetuate women's subordination.

Method

1 Hand out the story (**Handout 7**) to the participants. Ask each to read the story quietly for themselves.

(5 mins)

2 Ask three people to read the story again aloud to the group.

(5 mins)

3 Ask the group to discuss the following questions:

a What is Radha telling us?
b Is Radha's story familiar? In what ways?
c What are some cultural rituals, beliefs, and values that oppress women in our society?

(20 mins)

Facilitator's Notes

1 The questions can be adapted to suit the group you are working with.

2 In Kenya, women identified the similarities between the situation of Radha and their own lives. The major concern expressed was awareness of how women are marginalised and oppressed, so that the same situation was not repeated with their daughters. Some participants felt that to think that the attitudes of this present generation could be radically changed was but a dream, but wanted to explore ways in which things could be different for the next generation.

3 When used with girl students from East African nomadic people, this activity raised strong emotions, for some girls saw their mothers in the story, others saw themselves being forced into the situation by being sold into marriage; others shared their experiences of having escaped forced marriages.

4 This is a women-only activity.

Handout 7 *Activity 24*

Radha's story

'No sooner did I start understanding my surroundings than I realised that my preordinated role was to be a dutiful daughter. When I grew up it was emphasised again and again that I should be a dependent wife and devoted mother. Though I was a bright student I was allowed to educate myself only up to higher secondary level.

As soon as I started menstruating, the elders in my family got obsessed with the idea of marrying me off. Those years were extremely agonising. According to Hinduism, for those five days when a woman has her 'period' she is supposed to be impure. Hence, she is segregated and treated like an untouchable. The thought of being treated like an untouchable for one-sixteenth of my life made me feel horrible. For the first time, I understood the plight of the Harijans — 'untouchables', 'shudras', 'dalits' — the oppressed caste in India. Manu, the one who created the code of conduct of the Hindu civilization stated that the drum, the stupid, the untouchable, the animal, and the woman deserve beating.

For two years, the husband-hunting business occupied my parents. Prospective grooms and their relatives would come for an 'interview'. I was paraded in front of them like a decorative piece. For some, I was not fair-complexioned enough, for others, I did not look beautiful enough. They all wanted a sweet and smart, dainty and slim 'girl' who could resemble the goddess Laximi — the goddess of wealth and prosperity. At last, one family decided to choose me for their son to marry.

Haggling over the dowry then started. My family was middle-class. I have one sister and two brothers who were studying at that time. The demands of my in-laws were too exorbitant for my parents to fulfil. My father pleaded with my in-laws, and after some arguments they settled the matter. The arrangement was that my father gave Rs.1,000 in cash, one set of gold ornaments, 25 saris, one set of stainless steel utensils, a tape-recorder with radio, etc. My father had to incur so much debt for my wedding preparations. The atmosphere was tense. I wondered whether my marriage was indeed such a joyous occasion to celebrate. Despite the tension that prevailed, my parents consoled themselves by saying 'We will enter heaven now that we have donated our daughter'. This is termed *kanyadan*. In the Hindu customs, *kanyadan* is considered one of the best offerings. In this respect the daughter is reduced to an object that can be given away as a gift.

The wedding and the aftermath

On my wedding day, I was decorated with great care and concern by my friends. When my husband and I exchanged garlands to walk around the holy fire seven times, the Brahmin chanted Sanskrit holy verses. Some of them I remember very clearly, like:

'May the holy fire protect this woman
With a fertile womb may she be the mother of living children.
May she experience pleasure in her sons.
This am I, thou art you; the heaven I, the earth thou.
Come let us join and unite, that we may generate a son.
For increasing wealth, for blessed offsprings, for wealth.
Bountiful god, bless this woman with sons and happiness.
Give her ten sons and let her husband be the eleventh.'

After the wedding, I was to stay with my husband's family. At first I was scared of going to the new place. I heard talk about newly-wedded brides being ill-treated and sometimes even killed by their in-laws. On the other hand I had started weaving romantic bridal dreams.

At my in-laws' house, I got busy in my routine of washing, cooking, cleaning, scrubbing, putting up with scorn-taunts for bringing an 'inadequate' dowry, occasional beatings, and performing the duty of a wife. Hindu scriptures define a woman as one who is like a secretary in her work, a slave in her behaviour, a mother when it comes to feeding, and a sensuous partner in bed.

We have 3,600 million gods and goddesses. To fast for all of them would be impossible for a single woman. But I was made to observe as many rituals as possible for my husband's welfare and to beget a son. But my prayers were wasted when I had a baby girl. Everyone mourned her birth. My husband refused to talk to me for several days. He did not even look at my daughter for weeks. My in-laws taunted me for my bad luck. During my second pregnancy, I was threatened by my in-laws that if I failed to produce a son, they would throw me out of the house and have my husband re-marry another girl. Luckily, I bore a son and everyone rejoiced. My husband and in-laws distributed sweets. I then understood why my friend Sheela killed her daughter just after the birth.

Sometimes I feel very angry whenever my daughter is unfairly treated. In the last seven years that I have been married, I have realised that even if I remain weak, meek, submissive, and a masochist I am not going to be treated well and respected. I asked myself: 'Then why not assert yourself?' Now I have made up my mind, I will assert my daughter's rights. I want her to be well-educated, self-reliant, courageous, confident, and economically independent!'

(Source: Cited in *Awake — Asian Women and the Struggle for Justice*
Asia Partnership for Human Development, Sydney 1985.)

Time: 1-1¼ hrs

What are male/female stereotypes?

Objectives

1 To increase awareness of male/female stereotypes.

2 To initiate discussion about some of the consequences of stereotyping.

Method

1 Divide the group into small single-sex groups and give them two sheets of flipchart and pens.

(5 mins)

2 Explain that 'We are going to look at what we mean by sex stereotypes'. Ask each group to brainstorm all the characteristics of the opposite sex which they believe or which they have heard commonly expressed e.g. women are: talkative, patient. They should write at the top of the first sheet 'women/men are....'

(5 mins)

3 Ask them to repeat the list for their own sex. They should head the sheet 'men/women are ....' e.g. men are: aggressive, do not show feelings

(5 mins)

4 The small groups take five minutes to share initial reactions to these lists.

(5 mins)

5 Put up sheets and ask each group to present their ideas for five minutes.

(10-20 mins)

6 Ask 'If these are some of the images of men and women that are commonly believed in our society, what are the consequences for men and women?' e.g. if the male image is aggressive and the female image passive, what can happen?

Each small group lists up as many consequences as they can

(10 mins)

7 Put up sheets, and allow people time to read them.

8 With the whole group, lead a discussion on stereotypes and their consequences. (Include points in *Facilitator's Notes*.)

(10 mins)

8 Give out **Handouts 8 Masculine Boy** and **Handout 9 Dealing in Used Women**. Allow initial reactions and discussion.

(10-15 mins)

Materials

Flipcharts, pens
Handouts 8 and 9

Facilitator's Notes

1 This exercise is a useful introduction to the notion of stereotypes, but be aware that it may cause some tension between the women's and men's groups. If it does, follow with a game or activity to bring the group together again.

2 In the final discussion, bring out the following points:
a. We are looking at what is generally believed in society, and some of the results.
b. If these consequences are not as we would like them to be, what can we do to help change them?
c. We are not trying to prescribe — no 'oughts' or 'shoulds'.
d. Why be defensive?
e. There are 'personal' consequences.

3 Note that the handouts are very culture-specific; either adapt them or when you give them out, point out that they are very culture-specific and ask in what ways they correspond with participants' own experience, and what is different. What are the particular pressures and stereotypes in participants' own culture?

4 You may find it useful to ask a man to read out ***Handout 8 Masculine Boy*** *and a woman to read out* ***Handout 9 Dealing in Used Women****.*

(Source: This activity comes from a course for teachers and careers officers in a training project by Counselling and Career Development Unit, University of Leeds and Careers and Occupational Information Centre.)

Masculine boy

If I would have had the slightest inkling of what being a 'man' really meant, I am quite sure I would not have spent a great deal of my childhood waiting for the 'Rewarding Day'.

Before I could reach the accomplished state of being the 'Masculine Man', I had to suffer the repressive and agonising stage of being the 'Masculine Boy'.

I learnt fairly early in life that one of my first accomplishments was to be superior to that other little creature that inhabited the earth, 'girl'. My parents guided me through this difficult period well. They gave me some helpful pointers. If I cried they told me not to, as only little girls cried. I had to avoid the usual girlie things: bright colours (especially pink), skipping ropes, dolls, ribbons, etc. If my parents wanted to intimidate me because my hair was getting too long or untidy all they had to say was 'we will have to put a ribbon in your hair, won't we'. I would cringe at the mere thought. If I was too shy and quiet in company, I was being like a silly girl again (cringe). My name is Ian. If my father happened to be in a somewhat jovial, sadistic mood, he would call me Yvonne and my brother would give him a hand. I hated that so much I would end up throwing great boulders at my brother.

Then I started school, where I soon realised how weak girls were. If any heavy objects were to be lifted, teacher always asked us 'boys'. Whenever a girl got the cane she always cried. We were strong: we at least tried to choke the tears back inside our ears (figuratively speaking of course). That reminds me of a most humiliating experience. I was about eight years old: teacher called me out to give me the cane on both hands. Ha! he didn't make me cry. I turned to walk away, my ears swollen with excess water. Then... crash! I felt the cane against the back of my legs. My ears drained and the tears rushed down my face. It wasn't too long before I became quite proficient at containing my feelings during moments of stress or pain. Being a boy, of course, meant playing all the rough games; football, rugby, boxing, wrestling etc. I avoided such things by studying too hard. I avoided all physical contact with other boys. I avoided any display of my emotions. By the time I was 11, I felt I had achieved much success at being the Masculine Boy. But, alas, there was a small price to pay .... *repression.*

Ian Douglas, (excerpt from *Man Against Sexism*)

Dealing in used women

What do I do?
I deal in women,
Used and new.

I've many models
From which to choose.
I'm sure I have one
Just for you.

Here's a classic model:
She'll do as she is told,
Never acting knowing,
Never acting bold.

Here's a housewife model:
She really is a find.
She sews and cooks and cleans and
Mass-produces little minds.

Next, a secretary model:
Her typing can't be beat.
She makes good coffee, has good legs;
There's one word for her: 'sweet'.

There's an educated model:
In her class she's at the top.
She can hold a conversation,
But she knows when she should stop.

A recycled woman?

Yes, I have lots of those.
But she may be more challenge than you need.
She thinks … She feels … She loves …
She's real .... but she's not guaranteed.

(Source: Mary Ann Bornman, The Women's Center, Kean College of New Jersey, Union, NJ, USA).

Time: 45 mins — 1 hr

Stereotypes: self-disclosure

Objectives

1 To express some of our feelings about our own sex roles.

Method

1 Divide group into small groups of five (mixed men and women).

2 Explain that 'Within any situation in life, there are advantages and disadvantages; now is the opportunity to express some of our own feelings about being men and women'.

(5 mins)

3 Ask each person, individually, to complete the sentence:
'Sometimes I'm glad I'm a man/woman because.....'

Ask them to list as many of the advantages to being a man/woman as they can.

(5 mins)

4 Then, ask each person to complete the sentence:
'Sometimes I wish I were a man/woman because.....

Again they should list as many reasons as possible.*(5 mins)*

5 Ask each member of the group to share their lists for three minutes each.*(15 mins)*

6 Ask each group to consider:

a. Was one list more difficult to make, if so, which one?
b. What did it feel like to hear others' lists?
c. What does it feel like to hear statements about your sex from the opposite sex?

d. Did you want to challenge any of these statements?
e. How free were the lists from stereotyping?

(15 mins)

7 In the large group, ask what people learned from the activity..

(15 mins)

Materials

Pens, small pieces of paper
Flipchart with questions written on

Facilitator's Notes

1 Stage 6 of the activitycould be done in the large group. This might be especially important if the group was not evenly balanced for numbers of men and women. It is important that each sex hears the other sex's views, and that inaccuracies and stereotypes are challenged (e.g. if a man says he sometimes wishes he were a woman because then he wouldn't have to work).

2 This activity follows on well from the previous ***Activity 25 What Are Male/Female Stereotypes*** *and comes from the same source (CCDU/COIC). It is useful as an introduction to thinking about stereotypes and more personal issues.*

Time: 30 mins

Breaking the chain

Objectives

1 To give women time to think of themselves and their situation through symbolic action.

Method

Preparation

1 Collect a series of readings from women, some oppressive and some liberating. **Handout 10** gives some examples

2 Ask the group to sit in a circle with a circular paper chain laid out in front.

3 Ask four or five members of the group to read the passages aloud.

4 Tell the group to listen to the readings, and when they hear something that enchains women, to put their hands into the chain. When they hear something that frees women, they should take their hands out of the chain.

6 Conclude the session with background music, with women holding hands together.

(30 mins)

Materials

Series of readings **(Handout 10)**
A paper chain
Music

Facilitator's Notes

1 These readings have been provided as samples — you could seek out others, or ask the participants to produce stories about themselves or women they know. They should be short, so that the activity can move quite quickly.

2 Mix positive and negative stories, but make sure you end the session with stories which are liberating and help women 'unchain' themselves.

3 This is a women-only activity.

Readings

The Samities of Bankura

In a small village in West Bengal, a women's Samity (society) obtained a land donation in 1980 from private landowners who lacked the resources to develop the degraded land. With unwavering focus, and collective will, the Samity reclaimed the wasteland, and in three years the land was thick with trees on which tasar silk worms are reared. As news spread, other Samities were formed by women in surrounding villages, each with land donation from villagers and today, 1,500 women in 36 villages are members of such Samities. The groups have also organised supplementary income-generating activities, on an individual or group basis.

A freedom song

Atieno washes dishes,
  Atieno gets up early,
  beds her sacks down

In the kitchen
  Atieno eight years old
  Atieno yo.
Since she is my sister's child
  Atieno needs no pay
  While she works my wife can sit
  Sewing every sunny day,
  With her earning I support
  Atieno yo.
Atieno's sly and jealous
  Bad example to the kids
  Since she minds them like a school girl
  Wants their dresses, shoes and beads.
  Atieno ten years old,
  Atieno yo.

Atieno's had a baby
so we know that she is bad
Fifty-fifty it may live
To repeat the life she had,
ending in post-partum bleeding
Atieno yo.
Atieno's soon replaced
Meat and sugar, more than all
She ate in such a narrow life,
Were lavished at her funeral
Atieno's gone to glory
Atieno yo.

(Marjorie Mbilinyi, Kenya) (adapted)

Domestic violence

Every night for four months she was beaten brutally and burnt with a hot iron. The neighbours, unable to bear her screams, complained to the Kalachowki Police Station. But the police did not take action saying it was a domestic matter. She died on 2 October. Her body was full of bruises and burns. The complaint was made in August, and a month and a half later the young woman of twenty-two years dies because no-one has a right to interfere with what happens within the family.

(Kelkar 1983)

The Chipko Movement

A fight for truth has begun
At Sinsyari Khala.
A fight for rights has begun
At Malkot Thano.
Sister, it is a fight to protect
Our mountains and forests.
They give us life.
Embrace the life of the living trees and streams,
Clasp them to your hearts.
Resist the digging of the mountains,
That brings death to our forests and streams.
A fight for life has begun
At Sinsyaru Khala.

Ghanshyan 'Shalland, Chipko poe
t(Source: Chipko Information Centre, India IDOC *Internazionale*, March 1989)

A girl's life

Now we are faced with a ten-year-old girl. Her body has been mutilated to encourage chastity by destroying sexual feeling. She is handed over to a man twice as old as she is or more. She will have 14 children. Half of them will die. If too many of them are female she may be abused by her husband's family. She will spend her life within the narrowest possible radius, walled in by ritual and tradition. If there is scarcity she may watch her youngest daughter be systematically starved; the sons will be fed, the daughter will not. If she is divorced she will lose any claim to her children, since they are the property of her husband. What words shall we use to comment on the life of this girl?

(Cheryl Bernard
Edith Shlaffer 1981)

Kidan

My name is Kidan Gebre Tensay, and I'm twenty-seven. My family and others were helped a lot by the TPLF after the famine. We now live near Edaga Hiberet town in Marmaz Wahta village.

Before liberation we were highly oppressed and dominated; we could not even look at men. We would have to hide if we saw them coming. Women could not go to meetings or make any decisions or suggestions. Muslim women were even more oppressed than us. The revolution has put an end to all this and we have become free and equal like our class brothers. The organisation has shown us the way and now we participate in all areas. From my personal point of view, before, I was an insignificant woman and now I have been given political education and I am a *shig woyanit* — a torch of the revolution.

(Source: *Sweeter than Honey: Testimonies of Tigrayan Women*, Jenny Hammond with Nell Druce — Links Publications.)

A daughter pregnant by her father

When a mother discovered that her young daughter was pregnant the daughter said that she should ask the father about the pregnancy. When she ran off to Mombasa she was forced to return as she was unable to survive. When she returned she was told that she had brought disgrace and shame to the family by talking about this whole problem.

Sexual abuse

A man told his daughter that in order to lessen her period pain that she should have sex with him. An elderly woman, who was a neighbour of this family told the wife what was happening. The wife took the case to court, but withdrew the case due to the shame of the whole situation.

Ndugu Josima Machel

Ndugu Josina Machel, one of Africa's heroines died at the age of 25 — a militant in the struggle for liberation of Mozambique, she was dedicated and never faltered in her courage. Her own courage was a guiding force in the life of her husband. Yet she is remembered not for being the wife of Samora but in her own right. She is a symbol of women's contribution toward the liberation of Africa.

Women resist

In the Dangs district of Gujarat, India, there is constant conflict between forestry officials protecting the State forests, and villagers, who have lived in the forest for generations. In 1989, a forest officer, accompanied by six policemen, arrived in a village to confiscate timber. The carpenters ran away into the forest. The mother-in-law came out armed with a sickle, and stood at her door. She told the officials to stay where they were, or face the consequences. Meanwhile, the younger women had called others to join them. The officials were soon surrounded by a large crowd of women of all ages, carrying whatever implements they had been able to grab. The forest officer ordered the women to disperse, but nobody moved. The old woman declared that they could touch the wood only 'over my dead body'. The police threatened to open fire, but were challenged by the women . Finally, after a heated discussion, the official party left, escorted by the women for a kilometre.

(Source: Adapted from an article by Shirley Varghese, in Development in Practice, Oxfam, 1992.)

Time: 1 hr

Man to man

Objectives

1 To help men review and 'own' the implications of gender for men.

2 To develop ideas for positive action.

Method

1 Ask the participants to form small groups or pairs to discuss what they have felt about the training activities so far, such as what they have or have not enjoyed, agreed or disagreed with, or felt angry or hurt about.

(5 mins)

2 Ask groups to feed back their responses to the whole group.

(10 mins)

3 Lead a discussion in the whole group around the following questions:

a. Do most men find gender a difficult or easy subject to discuss? Why?
b. Why are discrimination against women, sexual harassment and even rape sometimes laughed off as trivial by men? If your own sister or mother experienced these things, how would you feel?
c. If a man is beaten up on the street, people do not ask what clothes he was wearing,or why he was out late — but women are asked these questions. Is it fair?
d. Is gender a minor issue, compared with, for example, world hunger?
e. Do you agree with this statement:
'We earn 90 per cent of the world's income and own 99 per cent of its property. We commit around 90 per cent of violent crimes.... (but) why should we be equated with men who run countries.... who rape and kill? We ask women not to lump us indiscriminately together with hostile men. But in return we need to recognise that we benefit from sexual discrimination every day of our lives whether we like it or not!' (*New Internationalist*, Sept 1987)

f. How can men share power with women in society?
g. In what ways does society pressurise men? *(20 mins)*

4 Ask the group to discuss **Handout 11Action Checklist** in pairs, considering the questions:

a. Do you disagree with anything?
b. What is left out?

(10 mins)

5 In the whole group, lead a discussion around the following questions:

a. Have you ever challenged sexism in other men? If so, what reactions did you get?
b. If not, why didn't you, and what would have helped you?

Encourage the participants to share experiences. Some of the situations could be role-played so participants can practise how to respond.

Materials

Handout 11

Facilitator's Notes

1 This activity must be led by a male facilitator. It is a man-only session.

*2 It must be preceded by group trust-building activities (see **Icebreakers**) and the 'ground rules' activity to help men to cope with the defensive and threatened feelings they are likely to experience.*

3 If done in a training for a mixed group, the men and women should come back together afterwards and briefly report from their own activities. It should then be followed by a physical trust game to build good relations between men and women, and mix them together for the next mixed-sex activity.

4 Stress that men have been encouraged to believe that to be 'real men' they have to oppress women. But this is not so. (e.g. slogan from Kenya 'Real Men Support Women's Empowerment'). Feeling guilty and defensive is not helpful to men or women. Action against sexism is.

5 The action checklist needs to be revised to be appropriate to the cultural context.

*(Source: **Class, Gender and Race Inequality and the Media in an International Context**: Focus for Change, 1992.)*

Action checklist on sexism: a code for men

1 Look out for ways you unintentionally threaten women. Don't walk behind a woman at night — cross the road. Don't loiter in a group of men or block the path. Approach a man, not a woman, for directions at night or in lonely places.

2 Don't comment, stare or whistle at a woman's looks or dress; it's sexual harassment.

3 Share domestic tasks equally. Housework and childcare should not be only 'women's work'.

4 If you have a woman partner, you should both have equal access to income.

5 Express your emotions and acknowledge your feelings.

6 Confront sexism in other men; do not rely on women to do this for you.

7 Challenge sexism at work, and in your dealings with the State (e.g. health, welfare).

8 Don't limit children; both boys and girls can enjoy football and sewing.

9 What you call 'normality' is based on male power and should be questioned.

(This checklist was developed in the UK, adapted from the *New Internationalist*, August 1985, and you may need to adapt the items to be appropriate to the country and culture in which you use it.)

Time: 50 mins - 1½ hrs

Feminist poker

Objectives

1 To enable men to identify the causes of women's oppression.

2 To enable men to discuss and rank these factors in order of importance.

3 To establish a consensus amongst the participants about which are the most important factors.

Method

Preparation: Make three identical packs of 40 cards, each one of the 40 with a different statement (see examples in **Handout 12**).

Explain the objectives of the activity, and tell the group that the session involves a card game and will be in two parts. In Part One, the players are divided into at least three groups, and have to complete the statement: 'Women are oppressed because...' according to the phrases on the cards which will be dealt to them.

In Part Two, the small groups of players will have to get together to agree on five completed statements from those which have been selected during the separate games. Players will be scored according to whether their judgements of the cards are accepted by the group or not.

Part 1

Divide the participants into three groups of eight players each. This may be varied according to the size of your group. The groups should sit around tables, or in a circle on the floor, and the facilitator deals out the cards.

Deal out five cards to each player. Explain that there will be five rounds, in which each player in turn will choose one card from their hand and decide whether it is a strong or weak phrase for finishing the statement about women's oppression. Each new round is started by a different person.

Once the cards are dealt, the players look at their hands and think about them, and then, in turn, each places one card face down in front of him declaring whether their cards are IN or OUT according to whether they are weak or strong completions of the statement.

Then in the same sequence all the players who declared OUT turn up their card, and explain and justify their decision.

The group debates each decision. If the group accepts the player's decision about the card, the player gains one point. If the group rejects the decision, the player loses one point and the card is placed in the centre of the table.

After all the OUT cards have been discussed and decisions taken, the process is repeated with the cards which players declared IN. If the group agrees with the decision, the card is placed in the centre, if they disagree, the player loses a point.

At the end of the round, one card is chosen from all those placed in the centre after discussion. This card represents the group's view of the most accurate reason for women's oppression for that round. The player who selected the card gains two points. If a card originally declared OUT is chosen, the player who declared it OUT loses two points and all others in the round gain a point.

Repeat the process for each round.

Part 2

Bring the three groups together.

Each group debates and discusses the choice of the five cards they have made. They have to defend their choice, challenge the choices of others, and finally all participants have to come to agreement on five statements about women's oppression.

Materials

40 cards with statements in **Handout 12**. There must be a full pack of cards for each group.

Facilitator's Notes

1 You may have to vary the size of the small groups according to the number of participants in the workshop, but there should be more than one group so that Part 2 of the activity can be carried out. You may also have to change the number of cards according to the size of your small groups. All the groups should have the same set of cards.

2 There are 37 statements given here. You may wish to add others, and replace some with your own.

3 This activity was developed for use with men, but you could use it with women, or for mixed groups — as long as you are confident of being able to deal with the debates which may emerge in a mixed group!

(Source: Karina Constantinos-Davids)

Women are oppressed because

They are last to be hired and first to be fired.
They play a secondary role in decision-making.
There is no sharing of household work.
They are stereotyped into secondary/subordinate roles.
Their intelligence and capabilities are undervalued.
They are not acknowledged to be breadwinners.
The law is biased against women.
They receive lower wages than men.
They are considered to be the weaker sex.
They must be submissive.
There are limited support services such as day-care centres.
They are used to sell consumer products.
Their self-worth is undermined.
Their place is in the home.
Men are the hunters and women are the hunted.
Their self-concept is based on men's perceptions.
Their contributions to economic production are not recognised.
Parenting is primarily a woman's concern.
They are treated as second-class citizens.
They are treated as sex objects.
They are victims of sexual harassment.
They are all potential victims of rape and other forms of violence.
They suffer from a double burden.
Of men.
There is a double standard in society.
They are economically marginalised.
Men are considered more capable than women.
Men have more privileges.
Societal institutions socialise women into subordinate roles.
They have less access to opportunities.
They have no control over their own bodies.
They have limited control over their own development.
They are brought up to serve men.
Their work is not valued.
Their primary role is reproduction.
They are forced to give sexual favours to their bosses.
They are discriminated against especially in leadership positions.

Time: 30-40 mins

Becoming a man

Objectives

1 To help men to see the pressures on them to adopt certain attitudes.

2 To enable men to become aware of some of the origins of their attitudes and feelings towards women.

Method

1 Explain the objectives of the activity to the group.

2 Hand out a copy of the list of questions (**Handout 13**) to each participant, and ask them to write completions of the sentences on the chart without consulting each other.

3 Then ask the participants to form pairs and to discuss with each other their answers, and their responses and feelings.

4 In the large group, draw out similarities in the responses and completions of the sentences, and discuss the following questions:

a. Do you feel your behaviour is limited by your peers? How and when does this happen, and why?
b. Are there some 'macho' attitudes towards women you would like to reject? How can you do this?

Materials

List of questions in **Handout 13**
Pens

Facilitator's Notes

Source: This activity was adapted from one described by Thompson:'As boys become men: learning new male roles' which was published in Update on Anti-Sexist Work with Boys and Young Men, *edited by Janie Whyld, Dave Pickersgill and David Jackson, (Whyld Publishing Group, 1990). The trainer described it as providing a good starting point for discussion of the way boys are socialised. Although used in a mixed group, with a similar chart for girls, the trainer felt it would be most useful with a men-only group. We suggest it could be a good introductory activity to other more challenging activities about male gender roles and attitudes.*

Sentence completions

The best thing about being a man is...

A man would never let a woman see...

Men would reject another man if...

Men would be praised by his parents if he...

Boys can't...

The parents of a boy let him...

Teachers expect boys to treat girls like...

Men get embarrassed when...

Parents expect boys to...

Men/boys are allowed to...

A boy would get teased if he...

Women really want men to...

Men don't like...

(Source: Thompson D. *As Boys Become Men: Learning New Male Roles.*)

Time: 50 mins-1½ hrs

Violence against women

Objectives

1 To enable women to discuss violence against women.

2 To identify the root causes of violence against women.

3 To create a climate where women can share freely their experience of violence.

4 To raise these issues in a Christian context, where appropriate.

Method

Part 1

1 Ask the group to look at **Handout 14** Our Experience..

(5 minutes)

2 In groups of three discuss the following questions :
a. Are these statements familiar in your community? Share some of your stories of wife-beating and other abusive treatment. Is violence on the increase?
b. Do you think the reasons men give for beating their wives are acceptable?
c. What are the consequences for women who choose to leave their abusive husbands? What are the consequences for their children?
d. What are some effective and life-giving solutions for women who are frequently abused by their husbands or male companions?

(15 minutes)

3 In the big group, ask small groups to share responses to questions b, c, and d. Give individuals who wish to do so the opportunity to share responses to question a. This should be optional. *(30 minutes)*

Part 2 For Christian groups

1 Give **Handout 15** Biblical background notes, and the appropriate texts to the group. (I Corinthians 13 1-13; Daniel 13 (Apocrypha); Judges 19; 2 Samuel 13: 1-21).

2 In small groups, discuss the texts and the background notes.

(30 minutes)

3 In the large group, bring out the main points in Handout 15.

Our experience

My husband comes home drunk nearly every night and always finds something to criticise or complain about! Sometimes it's my cooking, sometimes the noisy children, and other times it's money. And then he starts to beat me. I can't take much more of this treatment!

I know what you mean! My husband is just the same; beating! beating! beating! When I scream and complain, he just laughs and says that beating shows how much he cares for me. "It is a sign of love," he says! Frankly, I'd rather have less love and more peace!

Well, if beating means "love", I wonder if we can say that Margaret was "loved to death" last year when her husband beat her until she died from her injuries! How can you call that "love"?

Biblical background notes

A **1 Corinthians 13:1-13:** this passage from St Paul helps us to understand the Christian ideal of love better:

'Love is patient and kind... it is not ill mannered or selfish or irritable: love does not keep a record of wrong...'

Paul's definition of love leaves no room for such humiliating and brutal behaviours as wife-beating!

B **Daniel 13** (Apocrypha): this is a tale of 'sexual harassment', of threats and trickery. Susanna, a good, beautiful and faithful wife, is approached by two elderly men and harassed sexually, that is, she is disturbed or bothered by these men who demand sexual favours of her. If she refuses, they threaten to accuse her falsely of adultery with another man. Refusing to yield to these men and their threats, Susanna is falsely accused and faces death by stoning if proved guilty. She is brought to trial and is saved at the last moment through the efforts of the young prophet Daniel. The old men met their match in Susanna, a woman who respected herself more that she feared death. She was ready and willing to die rather than dishonour herself.

C **Judges 19:** in this chapter from the Book of Judges we read of the most tragic, degrading and violent abuse of women imaginable. It is the story of a concubine who was freely sacrificed to men in order to spare her husband the humiliation of sexual abuse by a gang of thugs. Her life was sacrificed for his honour and dignity. The host in the story refused to allow his male guest to be dishonoured by homosexual acts, for this was 'an evil and immoral thing.' But he did not regard the abusive rape of women as equally evil and immoral since he voluntarily offered his own virgin daughter and his guest's concubine to satisfy the sexual appetites of the gang. In the end it was only the concubine who was thrown to the men outside to be used for their pleasure, and

'They raped her and abused her all night long and didn't stop until morning...'

When day at last dawned, the concubine was found to be dead. No Bible story points out as clearly the low status of women in society. Versus 23-24 establish without any doubt the priority of value and the importance of men in that tradition and the inferiority of women. It was preferable, so men reasoned, to sacrifice a defenceless woman rather than allow a physically stronger man to be disgraced and abused.

D **2 Samuel 13:1-21**: here we read of incest-rape where one of King David's sons, Amnon, raped his own half-sister, Tamar. It is rare indeed when the Bible quotes the words of mere women, so it is all the more unusual to read here of Tamar's verbal as well as physical struggle with her brother.

After raping her, Amnon turned against her with hatred, throwing her out of his house. Tamar covered her head with ashes and tore her garments, symbolically proclaiming her deep sense of shame, mourning and sorrow. Another brother, Absalom, took Tamar into his own home and cared for her, later taking revenge on Amnon for destroying Tamar's life. She was apparently unable to marry because of the disgrace of being raped by her own brother. Her story ends pathetically. Tamar lived in Absalom's house, sad and lonely.

Points to ponder

1 Susanna in Daniel 13 is a remarkable example of a courageous woman who respected herself and honoured her marriage vows — even at the risk of possible death by stoning. She stood alone against corrupt men and their evil designs, resisting both sexual harassment and lies. And against all odds, she won! Susanna is a true sign of hope and resistance for women today in a patriarchal world that increasingly harasses and abuses women.

2 Men all too often abuse their God-given gift of strength by attacking and beating those who are physically weaker than they. Using superior strength to control and subdue others is behaviour worthy of a bully and a coward. A man who beats a woman in order to punish or control her shows lack of self-control as well as disrespect and contempt for women.

Today, unfortunately, we see evidence of wife beating all around us. Some of these battered women are so severely injured that they die as a result of such harsh treatment. So it is altogether incredible when we sometimes hear from women themselves that 'beatings show how much a man loves his wife; the more he beats, the more he loves!' This is total myth! How can the act of physically injuring another person be an expression of love? If a man beats his wife until she dies, does this then demonstrate the deepest love of all? It may help at this point to reflect once again on the Christian ideal of love as found in Paul's First letter to the Corinthians 13: 'Love is patient and kind...'

Nowhere does Paul mention physical abuse as a sign of love and caring. If we truly love someone, we will do everything possible to protect that person from injury and harm.

3 Violence against women wears many faces, aside from that of wife bashing or beating. Women are frequently abused at work through sexual harassment where their employers or male co-workers demand sexual favours in return for the woman's promotion or fair treatment. Women are violated on the streets when they are verbally or physically attacked and raped. Women are dishonoured and shamed in the media (press, TV, radio) through stories and advertisements that humiliate and exploit women and their physical attractions.

4 Women are also abused through prostitution, a 'profession' that humiliates and degrades men as well women. The majority of women who become involved in prostitution do so for economic reasons alone. Given alternative skills and ways of earning a living, most would probably give up prostituting themselves.

It is indeed strange how society condemns prostitutes as 'vulgar' and 'sinful', and in some countries, 'unlawful', yet winks playfully at the men who keep these women in business. How can it be wrong for one sex, but right for the other? This is patriarchal thinking at its worst!

5 Newspapers inform us that crimes of rape and incest are on the increase in our communities. Many, including the police and some women themselvesblame the female victims for this, claiming that they invite such treatment by their manner of dress or provocative behaviour. If that is so, how does one explain the rape of tiny children and elderly women?

Social scientists tell us that men frequently turn to rape, not so much out of strong and uncontrollable sexual urges, but rather, out of a sense of frustration and anger aimed at society in general and women in particular. Men who feel they have lost their role and status in society, men who are unemployed and impoverished, men who feel useless and no longer needed, all these frequently turn to crime and violence to help release their inner rage. And women are among the easiest victims to attack. Women become targets of male aggression.

6 In order to effectively to challenge male domination and aggression in the community, women need to join together in support groups, sharing their stories and designing new strategies for survival. But these strategies must include not only steps towards justice and equality between the sexes; they must also include plans for active peace-building that will serve to bridge the anger-isolation gap that presently exists between women and men. At present, support groups for women are essential; there is strength in numbers and courage in sharing.

7 **Violence against women is a crime!**
(Source: *Choose Life*: Jacqueline Dorr MM.)

Time:3- 4 hrs

Rape

Objectives

1 To create space and time to discuss rape and experiences of women who have suffered this crime.

2 To discuss myths held about rape.

3 To talk about the responses of courts, police, psychologists, doctors, family and community to women who have been raped.

4 To discuss the strategies and support mechanisms needed to support raped women.

Method

Part 1

1 Ask participants to walk around the room and study newspaper cuttings of rape cases that have appeared in the newspapers in the last three to six months. You can retype these (and see **Handout 16**) or photocopy articles to a larger print size to make them easier to read.

(10 mins)

2 Ask one participant to read out the newspaper cutting: 'A Night of Madness'(**Handout 17**).

(5 mins)

3 Ask the participants to form groups of five, and discuss the following:
a. What do these experiences of women make you feel?
b. What does the response of the deputy principal in the case we have just read make you feel, and tell you about people's views about rape?

c. Are there any cases in the newspaper cuttings that you want to talk about?
d. Are there experiences you know about of women who have suffered rape, that you want to talk about?(30 mins)

4 In the large group, share responses to the questions. Allow enough time. *(5 mins)*

Part 2

5 Give each participant **Handout 18** on myths about rape. Discuss again the striking issues that the handout provokes. *(15-30 mins)*

6 Ask participants to think about more myths that are missing in the Handout and list on a flipchart. Add any they omit. *(25 mins)*

Part 3

7 Give an input on women's experience of rape in your country.
Police procedures
Medical check-ups
Legal aspects and court proceedings
Psychological trauma — long-term and short-term

(If possible arrange for progressive, non-prejudiced experts to come and give the inputs.)
(30 mins)

8 Ask participants to form the same groups of five to discuss the following questions and write the answers on flipcharts:
a. What support do raped women need from:
family
community
doctors
police
lawyers/courts
b. What needs to change in the existing laws, court proceedings, medical and police procedures? *(30 mins)*

9 Each group then reports back in turn on one question, followed by discussion. *(30 mins)*

Materials

Newspaper cuttings
Handouts 16, 17, and 18.

Facilitator's Notes

1 Note that the timing in this activity is approximate; you need to be flexible, especially when women's personal experiences are brought out in the activity, or where there is prejudice. For example, in a workshop that took place in Kenya it was very clear how deep-rooted the myths were. It took a whole morning to demystify the myth 'She asked for it'. It is important for a trainer to realise a lot of cultures are silent on issues around rape. So the group needs time to build trust to be able to share their experience.

2 It is important at the end of the workshop to come up with ideas of ways for raped women to get support. Participants need to come with recommendations on what needs changing and how to channel this into legal reforms in their countries.

3 This activity was done with women only, but it could be tried in mixed groups. You would need to think carefully about the methodology, perhaps putting Part 3 first as it is less personal.

4 If time is limited the three parts could be done separately. In Part Two bring out the following:

Myths	***Facts***
Women are raped by strangers in dark places outside the home.	*Most rapes take place at home by someone known to the woman*
There is no rape in marriage.	*Women do get raped by their husbands.*
Women say 'No' when they mean 'Yes.	*'No' means 'No'.*
Men rape because they are overcome by sexual urges.	*Most rapes are planned for some time.*
Men who rape are obviously abnormal.	*Every man who rapes is somebody's son, brother, husband.*

5 You will need to prepare for this activity by collecting, before the workshop, stories about rape in the press. You could also ask participants to bring cuttings from their own countries or towns with them to the workshop.

Solicitor gets three years for rape attempt after Highland Ball

A solicitor who tried to rape a woman lawyer who was his guest at a Highland Ball was jailed yesterday for three years.

Angus Diggle, aged 37, of Bolton, Lancashire, attacked the 25-year old lawyer after they left the St Andrew's Day ball at the Grosvenor Hotel, London, last November. The terrified woman awoke to find Mr Diggle on top of her wearing nothing but the frilly cuffs of his Highland outfit and a green condom.

Judge David Williams QC told him yesterday as he passed sentence at Swansea Crown court: "I have come to the conclusion that your attitude to women leaves a great deal to be desired."

Diggle's barrister, Michael Borelli, told the court his conviction meant complete ruin and it was inevitable that he would be struck off as a solicitor. Describing him as sexually inexperienced and naive, Mr Borelli said Mr Diggle was wholly unsuited to prison life. "He is utterly terrified of what will happen to him."

The Old Bailey heard how after the rape attempt the woman's friends confronted Diggle as he was lying on the floor. He demanded that they help him get dressed, saying "A man should never have to dress himself."

Later he told the police: "Well, I have been out with her. I have spent £200 on her. Why can't I do what I did to her?"

A night of madness

Sometimes it takes a tragedy to startle people from the complacency of old — and destructive — attitudes. On July 13, Kenyans received such a shock, when 271 teenage girls were attacked during a rampage by dozens of their male classmates at St Kizito, a boarding school in central Kenya. Chased into a corner of the dormitory where they were trying to hide, 19 girls died of suffocation in the crush. Doctors say another 71 were raped. Last week 29 boys ages 14 to 18 were charged with manslaughter, two were also charged with rape.

The assaults were rendered all the more chilling because of the dismissive note struck by some officials. The *Kenya Times* quoted Joyce Kithira, the school's deputy principal, as saying, "The boys never meant any harm against the girls. They just wanted to rape." The episode is forcing Kenyans to re-examine attitudes that have long permitted rape to be a part of many girls' school years.

Handout 18 *Activity 32*

Myths and realities about rape

Rape is one of those crimes which causes emotional reactions in people. Some even think that rape is impossible, that a woman really wants it to happen. When a rape victim goes to the police station or to court, she will find that she has to prove that she did not provoke the rapist in some way.

Rape happens a lot these days because women have loose morals.

Yes, I think it does happen more often today.
But I don't think it is because women have loose morals.

MRS. KOFIA

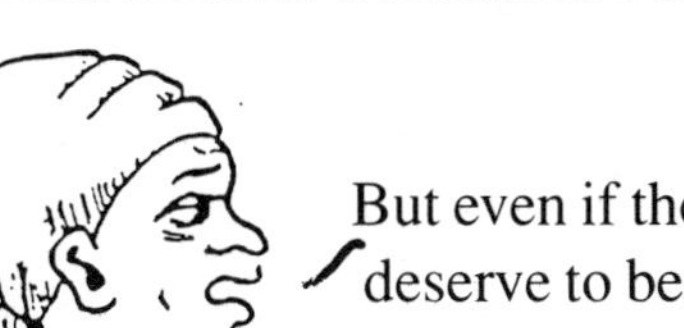

But even if they have loose morals, do they deserve to be raped?

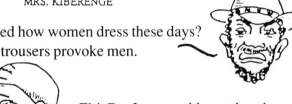

Have you noticed how women dress these days?
All those tight trousers provoke men.

Eh! But I am an old grandmother and even I was raped.

And my friend's daughter was raped
and she is only 9 years old.

Eh, you people! My neighbour's little 2 year old daughter was raped. Is she provocative?

Adapted from Oxfam Kenya: *Women, law and development legal guides*

C.4 Gender roles and needs

With the activities in this section the training programme moves into the phase of gender analysis. The first few activities explore gender roles and stereotypes about women and men; these are followed by activities introducing some of the tools of gender analysis first developed by Caroline Moser and now often used as an analytical framework in gender-sensitive appraisal and planning. Some of the key concepts briefly introduced in **Section A.2.** are expanded here, such as the gender division of labour, women's 'triple role', strategic and practical gender needs.

In this Manual we use the terms 'strategic' and 'practical' gender needs, thus following the Moser method of gender planning. Moser based the notion of strategic and practical gender needs on the distinction made by Maxine Molyneux in a paper published in 1985 between women's interests, strategic gender interests, and practical gender interests. Moser describes the translating of interests, or 'prioritised concerns', into needs or the 'means by which concerns are satisfied', as necessary for gender planning. For example,if a strategic gender interest, or prioritised concern, is for a more equal society, then a strategic gender need, or the means by which the concern may be satisfied, could be the abolition of the gender division of labour.

Whether the notion of needs or interests is preferred by users of this Manual, it is important to explain very clearly the difference between practical and strategic, and also to point out that these are not always easily distinguishable in practice. It is helpful to make the distinction in our attempt to understand more fully the range of women's needs and interests, which have been invisible in development and relief planning until very recently. (See **Handout 24** for more detail).

Some thought needs to be given to men's gender needs and interests. While it is not too difficult to identify men's practical gender needs, when we begin to talk about men's strategic needs, or interests, the question becomes more complex. Is it in the strategic interests of men to retain the *status quo*, whereby they hold the more powerful positions in all sectors of social life, and dominate women? Or is it in their strategic interests to work for a more egalitarian society, where women are not subordinate to men? And what can we say about men's strategic needs? Do men need the empowerment of women? Do men need to share in childcare so that they are closer to their children and build up more balanced relationships in their lives? Do men need to overcome the social expectation of them to be strong, aggressive, competitive and so on? Or is it really a gender need or interest of women that they do so?

Men, like women, are not a homogeneous category. Men oppress other men, and there are some men who feel it is not in their strategic interest to subordinate women.

There may, then, be areas where women can make alliances with men to achieve strategic goals. The point is that it is not only women who have to change: men have to change too, and for this to be addressed in development and relief planning, men's gender interests must be identified and analysed. Otherwise, men can present major, untackled obstacles to change.

C.4 Activities

Time: 40—50 mins

The story of Joan and John

Objectives

1 To examine the lives of women and men in a comparative way.

Method

1 Ask the group to form a circle and explain that they are going to construct biographies of two imaginary people, first Joan, then John.

2 Give a ball to someone in the group and ask that person to throw it, quickly, to anyone else in the group. As someone catches the ball, they say something about the life of Joan, beginning with her birth, the conditions of her life, her activities and aspirations, her achievements and finally, how she dies. Ask the group to repeat the game, constructing the life of John.

3 As this is going on, write the important elements of the stories on flipchart for discussion afterwards.

(20 mins)

4 In the whole group, go through the lives of Joan and John, and discuss the roles and achievements assigned to them.

(20 mins)

Materials

A ball, flipchart, pens

Facilitator's Notes

1 The ball should be kept moving rapidly for this exercise, so that participants respond spontaneously and say whatever comes into their minds at the time. This is also an energising activity to be used to vary the pace in the workshop and get people moving around.

2 The aim is to bring out, in discussion, the way that female and male roles are constructed from birth onwards.

(Source: CIDHAL, Mexico)

Time: 30-40 mins

Quiz on roles and activities of men and women

Objectives

1 To enable participants to be aware of their own (often hidden) impressions of men and women.

2 To start to look at roles and stereotypes in a non-confrontational way.

Method

1 **Preparation**: prepare flipchart reproducing the quiz sheet, and copies of **Handout 19** for group.

2 Explain that the group is going to do a quiz. It is important to stress that:
a. It is not a test of gender awareness.
b. There are no right and wrong answers.
c. Answers will be confidential.
d. First impressions are required, not thought-out answers.

(10 mins)

3 Hand out the quiz. Each person completes it individually as quickly as possible.

(20-25 mins)

4 Shuffle quiz sheets and then hand out again so each person gets a different sheet.

(2-3 mins)

5 Ask group to raise hands for answers to quiz. They indicate the answer on the paper in front of them, not their own answer. Write up on the flipchart the total number of answers 'men' or 'women' for each role and activity.

6 Discuss agreements (ask why all or most saw men and women in particular role or activity).

7 Discuss disagreements (ask why some thought an activity to be male others female).

8 Briefly discuss roles and stereotypes. Point out the contradictions and ask participants to discuss, bringing in the points in the Facilitator's Notes if they do not arise in the discussion.

(20-25 mins)

Materials

Handout 19, flipchart, pens

Facilitator's Notes

1 The reason for stressing that this is not a test of gender awareness, and for making the answers confidential, is to avoid participants becoming defensive, or trying to prove that they are gender-aware. The aim is to get at first impressions and stereotypes, not well-thought-out answers. You should encourage the idea that everyone (including yourself) will retain a stereotype, even when they have information to the contrary.

2 The roles and activities listed have been chosen for general relevance, but can be adapted to suit the particular context. With a very large group, it may be better to use a shorter list.

3 Use this exercise to reinforce the understanding of gender.

4 Bring out the contradictions between roles and activities e.g. the activity is often done by women, while the role is seen as men's

Men	***Women***
Tailor	*Do the sewing*
Farmer	*Plant the vegetables*
Chef	*Do the cooking*

An exception to this is the women's role of housewife, which includes budgeting and planning, yet these activities are generally seen as mainly men's activities. Similarly, men are generally seen to be the head of the household, yet in many societies up to 50 per cent of households have no man around on a regular basis, and even where a man is present, women often have the day-to-day responsibility for running the family.

5 Question why farmers are thought of as men when in fact women do most of the agricultural work (eg men own the land, men own the cash crop, farmer refers to trained men).

6 It seems that where there is money, power, or status attached to a role, and where it is performed outside the home, then men are more likely to be seen in that role.

7 Why are men assumed to be the ones to carry heavy loads, when in most countries a common sight is women carrying huge burdens? (One answer given at an East Africa workshop was that women carry food, while men carry important things — like beer!)

8 Note that the same activity may have different value when done by a woman and a man eg men talk, give speeches; women gossip. There may be cultural differences eg basket-making is done by women in some societies and by men in others.

9 End the session by pointing out that all the roles and activities could be performed by both men and women, and it is cultural and social norms which determine who does what. These norms lead to habits of thinking in fixed ways about men and women — stereotypes — even when in fact, roles can change.

10 A South African gender trainer (Michelle Friedman) added the dimension of race to this activity, by asking participants after they had answered the questions whether they had a particular racial group in mind. And then, asking them to think of a different race group and answer the questions again, to see whether the answers changed.

(Source: Janet Seed)

Quiz on roles and activities for men and women

This is not a test of gender awareness. It is not a test at all. It is just a way of looking at our first thoughts about people's roles and activities. Your answers will be confidential — we will be looking at group rather than individual answers. Please tick whether you think each role or activity is done mostly by men or mostly by women. Do not ponder your answer for a long time — your first thoughts are what we want. If you don't know or can't decide, leave that one and go on to the next one, in order to finish. You have 2 minutes. There will be a chance to discuss this fully after you have completed the exercise.

		Men	Women
Roles.	1. Chef		
	2. Housewife		
	3. Farmer		
	4. Nurse		
	5. Tailor		
	6. Community leader		
	7. Accountant		
	8. Mother		
	9. Union organiser		
	10. Refugee		
	11. Politician		
	12. Head of the Family		
	13. Breadwinner		
Activities	1. Sewing		
	2. Carrying heavy things		
	3. Operating machinery		
	4. Cooking		
	5. Selling		
	6. Basket weaving		
	7. Talking		
	8. Planting vegetables		
	9. Lighting a fire		
	10. Budgeting		
	11. Planning		
	12. Making decisions		
	13. Fetching water		

1½ - 2 hrs

Myths about women and men, and their effects

Part 1: Traditional Myths *(30 mins)*

Objectives

1 To look at the ways in which our own tradition and culture express beliefs about women and men.

2 To move about and have fun!

Method

1 Ask each person to list traditional and modern stories, songs, games, sayings, proverbs or rhymes from their own childhood which concern men and women's roles. Ask them to list as many as possible.

(5 mins)

2 Divide participants into 'country or region of origin' groups of three to six people, and share the most important songs, games, proverbs and the effect of these on them as girls/women, and boys/men.

(15 mins)

3 Ask each group to choose the most striking account, and to prepare a presentation to the whole group in a quick and dramatic way.

(5 mins)

4 Each group makes their presentation in turn. Explain that there is no comment or discussion at this stage. As this is going on, write brief descriptions of the stories or songs on one side flipchart.

(3 mins per group)

Part 2: Effects of myths *(30—60 mins)*

Objectives

1 To look at the messages behind certain traditional myths and see how these may influence our behaviour.

Method

1 In the large group, brainstorm the meanings of the presentations and record the ideas on the flipchart opposite the description of each song, story etc.*(10 mins)*

2 Discuss the implications of the ideas that come up.
(20 mins)

3 Summarise the discussion with input on the meaning and use of myths. (See *Facilitator's Notes*)
(20 mins)

Part 3: Learning gender roles *(30 mins)*

Objectives

1 To look at the ways in which our own tradition and culture determine beliefs about women and men.

2 To identify the origin of the messages.

3 To find out the effects of these today.

Method

1 Ask participants to break up into small groups again, and discuss the following questions:
   a. What did you learn about being a girl/boy? This should be written on separate lists for girls and boys.
   b Where did you learn it?
   c What are the effects on you today?

Materials

Flipchart, paper, pens

Facilitator's Notes

1 This activity, when used with both men and women, sets a good climate for discussing how gender roles are constructed, maintained and reinforced. Participants enjoy the songs, stories and proverbs told during the session. It helps participants to see the role of the socialisation process in constructing gender roles, and how deep-rooted these roles are. It has been one of the sessions best-received by both men and women.

2 Note that modern culture has its own myths. It is important to include these in order to avoid fostering racism or prejudice against traditional societies.

3 Myths address key issues relevant to the particular society, they provide norms of behaviour and reasons for these. They are told as entertainment at an early age, and thus have a great subconscious impact. We don't usually analyse myths for their meaning, and people may be surprised to discover the full implications behind myths.

4 You may find that participants are able to share more deeply if they are in single-sex groups, especially for Part 3. However, mixed-sex groups may be indicated where there is tension, hostility or misunderstanding between the men and women in the group.

5 It is important to point out that boys may have as much pressure to conform to their gender role as girls. Note that what is held to be 'proper' behaviour for men and women varies from culture to culture, and over time. The pressure comes from many places eg family, friends, school, religion, tradition, the media.

6 There are many effects on us as adults today from the messages we learnt as children. The messages are often internalised and thought of as natural, rather than learned eg it is seen as natural for women to be submissive, and men to be powerful and oppressive. People who do not act according to the stereotype may be criticised or ridiculed.

5 This activity is presented in three parts, but Part 1 could be followed by Parts 2 or 3 on their own. Part 3 could be used on its own, but Part 2 depends on Part 1.

[illegible]

Time: 1½ hrs

The 24-hour day

Objectives

1 To identify the daily tasks of men and women in low-income households in different regions of the world.

2 To raise awareness of men and women's workloads.

Method

1 Ask the participants to form small groups according to their country of origin, or areas/countries in which they have lived or worked. Ask each group to choose one low-income social group of which they have personal knowledge — such as fisherpeople, landless labourers, or an urban 'shanty-town' community.*(5 mins)*

2 Ask the groups to imagine a day in the lives of a wife and husband from each social group in a particular season, to be decided by the group.

3 Using the 24-hour day chart as a model, as on Handout 20, ask the groups to list the tasks performed by women and men in a household over 24 hours on flipchart paper. *(30 mins)*

4 Put the flipcharts up on the wall, and ask participants to walk around and look at each of them. *(10 mins)*

5 Help participants to draw out common points from the charts on the wall in a plenary discussion. *(25 mins)*

6 Give out **Handouts 21** Mr Moyo and **22** The Lie of the Land, and ask for comments. *(10 mins)*

Materials

Flipchart, pens, 24 hour chart, **Handouts 20, 21, and 22.**

Facilitator's Notes

1 The low-income groups chosen for this activity should be distinct from each other and provide contrasts. They should include both urban and rural examples. If there are participants from industrialised countries, ensure that one group selects one of these countries, to examine the common assumption that in the developed world, women's and men's workloads are equal.

2 Encourage the groups to include all activities, even those which might not be thought of as work eg breast-feeding, knitting, community meetings.

3 Some men, for whom gender is a new idea, may be shocked or surprised to discover the amount of work that women do, especially when the women are said 'not to work'. Some may feel threatened or unwilling to believe it, and thus may distort their information workload between the sexes. For example, in one training, one group chose nomadic people who keep slaves, and thus the women were said not to have much work, although the slaves were also women! In another training one group described the husband's role as being much fuller than had been experienced by one of the facilitators who came from that area. Following this activity with an activity from ***Section C.6 Women in the world*** *can be helpful.*

4 Despite the very considerable differences in the daily lives of the different groups, common points usually emerge:

Women and men do very different things during the day.
Women usually work longer hours.
Women have more varied tasks, sometimes doing more than one thing at once.
Work for the family is done by women.
Men's work is usually outside the home.
Men have more leisure time.
Women have less sleep.
Men are more involved in decision-making.
In some societies, traditional roles of men and women were more balanced in terms of workload, but changes have decreased men's traditional activities and increased women's.

5 This activity can start discussion on how to reduce women's workload and increase men's participation, or how to address any other imbalances.

6 This activity begins the analysis of gender roles, but deliberately ignores differences due to age, class, season, historical period, the effects of war etc. It can, be done to show up these differences, (eg comparing the work that boys and girls do, or older men and women) but be careful that you do not make it too complicated.

(Source: 24-hour Day exercise designed by C O N Moser (1993).)

Handout 20 *Activity 36*

Women	**Men**
01 a.m.	01 a.m.
02	02
03	03
04	04
05	05
06	06
07	07
08	08
09	09
10	10
11	11
12	12
13	13
14	14
15	15
16	16
17	17
18	18
19	19
20	20
21	21
22	22
23	23
24	24

Country:
Social Group:

Handout 21 *Activity 36*

A story: Mr Moyo goes to the doctor

'What is your job?' asked the doctor.
'I am a farmer' replied Mr Moyo.

'Have you any children?' the doctor asked.
'God has not been good to me. Of 15 born, only 9 alive,' Mr Moyo answered.

'Does your wife work?'
'No she stays at home'.

'I see. How does she spend her day?'
'Well, she gets up at four in the morning, fetches water and wood, makes the fire, cooks breakfast and cleans the homestead. Then she goes to the river and washes clothes. Once a week she walks to the grinding mill. After that she goes to the township with the two smallest children where she sells tomatoes by the road side while she knits. She buys what she wants from the shops. Then she cooks the midday meal.'

'You come home at midday?'
'No, no she brings the meal to me about three kilometres away.'

'And after that?'
'She stays in the field to do the weeding, and then goes to the vegetable garden to water.'

'What do you do?'
'I must go and discuss business and drink with the men in the village.'

'And after that?'
'I go home for supper which my wife has prepared.'

'Does she go to bed after supper?'
'No, I do. She has things to do around the house until 9 or 10.'

'But I thought you said your wife doesn't work.'
'Of course she doesn't work. I told you she stays at home.'

(Source: Presented by the Women and Development Sub-committee Ministry of Community Development and Community Affairs, Zimbabwe to Women's Regional Ecumenical Workshop, 26 June — 6 July 1989, Harare, Zimbabwe).

Handout 22 Activity 36

Agroforestry Today, Vol 1, No 2.

Time: 1½hrs

Analysing roles and needs

Objectives

1 To identify the three different roles of women.

2 To identify the two types of gender needs of women.

3 To illustrate which needs and roles different projects address.

4 To clarify and to practise identifying the roles and needs in different interventions.

Method

1 Continuing from the previous session (**Activity 36**: 24-hour day), draw out the different gender roles that the many different women's tasks represent. Give out **Handout 23** *(10-15 mins*

2 Explain gender needs. *(10-15 mins)*

3 Give out **Handout 24** and go through with group. *(15-30 mins)*

4 Give out **Handout 25**. Go through it in whole group, asking them to identify roles and needs. Debate the answers until there is agreement about the identification of roles and needs. *(30 mins)*

Materials

Flipchart
Handouts: 23 , 24 , and, 25.

Facilitator's Notes

1 This activity should be done after Activity 36. It should be made clear that this is the first step in learning the Moser method of gender planning.

2 All facilitators should have read, discussed and understood the handouts in order to be able to explain the roles and needs. In some cases, facilitators have found the terms 'family' and 'community' more acceptable to some groups than 'reproductive' and 'community managing', because of other connotations of these words. However it is important to keep the same concepts. Moser has now sub-divided the community role into two categories — community managing, and community politics. Community managing is the extension of women's reproductive role, and comprises activities such as organising collective provisioning of food, or education or health care. Their work is voluntary. Community politics is the public role of organising at community level for relations with other groups and organisations, including aid agencies, and with official representatives of the State. While women may participate in this, and be rank and file membership, men usually take the lead roles in community politics, often paid for their work.

3 Participants may ask why men's gender needs are not considered. One possibility is to explain that men's needs are usually seen as human needs or community needs and are thus taken into account. Women's needs are often not sought or acknowledged. The gender training is to redress the balance. Another possibility is to let the group work out men's gender roles and needs, making clear the previous point. Also point out that if women are ignored people may not notice, but leaving men out is always noticed. The analysis of men's gender needs is not part of the original Moser method. (C O N Moser, (1989) 'Gender planning in the Third World: meeting practical and strategic gender needs', World Development, *17, 11.))*

4 If the issue of men's practical and strategic needs arises, refer to the introduction to this section for discussion on women's and men's needs and interests, and ask the group to reflect on whether it is possible for women and men to share strategic interests and needs.

Handout 23 *Activity 37*

Types of work/triple role

Work can be divided into three main categories. Women's roles encompass work in all these categories, and this is referred to as women's 'Triple Role'.

Productive work involves the production of goods and services for consumption and trade (farming, fishing, employment and self-employment). When people are asked what they do, the response is most often related to productive work, especially work which is paid or generates income. Both women and men can be involved in productive activities, but for the most part, their functions and responsibilities will differ according to the gender division of labour. Women's productive work is often less visible and less valued than men's.

Reproductive work involves the care and maintenance of the household and its members including bearing and caring for children, food preparation, water and fuel collection, shopping, housekeeping and family health care. Reproductive work is crucial to human survival, yet it is seldom considered 'real work'. In poor communities, reproductive work is, for the most part manual-labour-intensive, and time-consuming. It is almost always the responsibility of women and girls.

Community work involves the collective organisation of social events and services: ceremonies and celebrations, community improvement activities, participation in groups and organisations, local political activities, and so on. This type of work is seldom considered in economic analyses of communities. However, it involves considerable volunteer time and is important for the spiritual and cultural development of communities and as a vehicle for community organisation and self-determination. Both women and men engage in community activities, although a gender division of labour also prevails here.

Women, men, boys and girls are likely to be involved in all three areas of work. In many societies, however, women do almost all of the reproductive and much of the productive work. Any intervention in one area will affect the other areas. Women's workload can prevent them from participating in development projects. When they do participate, extra time spent farming, producing, training or meeting, means less time for other tasks, such as childcare or food preparation.

(Source: *Two Halves Make a Whole: Balancing Gender Relations in Development* CCIC/MATCH/AQOCI)

Practical and strategic gender needs

Practical gender needs

- They are a response to an immediate perceived necessity.
- They are formulated from concrete conditions.
- They are derived from women's position within the gender division of labour (i.e. the women's role).
- They do not challenge the subordinate position of women although they arise out of it.
- They are needs mainly arising from and reinforcing women's reproductive and productive role.

Practical gender needs may include:
Water provision.
Health care.
Income earning for household provisioning.
Housing and basic services.
Family food provision.

They are needs shared by all household members yet identified specifically as practical gender needs of women, as it is women who assume responsibility for meeting these needs.

Strategic gender needs:
These are formulated by an analysis of women's subordination in society.

- When addressed, they should lead to the transformation of the gender division of labour.
- They challenge the nature of the relationship between men and women;
- They aim to overcome women's subordination.

Strategic gender needs may include:
Abolition of sexual division of labour.
Alleviation of the burden of domestic labour and child care.
The removal of institutionalised forms of discrimination such as rights to own land or property.
Access to credit and other resources.
Freedom of choice over child bearing.
Measures against male violence and control over women.

Examples of roles and needs

Intervention	R	P	CM	PGN	SGN
1 Training for employment					
a. Training for women					
Cooking cakes for family					
Tailoring — for sale					
Masonry/carpentry					
2 Basic services					
a. Introduction of creche					
Located in community					
In mother's workplace					
In father's workplace					
b. Primary Health Centre in area where women work on cash crops in the morning					
Open only in the morning					
Open in the evening					
3 Housing					
a. Tenure rights					
In man's name					
In women's name					
4 Community participation					
a. Project with community participation					
With unpaid women's time					
With paid women's time					

R = Reproductive; P = Productive; CM = Community Managing;
PGN = Practical Gender Need; SGN = Strategic Gender Need
(Source: Adapted from C O N Moser (1993) *Gender Planning and Development Theory Practice and Training*.)

Time: 1 hr

Balloons: practical and strategic gender needs

Objectives

1 To find out the gender needs of women.

2 To identify how those gender needs are linked.

3 To find out what needs NGOs respond to and whether they are practical or strategic gender needs.

Method

1 Divide participants into small groups of six, if possible according to common experience, or work in the same or similar area.

2 Give each group a set of marker pens and flipchart.

3 Ask each group to begin by drawing a picture of a woman from their area of work, in the middle of the paper.

4 Close to this picture they should draw a balloon in which they should note down one major problem affecting women in their area.

5 Ask them to reflect on one or more problems resulting from the first problem.

6 For each linked problem they should draw a new balloon and link it to the first.

7 They should continue drawing and linking other balloons representing a chain of linked problems, as far as they can go .*(30 mins)*

8 When a whole chain of balloons has been created ask each group to identify with an arrow the point in the chain where their NGO's intervention begins and to

highlight the consequences (how many other parts of the chain are impacted by this intervention).

9 Each group puts up their flipchart and has a 'gallery walk' looking at each other's balloon diagrams.

10 Discuss with the group:

a. What have you learned from this exercise?

b. What problems are being addressed by the interventions— do these represent practical or strategic needs or both?

c. What needs are being left out — are these practical or strategic needs? (Summarise practical and strategic needs — refer to **Handout 16**.)

d. (**Optional**) What interventions could be made to address more of women's strategic gender needs? What difference does the way in which practical needs are met, make to meeting strategic gender needs?

(30 mins)

Materials

Flipcharts
Felt pens

Facilitator's Notes

1 This is a good activity to help participants to conceptualise practical and strategic gender needs using their own experience. It gives a clear picture of NGOs' interventions and shows up whether they are addressing any strategic needs or only practical needs. This can lead to a discussion of the need for starting with practical needs of poor women and going on to address strategic needs; what these strategic needs are; and how they might be addressed.

2 If doing the activity with a group who do not have knowledge of the area, or if you want a particular problem to be included (eg. domestic violence or rape), you can work out the problems, draw them on 'balloons' and ask participants to stick them on the flipchart and draw the links.

(Source: This exercies was adapted from Lyra Srinivasan, by Colleen Crawford Cousins and Michelle Friedman NLC, South Africa.)

C.5 Women in the world

This section complements the previous section, contrasting facts and statistics about women with the 'Myths' explored in **Activity 35**, and providing material from the participants' own research to reinforce what has been learned about the roles and needs of women. It is important that participants in a longer gender-training workshop come well-prepared with facts about the lives of women and men in the countries or regions in which they work; or in relation to a specific theme, such as conflict, or the environment, if the training is theme-based. This will entail careful and detailed research on either a case-study basis, or in terms of compiling figures and facts about a country or region, and participants should be given plenty of time to prepare this material.

Guidelines should be given for this, such as those in **Activity 40 Women in Our Countries**. Guidelines for drawing up case studies are given in **Section C.7**, in relation to **Activity 56 Using Case Studies**.

Questions sometimes arise in gender training about the reliability of statistics — these have often come from men, suggesting that statistics exaggerate the worsening condition of women. It is useful to explore issues about statistics, and to point out that it is only recently, and in some forms of data, that women's real work and lives have been taken into account in statistical research at all. The handout attached to activity 38 outlines some of these issues.

C.5 Activities

Time: 2-3 hrs

Women in our countries

Objectives

1 To give an overview of the position of women in some of the countries where participants work.

2 To share the research carried out before the workshop.

Method

1 **Preparation**: before the training, ask participants to prepare presentations based on the following:

a. A short general overview of the situation for women in the countries under discussion, to enable the group to understand the differences (and similarities) in the position of women in different countries.

b. Data on women and men such as literacy rates; life expectancy; per day calorie intake for both men and women; women in decision-making; women's access to formal education and employment.

c. Child-rearing practices; preferences for boys or girls; the role of men and women, boys and girls in domestic tasks.

d. The role of both men and women in agriculture; paid and unpaid work; petty trade and other informal activities. Who has access to land (ownership or other resources) and who controls the land.

e. Different forms of discrimination against women (cultural practices such as dowry, bride price, etc).

f. Community and political participation. Where and how do men and women participate? Are there women leaders in the community?

g. Current legislation which has an adverse effect on women.

h. The relationship of the State to women, and women's rights.

i. The social and political changes that have occurred to alter, positively or negatively, the status of and value given to women.

(Time per presentation: 30-40 mins)

2 Ask two or three participants to make a presentation .

3 Allow time after each presentation for questions.

(10-20 mins)

Facilitator's Notes

1 The idea of this activity is to have comparable accounts of the situation of women in different countries. If all the participants are from the same country, they could divide the data collection amongst themselves, taking specific sectors such as health, legal and political rights, land and production and so on.

2 The material collected by participants for these presentations can be used at later stages in the workshop when methods of appraisal, analysis and planning are addressed.

3 You can ask participants to prepare full case studies, and give them clear guidelines, so that these can be used to practise using some of the analytical frameworks presented in **Section C.7 Gender-sensitive Appraisal and Planning***.*

4 The Handout on statistics for the following activity ***Handout 29 Why are women invisible in statistics?*** *may be useful to send to participants before the training; you could also send them* **Handout 28 Sources of data on women** *to assist them in their preparation.*

Time: 40 mins-1½ hrs

Facts about women and men

Objectives

1 To facilitate an understanding of gender imbalance worldwide and within countries.

2 To show how certain assumptions about men and women are reinforced in areas such as education, employment, and politics.

3 To help participants to see the importance of gender analysis in all aspects of development.

4 To consider gender bias in the collection of data and statistics. (Optional)

Method

1 Before the session, prepare factual information about men and women in your area/country/worldwide. Information should be simple enough for participants to read, understand and discuss. Write it onto flipchart or OHP-transparencies, dividing the information into sections on specific issues or aspects of life.

2 Present each information sheet. Then follow with a short discussion in pairs or large group on what is striking, before presenting another aspect.

(less than 5 mins)

3 After you have presented all the aspects ask participants to discuss the following question in groups of three:

a. What do the facts tell us about the situation of women and men in this area/country/ the world?

b. What assumptions about women and men are being reinforced or challenged?

(35 mins)

c. How can we ensure our data is gender-sensitive? (Optional)

Materials

Pre-prepared flipcharts or OHP transparencies. Handouts of key information (based on flipcharts). (See Handouts here as guide — you will need to do your own.)

Facilitator's Notes

1 The handouts included here are a guide. They give some idea of the type of information you need and the way it can be presented. Don't overload people with too much information. Don't try and fit too much onto one sheet. Make sure it is big enough to see — even for those with poor eyesight. Use graphics (graphs or pictures) where possible.

Possible subjects to include:
Wealth: income; property; land ownership
Paid work: farming/agriculture; industry; types of jobs; business/trade
Domestic activities: including child rearing practices
Education: formal; non-formal
Legal system
Migration and refugees
Violence and crime
Health, including mental health; life expectancy; maternal mortality; AIDS
Nutrition
Marriage customs
Community and political participation.

2 It may be difficult in some countries to obtain the relevant up-to-date information. UN agency sources are useful (UNDP reports, UN reports on The World's Women, UNICEF State of the World's Children, etc.) for general statistics — bearing in mind that these only give national, regional or global averages, and are thus restricted — and should be up-to-date. Information should also be sought from national and regional government and NGO sources, as well as from local groups who may have carried out small-scale surveys.

3 The presentation of facts can be done in many different ways, and the handouts attached to this activity can also be used in other contexts (gender and development, project analysis, gender planning).

4 This activity can also follow ***Activity 35 Myths about Women and Men, and their Effects*** *as a counterbalance to assumptions about the situation of women and men.*

6 You can also use this session to stress male bias in statistics and data collection methods i.e. the kind of information available from the usual official sources, at local, national and global level, is not usually disaggregated by gender. Nor are the methods of collecting such data gender-aware. Read ***Handout 29*** *and prepare notes from it if you intend to address this question in the training.*

Handout 26 — Activity 40

Higher mortality rates among girls between two and five years old have been found in demographic and health surveys in a significant number of countries

	Deaths per year per 1,000 population aged 2-5 years	
	Girls	Boys
Pakistan	54.4	36.9
Haiti	61.2	47.8
Bangladesh	68.6	57.7
Thailand	26.8	17.3
Syria	14.6	9.3
Colombia	24.8	20.5
Costa Rica	8.1	4.8
Nepal	60.7	57.7
Dominican Republic	20.2	17.2
Philippines	21.9	19.1
Sri Lanka	18.7	16.3
Peru	30.8	28.8
Mexico	16.7	14.7
Panama	8.7	7.6
Turkey	19.5	18.4
Republic of Korea	12.7	11.8
Venezuela	8.4	7.6

Compiled by UNICEF from national survey reports of the World Fertility Survey programme.

(Source: The World's Women: Trends and Statistics, 1970-1990, United Nations, New York 1991.)

Maternal mortality figures

Maternal mortality is much higher in developing regions, especially where women give birth with no trained attendant

(Source: The World's Women: Trends and Statistics 1970-1990, United Nations, New York, 1991)

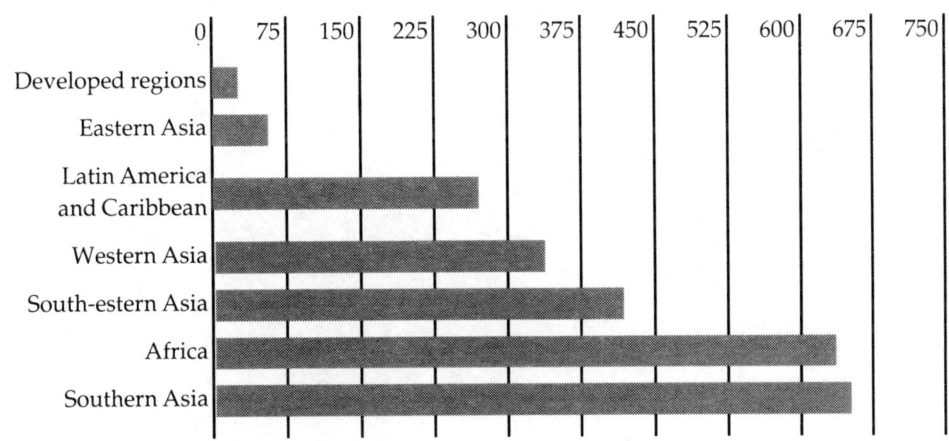

Estimated maternal mortality rate per 100, 000 live births, about 1983
(Note: Rates are based on estimated totals in each region, not country averages.)

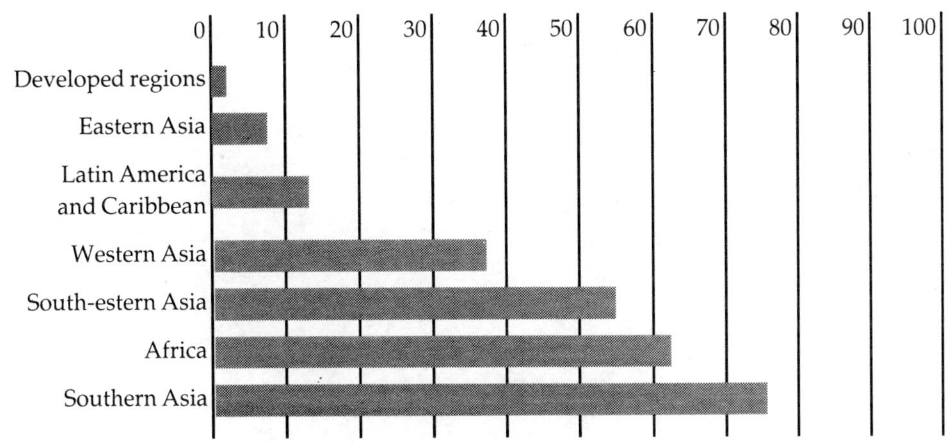

Estimated births without trained attendant, about 1985 (%)

Sources of data on the situation of women

	International	National	District/Loca
Agriculture	ILO Yearbook; Labour Force Statistics; FAO World Census of Agriculture	Population Census; Rural Labour Force Surveys, eg Kenya, India; Farm-Household Surveys.	Farm Management Data Bases; ILO Women, Work and Development series; Population Council Cases for Planners. 1985 Kumarian Press Village Studies.
Health	WHO Health Stats; ILO WEP; Population & Labour Policies; Working Papers	National Nutrition Surveys; Ministry of Health Records; Civil Registers	MCH Clinics. Local nutrition and health data. Hospital records. Civil Registers. Missions.
Education	UNESCO Education Statistics	Population Census; Household Surveys; Ministry of Education records	School and University records. Literacy class attendance.
Labour force.	ILO Yearbook; Labour Force Statistics; UN World Survey on the situation of women; ILO lab-force estimates and projections; USAID/US Dept. of Commerce 'Women of the World' 5 vols	Population &ensus; Household surveys; Lab/employment Surveys	Household surveys. Case studies. Employers' records. Village studiesLocal aid agencies & missions.

Source: Gender and Third World Development Module 1 (Alison Evans) Socio-Economic Statistics IDS, Sussex. Copyright: CEC

Why are women invisible in statistics?

Disaggregation — before and after

Until the 1970s, mainstream research, policy and planning virtually ignored the economic role of women. Development plans and policies were either based on men and then generalised to all people, or they prescribed a development future in which men were assumed to be the only breadwinners, and women and children their dependants. The practical outcomes of many of these policies and programmes adversely affected the welfare of many women and were shown to be in conflict with the interests of many more.

The dominant view was that women's participation in development was outside the economic mainstream and mainly restricted to activities for which women were stereotypically most suited: family and child welfare, household work, etc. On the other hand, case studies and qualitative research showed that most women in developing countries were crucial participants in economic and social life, although many were at a social and economic disadvantage in making effective contributions to growth and development.

In 1975, at the inauguration of the UN Decade for Women, priority was given to disaggregating by sex all national economic and social statistics. The aim was to make visible to planners the full extent of women's economic participation, particularly in areas traditionally considered to be male-dominated; and the status of women in terms of their income, health and education.

The process of disaggregating national statistics by sex has been fairly uneven, mainly because the changes that have had to be made in census and census-type procedures are slow, cumbersome, and often costly to manage. Data on women is nevertheless increasingly available at national and local levels for researchers and planners to see. However, many problems remain with this data. The process of disaggregation by sex does not in itself reveal the whole picture of women's lives and work. It shows only the tip of the iceberg. This is largely because of two assumptions which underlie the whole process of disaggregation by sex. These are:

• The assumption that all techniques for data collection and measurement are equally valid for men and for women. For example, techniques for eliciting information for men are also presumed to work for women. But the evidence is that women and men experience their economic and social environments differently, and this affects how they respond to questions about their situation.

• The assumption that conventional conceptual categories hold the same meaning for all people. The concept of work, for instance, is often taken to mean the same thing for women and men — and so their experiences in work are held to be adequately represented in unisex categories. *But* work for women may be largely subsumed within household or family unpaid labour; while for men it is socially visible and often economically rewarded.

Techniques of measurement

What is measured by statisticians — and, equally important, what is *not* measured — depends largely on the techniques of measurement that are chosen, such as the unit of enumeration;; and the dominant perceptions and attitudes about what is important or relevant information. For example, a number of recent studies criticise Census and National Income Accounting methodologies that exclude production outside of the market. These studies argue that some aspects of informal sector production and production for use within the household must be assessed in economic terms.

This approach holds particular significance for the economically developing countries, where a great deal of production continues to go unrecognised in estimates of national GDP. These economies are structured in such a way that if estimates of the national product exclude a measure of informal and non-market output, along with the labour effort involved, then the value and composition of national economic activity are grossly misrepresented. This problem is most acute where women's work is concerned For example, an analysis of the 1976 Peruvian Peasant Survey shows that once non-market production is measured, close to 86 per cent of women, rather than the 38 per cent initially measured, were engaged in agricultural production (Deere 1982).

There are several other factors which influence the accuracy and coverage of data collection, whether quantitative or qualitative data are being sought. These factors include:

- the timing of interviews;
- the length of the reference period;
- the language in which the interviews are conducted.

Example: In Africa, census enumerators usually visit rural communities in the dry season, when travel is easier. However, work is usually at its most intense in the rural areas during the rainy season. If the standard one- or two-week reference period is used, the volume and types of work normally carried out in the community will be underestimated. If rainy season activities are probed, accuracy of answers will depend on the ability of respondents to recall their work patterns. There is some debate as to how well people do recall annual patterns of work: both under- and over-reporting is suggested.

The choice of an unseasonal time of year and a limited reference period are amongst a number of technical explanations for the under-reporting and misrepresentation of women's work in agricultural statistics. Empirical research indicates that this underestimation problem is particularly acute for women whose current activity, at the time of enumeration, may not be on-farm work but domestic work. Consequently, women are classified as non-workers even though, at crucial points in the agricultural cycle, their main activity is in fact farm work.

Women and men also report differently. Generally speaking, it has been found that women report more accurately, as exemplified by estimates of harvest in Sudan, of water usage in Somalia, and food requirements in relief situations in Kenya.

Economic activity is not the only thing affected by seasonal fluctuation and recall difficulties. Cyclical changes also affect income and standard of living;health status; and household composition. Changes in these areas are frequently not visible in annual and decennial data because the information is averaged from a single reference period for the year as a whole.

Conceptual categories

The choice of conceptual categories in censuses and most census-type statistics is influenced by a 'way of seeing or looking at the world'. This generally undercounts and undervalues the position and contributions of women compared to men. Stereotypical 'ways of looking at the world' are best illustrated by some of the conceptual categories used to classify economic activity.

What is 'productive' activity?

The standard concept of economic activity refers to participation in a productive activity. Many aspects of women's work, particularly the unpaid services they provide as family labour, are not considered as productive activity. But why should preparing and processing food for own-consumption be considered any less productive than growing the food? Why should caring for children be considered less productive than caring for livestock?

One answer is that work associated with the household and own-consumption is rarely considered by economists or planners to be income-generating, and therefore essentially non-economic in character. Once this judgement is made, women's work loses its value and is marginalised from the economic mainstream.What would happen if women's 'domestic' work was reflected in national statistical surveys?

Example: A study from India shows that if, in the 32nd round of the National Sample Survey, all the activities assumed to be 'domestic' were deemed economic, the labour force participation rate for rural women above five years of age would rise from 30.5 per cent to 52.3 per cent (the male rate is 63.7 per cent). The state-wise coefficient of variation in the female labour force participation rate would also decline. The latter appears therefore to be an artifact of the exclusion of a wide range of women's tasks from so-called economic activity rather than to reflect real variations in their participation (Sen and Sen 1985).

Despite such evidence, there is general reluctance to change statistical conventions to meet new arguments about the value of women's work and economic activity. This reflects another conceptual obstacle — the assumption that gender roles, and the gender division of labour, are determined by sex differences. Data collection is limited by a stereotyped view of women's roles, and no consideration of gender relations.

Moving towards equity — the implications

Disaggregation by sex, then, does not ensure gender equity in data collection. Disaggregation can be a positive step but it is no panacea.

The equity-oriented model of gender presents new challenges in the collection and interpretation of statistical data. These challenges lie in choosing new concepts and methods with which to collect more accurate data on women, and in using and interpreting existing data in developing planning and policy making.

Two central issues stand out in the equity-oriented approach:

- **Quantitative and qualitative information about women and men can onlybe made sense of when studied in relation to its social, economic and cultural context.**

- **Disaggregating conceptual categories on the basis of sex is a *necessary* but not a *sufficient* process for improving the data on the situation of women.**

(Source: Adapted from: Gender and World Development Module 1: Socio-Economic Statistics, Alison Evans, Institute of Development Studies, Sussex University. Commission of the European Communities, 1991.)

C.6 Gender and development

This section builds on what has been learned in the sections on gender roles and needs, and introduces other concepts which make up a framework for understanding gender and development.

There are not many activities, but this is a fundamentally important section, as it tackles concepts such as participation and empowerment, which are frequently misunderstood, wrong assumptions, and ineffective policies related to women in development and relief work.

By the time workshop participants have completed the activities in this section, they should have a sound foundation for developing a gender perspective in development and relief work. This foundation is needed before moving on to the next section in this manual, section **C.7 Gender-Sensitive Appraisal and Planning**, which introduces a number of analytical frameworks for appraisal, planning, and evaluation of programmes and projects.

Please read all the handouts in this section carefully and **Section A.1 A guide to this manual,**, before starting to use the activities.

Policy approaches

The first three activities look at common assumptions about development and relief work, and introduce a framework of policy approaches to women and development. The Policy Approaches outlined in **Activity 42 Statements and policy approaches** are a framework for identifying and understanding the different ways in which official agencies and NGOs attempt to address the issue of women's participation in development. Although the framework is presented as a historical account, many of the approaches are recognisable in development policy today. These policy approaches are not comprehensive, and participants in the workshop may feel they are over-simplified: however, they provide an introduction to the analysis and planning which will be examined in more detail in section **C.7 Gender-Sensitive Appraisal and Planning**.

Empowerment and participation

The activities which look at empowerment and participation are crucial to an understanding of gender and development, and indeed to the understanding of development as committed to the equality of all people. These terms — 'empowerment' and 'participation' — have become part of the required discourse of development and relief agencies, and are frequently misunderstood and misused.

Participation in development is usually said to mean the full involvement of people in the development or relief programmes which affect their lives, regardless of gender, race, age, class, sexual orientation or disability. However, the concept is often taken for granted, leading to the dangerous assumption that people are participating, while in fact their experience is being marginalised, undervalued, or ignored. It is common for women to feel this, because it is often assumed that they will be compliant, and their views are not valued. Yet they may be defined as participating simply because they are present in a group, in a village community, in an organisation.

Genuine participation of women in development means women being able to make their views known, and to take decisions which affect their lives. It means that women's concerns influence development policy and project aims, and that women play a part in evaluating project impact.

'Empowerment' is also a very loosely-employed term. The most important thing to understand about empowerment is that, in a sense, no-one can empower anyone else. In the way it is used in relation to development, true empowerment is achieved by people themselves, through their own efforts (see **Handout 33).** When development and relief agencies use the term, they rarely mean this: they often claim to empower the poor, or women, through their interventions. In fact, agencies can only support people's own efforts to become empowered, and intervene in favour of the conditions people require to achieve dignity and control in their lives.

Participation and empowerment: two sides of the same coin

The 'Women-in-development' (WID) approach of the 1970s (still widely in use) illustrates the effects of participation without empowerment. After the beginning of the UN Decade for Women (1975-1985) women were said to have been left out of the development process. For development to work better (the 'efficiency' approach referred to in **Activity 42**) women's participation in development had to be assured by targeting projects at them. A gender analysis of *why* women had been ignored by development planners, and of what women's and men's roles were, was not part of this approach.

Women were not effectively consulted, and the result was a plethora of women's projects which gave women a great deal more work but less control than ever over their lives and basic resources.

The problem was not that women did not participate: of course they always participated in development, performing in some parts of the world, for example, 80 per cent of the work of food production. The problem was that they were not consulted directly about their needs, the aims and directions of new development initiatives, and were cut out of the decision-making processes.

In the WID approach, women's participation applied to development *work*, but not development *decisions*, led to women's disempowerment.

Development and emergency relief

This section also begins to look at gender issues in emergency relief work, for the insights of GAD analysis are central to the success of relief interventions. The incorporation of GAD analysis in the planning and implementation of relief work lags considerably behind its incorporation in development work. This is due to a number of factors:

- There is a false dichotomy between relief work and development work, due mainly to different operational styles, to the scale of work sometimes required and to the rapidity with which decisions have to be taken and interventions planned. This often means that relief programmes are planned and implemented from the top down.

- Relief work is commonly dominated by logistic considerations — how many tons of grain are needed, how many aeroplanes/trucks/barges will be needed, how many people have to be provided with shelter, water, food, health care and sanitation systems. This has meant that men tend to dominate the field, and that engineers and technical personnel (often short-term) with littleor no training in social analysis are brought in to manage highly complex social and cultural responses to disasters.

- The prioritisation of speed of delivery has often precluded proper discussion with the affected people, overlooked gender considerations, and resulted in inappropriate and therefore ineffective responses. Women especially face many barriers to participating in discussion and assessment of needs, and are rarely involved in planning or policy making in emergency situations.

Yet the majority of those affected by emergencies, such as refugees and displaced people, are likely to be women and children (see also **Handout 36).**

In this section we introduce the topic of emergency relief, and encourage participants to think about the commonalities and differences between development and relief work. The following section, **C.7 Gender-Sensitive Appraisal and Planning**, presents several frameworks particularly adapted to emergency interventions. **Section C.8 Gender and Global Issues** looks at gender in relation to conflict and presents a number of activities which address ways of analysing the issues and planning appropriate interventions.

C.6 Activities

Time: 35 mins

Wrong assumptions

Objectives

1 To identify common myths or wrong assumptions about gender and development.

2 To look at the consequences of believing these wrong assumptions.

3 To contrast myths and assumptions with facts.

Method

1 Brainstorm on as many myths (wrong assumptions about gender and development) as possible. Write answers on flipchart.

(10 mins)

2 Pick out two key myths. Write each on a separate flipchart.

3 Group brainstorms effects of planning development on the basis of these wrong assumptions. Write answers on flipchart.

(20 mins)

4 Give facts (supported by hand-outs) on issues related to the two myths.

(5 mins)

Materials

Flipchart
Handouts: See **Section C.5 Women in the World**.

Facilitator's Notes

1 You may join in the brainstorm and add in any key myths or assumptions which the group has left out. You can choose to pick out the particular myths or wrong assumptions which you wish to emphasise, rather than allow the group to choose them.

2 It is important to point out that development has its own myths, which have been harmful to development. There is always a great fear of imposing Western feminism, but this activity shows the dangers of imposing Western sexism. this activity ties up with ***Activity 34 Quiz on Roles and Activities***

3 Some key myths to include are:
All farmers are men.
Heads of household are men.
People live in nuclear families.
When you work with the community, you automatically take care of women's interests.
Refer back to **Activity 35** *Myths about Men and Women, and their Effects: in addition to traditional myths, development has its own myths.*

Time: 1¾ hrs

Statements and policy approaches

Objectives

1 To start discussion about different approaches to gender and development.

2 To introduce the topic of policies.

Method

Preparation: Make one set of cards for each participant, based on **Handout 30.**

Part 1: Statements

1 Introduce this activity and stress that it is not a test. Participants should not write their names on their sheets. Go through instructions on **Handout 32**. Make clear that top of the diamond is 'agree most strongly' and the bottom of the diamond is 'disagree most'. This does not represent total agreement or disagreement with the statements.

(5 mins)

2 Ask each person to sort 16 cards, with statements A to P (**Handout 30**) and put their answers on **Handout 32.** At the same time prepare the 'diamond' on flipchart.

(15 mins)

3 Ask participants to form small groups of three or four for discussion. Each group has to try to reach agreement, and write the group answer on a group 'diamond' (**Handout 32**). Also, give each person a copy of **Handout 30** to reflect on.

(20 mins)

4 Reconvene the whole group for discussion. Write up answers on flipchart for each group

.*(30 mins)*

Raise the following questions:
a. How did you feel doing that exercise: was it easy?
b. Were there wide variations?
c. Look at similarities and differences in 'agree' and 'disagree' and discuss the reasons.

Points for discussion:
a. The statements are examples of real statements.
b. They have been chosen to reflect particular policy approaches.
c. They are over-generalisations.

Part 2: Policy Approaches

1 Explain that this part of the activity will relate the statements from Part One to policies that exist about gender and development.

2 Show prepared flipchart (as **Handout 31**) with five major policy approaches and important points noted.

3 Ask participants to indicate which statements reflect each of the different policy approaches; and fill these in on the flipchart.

4 Ask about other statements with no policy approach.

5 Ask about statement M. What does it represent?

6 Distribute **Handout 31** on policy approaches. *(20-25 mins)*

Materials

1 set of 16 cards, for each participant, on each of which is written one statement. These can be produced by photocopying and cutting up copies of **Handout 30**. They can then be retained for future training workshops.
1 grid for statements for each participant (**Handout 32**) plus one for each small group.
1 page of 16 statements for each participant (**Handout30**).
1 handout of policies for each participant (**Handout 31**).
Prepared flipchart of **Handout 32** and **Handout 31**.
Flipchart, pens etc.

Facilitator's Notes

1 The statements reflect five policy approaches to WID:
a. Welfare (K, B)
b. Equity (H, N)
c. Anti-poverty (F, O)
d. Efficiency (E, L)
e. Empowerment (G, D)

2 Gender analysis (represented by statement M) is a necessary starting point for putting any of these strategies into practice. It does not indicate which approach to adopt.

3 The statements have been taken from published documents or overheard remarks. This activity can be adapted for different cultural contexts, by substituting some commonly heard views; but statements B, D, E, F, G, H, K, L, M, N, and O must always be included.

4 People may find it difficult to reach agreement: but that is part of the learning experience. Try to move people from disagreements about the words to discussing the ideas. This activity shows that having a gender perspective can mean many different things. Often statement G, representing empowerment, is a favoured statement; it is important to remember this when analysing projects, using the Moser method. While people theoretically want to support an empowerment approach, in practice this is less likely (see ***Activity 43 Empowerment and Participation****).*

4 This activity can be used to teach the policy approaches for the Moser method of gender planning. However, if you are conducting a more basic training and do not need to teach specific methods of project analysis, this activity works well using Part 1 only.

(Source: Janet Seed.)

Handout 30 *Activity 42*

Statements about gender and development: statement sheet

(See over)

A A good development project will benefit the whole community which will automatically include women.	B We aim to help the poorest of the poor. Poor women are particularly disadvantaged, so they should be specially helped.	C I agree that Southern women have a hard time, but it's not up to us to change their culture.	D Women (in any society) often find it difficult to speak in the company of men. Therefore it is important to devise ways of enabling their voices to be heard.
E Women do the main farming work. Therefore women must be involved in any agricultural project if it is to succeed.	F There should be some aspect of income-generation in all schemes for women. The aim should be that such schemes should be self-financing.	G True development for women would enable them to have the power to make meaningful choices and changes in their lives.	H Equal Opportunities policy and practice in Northern NGOs should be directly relevant to, and can provide guidelines for, the projects we support in Southern countries.
I When the situation is serious you can't afford the time to stop and think about gender issues.	J If a community is involved in a national liberation or class struggle, then this has to be the priority for both men and women. To focus on women's specific needs is divisive and disruptive.	K Women as wives and mothers are responsible for the health and well-being of the whole family. Therefore we should help them to help the whole family.	M All aspects of development will affect women and men differently. Therefore we need to look at everything for its different impact on men and women.
N Within each culture, women are subordinate to men. The aim should be to eliminate this inequality and subordination.	O If women had more education they could catch up with men to become more economically self-sufficient.	P The important thing is to help the people most in need, not just the women.	

Policy approaches to women's involvement in development

(see over)

	Welfare	Anti-poverty	Efficiency	Equity	Empowerment
Cause of the problems.	Circumstances that are beyond control.	Lack of resources, causing low standard of living	Failure by development planners to recognise women's key role in production, and necessity to involve women	Patriarchy, exploitation, subordination, and oppression of women by men.	Women's subordination not only by men but as aspect of colonial and neo-colonial oppression
Goals or purpose.	To support motherhood as the most important role for women in society. To relieve suffering.	To raise production to ensure poor women increase their productivity. To integrate women into development	To ensure that development is more efficient and more effective. 'Feed the nation.'	To gain equity for women in development by grafting gender into the development process	To empower women through greater self reliance. Building new political, economic and social structures. To challenge/overcome exploitative structures
Service programmes.	Famine relief programmes. Family planning. Nutrition (improving family health, especially of children through maternal care). Activities to meet Practical Gender Needs	Training women in technical skills. Small-scale income-generating activities to meet basic needs (practical gender needs)	Programmes that meet PGN in the context of declining social services. Rely on all 3 roles of women and elasticity of time	Organise to reform structures. To meet SGN in terms of Triple Role.	Programmes that address themselves to SGN in terms of Triple Role — through bottom-up mobilisation around PGNs to confront oppression.
Type of change	FUNCTIONAL CHANGE (Non-challenging)	FUNCTIONAL CHANGE (Non-challenging)	FUNCTIONAL CHANGE	STRUCTURAL CHANGE (Challenging) Equal Rights/Opportunities	STRUCTURAL CHANGE (Challenging)
Type of leadership	Strong reliance on authority (patriarchal in nature) — residual model of social welfare with the modernisation ideology with roots in colonialism.	Consultative — ideological reproduction of values that reinforce patriarchy and women's subordination.	Authoritarian/consultative. Women seen as resource	Participatory to reform structures. Top-down state intervention to reduce inequality	Enabling, participatory, build solidarity, overcome fear (alternative m/f balanced structures). 'Bottom-up'
Type of service	WELFARE — Assuming women are passive beneficiaries of development	ANTI-POVERTY — Development (integrating women into development). Poor women isolated as a category. Recognition of the productive role of women	EFFICIENCY — Policies of economic stabilisation and adjustment rely on women's involvement.	EQUITY — Reforming, liberating. Women seen as active participants in development.	EMPOWERMENT Transformation, liberation Largely unsupported by Government or agencies. Slow steady growth of under-financed voluntary organisations.
Period most popular	1950-70, but still widely used.	1970s onwards. Still limited popularity.	Post 1980s — Now most popular approach (ODA, USAID)	1975-85 — Attempts to adopt during Women's Decade	1975 onwards, accelerated 1980s. Still limited popularity

Adapted by Adelina Ndeto Mwau from C.O.N. Moser 1989

Handout 32 *Activity 42*

Statements about gender and development: diamond ranking

Please read the statements carefully and judge them on how much you agree or disagree with them.

Then please sort them into order, in seven levels from level 1 (Agree most strongly) through to level 7 (Disagree most strongly). Please sort them so that they form a 'diamond' shape as indicated below.

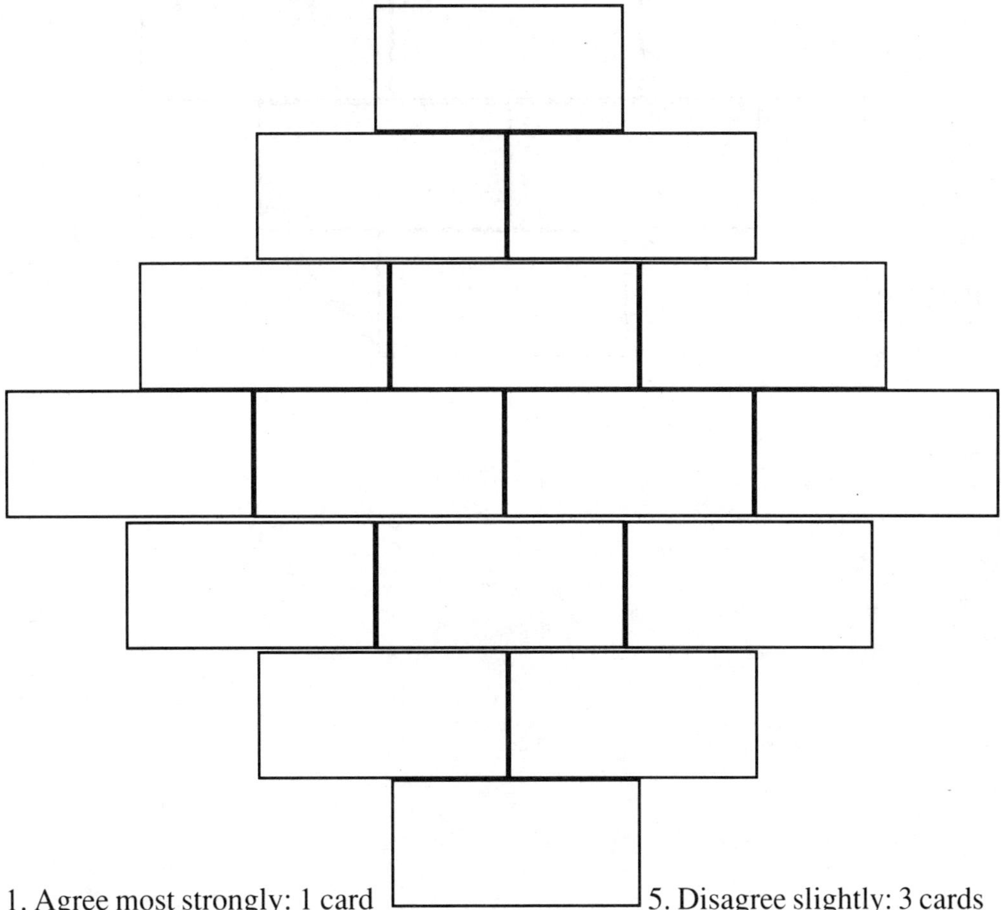

1. Agree most strongly: 1 card
2. Agree moderately: 2 cards
3. Agree slightly: 3 cards
4. Neither agree nor disagree: 4 cards
5. Disagree slightly: 3 cards
6. Disagree moderately: 2 cards
7. Disagree most strongly: 1 card

The cards are labelled **A** through to **P**. Please write the appropriate letters in the spaces provided on the diamond below. Please write only one letter in each box.

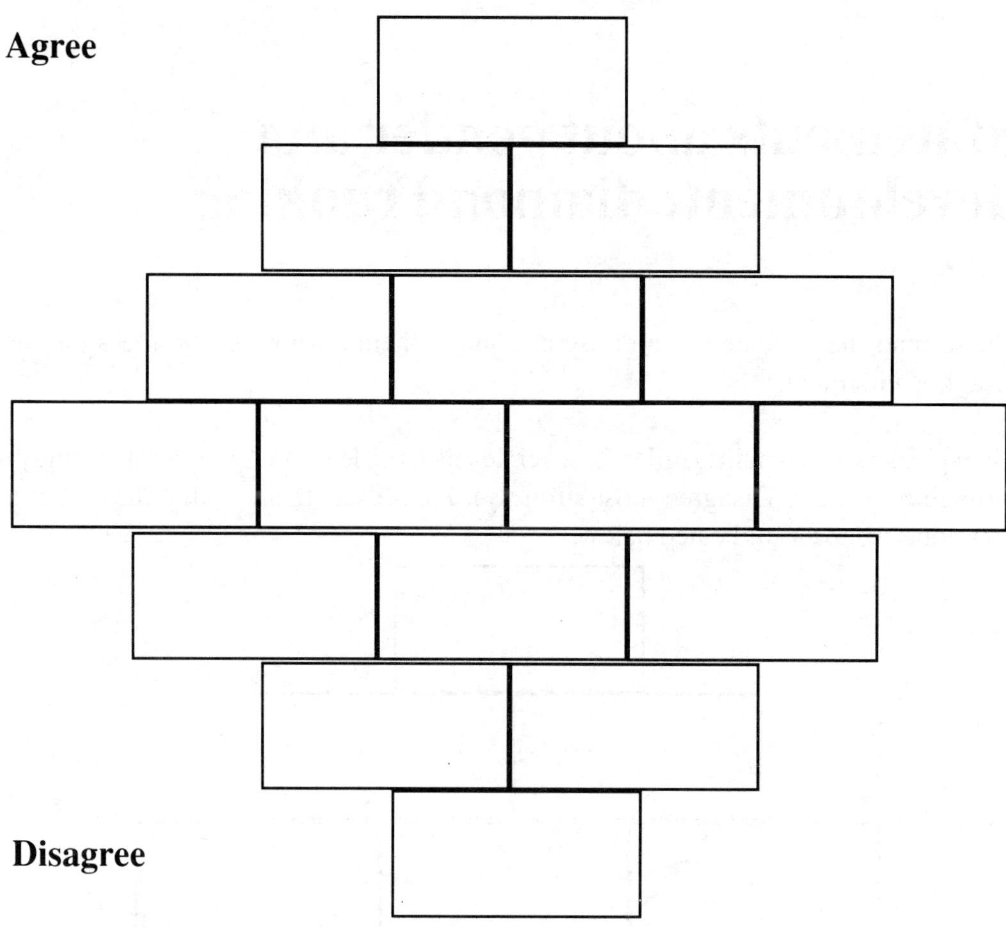

Time: 1 hr

Empowerment and participation

Objectives

1 To highlight the importance of women's empowerment and participation.

2 To analyse what is meant by these concepts

3 To provide a space for participants to share their experiences of empowerment and disempowerment, and to link their personal experience with their development role.

Method

1 Read out the excerpt from the EC-NGDO General Assembly 'Gender and Development' (see *Facilitator's Notes*). Point out that the linked issues of women's participation and empowerment are crucial for development. Make reference to **Activity 42**. This activity looks at what we mean by the concepts of empowerment and participation and how they can be put into practice. Look at the Introduction to this section and draw out relevant points.

(5 mins)

2 Ask individuals to reflect on two incidents in their lives: one where they themselves felt disempowered or were prevented from participating; and another where they felt empowered and able to participate.

(5-10 mins)

3 Divide people into small groups by asking who likes talking/writing/singing/creating (one group for each, but the groups should be of roughly equal size). In the small groups, participants share their two experiences, note common elements, and work out a way of presenting these to the large group, in different ways. Talking group — role play; writing group — written definition of concepts; singing group — song or rap; creating group — group sculpture. (See **Activity 92** for details of method of group sculpture.)

(30-35 mins)

4 Ask each group to present their representation of disempowerment/lack of participation and empowerment/participation to the whole group. (The timing of this will depend upon how many groups you have.)

(10-20 mins)

5 Facilitate full group discussion on the following points:
a. What are the common aspects of empowerment and participation brought out by the different presentations? List these on a flipchart.
b. What are the differences and why?
c. Is it easier to be clearer about disempowerment and lack of participation, than empowerment and participation?
d. What do we mean by power? Is it oppressive to be powerful? Look at the different types of power, using **Handout 33**.
e. Do participants feel that there is a real clarity and understanding about participation and empowerment in their organisation, or are they just sometimes used as 'fashionable buzz words'?
f. Can external agents empower and disempower people?
g. Bring out other points from the Introduction to this Section.

6 Give out **Handout 33** at the end.

Materials

Flipchart, marker pens
Handout 33

Facilitator's Notes

1 Note to read out:

The EC-NDGO General Assembly in Brussels in 1989 made a number of recommendations under the headings of: Women and food matters, debt, emergency situations, population and images. The report of this Assembly (Gender and Development) states that:

'Despite the diversity of areas covered, it can be seen that two key words recurred throughout the General Assembly discussions: empowerment and participation. In all the policy recommendations, therefore, featured the common underlying message: the need to empower women and ensure their equal participation at both project and policy levels.'

2 When we did this activity, we asked for a group who liked 'talking' rather than 'role-play' in view of the notorious reluctance of this cultural group (mostly British-based NGO staff) to get involved in role-play.

3 It proved to be easier for people to come to agreement about what represented disempowerment and lack of participation, than empowerment and participation in the positive sense.

4 There are different meanings of power and empowerment e.g. the difference between 'power over', 'power to do something', 'power within'. *(See **Handout 33**)*

4 This can be a creative, enjoyable session. However, it can also be emotional and difficult depending to some extent on the pre-existing relationships (e.g. manager-staff) of participants. In such cases people in authority roles should not be in the same small groups as those they manage.

Handout 33 *Activity 43*

Power and empowerment

Behind most attempts to increase women's power has been the notion that power is a limited quantity: if you have more, I have less. If I have power over you, increasing your power comes at the expense of mine. This power is an either/or relationship of domination/subordination or **power-over**. It is ultimately based on socially sanctioned threats of violence and intimidation, invites active and passive resistance, and requires constant vigilance to maintain.

There are alternatives. We can conceive of power as **power-to**, power which is creative and enabling, the essence of the individual aspect of empowerment. Most people describe situations where they felt powerful as those in which they solved a problem, understood how something works or learned a skill.

Collectively, people feel empowered through being organised and united by a common purpose or common understanding. **Power-with** involves a sense of the whole being greater than the sum of the individuals, especially when a group tackles problems together.

Yet another kind of power is **power-within**, the spiritual strength and uniqueness that resides in each of us and makes us truly human. Its basis is self-acceptance and self-respect which extend, in turn, to respect for and acceptance of others as equals. In traditional cultures, shamans, healers and wise elders were felt to have this type of power, and were often called on for advice. Use of the talking stick in North American native councils reflects appreciation of the power-within every speaker.

Power-over requires the creation of simple dualities: good/evil, man/woman, rich/poor, black/white, us/them. There *are* differences and different groups do have very different interests. But power-within recognises the strengths and weaknesses that exist in all of us and does not automatically condemn difference, or categorise in either/or terms. Power-within stresses self-acceptance and self-respect, complementarity rather than duality, recognition of aspects of the other in ourselves.

In a gender context, women and men are socialised differently and often function in different spheres of the community, although there is overlap and interdependence. As a result, women and men have different life experience, knowledge, perspectives and priorities. **One cannot necessarily represent the interests of the other, and neither alone can fully represent their community.** A healthy society will appreciate and value the positive aspects of these differences, and use them for its betterment.

Strategically, **we need to transform our understanding of power and resist power-over creatively.** Gandhi's non-violent resistance is an outstanding example. **We need to explore the concepts of power-to, power-with, and power-within** and their inter-relationship. In our development work, this means building problem-solving and conflict-resolution skills; strengthening organisations; and building individual and collective skills and solidarity. **We need to be aware when our actions may increase divisions and conflict and be sure that those who will bear the consequences understand and accept the risk.**

(Source: *Two Halves Make a Whole: Balancing Gender Relations in Development*, CCIC, MATCH and AQOCI.)

Time: 1–1½ hrs

Visions of empowerment

Objectives

1 To locate the introduction of gender training in a specific organisational context.
2 To highlight the continuity between internal organisational processes and field practices regarding gender.

Method

1 Tell participants that they are going to draw a picture which shows what activites they would see and what people would be doing in the communities where they work, as a result of their work in ten years' time. Give them five minutes to think about this on their own. let them refer to the organisational mission statement if there is one.

(5 mins)

2 Divide them into small groups of colleagues (as homogeneous as possible in terms of job, status, area, sex, race, etc.). Each group produces a group drawing.

(20 mins)

3 Check that each group is drawing indicators of empowerment. If not, ask them to include in that drawing, or a new one, indicators of what people would be doing if they were empowered.

(20 mins)

4 Put up all the drawings, and have a 'gallery walk' with each group explaining any part of the drawing that is not clear.

(10 mins)

5 Draw out what is common and what is different. One option is to ask the group to make one single collage representing the joint vision. List the relevant indicators of empowerment and refer to them during the rest of the workshop.

(30 mins)

Materials

Felt-tip pens, flipchart
Organisations's mission statement, if applicable.

Facilitator's Notes

1This activity and notes are adapted from a paper by Michelle Friedman. She used the activities in South Africa with groups used to thinking about empowerment in terms of race but less so in terms of gender. It could also be useful with other groups for whom resistance, liberation, and empowerment on the basis of class is their starting point. In workshops where there was resistance from men and time constraints, it has been a useful way of showing links between gender issues and their ongoing work.

2It has been used with participants from a single organisation, but with a mixture of races, sexes, job, and status. It has been the first exercise in a one-day workshop after introductions and objectives; but could equally be used later to explore empowerment further.

3The activity gives the facilitator information about the group. It also highlights differences between the participants' views of empowerment, based on their own experiences and perspectives from within the organisation.

4Once they have overcome their initial terror at the thought of drawing, this activity helps people relax into the workshop. Drawing usually acts as an equaliser and removes some power from the most literate and articulate.

5This activity can be used to help people to identify their own indicators of empowerment. These can be referred back to in the course of the workshop. These indicators tend to fall into four categories:

- *general material improvements*
- *political changes*
- *changed relationships between women and men*
- *changes within participants; organisations.*

Time: 1 hr

Finding the balance

Objectives

1 To share experience of women and men's roles in various kinds of work and decision-making.

2 To identify obstacles women face to full participation in decision-making, particularly in development programmes.

3 To think about strategies for creating an equal gender balance in decision-making and workloads.

Method

Part 1

1 Distribute **Handout 34** to all participants. Those who work in the same area can work together in a group.

2 Explain that the participants should reflect on the roles women and men play in a developing country with which they are familiar, and consider particularly gender differences in workloads and participation in decision-making.

3 Ask participants to fill in the grid with reference to the country or area they know, using a diagram of a balance to indicate whether the degree of involvement is weighted in favour of women, or men, or equally balanced (see diagram over the page).

(15 mins)

This indicates women are
more heavily involved:

W M

This indicates men are
more heavily involved:

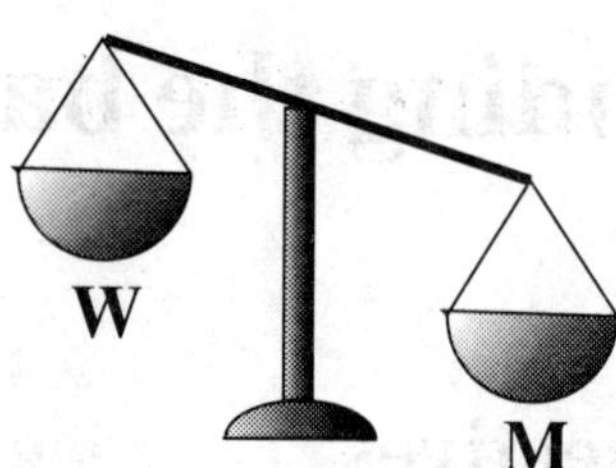

This indicates a balance
in involvement:

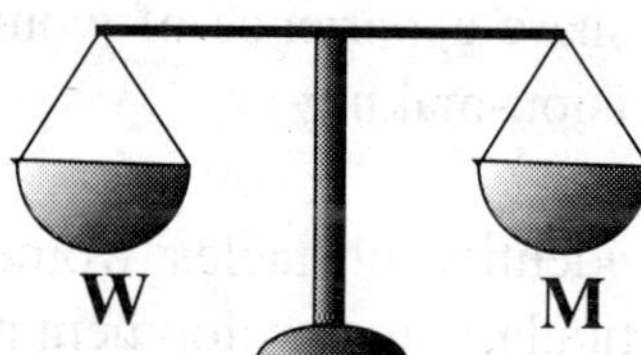

Part 2

1 Ask the participants to consider the list of possible obstructions women may face to their full participation in community decisions and development programmes. **(Handout 35).**

2 Ask them to rank these factors in order of priority according to the situation and social group with which they work. *(15 mins)*

3 In the whole group, ask participants to reflect on the issues raised in the ranking activity. Make notes on the flipchart of common points which emerge.

4 Bearing in mind the obstructions identified, ask participants to refer back to the categories highlighted in the 'balance' grid. Ask the questions:
a. Are there any ways in which an equal balance can be created between workloads and participation in decision making, for women and men; what changes will have to take place?
b. Are these changes feasible in the social group you have been considering, and work with? *(30 mins)*

Materials

Handouts 34 and 35
Flipchart, paper and pens

Handout 34 *Activity 45*

Areas of involvement	**Comment**	**Women and men balance**
Decision making:		
a.. finance in the home		
b education of children		
c. family planning		
Contributions to:		
a. health of children		
b. feeding of family		
c. production of food for family consumption		
d. production of food for cash payment		
Community Discussions		
a. agriculture		
b. water/sanitation		
c. school/education		
d. neighbourhood construction		
Nationally		
a. political representation		
b. political involvement		
Employement outside the home :		
a. industry		
b. business		
c. medical/nursing		
d. law		
e. service industries		

Handout 35 *Activity 45*

Ranking exercise: the factors obstructing women's involvement in community affairs and development work

Lack of formal education

Limited involvement in community action/discussions

Poverty

Malnourishment

Heavy domestic workload

Mobility requires permission from males in the household

Religious practice/beliefs

Inequality in national laws

Previous negative experience of development projects

Difficulty in recruiting female field workers

Child-rearing responsibilities

Government austerity programmes resulting in less time and finance

Time: 45mins-1 hr

Development and relief: common elements

Objectives

1 To explore participants' perceptions of the differences and similarities in development and emergency relief interventions.

2 To start thinking about gender and emergencies and to enable people to see the relevance of gender issues to emergency work as well as to development work.

Method

1 Ask the group to brainstorm for five or ten minutes on the differences between development interventions and emergency relief interventions. Write key points to emerge on flipchart, in two columns *.(5-10 mins)*

2 Divide the participants into groups of four or five people, and ask them to discuss the common elements in development and relief work and make a list of them. They should keep in mind the work already done in the workshop on roles, needs and policy approaches in Section C.5. *(15 mins)*

3 Bring the group together again and ask each sub-group to report back. Make a note of the main points on flipchart. *(20 mins)*

4 Lead a short discussion on the common elements in development and relief work and the integration of gender into both kinds of intervention. At the end of the session, distribute **Handout 36**. *(10 mins)*

Materials

Flipchart, paper, pens, **Handout 36**.

Facilitator's Notes

1 This is an introductory activity for development workers who may not be familiar with emergency relief work and for relief workers who have little understanding of gender issues. It is important to include this activity at this point in the training if you plan to include the activities in the manual which use examples and case studies referring to emergencies. It is also important to follow it up with one of the activities about emergency work.

2 Staff working in emergencies are predominantly male, with technical rather than social expertise in their work. If this is the case in your group, the discussion may be sidetracked along only technical/logistic aspects of relief work; you may need to make sure that the social aspects of the work are fully brought out and understood.

3 You may find that participant see development and relief at opposite poles: if so, this assumption needs to be explored. Participants may also hold a view that development is the 'real' work and disaster relief a kind of necessary evil. Point out that people experiencing the situation make no such distinction. For example, people in a disaster-prone area may be unwilling to take risks in a development programme, such as the introduction of new crops, because they take disasters into account; or during a disaster, people take a long-term view, wanting to get their children back into school as soon as possible, for example.

Handout 36 *Activity 46*

Gender and emergencies: some key issues

1 Women and children form up to 85 per cent of the people displaced by conflict and disasters. As men leave to fight or seek work in times of famine, the number of women solely responsible for the household increases dramatically. 80-90 per cent of households or family groupings in refugee settlements are headed by women. As heads of households, facing the breakdown of kin, village or community support networks, the destruction of crops and food supplies, women assume sole responsibility for the survival of children, the elderly, the sick and the disabled.

2 Women are generally excluded from most formal decision-making processes within their village or urban community. When women refugees arrive at a camp or settlement, little is likely to be known about them or their lives, and they will probably not be consulted about methods of delivering aid by the implementing agency. Thus it is crucial to:

- consult women directly, and involve them in planning;
- consider women's roles in the distribution of food, water and fuel and build on these;
- obtain information about the gender division of labour: has it changed in the emergency?
- learn about women's organisational and leadership roles and build on these;
- look at ways in which meeting women's practical needs will also contribute to meeting their strategic needs;
- find out how women's productive role may change in the emergency;
- look for ways in which the changing status and role of women in the emergency may become a force for improving women's position;
- consider how space is used; how women's lack of access to public space because of cultural factors affects the need for private space;
- identify women's particular needs — such as protection from violence, rape and sexual harassment; documentation in their own right; assistance with childcare; needs related to menstruation and pregnancy.

3 Women also play a pivotal role in holding a social group together and helping it to recover. It is important not to undermine them by casting them only as victims:

women's strengths and capabilities — as well as men's — should be supported and built upon.

4 A gender perspective is essential in any emergency response. To ensure this, all emergencies personnel should be gender-aware and be given appropriate training; and women should be part of all assessment and relief teams, in equal numbers with men, to ensure direct access to the women for consultation. Men, however, must take equal responsibility for ensuring that gender issues are raised and built into planning.

C.7 Gender-sensitive appraisal and planning

This section is about the appraisal and analysis which is essential to gender-sensitive planning for development or relief interventions. It includes a number of analytical frameworks developed in different parts of the world by institutions and individual trainers, and a variety of checklists. All of these are tools for the initial appraisal of situations or projects as well as tools for assessment of gender needs at any stage of the project cycle. There are other frameworks and analytical tools which we have not included because we have not used them: but references to them (such as the Gender Analysis Matrix, GAM) will be found in the Resources Section at the end of the manual.

This section is divided into two parts:
Analytical frameworks
Case studies

Analytical frameworks

The 'package' of GAD analytical tools presented in this Manual will be completed with this section, which introduces a number of analytical frameworks which have been used in gender training in Oxfam-run workshops.

It is important to realise that you can only provide an *introduction* to an analytical framework in the course of a short gender-training workshop, illustrating its use through analysing case studies. Participants who learn these frameworks need to use and practise them in concrete situations before they will feel completely comfortable with them, and learn how to adapt them to their own needs. It is not advisable to try and teach too many frameworks in a training — select one or two that are most appropriate to your group, and concentrate on helping participants to learn them thoroughly.

This section completes the full **Moser Gender Planning Framework**, a cluster of inter-related methods which Oxfam has used extensively and whose components have already been introduced in **Sections C.5 and C.6.**

Summaries of some of the other frameworks, and their strengths and weaknesses, are presented below:

1 The Harvard analytical framework (see Handouts 38 -45)

The **Harvard Framework**, sometimes called the **GFA (Gender Framework Analysis)**, is designed to provide the basis for a gender profile of a social group. It is very adaptable and is composed of three basic elements:

- an **activity** profile, based upon the gender division of labour, which lists the tasks of women and men, allowing for disaggregation by age, ethnicity or class, as well as where and when the tasks are performed. Activities are grouped under three headings: productive activities, reproductive or household activities and social/political/religious activities;

- an **access and control profile**, which lists the resources needed to carry out these tasks, and the benefits derived from them. The resources may be material or economic, political or social, and include time; access to these resources and benefits, and control over them is disaggregated by gender.

- the **influencing factors** which affect the division of labour and the access and control profile of the community.

In a version developed by the United Nations High Commissioner for Refugees (UNHCR), known as the **Framework for People-Oriented Planning in Refugee Situations**, the profile is completed twice, the first relating to the situation of the refugees before the flight, the second to their actual situation. The second profile indicates not only what the refugee group does and does not have, but also who has lost what and who has gained what. The comparison underlines the fact that a refugee or displaced group is unlikely to be totally destitute: people bring with them skills, knowledge, attitudes, values and means of organising themselves, even if they have lost all their material resources. Refugees and displaced people can be active participants in the solution of their own problems. This framework brings out a crucially important issue for women — **protection —** often jeopardised during a crisis.

Particularly useful elements of these frameworks are:

- the differential access to and control over resources and benefits in relation to women's and men's responsibilities, and the distinction between access to resources and benefits, and control over them.

- a broad view of what resources means, not just material resources but also less tangible things like skills and social organisation, and — most importantly for women — time.

- the idea that individuals and groups lose resources over time but also retain some and gain others. This aspect is particularly important for long-term development work with strategic aims, and also in relation to emergency relief work. For while sudden disaster may rob women and men of some resources, others may arise and provide sources of strength: these are opportunities for relief work to focus on people as actors in, rather than victims of, their situation.

The weakness of the Harvard Framework is that while it works well when used by people who have detailed knowledge of the social group in question, it is difficult to use without access to accurate detail. It is also difficult to use across a region where people's social and economic circumstances differ widely.

2 Capacities and Vulnerabilities Analysis (CVA)

The CVA framework was developed as a tool for predicting and/or assessing the extent to which relief and development projectssupport or undermine development. The central question it poses is 'how can agencies plan and implement interventions which meet the immediate needs of people affected by a disaster and also promote long-term development?'

The CVA framework enables agencies to map the **vulnerabilities** of women, men and children in an emergency, and their **capacities** to deal with their situation. It is based on a matrix which sets out the different categories of factors which affect people's lives, and the relationship between the factors. The categories are:

- the physical and material category: resources which people need to gain their livelihoods, such as land, climate, health, skills, technologies;

- the social and organisational category: social networks, political organisations, systems of distributing goods and services, social resources such as education;

- the psychological or attitudinal category: the complex of beliefs, attitudes, aspirations or dependencies which influence how people react to situations.

The CVA matrix allows all these categories to be differentiated by gender, race, class, ethnicity and any other social factor, and can also be used for analysis over time.

Its greatest value is that it brings into focus people's strengths in times of crisis, so that they are not considered as just victims of the situation. This is particularly important to women, who not only constitute the majority of refugees and displaced people, but whose strengths are so often overlooked.

(This framework is presented in **Section C.8 Global Issues**, for use in relation to conflict.)

3 The Longwe hierarchy of needs

This framework may be applied to any situation as a guide to where to focus future activities. It looks at equity between men and women in relation to certain key development indicators. They are:

- Control over resources
- Participation in decision-making
- Conscientisation
- Access to resources
- Well-being

These are arranged in a hierarchy. The framework assumes that the objectives of women's development are ordered according to this hierarchy, so that equality of control of resources is not truly possible unless equality in the other four spheres has been achieved.

The Longwe grid thus presents a progression. It permits an assessment of the existing advantages in women's situation and what remains to be done.

Its disadvantage is that it can be rigid, not allowing for the way situations change over time. Some of its basic assumptions (for example that the different stages have to be worked through in order) have been questioned.

4 Participatory Rural Appraisal (PRA)

A number of appraisal methods have developed since the late 1970s to overcome some of the problems inherent in formal data-collection methods — such as slow, cumbersome and often inaccurate questionnaire-based survey methods, and the seasonal, geographical and social biases which resulted from the way development personnel conducted their field investigations.

Rapid Rural Appraisal (RRA) was the first. It gave rise to Participatory Rural Appraisal (PRA) and a number of other variations, such as Participatory Action Research (PAR), Participatory Learning Methods (PALM) and Participatory Assessment, Monitoring and Evaluation (PAME). This Manual does not attempt to teach any of these methods — they are complex and require specialised training.

However, the emphasis on participation in all of the practical methods of information-gathering means that gender sensitivity should be central to all of them. Indeed, if women are in any way excluded or marginalised in PRA or PALM processes they cannot be said to be participatory, and cannot fulfil their own objectives. What this Manual offers are some guidelines to ensure that if participants are using PRA/RRA or other field-based information-gathering techniques, they integrate gender into the process.

The Munro method (**Activity 49**) includes some PRA tools, and the PRA 'Timeline' method is used in **Section C.8 Activity 63**. **Activities 52** Mapping for mars and **53** Bangladesh maps are examples of mapping activities often used in PRA. There are now a number of resources on PRA and gender available: these are listed in the Resources section of the Manual.

Case studies

We present with this section a number of case studies, which have guide questions, and can also be adapted for training use with the analytical framework and appraisal tools. You can of course provide or design your own case studies. **Activity 56** offers a general method for using case studies, with some notes on adapting case studies to bring out particular gender issues. We also include with this Activity, some guideline for writing case studies (**Handout 59**).

Please read all the handouts in this section before embarking on the activities.

C.7 Activities

1 Analytical frameworks

2 Case studies

Time: 2 hrs

Moser method

Objectives

1 To relate the concepts learnt about gender roles, needs and policy approaches to real examples from the day-to-day work of development agencies.

2 To introduce the Moser method of analysis that can be used by development and relief workers to help to assess projects and programmes.

Method

1 **Preparation:** Well before the training, ask participants to provide two project application forms used in their programmes, one filled out for a women's project and the other for a project not specifically for women. Ask the participants not to include model projects, but the most recent projects approved in each category.

Before the training begins, the facilitation team has to meet and analyse all these projects using the gender planning summary tables (see **Handout 27**). Choose five projects for the training. The selection criteria are:

- Simplicity: at least the first two should be simple and clear in their objectives.
- Variety: a range of areas or countries and types of project.
- Gender mix: there should be women-only, mixed projects, men-only.
- Range of needs, roles, and policy approaches.
- Agreement amongst the facilitators on the analysis of the projects.

(this preparation may take 1 day)

2 If possible, give a copy of the five project write-ups to each participant to read the day before the activity.

3 Divide the participants into three to five small groups, representing a mixture of country teams or work experience in each group.

Give out handouts (project application forms and gender planning summary tables. Ask the groups to complete the table as outlined in **Handout 28**. All groups should finish four case studies. Those who finish early should go on to the fifth case study.

Prepare flipchart for answers. Go round the groups, sitting-in on discussion and assisting. *(1 hour)*

4 Lead discussion in the large group and write the correct answers on flipchart. Make sure each person understands why a project is classified in a certain way, and is prepared to change their classification in the light of new facts or arguments. (This includes the trainers if new information has come to light in the discussion.) *(30 mins)*

Materials

Five Project Application Forms
Handout 37
Flipchart, pens

Facilitator's Notes

1 This activity is the final step of learning the Moser method. ***Activites 36, 37****, and* ***42*** *on gender roles and needs and policy approaches must be done first.*

2 It is very important that there is no value judgement implied in relation to projects. At this point participants are there to learn a method, not to judge, or be defensive about the project or the way the project document is completed.

3 If any participant is closely involved with the project they may either be defensive or add information that changes the classification. This is particularly likely to happen if the project is analysed as being 'welfare', when the person involved hoped it was 'empowerment'. This may lead to discussion about whether and how projects can actually lead to empowerment, and how we can judge this. It may also show up shortcomings in the way project documents are completed, and lead to calls for their redesign to incorporate specific references to these concepts.

4 Some people working for NGOs feel uncomfortable applying the policy classifications to their projects, because NGOs may not have a unified policy approach, or the policy may not refer to gender, or they may not apply gender policy to all projects. Nevertheless, people do find this a useful activity and it is important to show that all projects have a gender implication whether explicit or implicit.

Handout 37 *Activity 47*

Gender planning summary table

Project Title/Number	Roles on which focussed?			Gender needs met		Policy Approach	Further information/ comments
	Reproductive	Productive	Community	Practical	Strategic		

Source: Caroline Moser

Time: 2-2½ hours

The Harvard framework

Objectives

1 To introduce the participants to the Harvard method of analysis.

Method

1 Introduce the main features of this form of analysis using prepared OHP transparencies or prepared flipcharts. (See Handouts)

(20 mins)

2 Distribute a copy of the case study in **Handout 38** to each participant and ask them to go through it thoroughly, referring to the **Handouts 39, 40and 41**

(30 mins)

3 Divide the participants into groups of three to five, who discuss the case, making notes for discussion in the whole group.

(30 mins)

4 Reconvene the whole group and jointly analyse the case study with the participants, filling in the charts on prepared flipcharts.

(30 mins)

5 If you are doing the UNHCR version of this framework prepare two versions of each chart on **Handouts 43 and 44** for pre- and post-flight situations. Use **Handout 46** as a case study and **Handouts 42 and 45** as a guideline to the method.

Materials

Flipchart, paper, pens, transparencies
Handouts 39, 40 and 41(for Harvard Framework)
Handouts 42, 43, 44, 45, and 46 (for UNHCR version)

Facilitator's Notes

*1 The tables for the original version of the Harvard framework are provided in **Handouts 39, 40** and **41.**They are useful in that they contain the crucial categories of time spent on different kinds of work, and where the work is done. This is most important for women who spend much of their time on work in the home as well as on the land or in markets, factories or in the village or urban community. It is useful to consider the Activities Profile in conjunction with the triple role concept.*

2 Disaggregation by ethnic identity, economic status, caste and race can add further dimensions to this framework, and it can be adapted to any level.

3 The framework is best suited for individual projects, or easily-delineated areas, where it would be possible to gather information and data in all the categories. In all cases, it is crucial to stress that information should be gathered directly from the women themselves. The category of Influencing Factors requires a broader analysis of socio-economic, political and cultural factors than may be readily available, but participants should nevertheless be encouraged to put down all they know that is relevant in this category.

*4. The People-oriented Framework (**Handouts 42, 43, 44 and 45**) developed for the UNHCR for use in the planning of refugee programmes, is based on the Harvard Framework. It can thus be introduced to participants using the same activity as for the Harvard Framework, using a case study of a refugee project (**Handout 46**). Participants need to fill out a 'before and after' analysis for each of the charts for this framework, so you need to ensure that your case study has information about the lives of the refugees before the crisis as well as in their current situation.*

*5 If the participants are to prepare the case study, they should have clear guidelines from facilitators about the level of information needs. You could also use one of the long case studies from the original book, **Gender Roles in Development Projects: A Case Book**, edited by Overholt, Anderson, Cloud and Austin.*

*6 The checklist of questions linked to this framework is found with **Activity 54 Checklists**.*

Handout 38 *Activity 48*

Programme planning and implementation in community forestry

Background: Forestry in Indonesia

Conventional forestry projects (concerned with planting and maintaining or cutting forests) usually have two objectives: wood production for commercial use or tree growth for environmental protection. Commercial forestry in Indonesia involves the logging of timber, processing into saw logs, plywood and veneers for export, also for fuel wood, building material, and non-timber forest products for trading and domestic use. Intensive silviculture is done only in the teak forests of Java. Forests maintained for environmental objectives prevent soil erosion, and control run-off and water supplies. Conventional forestry projects are the major activity of the Indonesian Ministry of Forestry, and are also undertaken through the State forestry management company.

'Forests for People', an Indonesian programme developed by the Ministry, has recognised that, especially in adjacent areas, forests should benefit the community as well as State and corporate interests. A different set of objectives, activities and management style from traditional forestry projects has evolved.

Community forestry may involve activities similar to those in conventional forestry, but most community forests are for consumption by rural people. Community forestry objectives may include production of fuel wood, animal fodder, poles and timber for building, food products (leaves, nuts, fruits, herbs) as well as environmental protection. As rural development activities, these projects may also aim to increase rural employment, raise the standard of living of the rural poor (through increasing forest output and income), and involve the rural community in local self-help activities. Institutional inputs may include extension, training, guidance, technical help, the provision of materials/tools, and training.

In Indonesia, the community forestry approach has had good results. Since 1964, Gadjah Mada University has been involved in reforestation based on a participatory approach to communal development. In West Java, participatory action research has been used to involve the rural population in dealing with problems of soil erosion, increasing resource management, and improving the livelihood of rural people. WALH, a federation of 15 Indonesian environmental organisations, worked with government and NGOs to promote tropical forest conservation, soil protection, and community forestry.

The pilot project area

In February 1983, the village of Biyasan (not its real name) was given approval for a community forestry project, one of several villages in three neighbouring *kecamatans* targeted by government for community forestry programmes. The village, located in an upland area of East Kalimantan near the headwaters of a major river, is made up of seven hamlets, scattered within walking distance. It covers 1200 hectares of hilly terrain.

In 1983, Biyasan had a population of 3843, 1680 males and 2163 females, withan average of 5.9 people per household. Over the previous 15 years, the area had seen considerable population growth and then a decline. Population growth, at 1.6 per cent per year, was low due to migration. Most villagers (600 households) had been in the area for generations. Twelve years ago farmers from elsewhere (50 households) were resettled in Biyasan and given small (0.5 ha) plots of land.

Though the soil was stony and shallow in places, there was good seasonal rainfall, and farmers harvested one crop of sawah rice each year. They also grew dryland crops. 38 per cent of the land was in agricultural production, 12 per cent home gardens, 7 per cent private woodlots, 15 per cent fallow and 33 per cent unproductive due to the river, the slope of the land, previous clearcutting, and poor soil. The main crops in the area included rice, and *palawija* (cassava, corn and peanuts). Tree crops included cashews and coffee, and were primarily cash crops, as were peanuts.

Women and men both owned and inherited land. Men owned 68 per cent of all productive land, women the remaining 32 per cent — a result of traditional inheritance patterns. The average size of landholding per household was 0.7 hectares, when 6 per cent holding more than 3.5 hectares. Twenty per cent of households were headed by women, and in another 10 per cent of households, the men had migrated in search of waged employment.

Wealthy farmers might employ wage labour at harvest time, as well as using family labour. Many of them obtained credit for fertilisers and some had access to machinery for weeding and hulling. They were also converting fallow fields to cloves, chocolate and coffee tree crops. Because of poor soil quality, steep slopes and soil erosion, wealthy farmers' fields expanded further and further from the village.

The poorer farmers had significantly poorer yields in recent years, and had not been able to benefit from commercial inputs. Few farmers, however, were landless sharecroppers. Seasonal agricultural labour was primarily unpaid family labour, and *tolog menolong*. For poor farmers, returns on family land were not usually enough to provide for a household, and other income had to be earned.

In nearby timber estates, trees were, and continue to be, cut and sawlogs shipped to urban areas. Depletion of the nearby forest because of widespread clearcutting resulted in problems. A number of necessary ingredients for natural medicine were becoming scarce. It was harder to find choice trees for wood forest products. Reforestation had provided employment for a number of men and women over the last 10 years, but at the time of the case study, these jobs had decreased because of concession holders' low priority on reforestation. Women's earnings traditionally came from making rattan products and other non-wood forest goods and trading in the market. During reforestation efforts, women were the main wage labourers in tree nurseries.

Wage labour accounted for 30 per cent of male income, (down 10 per cent in five years), and 17 per cent of female income (down 15 per cent in five years). The drop reflects a decline in local forestry employment, increased mechanisation by wealthy farmers, and land-use changes by large landholders — from increasingly unprofitable agriculture to private woodlots — which decreased the need for hired labour.

Farmers had not concerned themselves with planting and maintaining private woodlots, because there appeared to be abundant forests which could be cut, with or without licenses. Their concern was food production. But, clearcutting, the resulting soil and water losses, and a growing need for building material and fuel wood, made private woodlots desirable for those who could afford it. At the time of the case study, no income had been generated from private woodlots.

Activities

Local men who had not migrated for work were involved in agriculture, either on family land or as hired labour. Men carried out field preparation, terrace construction, and ploughing with oxen. They were also involved in animal care and feeding. Their daily work might also include some artisanal craft production, (making rattan furniture), and trading. From time to time, men raided the reforested area for building material, or additional space for home gardens. Families planted trees for fencing around their gardens, and for soil conservation; but more trees were needed for home construction and other building.

Women managed the households. They were involved in seasonal rice planting, transplanting, hoeing, weeding and harvesting, rice processing and storage, and work in their gardens. Many women worked as unpaid labourers alongside their husbands who were employed by the state forestry company. Some also worked seasonally for wages, picking and drying coffee and tobacco for wealthy farmers.

Year-round, women collected fuel wood and natural medicines, made non-wood forest products from rattan, and traded at the market. They collected wood from the piles made when fields were cleared (often with their children), or walked further into the hills. As clearing moved further away from home, women walked greater distances for fuel wood. Sometimes they collected it from the reforestation area closer to home. As they returned home, they also collected leaves and fruit along the way. Women were active in traditional wedding and funeral activities, and found alternatives to institutional credit by raising money through participation in the local *arisan*.

Girls were involved in household work from an early age. At seven, they helped feed animals, carry water, gather fuel wood. By the age of ten, girls were helping to plant and harvest rice. Boys were active in feeding and caring for the animals, and helping with their fathers' work. There was a primary school in the village which both boys and girls attended, but, as they got older, girls were needed to help at home for longer hours than boys. Girls, especially those whose mothers worked as labourers or traded in the market, had to drop out of school.

Poverty in the area was a result of the complex relationship between high population density, poor quality soil, inequitable land tenure arrangements, and migration of men. The poorest people tended to be women and their families in single-headed households. Women traditionally did not benefit from credit and extension programmes for farmers as much as men. Women's incomes had declined and, because of a multitude of factors including lack of education, there were few employment opportunities for women.

The project: integrated community forestry

The pilot project in Biyasan was initiated by the Ministry of Forestry in conjunction with Walhi (environmental organizations). Village involvement was enlisted in the planning stages through a bottom-up planning process, and the LKMD.

The present objectives were to:

- improve the living standards of rural people, especially the poorest: through cash income or home consumption, encouraging increased village production of fuel wood, fodder, timber, and non-wood forest products;

- decrease consumption of fuel wood by testing, manufacturing and distributing improved stoves;

- promote rural self-reliance through active participation in forest resource management, including individual woodlots and communal forests;

- reduce environmental destruction, through including soil conservation, terracing, and protecting water resources; and

- improve women's role in rural development, and increase their productivity.

The objectives were to be accomplished through specific project strategies:

- Re-establish nurseries for seedling production and distribution; establish forests estates for communal use, as well as household woodlots and windbreaks.

- Develop and distribute improved stoves.

- Increase forestry extension services to improve tree planting and maintenance, encourage the use of the stoves, and promote better farming methods (including increased forage production within forest estates).

- Encourage more active participation of rural people in the project activities and their management.

- Enhance income-generating possibilities for rural women through the expansion of non-wood processing.

A number of objectives were not stated in the project outline but were understood. These were implicit assumptions.

- Men and women would contribute equally to project management.

- Both villagers' leadership skills and farmers' sense of responsibility and participation would be developed.

- Credit was not offered, but incentives would be offered at the discretion of the Village Head.

- The work efficiency of women in cooking would be increased and more time could be spent on making rattan mats and baskets.

- The market for non-wood products had potential for expansion.

- More intensive land use would be encouraged (more agroforestry).

- Farmers' incomes would improve, as would living standards from more productive land and less soil erosion.

- Little social change would occur in the village, except improved economic position for all.

The project involved a number of management levels. Watershed rehabilitation and reforestation of State-owned forests were part of the [State] Programme for the Preservation of Forest, Land and Water. Activity on farmers' land was considered 'regreening'.

The official responsible for the project was the District Head, assisted by Walhi for many of the activities, and a regreening specialist. The project manager was Head of the District Forest Service. Head of Implementation was the Subdistrict Forest Service staff person and implementers were the farmers' groups. The farmers formed groups of 20 to 40 people, each groupled by a key farmer and a Walhi community development officer. They served as project contact for the extension workers, and handled instructions, distribution of materials and incentives. Meetings were held regularly to discuss problems. Extension was done through demonstration plots.

Women were involved with local decision-making, through the PKK which was consulted for this project. It was an enthusiastic supporter, since the project fitted into its concern with village beautification and the home-garden movement. A PKK representative was assigned to each farmers' group.

Project activity

After the project was approved, stage one began and a survey was conducted.

- An inventory was done of male and female farmer holdings, noting home gardens, and agroforestry activity (pekarangan). Species and numbers of trees and plants were enumerated.

- Fuel wood needs and patterns of collection were surveyed.

- Data was collected on both men's and women's roles and needs in forestry development activity.

Stage two was more difficult. Initially it was hard to enlist farmer support for long-term tree planting. With little land, little time, and few resources — and because forests surrounded the village — poorer farmers did not see tree planting as a priority. The poorer women were too busy to be concerned with beautification, and had little contact with the PKK. Since the forest estate nearby had employed labourers, people felt that it was the state forest company's responsibility to do the work or at least pay for it. Incentives became important.

The project's nursery-based seedling production, previously wage labour done by women, became a job done by men because the incentive was donation of seedlings for private planting instead of wages. Women were too busy producing handicrafts and training to engage in non-remunerative work. The incentive was appropriate to enlist the involvement of men, the dominant landowners, not women. Those with more land could use fallow and marginal (non-productive) land for tree planting. Because tree maintenance involved low labour and low risk, the larger landowners were more easily convinced of the benefit of establishing woodlots.

Input into choice of seedlings to be grown and planted was open to all. With assistance from the extension workers, the final decision was made at the farmers' group level. Men were concerned about fodder for animals, building materials and fuel wood; women were interested in fuel wood and in varieties for non-wood processing. Fast-growing pine trees were not preferred for fuel nor for use in cottage industry, but were thought to be most useful for short-term environmental protection and faster economic returns for sale as building materials.

Since the government had further plans for resettlement, some people were uncertain about security of land tenure and whether trees planted as woodlots would remain theirs. It was unclear who would have the use of trees planted for erosion control along the river and in some steeper areas on the hillside.

Extension activity was aimed at both men and women, although there were few female forestry extension workers, and the timing of training did not consider whether men or women could attend. Providing female extensionists and timing to suit women became a priority, in order to enable more women to have training in the areas that affected their work in home garden, food production and non-wood processing. As gatherers of fuel wood, women's learning about forest maintenance was also seen as important, but a low priority because of their busy schedules. Their previous expertise in tree nursery skills was overlooked.

Incentives were assigned to heads of households for household participation in the forestry programme, equal to the value of the tools and materials. Wages for tree planting were borne by the farmers. Establishing nurseries, tree planting and forest maintenance were not waged work. Family members who had time to participate were generally older sons and the male head of household.

Skills training and information on the improved stoves and their construction was directed at the men, since it hadn't been specified in the project proposal who should be involved. The timing of the training also meant women would not be able to attend because of work in the rice cycle (post harvest processing).

(Source: *Two Halves make a Whole: Gender Relations in Development*, MATCH. This case study was especially prepared by MATCH for teaching the Harvard Analytical Framework.)

The Harvard analytical framework

This framework was developed in the 1980s in the Harvard Institute for International Relations to facilitate the integration of women into project analysis. It is outlined in *Gender Roles in Development projects: A Case Book*, edited by Catherine Overholt, Mary B. Anderson, Kathleen Cloud, and James E. Austin. It is a useful tool for gathering data, understanding women's and men's roles in a society, and taking account of external forces which affect development planning. It is a flexible instrument which can be used at many different levels of planning and analysis, and can be expanded to disaggregate data according to cultural, ethnic and economic factors as well as gender and age. The framework can also be used as a planning and implementation tool for programmes and projects.There are four inter-related components:

- **The Activity Profile**, which is based on the gender division of labour and delineates the economic activities of the population in the project area. It provides for disaggregation by sex, age, and other factors, and for recording the amount of time spent on activities, and the location of the activities. (See Table 1, **Handout 41**)

- **The Access and Control Profile**, which identifies the resource individuals can command to carry out their activities and the benefits they derive from them. By distinguishing between access to resources and benefits, and control over them it is possible to assess the relative power of members of a society or economy. (See Table 2, **Handout 42**)

- **Factors Influencing Activities, Access and Control**: factors (such as gender division of labour, cultural beliefs) which create different opportunities and constraints on women and men's participation in development. The impact of changes over time in the broader cultural and economic environment must be incorporated into this analysis.

- **Project Cycle Analysis** is the final component which consists of examining a project proposal or area of intervention in the light of gender-disaggregated data and social change.

Note on the use of the tables: The Activity Profile charts productive activities, such as those related to agriculture or employment and then lists specific activities under the headings of each area.. There can be a large number of categories, depending on the nature of the situation. Under 2, Reproductive Activities are listed. These may be related to water, fuel, small livestock, child care etc

The influencing factors would include political, economic, cultural, legal, international factors..

Handout 40 *Activity 48*

Table 1 — Activity Profile

	Gender/Age[1]							
Socio-economic Activity	FA	MA	FC	MC	FE	ME	TIME	LOCUS[3]
1 *Production of Goods and Services*								
a Product/Services								
1. Functional Activity								
2. Functional Activity								
3. Functional Activity								
b Product/Services								
1. Functional Activity								
2. Functional Activity								
3. Functional Activity								
2 *Reproduction & Maintenance of Human Resources*								
a Product/Services								
1. Functional Activity								
2. Functional Activity								
3. Functional Activity								
b Product/Services								
1. Functional Activity								
2. Functional Activity								
3. Functional Activity								
4. Functional Activity								
5. Functional Activity								

Code:[1] FA = Female Adult MA = Male Adult FC = Female Child
MC = Male Child FE = Female Elder ME = Male Elder
Code Percentage of time allocated to each activity; seasonal; daily
Code:[3] Within home; family, field or shop; local community; beyond community
(Source: *Gender Roles in Development Projects: A Case Book* edited by Overholt, Anderson, Cloud and Austin.)

Handout 41 — Activity 48

Table 2 — Access and Control Profile

Resources	*Access (M/F)*	*Control (M/F)*
Land		
Equipment		
Labour		
Production		
Reproduction		
Capital		
Education/Training		

Benefits	*Access (M/F)*	*Control (M/F)*
Outside Income		
Assets Ownership		
In-kind goods (Food, clothing, shelter, etc)		
Education		
Political Power/Prestige		
Other		

(Source: *Gender Roles in Development Projects: A Case Book* edited by Overholt, Anderson, Cloud and Austin.)

The people-oriented analytical framework

The Framework for People-Oriented Planning in Refugee Situations was devised by Mary B Anderson and the UNHCR Senior Coordinator for Refugee Women following the adoption by the UNHCR of a Policy on Refugee Women which called for the improvement of participation and access to resources of refugee women in all programmes. It is based on the Harvard Analytical Framework and is intended as a practical planning tool for refugee workers.

There are two key elements (common to all human experience, and centrally important to women), that are particularly acute in refugee populations: change and protection. When people flee from disaster or conflict, their lives change rapidly and dramatically. Even in long-term refugee settlements where women's and men's roles may stabilise, they will be different from those pre-flight, and may be regarded as temporary by refugees themselves. Protection is both a legal and social concern, and refugees lose their national status and the social networks which may have offered them some protection. These issues will be very different for women and for men, and this framework should help to identify these differences.

The Framework has three components:

- **The Activities Analysis**: because the existing gender division of labour and roles is disrupted by flight, it is essential to find out what women's and men's roles were before flight, and how they have changed for women and men as refugees. Protection, legal, social and personal is a crucial activity to be highlighted, particularly for women and girls. (See Table 1, **Handout 35**).

- **The Use and Control of Resources Analysis**: this provides for gathering data on resource used and controlled by women and men before flight, and which they control as refugees. Women and men may have lost control permanently over resources in their place of origin and be unable to regain it. The new situation will affect gender relations and may introduce opportunities for positive change for women. (See Table 2, **Handout 36**).

- **The Determinants Analysis**: these are the factors both within the refugee groups and in the receiving country which determine or influence the roles and responsibilities of women and men and change their use and control of resources. They include economic and demographic factors, institutional structures, socio-cultural factors in the refugee group and the host country/population, legal factors and international political events and trends. This helps to identify the external opportunities and constraints which it is necessary to consider in planning.

(Adapted from: A Framework for People-Oriented Planning in Refugee Situations: A Practical Planning Tool for Refugee Workers, United Nations High Commission for Refugees, UNHCR)

Handout 43 *Activity 48*

Table 1 Activities analysis

(Complete for both the pre-refugee experience and the present situation)

Activities	Who	Where	When/ how long	Resources used
Protection				
Production of goods... e.g. carpentry metal work				
...and services e.g. teaching domestic labour				
Agriculture e.g. land clearance planting care of livestock				
Household production e.g. childcare home garden water collection				
Social/political/religious e.g. community meeting ceremonies				

Source: UNHCR

Table 2 Resource use and control

Lost		
Resource	*Who used*	*Who controlled (men/women)*
land		
livestock		
shelter		
tools		
ediucation system		
health care		
income		
Brought by refugees		
Resource	*Who has*	*Who uses (men/women)*
Skills		
e.g. political		
manufacturing		
carpentry		
sewing		
cleaning		
agricultural		
animal husbandry		
Knowledge		
e.g. literacy		
teaching		
medicine/health		
Provided to refugees		
Resource	*To whom*	*How (male heads of household (female heads of household)*
food		
shelter		
clothing		
education		
legal services		
health		

(Source: UNHCR)

Determinants analysis

A final stage in the analytical framework is to look at determinants. These are the factors both within the community and in the receiving country which determine or influence the roles and responsibilities — and the resource use — of women and men and which, therefore, can affect the outcome of your planned activities. They are broad and interrelated and include such factors as:

general economic conditions, such as poverty levels, inflation rates, income distribution, international terms of trade, infrastructure;

institutional structures, including the nature of government bureaucracies and arrangements for the generation and dissemination of knowledge, technology, and skills;

demographic factors;

community norms and social hierarchy, such as family/community power structure and religious beliefs. These can be particularly important among refugee groups where men's and women's roles are changing;

legal parameters;

training and education;

political events, both internal and external;

national attitude to refugees; and

attitude of refugees to development/assistance workers.

We do not provide a table for this analysis because the purpose of identifying these *determinants* is to consider which ones affect activities or resources and how they affect them. This helps you to identify external constraints and opportunities that you should consider in planning your programmes. It will help you to anticipate and predict the inputs of your programmes.

Women refugees in Bangladesh

In 1991-2 about 300,000 Rohingya refugees from Mayanmar (Burma) took shelter in south-east Bangladesh. Muslims from the Rakhaine state, numbering between one and two million, are distinct linguistically from the Buddhist Burman majority of Myanmar. The repression of Muslims is part of a consistent pattern of human rights violations against all political opposition and dissent, and against vulnerable and weak sectors of the country's population, such as ethnic minorities, who the military authorities suspect may not support its nationalist ideology. Muslims from the Rakhaine state fled in similar numbers (two hundred thousand plus) to Bangladesh in 1978 and were later repatriated after an agreement between the two countries was reached.

At first the government of Bangladesh showed remarkable hospitality and provided land and shelter to this large-scale influx. UNHCR was requested to assist in mid-February 1992.

Oxfam's involvement was at first to fund health services, then at the urging of UNHCR, Oxfam brought in water equipment and engineers in April 1992 to provide water for some of the camps. Later Oxfam took on another wide-ranging project in the sector of sanitation and environmental health services in two of the camps where it had helped instal water supplies. This is rounded out with a health education programme.

Repatriation agreement

An agreement signed by the Governments of Bangladesh and Myanmar in late April of 1992 to repatriate all refugees over six months provided no provision for UNHCR supervision or involvement in the repatriation process on either side of the border. After several attempts by the UN at different levels the government of Bangladesh allowed UNHCR's protection officers to verify the 'voluntary' repatriation through individual interviews and access to repatriation transit camps in Bangladesh. Refugees wish to remain in Bangladesh until they are sure of their future safety in Myanmar and UNHCR's active involvement on the other side of the border. The government of Bangladesh is encouraging refugees' departure by ordering all NGOs to terminate employment of refugees, restricting movement between camps, and closing down the small makeshift shops inside and around the camps. Refugees are increasingly being confined to their camps and actively discouraged from using local markets.

Myanmar signed a Memorandum with UNHCR in November 1993 allowing them to monitor repatriation in Rohingya areas in Myanmar. UNHCR is now working out the detailed tasks and activities to implement the memorandum. Both UNHCR and Government of Bangladesh are expecting January 1994 to see the start of the accelerated repatriation.

Forced to 'volunteer': Amina's story

'When they started pushing they pushed us first, now you start pushing and again we are the first,' said Amina, a widow in her early forties with five children under 12, when armed police'helped' her pack her belongings hurriedly on the way to a transit camp for 'voluntary repatriation' in September, 1992.

After the repatriation agreement between the two governments, the authorities instructed each 'camp-in-charge' to arrange for volunteers for repatriation. Each camp-in-charge had to fulfil a fixed quota by producing a weekly list of the refugees who were 'willing' to go back. The camp-in-charge have used a 'carrot and stick' policy to fulfil their quota. Most of the time they are so desperate that they start with less carrot and more stick and end up with no carrot and all stick. Widows with children are the easiest victims of this voluntary repatriation operation.

I met Amina first in January 1992 in Dhechuapalnog area among the first group of refugees. At that time only the workers of Gonoshastya Kendar, an NGO with a long history of medical work dating back to the Liberation War, was working with the refugees. Its workers had started a survey and needs assessment. I asked a worker to help me as an interpreter as I wanted to talk with some women who came without husbands, father or a male guardian.

Amina had had to cross the border with her children as the members of the Burmese paramilitary force 'Lone Htein' started raiding their villages to collect the able-bodied people as forced labour. 'Lone Htein' were not happy with only able-bodied men, they took the women as well in their camps for 'household' work. They targeted women-headed families as the easiest sources when they were looking for young girls to take advantage of. First they asked for money in lieu of male labour, then livestock, then poultry. If nothing was available, they would take a girl. This happened to Amina. At first they took her life-savings of 500 kyats, two goats, and gold earrings. The second time, when she had nothing to offer, they asked her to hand over her 12-year-old daughter just for two or three days. 'I refused and cried. Then they took me to their camp and they kept me there the whole night. Next day they released me but took me again the following day for another two nights.'

Amina took a decision and crossed the River Naf for a secure life in Bangladesh and to protect her children from the hands of 'Lone Htein'. Crossing the border was not a pleasant event. 'Lone Htein' confiscated her money (which she had borrowed from the village head man to meet the costs of the journey), her national registration cards, and her few possessions.

After eight months of refugee life in Bangladesh, moving from one shelter to another, Amina found herself again trapped by authorities against whom she was powerless. This time her 9-year-old son was caught red-handed by the Camp Guards breaking the law when he was trying to sell some pulses (which the refugees are given but don't like as food) to buy some vegetables and dried fish. (At that time dried fish was not in the food basket of UNHCR.) They confiscated the pulses and took him into custody. Hearing of the incident, Amina with their Mahjhi (head man), rushed to the camp office to plead for her son. The guards asked her to choose one of two options — either face the policecase as her son broke the law, in which case the authorities would send him to jail; or list her name in the voluntary repatriation list and get herself ready for repatriation within a week. 'Go back or face the trial': the solution was as simple as that. What could Amina do in such a situation? She was not ready to leave her only son in the hands of foreign police so she opted for repatriation. There are so many such Aminas still struggling in the camps.

The vulnerability of women refugees

Many of the women arrived with a history of rape, and came from divided families with lost husbands or children. They may have been unaccompanied, possibly pregnant or with VD, but they had little hope of being treated sympathetically by male doctors. They have found themselves in camps where the space for them to lead anything but the most restricted lives is unavailable, and where the level of curiosity at what they had been through made them the object of unwelcome attention from the media and local population.

It became very hard to find a safe place for women who suffered at the hands of the forces on the other side of the border; the same vulnerability followed them like a shadow, even in a friendly country. We have heard allegations of harassment of women by security forces at the water collection points, and regular sexual abuse of refugee women by the security forces has also been reported. It is not easy to address these problems in a situation when all the camp officials are men and they work entirely through the — mostly male — Mahjhis.

Recognising gender issues

There was no specific gender component in our initial water programme but gradually we started responding to the gender issues. It is difficult to work in a gender-blind situation, where every decision is taken and implemented by male officials living in the bachelors' dormitory far from their family, with no positive motivation to work with distressed people. As the only organisation whose staff live in the camp, we have some advantages over other organisations whose workers are only available during the day. Moreover, from the very beginning, we tried to stick to the principle of 'more female, less male' in the working team. Female engineers and health educators became our strength in pointing out and responding to women's concerns. Moving the tap-stands to a safer location, to avoid harassment of women by a section of the security forces, and changing the timing of supplying water to suit the routines of both the women and the men was the first attempt to change the gender-blind situation into a positive gender-sensitive approach.

Setting up women's health centres

Health Educators tried to make it possible for the women to benefit from the services and health education programme by arranging women's gatherings and group meetings. Later on this became difficult, when camp officials banned all group meetings and gatherings to prevent any anti-repatriation activity. Then the team took new initiatives to reach the women by setting upwomen's centres in the camp. In the first phase the women's centres, which were called 'health education centres' to make them more acceptable, were constructed by a mixture of voluntary and paid labour. Later on we supplied the materials and women managed the construction on their own. Gradually these centres became a refuge for the women, a place of talking, sharing of emotions and releasing of tensions. Health educators also benefited from these centres as a place of contact and discussion.

Refugee women proposed to use the centre for their children as children's health education centres (schools were not allowed), in the morning while the women were busy with cooking and other domestic activities. That gave birth to our 'child to child' programme.

Ultimately these centres became the learning place for the Health Educators as well. New ideas for garbage disposal, construction of women's bathing places using refugee voluntary labour, ways of using the refugee labour in desludging full latrines, watching the water sources, guarding and protecting the latrines and other communal areas, all came up from the discussions at the women's centres. The original idea behind these centres was just to make better contact with families, and hence the refugee community at large, through the women and children; but gradually they became more than that. Individuals who are attending the centres are also getting benefits personally. The benefits are often intangible — some comfort or ease, perhaps, from the informally organised activities in congenial company.

Attempts to close the health education centres

When the health education centres became the women's centres in a real sense, the male folk, both officials and refugees, felt threatened and started plotting a conspiracy against them. It has become a common practice of chief camp officials to issue verbal orders to our Health Educators and sometimes to our coordinator to close down the centres, claiming that they are the breeding ground of conspiracy against repatriation, and other anti-law-and-order activities. This has never been backed up with evidence, and we continue. A desperate and very organised attempt was made in the last 'Ramadan' (the Muslim holy fasting month), when a group of male Mahjhi sought permission to convert a centre into a mosque (where women's entrance is not encouraged). The women resisted from the very beginning when they heard about it. Giving up the attempt, the Mahjhis changed their strategy and sought permission for using the centres just for one month. Again, it was the women of the centres who uncovered the plot. They warned the Health Educators about the consequences of the proposal if we endorsed it. 'We will never be able to change the status of a mosque into a women's centre no matter what the agreement was.' This is how a mere sitting and chatting place of women become a source of power and learning for both parties.

Protecting the rights of women refugees

It is true that as refugee workers with the limited responsibility of supplying water and ensuring sanitation we have very little scope to play a substantial role to protect women like Amina or to allow them repatriation with dignity, but I don't think we should not try. If we can organise the refugees, especially the refugee women, through women volunteers and workers and achieve some confidence among them I think nothing is impossible.

It is also high time to detail the requirements to protect women's rights in refugee camp situations, on behalf of NGOs who are willing to be involved in future refugee programmes managed by UNHCR in a situation where local authorities have different attitudes and conceptions. Otherwise NGOs will remain the enlisted or pre-qualified subcontractors of UNHCR, with no choice. Nobody will be there to ensure UNHCR actually achieves its own intention of ensuring gender issues are addressed in a positive way in every programme.

(Source: Gawher Nayeem Wahra in *Focus on Gender*, 2:1, Oxfam.)

Time: 1 hr

Comparison of methods

Objective

1 To help participants to compare the salient features of two methods of analysis, e.g. Moser and Harvard methods, and their usefulness in the field.

Method

1 Divide the participants into small groups to discuss each method, based on the introduction to these methods in **Activities 47and 48** . Ask the group to prepare a chart listing the most important features of each method on a chart.

(15 mins)

2 Using their chart, ask the groups to discuss the usefulness of these methods in project analysis.

(25 mins)

3 Reconvene the whole group, and ask a spokesperson from each group to report back. Ask each group to report one salient feature until the list is complete.

(20 mins)

4 List main features on flipchart.

Materials

Flipchart, paper, pens

Facilitator's Notes

*1 This exercise can only be done after doing both the Moser method (**Activity 47** and the Harvard method (**Activity 48**).*

2 The facilitators should have studied the two methods and be able to add any key features that the group omits.

3 This activity is useful if you have studied more than one analytical framework — it helps participants to think about them in a comparative way, and identify relative strengths and weaknesses.

4 It can be used to compare any two analytical frameworks.

Time: 2 hrs

Longwe method

Objectives

1 To provide a method of analysis to assess projects and programmes.

2 To show the possible negative as well as positive effects of considering or failing to consider gender issues.

3 To provide greater understanding of what equality and empowerment mean in practice.

Method

1 **Preparation:** Before the training ask participants to provide two project application forms used in their programmes, one for a women's project, the other for a project not specifically for women. Ask participants not to include model projects, but the most recent projects approved in each category. If you are doing the Moser method, you can use the same documents.

Before the training begins, the facilitation team should read **Handout 47**, then meet and analyse the projects, using the Women's Development profile (**Handout 48**).Choose five projects for the training. (See **Activity 47** Moser method for criteria for selection).

2 If possible, give a copy of each of the project documents to the participants the day before the activity.

3 Present the Longwe method based on **Handout 47,** using OHP or flipchart where applicable. Distribute the handout. Invite questions and discussion.

4 Analyse the first project with the group. Choose one that has some negative, neutral, and positive elements.

5 Divide the group into four groups. Give each group four copies of the Gender Profile Chart, **Handout 48**. Ask the group to fill in one for each project.

6 In the large group, each small group presents their profile of one project. Write this on the prepared flipchart. Other people in the group can then add their comments. If you and other facilitators disagree with groups' analysis, explain why.

7 Lead a general discussion. Hand out one copy of the charts (**Handouts 48 and 49**) to all participants for future reference.

Materials

Handouts 47, 48 and 49
Prepared flipcharts, pens

Facilitator's Notes

1 Sara Hlupekile Longwe is a consultant on gender and development based in Lusaka, Zambia. She has introduced the 'Women's Empowerment Framework' as a basis of her own distinctive method of gender analysis of development projects. This method of analysis is based on the approach that gender awareness means an ability to recognise women's issues at every stage of the development cycle. It emphasises that development means overcoming women's inequality with men in every respect.

2 The method is particularly useful in explaining the role of empowerment as intrinsic to the process of development, and therefore to illuminate aspects of development work which had previously not been sufficiently recognised or appreciated. It is a method to change attitudes.

3 For those groups who are committed to equality and empowerment, but whose projects may not reflect this, this is a particularly valuable method of analysis.

4 There is a strong ideological component and the training aims at conviction - and liberation from more limited theoretical perspectives.

5 The handout is based on an earlier account of the Longwe method, which appeared in an Oxfam publication. Sara Longwe now prefers to use the phrase 'Women's Empowerment Framework' to characterise her method.

Gender awareness: the missing element in the Third World development project

Introduction

Although development agencies and Third World governments are trying to formulate and implement new policies on women's development, success with these policies depends on increased gender awareness amongst development personnel. This paper therefore considers at what gender awareness means in looking at women's development in the Third World, and defines this awareness in terms of an ability to recognise women's issues at every stage of the development project cycle.

The paper presents a five-point Women's Development Criteria as an analytical framework for understanding what Third World development projects ought to be doing in order to contribute towards women's development.

The need for gender awareness

The general lack of attention to women's needs within the development process stems from a general lack of gender awareness amongst those who plan and implement development projects. The project target group is often treated as an undifferentiated group of 'people' without recognising the special needs of women; more likely, and worse, a male-biased vocabulary is used to describe the target group which becomes 'men' rather than 'people': in this way the women actually disappear from sight — and from thought. Typically a project document describes the Third World farmer as 'he'; but in actuality, the Third World farmer is usually a woman.

Development in the Third World is not merely about increased productivity and welfare, although these things are important. Development is also about meeting the needs of those who are most in need, and about increased participation, and equality.

Development is therefore also concerned with enabling people to take charge of their own lives, and escape from the poverty which arises not from lack of productivity but rather from oppression and exploitation. The typical rural woman in the Third World is a hard-working producer of food who remains, with her children, short of food and malnourished: the food is consumed by the husband rather than the wife; by men rather than women and children; by landlords rather than tenants; by townspeople rather than rural people; by rich consumers rather than poor producers.

Thus, the problem in women's development is not primarily concerned with enabling women to be more productive, more efficient, or to use their labour more effectively. The central issue of women's development is women's empowerment, to enable women to take an equal place with men, and to participate equally in the development process in order to achieve control over the factors of production on an equal basis with men.

Criteria for recognising women's issues

Women's development is here defined as being concerned with women's issues, where the overall issue is equality with men, and overcoming inequality.

There is a need to spell out the different forms and levels of equality that constitute development. Much of the development literature on this subject is concerned with defining equality according to the conventional sectors of the economy and society: equality in education, employment, under the law, and so on. The difficulty with this system of analytical division is that it provides a focus on areas of social life, rather than the role of increased equality in the development process. I shall therefore introduce five different levels of equality as the basis for criteria to assess the level of women's development in any area of social or economic life.

Women's Development Criteria (Women's Empowerment Framework)

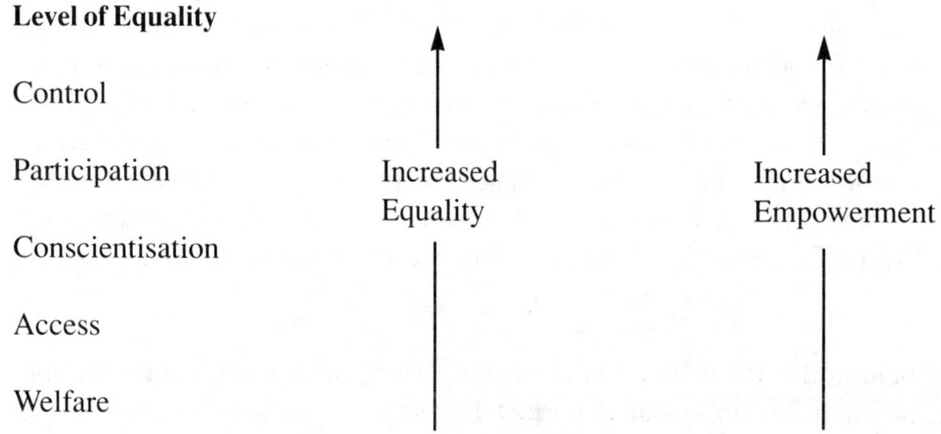

These levels of equality are in hierarchical relationship, so that equality of control is more important for women's development than equality of welfare. The higher levels of equality are automatically higher levels of development. This is a hierarchy of empowerment, since the higher levels are concerned with providing women with the means towards increased control over their own lives.

These five levels are presented as criteria for measuring the extent of women's development in any area of social life. They are:

i) Welfare. The level of material welfare of women, relative to men, in such matters as food supply, income and medical care. This level of equality is concerned purely with relative level of welfare, and is not concerned with whether women are themselves the active creators and producers of their material needs: such involvement would suggest a higher degree of empowerment and development, which is considered in the higher levels of the criteria.

ii) Access. Women's access to the factors of production on an equal basis with men: equal access to land, labour, credit, training, marketing facilities and all publicly available services and benefits on an equal basis with men. Here equality of access is obtained by ensuring the principle of equality of opportunity, which typically entails the reform of the law and administrative practice to remove all forms of discrimination against women.

iii) Conscientisation. The understanding of the difference between sex roles and gender roles, and that the latter are cultural and can be changed; conscientisation also involves a belief that the sexual division of labour should be fair and agreeable to both sides, and not involve the economic or political domination of one sex by the other. Belief in sexual equality lies at the basis of gender awareness, and provides the basis for collective participation in the process of women's development.

iv) Participation. This level of equality is concerned with women's equal participation in the decision-making process; this means participation in the processes of policy making planning and administration. It is a particularly important aspect of development projects, where participation means involvement in needs assessment, project formulation, implementation and evaluation. Equality of participation means involving the women of the community affected by the decisions taken, and involving them in the same proportion in decision making as their proportion in the community at large.

v) Control. This level entails not only the participation of women in the decision-making process, but a utilisation of this participation, through conscientisation and mobilisation, to achieve equality of control over the factors of production, and equality of control over the distribution of benefits. Equality of control means a balance of control between men and women, so that neither side is put into a position of dominance or subordination.

A development project is concerned with women's development when it is concerned with a women's issue, defined in terms of the above five levels of equality. The term women's issue is here defined differently from a women's concern, which is here used to denote matters connected with women's sex roles, or their traditional and subordinate sex-stereotyped gender roles. By contrast a women's issue is concerned with equality with men in any social or economic role, and involving any of the above five levels of equality. Therefore, a main purpose of the above five-point criteria is to distinguish between women's issues and women's concerns.

In terms of the above criteria, poverty relates to the basic level of welfare, where family income falls below the level necessary to meet basic needs and subsistence. There is nothing in this definition of poverty which necessarily means that poverty is a women's issue. Poverty is, first and foremost, a general concern which affects both men and women. It becomes more of a women's concern where women have the main responsibility of producing the food crop, and where women have the responsibility of ensuring the welfare of children. Poverty becomes a women's issue where food and income is not fairly distributed between men and women, and where women do not receive a fair share of the fruits of their labour.

With the above Criteria as our analytical tool, we are now in a position to take a critical look at any Third World development project, and to analyse the prospects for better attention being paid to the requirements of women's development.

Women's issues and the project cycle

This method here can be used at each stage of the project cycle, to consider typical inadequacies in terms of the Women's Development Criteria. But we shall look only at the inadequacies which seem to be most important, or which point to the current obstacles to women's development.

1 Assessing women's needs

Project formulation ought to begin with an investigation into people's needs, both by considering the needs which are implicit in their situation, and by asking them about their felt needs and priorities. The first and perhaps most important reason why women's issues are overlooked is that no needs assessment is carried out; it is not merely that women's needs are overlooked in a needs assessment, but rather that no needs assessment of any sort takes place.

Typically a project is formulated by a consultant or programme officer who has no detailed or specific information on the situation or particular needs of the affected community, but who identifies project objectives on the basis of knowledge of the overall national situation and development priorities and objectives. Typically, this background knowledge includes little or no information on the general situation of women in the country, or the main issues which need to be addressed in women's development.

The stage is set for the formulation of a project which overlooks the position of women entirely, and which is likely to have a negative effect on women's development, especially by increasing the burden of labour upon women, whilst allowing project benefits to be controlled by men.

Such a project is well set for failure, since many women will quietly opt out of project activities as they see the extra burdens put upon them, and the lack of benefit to themselves and their children.

The implication of the Women's Development Criteria is that the needs of women in a target group and affected community must be assessed at all five levels: welfare, access, conscientisation, participation and control, with a view to suggesting how the project intervention can make a meaningful contribution to women's development at each of these levels. It is also necessary for the needs assessment to identify priority target groups, such as female heads of household or landless widows, who are more in need of development assistance in terms of the criteria, and who are more at risk if the project intervention does not take account of their special position and needs.

2 Women's issues in project identification

The usual situation is that women's issues are completely overlooked when identifying the project objectives. If the agency responsible for formulating the project is asked why there is nothing concerning women's development in the project document, a typical answer is that 'This project is not concerned with women, it is a forestry project', or simply 'This is not a women's project'.

There is still a common perception amongst development personnel that women's development is confined to separate and special women's projects, and that these separate projects should be concerned with income-generating activities, especially in women's clubs and in the sex-stereotyped activities of knitting, sewing and cooking. However, in terms of the Women's Development Criteria introduced in this paper these 'women's club projects' cannot be seen as a contribution to women's development, but rather as a subtraction from it.

In addition to the levels of women's development according to the Criteria, it can be useful to identify the extent to which the project objectives are concerned with women's development purely in terms of whether women's issues are ignored or recognised. From this point of view it is possible to identify three different levels of recognition of women's issues in project objectives, as shown below:

Level of recognition of women's issues

i) The Negative Level, where the project objectives make no mention of women's issues. Experience has shown that Third World women are very likely to be left worse off by such a project, in that its effects are negative for women's development.

ii) The Neutral Level, where the project objectives recognise women's issues, but concern remains at the neutral and conservative level of ensuring that the project intervention does not leave women worse off than before.

iii) The Positive Level, where the project objectives are positively concerned with women's issues, and with improving the position of women relative to men.

From this categorisation, we may go on to talk of negative or positive projects, according to the overall balance of the project objectives.

Neither the above Levels of Recognition nor the Women's Development Criteria say anything about whether the project target group is women only, men only, or partly women and partly men. Women's development is defined in terms of whether it addresses women's issues, as defined in the Criteria; these issues of equality between women and men must be the concern of both women and men.

It is now possible to produce a project profile which categorises the project objectives in terms of the Levels of Equality, and the Levels of Recognition, using the charts shown in Handout 48 **Chart for the Gender Profile of a project.**

Since the women's development component is typically missing at the stages of needs assessment and project identification, it follows logically and unsurprisingly that there is usually little to be found at the final stage of project formulation — project design.

The main point is that the Criteria interpret women's development as a process of women's increased welfare, income, production and skills. The development project is part of this process, and must remain true to it. Therefore the strategies and methods of implementation must exemplify the process of women's empowerment in such matters as the proportion of women in the team concerned with implementation, the level of gender awareness within the team, the proportion of female members of the target group who are members of the project management committee, equal conditions of employment for men and women, and so on. Conversely, a male dominated and patriarchal style of project administration contains implicit lessons and messages which negate project objectives concerned with women's development.

4 Women's issues in project implementation

For the few projects whose design is seriously concerned with making a contribution to women's development, it is sad to see this concern evaporate at the stage of implementation. One reason can be that the members of the implementing team are themselves not gender aware, and not committed to the process of women's development, and fall easy prey to various forms of bureaucratic resistance. Therefore it is common to hear the excuse that 'we are trying to do things which are against the local custom, and nobody seems interested, so why should we bother?' At the stage of project implementation the most important level of the Criteria is conscientisation — amongst the implementing team!

5 Women's issues in project evaluation

There is a general lack of know-how on how to evaluate a project's contribution towards women's development. This is compounded by the confusion of different methodologies in project evaluation, as well as the domination of the field by cost-benefit analysis — a method which has little relevance to the field of women's development. Cost-benefit analysis is concerned with measuring project outputs, whereas the evaluation of a women's development project must be concerned with assessing whether the social and political processes of empowerment are taking place. The evaluation of women's development must take place at each stage of the project cycle, and the Women's Development Criteria can provide the basis of the evaluation criteria.

Taking as an example the Criteria's concern with participation, the projectappraisal must consider the proportion of women amongst those who will be providing project inputs, and amongst those who will be receiving project benefits. It should look at the proposed proportion of women, including especially local and target group women, who will be involved in decision making in project planning, management, implementation, and evaluation.

During the implementation stage it is important to monitor and evaluate progress towards women's participation and empowerment. It is necessary to set actual development against the original objectives and project design, to see if the women of the target group and affected community are participating in project activities and decision-making activities in the numbers and proportion (relative to men) that were originally intended. If the intended participation is achieved, the next thing to monitor is the evidence of women recognising women's issues and interests, mobilising to pursue their interests, influencing the decision making and changing the course of events to achieve increased access to and control over the factors of production.

It is only towards the end of the implementation period that it will be possible to measure project outcomes in terms of whether women's position, relative to men, has improved in such matters as increased income and welfare, and reduction of the burden of labour. More important, as long-term effects, are women's continued participation in the development process, and their continued collective mobilisation to recognise and address women's issues in development. It is in this sense that any material benefits are secondary: the main purpose of the women's development component of the project should be concerned with enabling and promoting the process of empowerment, so that women can act collectively to improve their own situation and not remain the passive recipients of decisions made by others.

Women's issues in a development programme

Typically the individual development project is part of an overall programme of projects — the so-called Country Programme. Such a programme is guided by overall policies, and has its own priorities and themes. The question here, therefore, is whether women's development is a strong element within the overall theme, or is seen as a side issue.

The Women's Development Criteria provides the potential basis for evaluating a whole programme. For instance, an appraisal of the women's development component within a programme may be done by drawing a Gender Profile Chart for the whole programme which shows the level of concern with women's issues in the objectives of each individual project, as shown in **Handout 49**.

Women's development would become a strong theme at the programme level if there is a programme level commitment to include women's development in all projects to ensure that a range of levels of women's development are addressed in various different projects, and if the programme includes some projects which have a priority interest in addressing particular aspects of women's development.

It is also important for the programme as a whole to take account of the overall situation of women in the Third World country, to take account of the policies on women's development of the Third World country, and to work out feasible starting points for introducing more projects concerned with women's development into the programme.

Such considerations might suggest quite different sorts of projects from anything which arises from attempting to bolster the women's developmentcomponent in general development projects. For instance, if the low level of gender awareness amongst development planners and implementers is an obstacle to progress, then a women's development project might take the form of providing training workshops for development personnel within the implementing agencies. Similarly, a contribution towards women's development may be made by assisting with the improvement of institutional capacity to plan, implement and evaluate projects concerned with women's development.

However, it may be difficult for individual agencies to tailor a Country Programme around particular development priorities, and a Country Programme is always in danger of being a mere collection of projects without inter-connections or common theme. The building of a balanced and purposeful theme concerned with women's development suggests close collaboration with other development agencies which are operating in the particular Third World country. It is this sort of close collaboration which will enable the local office of the development agency to achieve a better Third World perspective on women's development, and make a more appropriate and meaningful contribution to this area of great need, but small progress.

(Source: This paper by Sarah Hlupelkile Longwe is an edited and slightly abridged version of the paper that was previously published in GADU Newsletter No. 11. A much shortened version appeared in *Changing Perceptions: Writings on Gender and Development*, Oxfam, 1991)

Handout 48 *Activity 50*

Chart for the Gender Profile of a Project

For photocopyable tables see re

Project title:______________________________

Level of Recognition / Levels of Equality	Negative	Neutral	Positive
Control			
Participation			
Conscientisation			
Access			
Welfar			

Project title:______________________________

Level of Recognition / Levels of Equality	Negative	Neutral	Positive
Control			
Participation			
Conscientisation			
Access			
Welfar			

Project title:______________________________

Level of Recognition / Levels of Equality	Negative	Neutral	Positive
Control			
Participation			
Conscientisation			
Access			
Welfar			

Project title:______________________________

Level of Recognition / Levels of Equality	Negative	Neutral	Positive
Control			
Participation			
Conscientisation			
Access			
Welfar			

Gender Profile for a Country Programme

		Level of Concern with Women's Development				
Sector	**Project**	**Welfare**	**Access**	**Consciencious**	**Participation**	**Control**
Agriculture						
Education and Training						
Commerce and Industry						
Women's Projects						

Time: 45 mins—1 hr

Gender awareness in projects: overview

Objectives

1 To provide an overview of gender issues in project-planning.

2 To link project planning and appraisal with work with groups.

3 To provide a framework for linking different activities.

Method

1 Before the training, read **Handout 50** Ensuring Gender Awareness in the Planning of Projects. Write the main elements on four flipcharts:
A. Introduction and entry strategy.
B. Improving awareness of gender relations.
C. Improving ways of consulting women.
D. Improving quality of information for planning.

2 Give input based on flipchart A and Handout. *(10 mins)*
Allow discussion and questions.

3 Give input based on flipchart B. *(10 mins)*
Refer to **Activity 48** (Harvard method)

4 Give input based on flipchart C. *(10 mins)*
Then do, for example, **Activity 82** Finding out about Women.

5 Give input based on flipchart D. *(10 mins)*
Then do **Activities 52** Checklists.(+)

6 Summarise and give out **Handout 50**. *(10-20 mins)*

Materials

Handout 50 Ensuring Gender Awareness in the Planning of Projects.
Four flipcharts based on this Handout

Facilitator's Notes

1 This paper is particularly useful for groups who have some specific knowledge and experience of gender analysis and need a broader overview to link the elements of their knowledge.

2 It can be used in the way described, or can be used as an introduction to project appraisal (with groups with some previous knowledge of gender) or as a summary. The Handout can be given out prior to the session for overnight reading, if preferred.

3 The timings should be adjusted depending on how you use it.

Ensuring gender awareness in the planning of projects

Planning for rural development is too often shaped by a primary focus on the output of the plan at the expense of the process through which the plan is prepared and designed. This process involves people; their perceptions of how they fit into plans can take radically different directions. This fit between beneficiaries' needs, project performance and the role of the NGO (non-governmental organisation) begins with the learning capacity of the agency: how well it copes with mistakes and contingencies, how it uses its experience to strengthen institutional capacity and to what extent it shares the knowledge gained with the community.

The way an NGO approaches and works with the community at the planning — and subsequent — stages is crucial; the importance of the entry strategy cannot be over-estimated. This strategy must be based on adequate knowledge, understanding and communication with the community, and women are vital to this process.

The importance of the entry strategy

A productive relationship between a rural development agency and a community will depend on the agreement reached between them at the planning stage, about the process of change. This will determine the entry strategy to be adopted. Three stages are important:

agreeing with the population on the values and goals which will guide the intervention;

negotiating an agreement on what the population and the agency have to offer each other; that is, how participation is to be organised and the role each will play in achieving the outcomes which are jointly planned;

arriving at a common analysis of the situation so that not just the problems and needs are identified but the reasons for them are jointly understood.

What must be avoided is the imposition of values important to the agency alone. For example, a Western feminist policy may not be easily or desirably transferable; but a commitment to security of livelihood for the poorest groups may stimulate development for both men and women which may bring about a desired shift in the balance of power between the genders, in favour of women.

Implicit in this approach is the establishment of a partnership in which the agency listens, learns and consults. This is important not just because the poorest groups in a community — particularly women — are easily overlooked, but because every community exists within a wider context. Developing an informed perspective on the links women have to wider environmental, political and socio-economic systems implies the agency's willingness, and ability, to appraise both women's practical and strategic interests.

However, identifying both women's practical and strategic interests must be a process which is sensitive to the community, and to the capacity of that community to work with the agency's different cultural perspective on relations between men and women, and vice versa.

Any jointly-negotiated and agreed plan of action which details what it is possible to achieve for the benefit of women, should contain the ingredients for policy, project design, and implementation. Moser and Levy (1986) identify two factors which are very important for a gender-conscious entry strategy: the first is an informed judgement about which practical and strategic needs can be met in the socio-economic and political conditions of a particular place and time. The second is an assessment of the extent to which women have access to local institutions and whether these institutions can be used to meet some or all of the particular practical and strategic needs.

There are three approaches which an agency might consider in order to develop this informed judgement and accurate assessment. These are to improve its understanding of how gender relations work within the community; to improve its ways of consulting women; and to improve the quality of information used for planning purposes.

Improving awareness of gender relations

Understanding the relative access to and control over resources and benefits has to include an awareness of the differential access to power which is integral to the division of labour by gender. In conventional project appraisal the unit of analysis is the household, represented for purposes of estimating costs and benefits by assumptions about the behaviour of a male head of household. But it is a major misconception in project planning to see the household as a homogenous decision-making unit; this is clearly not the case in many rural societies where different members have separate productive and entrepreneurial roles and there are competing, unequal and often conflicting claims on resources and outputs for the satisfaction of basic needs.

There is an argument for an increased understanding of gender relations within a household structure, in order to prevent a distortion of the entry strategy. There is a danger of being swamped by diversity and of looking at increasingly complex social relations without testing their impact on what happens outside the household. For example, women may have to get men's permission to work co-operatively with other women in an all-female organisation or they may want to receive men's sanction on their separate activities; this will not necessarily mean that the decision making is male-dominated. At the same time, male control of financial gains from a women's group may be detrimental to the group's autonomy and growth and may also undermine individual women's decision-making power in the household.

How is it possible to arrive at an understanding of gender relations within a rural household? A key principle is to consult both men and women, most simply by documenting their different activities, resources and responsibilities which can then be compared. Indicators of how, for example, women and men experience changes to the environment, seasonality, access to preferred technologies, large family size, increasing costs of inputs for production, and an agency's style of intervention, can contribute to a body of qualitative information about women's activities, the resources they command, and the responsibilities they manage. What has to be avoided is placing an exclusion zone around a target group of women, both during and after the planningphase, simply in order to reinforce their target-group status.

Improving ways of consulting women

Women are not a homogenous social group and their needs will differ according to their relative ages as well as their different activities, resources and responsibilities. A needs assessment should therefore take into account this social and personal heterogeneity. Women may well need support in defining their needs, and various techniques have been employed to facilitate this process: documenting and sharing life histories; stimulating discussion around a series of photographs of the women themselves and other women; using a situational analysis or other data collection tools to highlight inequalities in the gender allocation of tasks. This is also a learning process for the agency.

It is important that the context and style of discussion should be accessible to women for whom speaking out may be an unfamiliar event; the location, materials used, the size and membership of the group may all be significant. A group action may require organisational skills. Providing women with enabling skills for group management or supporting existing organisations that women use may be a vital investment in the development process even before the entry strategy is agreed.

As Moser and Levy say, consultation on issues that perpetuate gender inequality, and the active participation of women in the planning process is desirable not only as a means of achieving development objectives, but as an end in itself. At the same time, women's expression of their situation and their demands for the fulfilment of certain practical interests may well provide a more accurate appraisal of what assistance would be appropriate than blueprinted objectives developed by outsiders based on strategic interests. How the meeting of practical needs is linked to longer-term strategic needs must be decided as a result of frequent consultation and monitoring with the women concerned, and then a testing of solutions within the community.

Improving the quality of information for planning

A balance has to be struck between spending time on diagnosing gender inequalities and formulating proposals. Participative techniques can provide the means for the community and the agency to learn about each other's values and criteria. Testing this data in an interactive way is part of the process of building up a body of planning and monitoring information. The employment of Rapid Rural Appraisal techniques in a range of situation is beginning to show the importance of using a portfolio of methods. Three of these techniques are as follows:

i Direct matrix ranking and preference ranking:
In situations where women hold particular indigenous skills and knowledge, it is important to understand the criteria leading to their decisions and preferences regarding productive or organisational practices. Ranking methodologies have been used with some success to identify local knowledge. Direct matrix ranking involves the respondent(s) listing criteria which are important to them when considering the value of a resource or when considering why one type of the resource is preferred to another. Scores are allocated to each criteria for each resource type and a matrix is constructed which can pinpoint the preferred type as well as indicating why one type, forexample, a high yielding variety (HYV) or a traditional variety of the same crop, is not preferred for that particular locality. The ranking of preferences can be conducted between two types of an item or between several types, thus building up a scoring matrix of ranked preferences. Two characteristics of the method seem potentially important:

The quality of discussion required to arrive at a consensus within the group on the criteria to be ranked and then scored is a valuable learning process for all concerned, and yet one that is conducted under the control of the group.

The criteria chosen by the group are often indicators of links in the system of resource management and decision making, which might not otherwise appear. Once these links are known they can be a further reinforcement of a shared analysis.

ii Situational analysis and food paths:
Gathering data through group interviews is a method requiring training and

practice. A methodology which focuses on the stages and sequences of an activity can facilitate the process of acquiring gender sensitive data in a group interview. The situational analysis builds up a diagrammatic representation of a sequence of activities by focusing on the situation (e.g. introducing contour ploughing or allocating irrigation water). Each stage of the sequence can be examined and discussed to highlight the gender allocation of labour, resources and responsibilities. Using this technique for a 'food path', focusing on one crop, tracing the production of food from the purchasing and planting of the seed to the sale or preparation of the food, enables further layers to be added, such as hours spent, technology used, and seasonal variations identified, throughout an interactive process of discussion.

iii Checklists
Although checklists have become established as gender-conscious tools for planning a project, the checklist can become a barrier to effective interaction between agency and community unless, like any tool, it is frequently refined and sharpened in the context in which it is used. Our understanding of this context is, after all, only the first step in the process through which women may come to realise the benefits from jointly planned interventions.

Conclusion

The importance of fitting projects to the real needs of a community cannot be over-emphasised; and to achieve this it is essential for agencies to discuss and negotiate fully with the community. In order to ensure that women are an integral part of the process it is important to improve gender awareness among all the participants, to find ways of communicating with the women directly, and to base planning on the best level of information possible.

(Source: Adapted from 'Ensuring Gender Awareness in the Planning of Projects' by Miranda Munro, in *Changing Perceptions*, ed. Wallace and March, Oxfan 1991.)

Time: 1½-2 hrs

Mapping for Mars

Objectives

1 To enable participants to experience for themselves the variety of perspectives on an issue.

2 To enable participants to recognise the importance of acknowledging and encouraging expression of the diversity of perspectives, particularly in relation to gender.

Method

1 Explain to the group that you are a development worker from Mars. Tell them that you are developing their country or region this month, and you are trying to understand the issues that are important to them.

2 Divide the group up into groups of about five according to gender and geographical origin, or other criteria which will ensure that the members of each small group have strong characteristics in common.

3 Ask each group to use flipchart papers and marker pens to draw a big map of the *same* and with the same title. For instance, you could ask them all to draw the same village, town, country, or continent. Explain that each group is to draw on their own map 5-10 issues of particular importance to their group. Ask them to use no writing as you do not read earthscript, and use symbols and drawings only

4 Go around to each group as they are working on the maps, and point out:
   a. The importance of drawing on the ground, where all can see clearly;
   b. The importance of the use of symbols, not words, so as to include everyone, whether literate or not;
   c. The importance of letting the people in the community do the discussion and analysis, while the development worker observes;
   d. The opportunity this gives the development worker to observe group dynamics, including leadership, disputes, those excluded, etc.

e. The opportunity it gives the development worker to listen to people's process of analysis. *(50 mins)*

5 Bring the groups together again, and put the maps up on the wall, or leave them on the floor if there is space. Ask one member of each group to present their map to the whole group, explaining what the symbols mean and what information is on the map.

6 Then ask the group to decide which map is the best. Explain that you will take the best one back to your head office on Mars. If the group cannot decide, choose the map of the most vocal group.

7 Then ask those whose maps were not chosen how they felt about their maps being left out. Point out that there are more people in the room whose ideas are not represented, than there are those whose ideas are represented on the chosen map.

8 Allow a discussion to develop about finding a solution to the problem.

(40 mins)

Materials

Flipchart, pens

Facilitator's Notes

1 Emphasise throughout that the quality of the drawing is not important: it is what is portrayed that is significant. Once symbols are explained to us we can all remember and understand them.

2 Often a woman's map will include an issue which is of importance to women, but which will not even appear on men's maps: and vice versa. It is important in this activity to keep emphasising that we learn more from several separately collected perspectives than we would from one general meeting where the dominant view would prevail.

3 When this activity was tried out in Zimbabwe, the maps drawn were all very different. One map emphasised literacy, one AIDS, another environmental problems. When the trainer suggested taking one back to Mars, the group discussed this and asked her to take all the maps, to ensure that all perspectives would be taken into account. Each one had its own story to tell and, like pieces of a jigsaw, filled in a fuller picture of Africa. It was concluded that there was ***no best map****.*

(Source: Alice Welbourn)

Time: 25 mins

Bangladesh maps

Objectives

1 To enable participants to test their own assumptions about other societies.

2 To use maps drawn by people of a village or community to give participants an example of the different perceptions and priorities of different people.

Method

1 Explain the objectives of the session. Then ask participants to break into small groups of four or six, and give each participant a copy of the three maps on **Handout 51**.

2 Tell participants that one map was drawn by women, another by old men, and another by young men, but do not reveal which was drawn by which people. Ask the small groups to try to work out which map was drawn by whom, and give their reasons.

(10 mins)

3 Next, ask each group to present its conclusions. Then tell them the story of the village, as it was told by the people drawing the maps.

The villagers are squatters on the banks of the Jamuna river. Old men, young men and women respectively were asked to draw a map of their village.

The old men, through their map, told the story of their ancestral land, which now lay under the flooded river. They said 'we must stay squatting here, so that we can reclaim that land, once the flood has receded'. The Law states that villagers must continue to pay tax on the land, otherwise it reverts to the Government. How could they make sure that they could stay?

The women gave most detail of the immediate settlement, stating that 'we need to earn money here, but can't move from our settlement because we are women. What do you suggest?' What work could they do?

The young men emphasised the road and the railway, which links them to the far-away places where they seek migrant labour. They get sizeable advance loans, which then must be repaid with interest. They spend about eight months of the year away. How could they find work nearer home?

4 Tell the group which map was drawn by which people, and lead a short discussion, bringing out the importance of finding out about people'sdifferent concerns and priorities. Draw out especially the gender issues, related to women's mobility, opportunities for income-earning etc. in contrast with men's. Draw out how incomplete a picture would have been obtained if only one map had been used to assess possible interventions to help the villagers. *Emphasise that there is no best map.*(See Activity 52 Mapping for Mars.)

(15 - 20 mins)

Facilitator's Notes

1 Map A was drawn by the old men; Map B was drawn by the women, and Map C was drawn by the young men. Let the participants work out who drew them and why they think that. They rarely get it all right!

2 You may use your own maps, if you have suitable ones available.

(Source: Alice Welbourn/ActionAid Bangladesh.)

Handout 51 *Activity 53*

Bangladesh maps

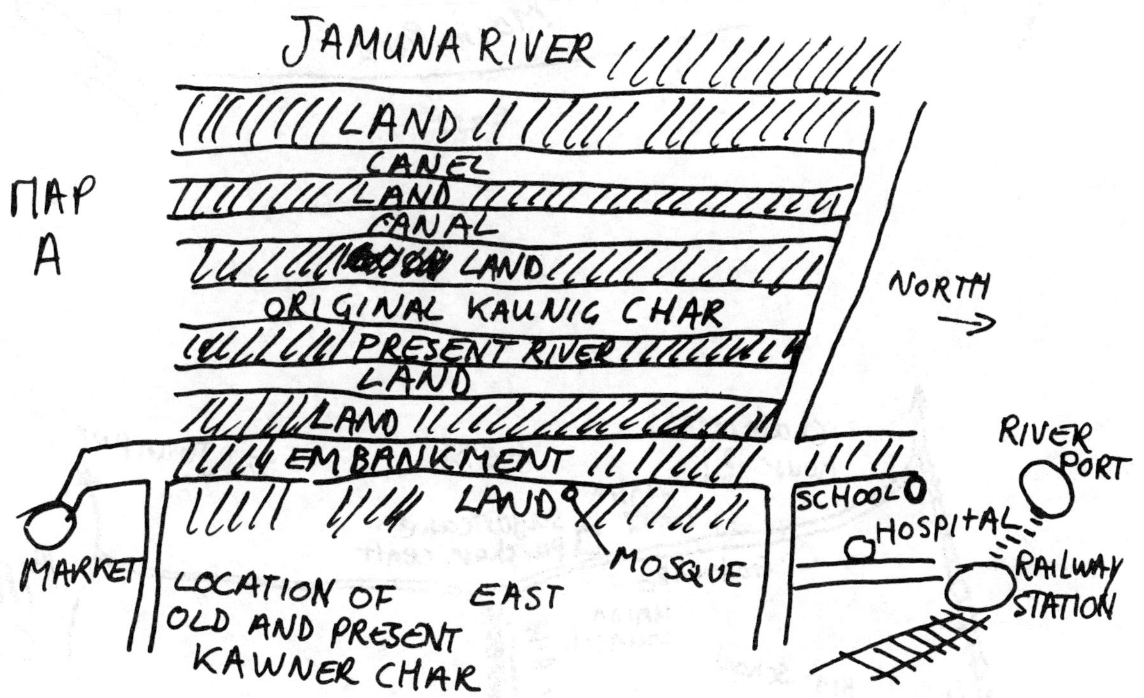

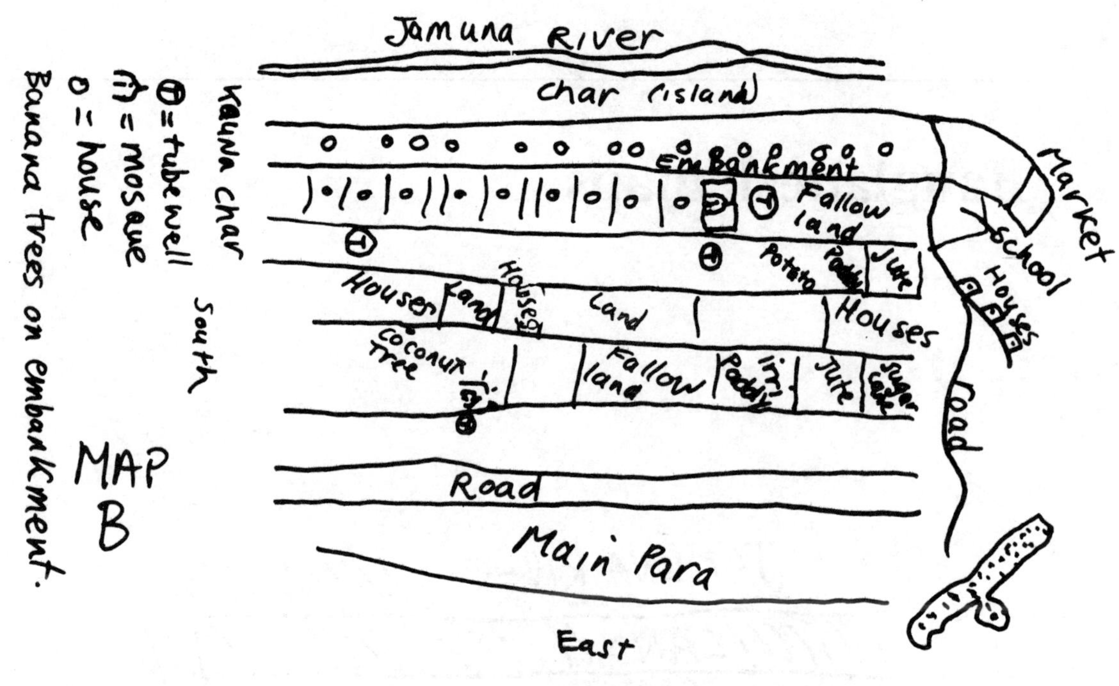
Jamuna River
Char (island)
Embankment
Fallow land
Market
School
Houses
Potato Paddy
Jute
Houses
Land
Houses
Land
Houses
Coconut Tree
Fallow land
Paddy
Jute
Road
Road
Main Para
East
South
Kauna char
= tubewell
= mosque
o = house
Banana trees on embankment.
MAP B

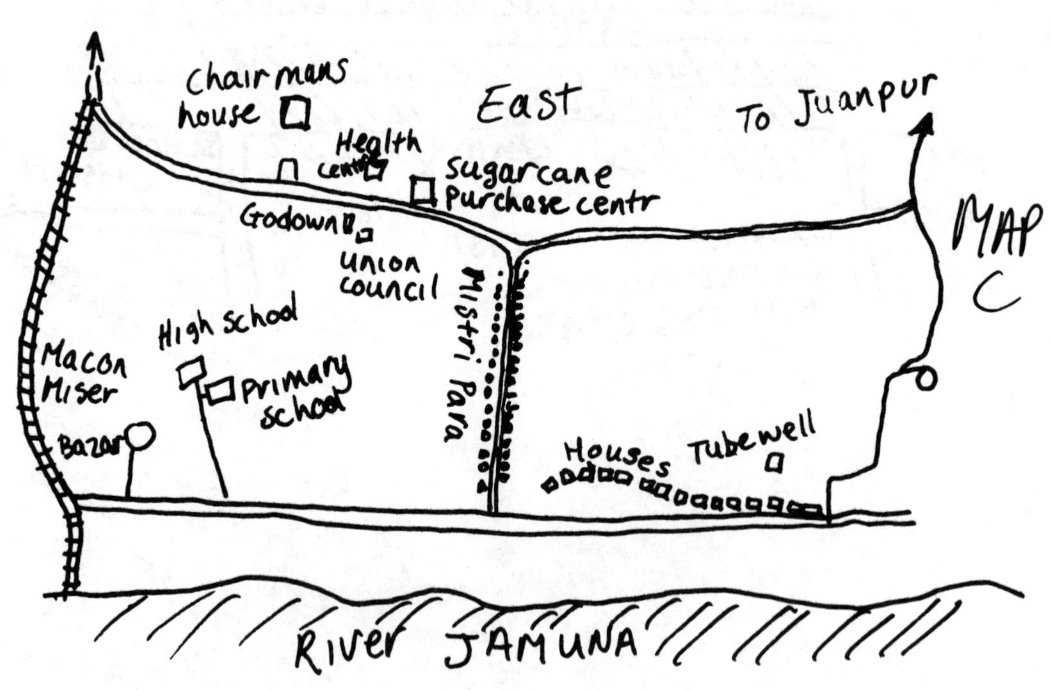
Chairmans house
East
To Juanpur
Health centre
Sugarcane purchase centr
Godown
Union council
Mistri Para
MAP C
High School
Primary school
Macon Miser
Bazar
Houses
Tubewell
River JAMUNA

Time: 1-1½ hrs

Checklists

Objectives

1 To introduce a variety of checklists, their uses and limitations.

2 To enable participants to write or adapt a checklist for their own use.

Method

1 Divide the group into small groups, and give out two or three of the checklists from **Handouts 52 to 56**.

(5 mins)

2 Ask each group to discuss the uses and limitations of these checklists.

(20-30 mins)

3 Ask each group to design a new checklist based on their own needs, using ideas from the checklists and any other methods taught.

(30 mins)
(alternative 2 hrs +)

Materials

At least two or three handouts from **Handouts 52 -56** for each participant.

Facilitator's Notes

1 This activity can be used either as a short introduction to checklists, or as a much longer exercise where the aim is to write a checklist which the team will actually use in practice.

2 If the aim is to write a 'real' checklist, the small groups should be teams of people who work together, and the people should have the power to be able to use it.

3 Checklists are always both too short (in that it is impossible to ask every relevant question), and too long (in that they take a long time to fill out, and there is a danger that they will not be used).

4 A checklist is most effective when used by the people who have been involved in drawing it up, and who thus understand the concepts and rationale behind it. It then serves as a reminder in the training process, rather than an outside imposition.

5 As an additional exercise, an existing or new checklist can then be tested out using a case study.

6 The Harvard Method checklist is presented here as ***Handout 52****. You can use this in conjuction with the Harvard Analytical Framework in* ***Activity 48***

Handout 52 *Activity 54*

Harvard method: checklist

The following sets of questions are the key ones for each of the four main stages in the project cycle: identification, design, implementation, evaluation.

Women's dimension in project identification

Assessing women's needs

1. What needs and opportunities exist for increasing women's productivity and/or production?
2. What needs and opportunities exist for increasing women's access to and control of resources?
3. What needs and opportunities exist for increasing women's access to and control of benefits?
4. How do these needs and opportunities relate to the country's other general and sectoral development needs and opportunities?
5. Have women been directly consulted in identifying such needs and opportunities?

Defining general project objectives

1. Are project objectives explicitly related to women's needs?
2. Do these objective adequately reflect women's needs?
3. Have women participated in setting those objectives?
4. Have there been any earlier efforts?
5. How has the present proposal built on earlier activity?

Identifying possible negative effects

1. Might the project reduce women's access to or control of resources and benefits?
2. Might it adversely affect women's situation in some other way?
3. What will be the effects on women in the short and longer term?

Women's dimension in project design

Project impact on women's activities

1. Which of these activities (production, reproduction and maintenance, socio-political) does the project affect?
2. Is the planned component consistent with the current gender denomination for the activity?
3. If it is planned to change the women's performance of that activity, (ie locus of activity, remunerative mode, technology, mode of activity) is this feasible, and what positive or negative effects would there be on women?
4. If it does not change it, is this a missed opportunity for women's roles in the development process?
5. How can the project design be adjusted to increase the above-mentioned positive effects, and reduce or eliminate the negative ones?

Project impact on women's access and control

1. How will each of the project components affect women's access to and control of the resources and benefits engaged in and stemming from the production of goods and services?
2. How will each of the project components affect women's access to and control of the resources and benefits engaged in and stemming from the reproduction and maintenance of the human resources?
3. How will each of the project components affect women's access to and control of the resources and benefits engaged in and stemming from the socio-political functions?
4. What forces have been set into motion to induce further exploration of constraints and possible improvements?
5. How can the project design be adjusted to increase women's access to and control of resources and benefits?

Women's dimension in project implementation

1. Are project personnel sufficiently aware of and sympathetic towards women's needs?
2. Are women used to deliver the goods or services to women beneficiaries?
3. Do personnel have the necessary skills to provide any special inputs required by women?
4. What training techniques will be used to develop delivery systems?
5. Are there appropriate opportunities for women to participate in project management positions?

Organisational structures

1 Does the organisational form enhance women's access to resources?
2 Does the organisation have adequate power to obtain resources needed by women from other organisations?
3 Does the organisation have the institutional capability to support and protect women during the change process?

Operations and logistics

1 Are the organisation's delivery channels accessible to women in terms of personnel, location and timing?
2 Do control procedures exist to ensure dependable delivery of thegoods and services?
3 Are there mechanisms to ensure that the project resources or benefits are not usurped by males?

Finances

1 Do funding mechanisms exist to ensure programme continuity?
2 Are funding levels adequate for proposed tasks?
3 Is preferential access to resources by males avoided?
4 Is it possible to trace funds for women from allocation to delivery with a fair degree of accuracy?

Flexibility

1 Does the project have a management information system which will allow it to detect the effects of the operation on women?
2 Does the organisation have enough flexibility to adapt its structures and operations to meet the changing or new-found situations of women?

Women's dimension in project evaluation

Data requirements

1 Does the project's monitoring and evaluation system explicitly measure the project's effects on women?
2 Does it also collect data to update the Activity Analysis and the Women's Access and Control Analysis?
3 Are women involved in designating the data requirements?

Data collection and analysis

1 Are the data collected with sufficient frequency so that necessary project adjustments could be made during the project?
2 Are the data fed back to project personnel and beneficiaries in an understandable form and on a timely basis to allow project adjustments?
3 Are women involved in the collection and interpretation of data?
4 Are data analysed so as to provide guidance to the design of other projects?
5 Are key areas of WID research identified?

(Source: *Gender Roles in Development Projects* edited by Overholt, Anderson, Cloud and Austin. Kumarian Press Inc, Connecticut, 1985.)

Checklist for disaster relief

While there has been increasing understanding that gender planning is a vital component of development programmes, it has been less widely recognised that gender awareness is also central to effective planning and implementation of relief and emergency programmes. The need for rapid response and short-term specialist inputs has often meant that relief programmes are conceived and implemented in a top-down manner.

Complex logistics requiring co-ordination with a wide range of governmental and non-governmental organisations, political sensitivities, and the very large numbers of people often involved are also factors which affect organisational responses to emergencies.

In practice, the approach whereby speed of delivery is a priority, has often precluded proper discussion with the affected people, overlooked gender considerations, and resulted in an inappropriate and therefore ineffective response.

Women, especially, lack access to discussions about their needs, and are rarely involved in planning or policy making. Yet the majority of those affected by emergencies, for example refugees or displaced, are likely to be women and children.

It is therefore essential to understand the gender dimensions of an emergency and to find ways of working with women and involving them at all stages in the response.

Data collection

1. Gather information from women and men separately.
2. Involve women in data collection, in survey teams etc.
3. Disaggregate data by sex and age — this may reveal a high proportion of women-maintained households, or groups of unaccompanied children.

Basic gender needs

Gather information from women about their concerns:

Water: siting and maintenance, distribution mechanisms, methods and times of collection, containers and storage facilities; cultural practices in water use; washing/bathing sanitation facilities;

Food: involve women in targeting, monitoring and distribution of food rations, allocation at household level, needs of vulnerable groups. Will processing/cooking of food give women more/less work? Is fuel easily available?

Shelter: consult women about siting and design, bear in mind women's needs for security, privacy, safe access to facilities eg washing/bathing/sanitation. Camp design should take account of women's vulnerability to sexual harassment.

Health: involve women as health workers, consult women directly about health needs and to identify target groups eg for nutrition, health care and support; rape is a tool of war and women survivors will need medical help, moral support and a safe environment.

Empowerment and disempowerment: changing roles and responsibilities

Refugees and displaced people are experiencing change which will also have an impact on gender relations. Women and children are among the most vulnerable in most communities. In an emergency situation their vulnerability will be increased but there may be new opportunities. Relief programmes must be designed in such a way as to reduce vulnerability and strengthen the capacity of both women and men to cope. It will be useful to remember that *women may be further disempowered*:

if they are deprived of their customary authority over the management of water and food (eg men control access/distribution);

in the home (often culturally their place of authority) if shelter is inadequate, inappropriately designed, increases their vulnerability to harassment and violence;

in their community leadership roles. These are often less formal and therefore less visible than those of the men, and outsiders such as camp authorities/agency workers may overlook/bypass women's community groups through lack of awareness and thus reduce women's authority.

Women may be empowered:

if they are treated with respect, and their needs, views, skills and experience are regarded as important;

by being consulted directly about their needs;

by being involved in programme design and implementation;

by having positions of authority in their traditional sphere e.g. in food distribution mechanisms, health care services;

by also receiving support, encouragement and skills training for the new roles they have taken on in the new situation.

Conclusion

The above suggestions are not exhaustive but are intended as guidelines for the development of gender-sensitive programming in emergency situations. Although situations will differ depending on context it is crucial for the success of emergency and relief programmes that gender issues be raised, included, and monitored at all stages in the response.

(Source: Adapted from Oxfam's *Working Guidelines on Gender and Emergencies*, adopted in 1991.)

Integrating a gender perspective into emergency work

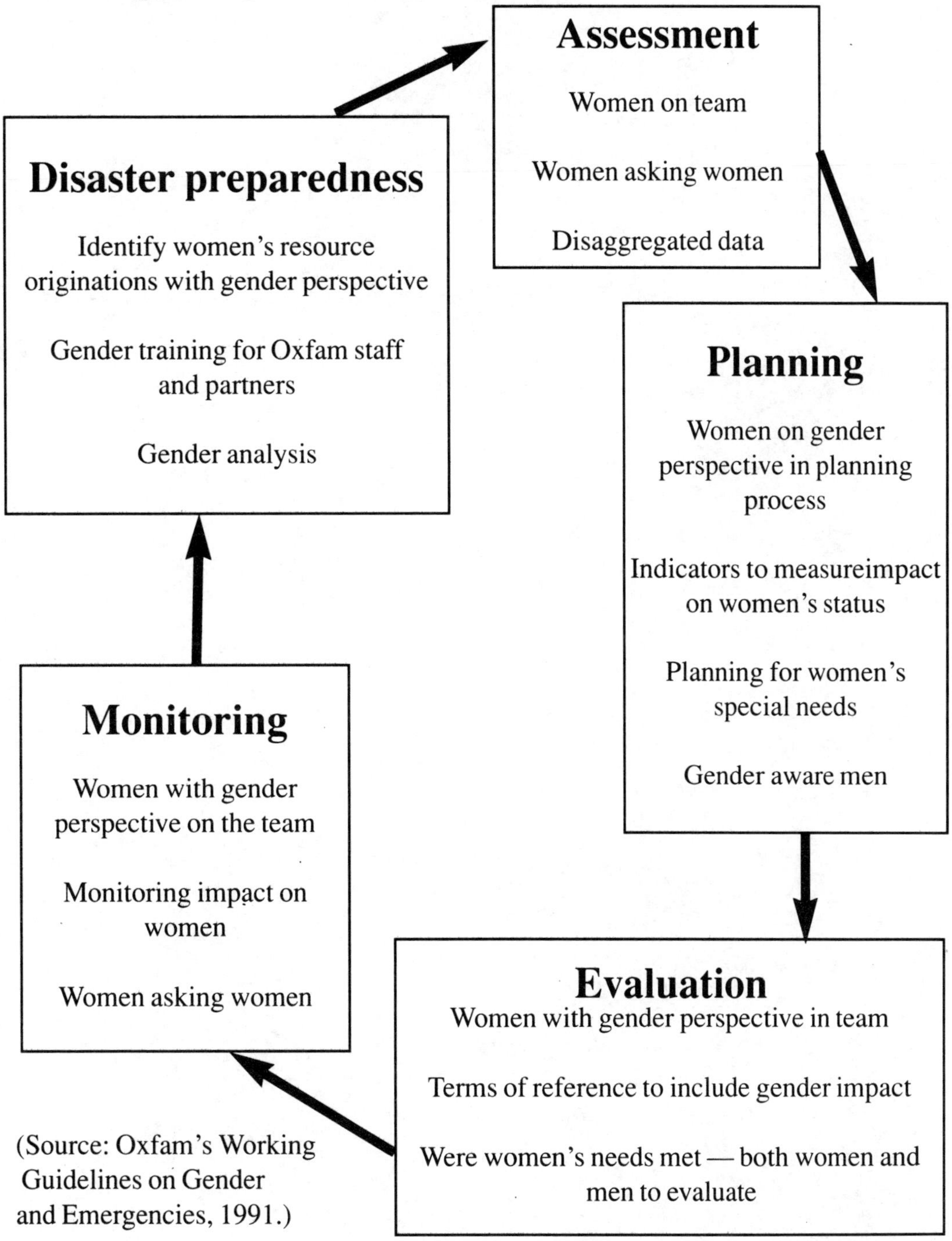

Disaster preparedness

Identify women's resource originations with gender perspective

Gender training for Oxfam staff and partners

Gender analysis

Assessment

Women on team

Women asking women

Disaggregated data

Planning

Women on gender perspective in planning process

Indicators to measureimpact on women's status

Planning for women's special needs

Gender aware men

Evaluation

Women with gender perspective in team

Terms of reference to include gender impact

Were women's needs met — both women and men to evaluate

Monitoring

Women with gender perspective on the team

Monitoring impact on women

Women asking women

(Source: Oxfam's Working Guidelines on Gender and Emergencies, 1991.)

Checklist for development projects: if integration of women in development is an objective

Project objectives

1 What are the objectives of the project?

2 Are women specifically mentioned as either agents or beneficiaries?

3 What, if any, are stated benefits for women? eg:
acquisition of skills
increased productivity
opportunity to earn cash income, etc

4 What assumptions are made in believing that project inputs will lead to these benefits?

5 If women are not specifically mentioned as participants, would their actions be relevant to the objectives of the project? Would a component for women be a useful addition to the project?

Availability of basic information

1 What socio-economic information is already available which is relevant to the target group in general and women in particular?

2 Is information on economic arrangements at household level, including role of women, adequate for purposes of project:
structure and size of households, and developmental cycle
division by sex/age of labour, decision making, rights to land control over saleable products, sources of cash incomes, including off-farm activities, of household members; seasonality of labour demands.

3 If more information is essential, what arrangements are being made to obtain it?

4 If consultants are assisting with feasibility studies, have they been briefed to consider situation and contribution of women, as appropriate?

Project design and preparation

1 Has there been consultation with people whose lives will be affected by the project, and what attention has been given to women in this?

2 Are women involved at any level in the professional planning and implementation of this project?

3 Are women to be given access to the new opportunities and services which the project provides? (local training and overseas fellowships; agricultural extension; new allocation of land rights; credit arrangements; membership of cooperatives; employment during either constructural or operational phase)

4 If not, what are the reasons?

5 Are resources adequate to provide these services for women? Are women extension staff available in sufficient numbers if approached by male staff is not culturally acceptable?

6 If project is likely to have adverse effects for women (see below) what actions are planned to counterbalance this?

Anticipated impact

1 How will project affect women's access to economic assets and cash incomes? (access to land; opportunity for paid employment or other income-earning activity; assistance with economic activities from other members of household; control over sale of product) Are there gains expected other than those stated in Objectives (see above)?

2 How will project affect women's allocation of time?
Will their workload increase/decrease as a result of innovation or changes? (mechanisation; new agricultural inputs and cropping patterns; withdrawals of labour by other household members; agricultural advice, nutritional or health teaching, if implemented; changes in distance to farms, workplaces, water supply, firewood supply) If workload is decreased, does this involve loss of income for women?

3 How will project affect subsistence within the target group, and women's control

over food supplies for household?
Will promotion of commercial agriculture affect availability of land for food grown mainly for family use; women's access to land; labour inputs (male and female) on foods crops?

Will any sources of food be removed or decreased?

Will women be increasingly dependent on partner's cash income for household food and necessities? If so, will this income be sufficient to make good subsistence losses? How subject is it to fluctuations according to world market, climatic conditions? Can it be assumed that male income will 'trickle down' sufficiently to meet basic household needs?

Will there be a change in staple diet? Will this be acceptable? Will it involve increased time in preparation?

Will changes in labour allocation alter nutritional needs of any members of household? Are subsistence resources or increased cash incomes sufficient to meet them? If not, what are probable consequences for women and children, especially if unequal food distribution patterns are customary?

4 Is the project likely to have any adverse consequences for women within groups and categories not immediately affected?

Evaluation

1 Is provision being made to monitor and evaluate the impact of the project on women?
2 Will available baseline date be adequate for this purpose?
3 What factual indicators would be relevant

(Source: *Women and Development: Guidelines for Programme and Project Planning*, Caroline Pezzullo, consultant to CEPAL, 1982)

Women's status criteria

A woman's development project may be counted as improving the status of women to the extent that progress may be seen in the following indicators:

Basic needs: better provision for women of such basic needs as food, water fuel, housing and health care; proportional distribution of basic needs between men and women.

Leadership roles: proportion of women to men in leadership roles in the community; involvement of women as women's leaders on women's issues.

Consciousness: awareness amongst women of women's needs and women's issues; awareness of discrimination against women; ability to analyse issues in terms of women's interests and women's rights.

Needs assessment: involvement of women in identifying the priority needs of the community, and in identifying the special needs of women.

Planning: involvement of women in project design, implementation and evaluation.

Sexual division of labour: involvement of women in tasks traditionally performed by men; level of involvement of men in tasks traditionally performed by women; number of hours per day worked by the average working woman, in comparison to the number worked by the average working man.

Control over the factors of production: women's access to, and control over, land, credit, distribution of income and accumulation of capital.

The order in which these indicators are presented is not intended to imply an order of priority, nor a sequence of what should come first and what should come later. It is merely suggested that a successful project should be making progress across several of these indicators, and that a successful programme should include projects which seek to improve women's status across the full range of these indicators.

(Source: Zambia Association for Research and Development (ZARD) workshop) .

Time: 1½-2 hrs

Design a project

Objectives

1 To design a project which aims to empower women.

2 To consider the processes which would need to be used to ensure women's participation and empowerment.

Method

1 Ask participants to divide into small groups (three to six people), preferably from different work teams). Remind them of the empowerment exercise (**Activity 41**). Ask them to design a project with the above objectives, and to list on flipchart the main features of the project and the processes used. They should choose one person to report back.

(30-45 mins)

2 In the large group, each small group reporter puts up their flipchart and presents the project and the process, and invites questions.

(5-10 mins per group)

3 Lead a group discussion on the following questions:
a. How do these projects actually empower women?
b. Are the same criteria being used to define empowerment in a project as in our own lives?
c. Does participation mean increased work-load? *(20-30 mins)*

Materials

Flipchart, marker pens

Facilitator's Notes

1 Empowerment has become a fashionable word among official and non-governmental development agencies, but it is very difficult to define and to realise. It is much easier to criticise existing projects than to design a new one.

2 When this exercise was done with one group, the examples given of what empowerment was for themselves (in ***Activity 43****) were different from the ideas for 'empowering' projects, which tended to use ideas from existing projects. There was a long discussion about whether, for example, a new type of stove could be empowering. In the end it was said that adequate income and food might be necessary prerequisites of empowerment, rather than being empowering in themselves.*

3 It needs to be acknowledged that a project that was really empowering would not be designed by people outside the situation.

4 This also raises the question as to what extent it is possible for women or any other powerless group to be empowered before coming up against forces of opposition whether at local, national or international level.

5 This activity could immediately follow ***Activity 43*** *on Empowerment and Participation.*

Time: 1-2 hrs

Using case studies

Objectives

1 To enable participants to analyse a project or situation from a gender perspective.

2 To help participants to think of ways to change the situation where gender issues have not been addressed.

Method

1 Give participants the case study and allow them to read it on their own, or read it aloud to the group.

(15 mins)

2 Divide the participants into small groups to discuss the case study and answer the questions. One person should be chosen to report back from each group.

(15-25 mins)

3 Ask the small groups to report back, writing their answers on newsprint. Take one idea from each group at a time. Add any remaining answers yourself after all groups have finished.

(30 mins)

4 In the large group, lead a discussion on:
a. How easy or difficult was the activity?
b. Has anyone known of similar situations?
c. Did you have sufficient information to answer the questions?
d. Key learning points from this activity. *(30 mins)*

Materials

Handouts 57, 58 and **59.** Flipchart, pens

Facilitator's Notes

1 Case studies, like any other method, can be used for different purposes. Work out what your objectives are, and then choose a case study and questions that meet those objectives. In some cases you may need to write additional questions — but do not have too many.

2 Make sure that the case study is relevant and comprehensible to your group. All facilitators should have read the case study and answered the questions as part of the preparation for the training. At this stage required timings should be calculated.

3 Be aware of differences and difficulties in reading ability and language comprehension, particularly where people are reading in a language that is not their first. It may be better to read the case study aloud, if it is not too long. It is important that some people in a small group do not start answering the questions while others are still reading the case study.

4 The timings on this activity are approximate, and will vary according to the length and complexity of the case study, and the depth and range of the questions.

5 You may need to adapt or re-write case studies to make them culturally relevant. Where possible, use case studies that match the experience of the group. People should be able to recognise the situations described in the case study.

6 If you decide to write your own case study, make sure that it illustrates a real issue, which you have heard people describe and which will generate discussion.

7 Include clues to the key issues, but don't spell out all the answers.

8 If you write case studies, as with any exercise, be very clear in your objectives, test out the exercise on colleagues or co-fieldworkers first, and re-write. See ***Handout 59*** *Designing case studies.*

9 If the nature of your workshop requires preparation of reports on situations, programmes or projects from participants, it would be useful to send participants the ***Handout 59*** *on preparing case studies, and the Timeline* ***Handout 75****, to assist them in preparing their information.*

10 The Mozambique case study is a fairly typical report on a refugee situation. Often such reports have major gaps in information, and do not provide you with what you need to assess a situation and plan interventions. Frequently this is precisely because gender-sensitive data collection methods have not been used.

11 This case study has been used as the basis for a full day's training — the case study was presented, and Question 1 discussed in small groups. The groups reconvened to share ideas. They repeated the process with Questions 2 and 3. Question 4 was only tackled at the end of the day, after a number of sessions on assessment and appraisal, and planning interventions.

Case study: Ngwee nutrition group and the co-operative

The women of Ngwee were very worried about malnutrition in their area. It seemed that more and more of their children were weak and sick and many died from simple causes such as diarrhoea. Others had symptoms of kwashiorkor or marasmus.

Then they heard that the church was giving free milk to nutrition clubs, so they decided to form a group. Twice a week they met at the church to receive and distribute the milk. This helped them a little bit, but it was not enough to solve the problems. When they met, the women started discussing what else they could do to improve the situation. In that area, there is a Development Committee which is made up of representatives of all the various development projects in the area including church groups. The Development Committee is responsible for all the projects, including obtaining funding from international donor agencies.

When one of the women from Ngwee Nutrition Group spoke to someone from the Development Committee about their problems, he told them about a nutrition club in town which could teach them new recipes and help them to start vegetable gardens. Before long, the women had managed to contact the nutrition club, who sent someone to teach them how to make buns and fritters, and to explain that for a good balanced diet you need energy-giving foods such as starch and fats, vitamins, and body-building proteins.

Unfortunately the group was unable to follow the recipes, due to shortages of cooking oil and the high price of flour. They understood about a balanced diet, but this could not help them buy meat, chicken or even fish, which few people in Ngwee could now afford. Groundnuts had also been suggested as a good food, but they did not grow groundnuts any more. The land on which they previously grew groundnuts is now used to grow cotton and tobacco.

The vegetable gardens were also a failure due to lack of water. The nearest stream was 2km away and the women had no time to go and fetch water for the garden. Many of the women would spend long hours buying vegetables from a local farmer and then travelling to market to try and resell them for a small profit. At other times of the year they were too busy in the fields evem to do this.

Also in Ngwee was a co-operative, started by some people trying to earn an income by working together. First of all, they dug a fish pond, near the stream. This project was going well and they managed to sell a lot of fish in town. Now they wanted to start rearing small livestock — chickens or ducks.

Some of these co-operative members were men who had wives in the nutrition group. But the men themselves never attended the meeting and knew nothing about nutrition.

Of the profit from selling fish, some men gave a little money to their wives, and some of the money was saved towards the new project for small livestock. The rest they spent on trips into town, and beer.

Whenever the men were at home, they expected their wives to prepare a proper meal for them — even if there was not much food and the rest of the family were sometimes left out. It seemed to the men that many of their children got ill and died and they wondered if their wives learnt anything at all in their nutrition group!

Discussion questions

1 What are the gender issues here? (Strategic and practical gender needs, issues related to access and control.)

2 How would you raise them with the partners (development committee) or groups?

3 How could the situation be improved?

(Source: adapted from Zambia Nutrition Group training)

Case study: Mozambican refugees in Eastern Transvaal, South Africa, update report (1989)

In two separate districts Mhala and Nkomazi the figure for registered refugees is now about 33,000. In the last three months new refugees arriving at between 1,600 and 2,400 a month, as a result of intensified conflict in Southern Mozambique. Approximate breakdown of registered refugees is 62 per cent children, 30 per cent women.

Reception arrangements

New arrivals come to one of three reception points to register. Most have walked for over a week with little food en route. Many come direct from scene of conflict. Most have witnessed or suffered violence — high incidence of reports of rape. Families often split in transit. Reception camps have health workers (MSF doctor in Nkomazi, nurses from Tinstwalo hospital in Mhala) and relief-committee worker, with other assistants. New arrivals screened for malaria, children immunised. Given blankets and minimal set cooking utensils and (ICRC) food to take them up to first distribution date. In Mhala can stay at reception area for several days. In Nkomazi have to find other shelter immediately.

Settlement

About 70 per cent of refugees live in separate all-Mozambican settlements, close to local communities. Shelter is self-built huts — no agency assistance given with shelter. The other 30 per cent (in Nkomazi area) are taken in by local families. No land available to refugees for cultivation. Where refugees share with local families concern that food supplies are diluted across both families. Some concern about abuse of position of some refugees within local families.

Food distribution

Food distribution organised by Hlanganani (Nkomazi) and Phalalani (Mhala) Relief Committees. Both bodies made up of local political figures (mainly local chiefs), agencies involved in work with refugees, ICRC and homeland government reps. No Mozambicans on committees — committees invite 'representatives' in for some discussions. This usually means the few Ndunas (traditional chiefs) present among refugees.

Food distributed to over 50 different 'points' in districts on a monthly basis. Control through the family card issued at reception. Ration is felt to be 'adequate' to 'generous' (ICRC): basics are mealie meal, cooking oil, salt, sugar, soap with variable 'extras' (soup, beans etc). Irregular distribution of seeds for cultivation.

Recent decision to reduce food supply to family through distribution point. Target food resources instead at schools and pre-schools in the districts to reach both local and refugee children..

Water

Access to water varies considerably. No distinct Mozambican settlement has its own water supply. For some settlements relatively good access with waterpump half to 1 kilometre from settlement. But many areas water source over 1km and up to 3 or 4km from settlement (especially small Mozambican settlements). All water is borehole source. All water points shared with, located in, local communities. In recent months several points of tension and conflict over water when two out of three borehole pumps near big settlements have broken, leaving pressure on remaining source. Control of water through local chief structures, particularly when conflict.

Health

Health of arriving refugees is often poor but usually linked to immediate problems of travel with little food. Increasing incidence of malaria amongst newly arrived in recent months has caused concern. Amongst settled refugees persistent low grade malnutrition in young children reported in Nkomazi district (also in local children). Several outbreaks of diarrhoea reported in last month. Sanitation facilities are still inadequate in most settlements — pit latrines now provided in most but not in sufficient numbers. Health-care provision is varied. At Reception areas MSF presence and local health-care back-up ensures good initial care and screening.

Once in settlements refugees have access to local health care facilities which are generally thin on the ground and overstretched. Some concern that drug and other supplies to local clinics are irregular and not sufficient to meet new pressures from population increase. Main hospital — Shongwe — for Nkomazi is 40 kilometres from main refugee concentrations. Tinstwalo Hospital in Mhala more central to settlements.

Economic possibilities

No refugees have significant land for cultivation. Most grow some crops around shelter (maize and some root crops) but with poor results this last year due to lack of rain in key months. Some temporary work opportunities on latrine construction through World Vision — this programme is now coming to an end. Main work opportunities are as farm labourers on 'white' farms. Poorly paid however and with constant risk of deportation — means leaving 'homeland' area. (In recent incidents 19 women denounced to police by farmer employing them — to avoid three weeks' pay — are deported). In longer-established settlements several sewing projects set up but as yet not financially successful.

Educational provision

Limited educational and child care provision, mainly at pre-school level. Some seven creches in Mhala and Nkomazi take in about 1,100 children from age two to six. Creche workers are all young Mozambicans. Older children can enter local schools at about seven or eight — in Nkomazi with language problem (taught in Siswati not Shangaan). Teenage entry into school system particularly problematic. Pre-schools have their own feeding programme. No adult education or awareness programme around health, nutrition etc.

Status and harassment

All refugees on six-month 'visas' from homeland governments. Not valid in 'white' South Africa. SADF (army) patrols settlement areas in Nkomazi and regularly detains and deports refugees found 'without documents'. Instances of harassment and beatings common in Nkomazi with two deaths in last three months. In Mhala situation is more settled with little SADF presence but refugees leaving the district for work are liable to deportation. Some local hostility and resentment in recent months over food distribution, firewood and water issues.

Agencies involved

Direct work with refugees is done by local agencies. Catholic Church, Operation Hunger and SCF (South Africa) main actors in food-distribution programme. South African Council Churches (Protestant) less direct programme involvement but has funded creche construction. World Vision solely responsible for sanitation programme. Health-care programme monitored (but rather informally) from two local hospitals. No UNHCR presence in South Africa. ICRC has overview role and particular concern for status of refugees. Some local coordination through two relief committees but no central coordinating body across different districts. No South African government involvement. Homeland governments — KaNgwane and Gazankulu — sympathetic but increasingly concerned about pressures on local services.

Questions:

1 What do you think the gender issues are here?

2 What additional information do you need?

3 How will you get the information?

4 What would you do, as an NGO, and why?

Handout 59 *Activity 56*

Designing case studies

The usefulness and limitations of case studies

We use a number of case studies in this Manual, to teach specific frameworks of analysis (such as the Harvard Method, a Timeline, or the Capacities and Vulnerabilities Analysis); to draw out learning points with relation to gender from a "real" situation (such as the Ngwee Nutrition Group, the Bangladesh Refugees studies); to pose problems to participants which they can relate to their own experience and attempt to solve.

Case studies are useful because they give participants in a training course the chance to practice their skills in the kind of situation they may encounter. The way they are used in this Manual allows for discussion in groups and collective learning, so that participants can share their experience and knowledge with reference to a particular case. Where the case study has been drawn up and is presented by one or more of the participants, this aspect of learning can be stronger and more effective.

The limitations of case studies is that they give the illusion of being real, but if fact they are a small snapshot of reality, using highly selected facts. Because this is a gender training Manual, the case studies focus on information relevant to gender issues, necessarily reducing the focus on other issues. Reality is much more complex than is apparent in a case study — but this is also part of the learning. Participants may be frustrated because the information they require for analysis or for planning is not in the study — this is often the case in real life, and points to the need for gathering more relevant information, in more effective ways.

The case studies we present here are drawn from a variety of sources, and apart from those developed specifically for use with an activity (such as the Mwea Case Study), are examples of the kind of study you may need. They are of course chosen because they are relevant to the analysis you are teaching, but we would recommend that wherever possible, you prepare for the workship by asking participants to write up their own case studies and bring them. This way other participants can ask the presenter for information which is lacking, and the case becomes much more alive and immediate.

Writing case studies: general points

Writing case studies is not easy. They have to be tailor-made for their teaching purpose, as much as possible. If you are asking participants to write them, they will need guidance. So will you, if you plan to write case studies yourself for the workshop. Here are some questions to ask before starting to write:

- **What is the case study for?** Make sure you are clear about this. Why do you need one? How will you use it?
- **Who is the case study for?** What are the needs of your users/readers? What information do they require? How is the case study going to be relevant to their work?
- **How long have you got?** The length of the case study will depend on the time you have. Short ones can be as effective to teach particular things as long ones.
- **What is the experience of your training group?** You may be able to ask participants to prepare their own. If you are going to write them yourself, make sure that the cases you use are relevant to the work of your group.
- **Are you going to use a real or a hypothetical situation?** If you want to teach a very specific analytical framework (for example, the CVA framework) you could draw up a hypothetical case study which will contain all the information you need to complete the exercise of analysis. However, reality is not like that, and people will have to analyse real situations, which do not present all the relevant information in the form you need it. If you are going to use a real situation, you need to do careful research, bearing in mind all the points above.

How to prepare a case study of a real situation

Below are some guidelines Oxfam has found useful in researching and preparing case studies of development or relief interventions. They are not comprehensive, and the way you go about the research will depend very much on your specific needs.

- Clearly identify the main issue you want to bring out in the case study (for example, the effects of structural adjustment policies on women), and any sub-issues related to it (for example, problems in NGO development interventions attempting to address the situation).
- Collect background data from research papers, newspapers, surveys and reports, and your own work in your organisation in analysing projects and discussing issues.
- Plan your research: the meetings you will need, the people you want to interview, who you will have to contact to set it up. Explain clearly to the NGO or other organisation who will help you set up the visit what your interests and intentions are in preparing the case study.
- Think about information-gathering techniques. You may wish to use informal interviews, formal interviews, checklists of questions, participatory techniques such as village mapping or seasonal calendars. Make sure the techniques are appropriate to the people you will talk to. Make sure you are clear about the information you are

looking for, but also open to information you may not have anticipated.

- Make sure you talk to a range of people, both women and men. They may include NGO staff, government officials, local organisations, women and men from villages or urban communities, health or agricultural workers, teachers and so on. Try and talk to different ages, and people from different ethnic or caste groups, and record different views of the situation;
- Incorporate **change** into your research: how has the situation changed over time? (you could use the Timeline activity presented in this manual) What are the expectations of women and men for future change?
- Make sure that you have a strong section on the **results** of any project intervention you are looking at. This is the heart of the case study. It must show clearly **what** happened, and give clear indicators of **why** it happened — from a gender perspective. What happened to the women, and what happened to the men? What were the similarities and differences?

What a case study should cover

Your case study should include the following:

- A section on the international, national and local context of the intervention (political, cultural, socio-economic), and implications for women and gender relations;
- A section on activities of the key actors in the situation, such as local NGOs, local organisations of women and men, local authorities, national and regional government, external agenciessuch as foreign funders, and what the impact of these are on the lives of women, and on gender relations;
- A section on gender relations in the context of the development or relief intervention, including an account of the gender division of labour, access to and control of natural resources and to project benefits, decision-making in the urban community or village, the influence of other social variables such as age, class, ethnicity, caste, and so on;
- An account of the aims of the intervention, and its operational strategies;
- A section on the results of the intervention in terms of changes to the lives of women, and changes in gender relations.

Time: 1½ -2 hrs

Mwea rice scheme

Objectives

1 To enable people to work out for themselves the likely impact of a project which was not focused on women and which took no account of gender needs or roles.

2 To compare predicted and actual results.

3 To try and redesign a project to incorporate gender needs.

Method

1 Hand out copies of the Mwea Rice Scheme case study (Part 1 only: **Handout 60**) to the participants, and ask them to form small groups of five or six, and discuss Part 1 of the Case Study. This describes the objectives, expectations and plan of implementation for a rice-irrigation settlement scheme in Kenya. It also describes the pre-existing farming system and gives other background information. Ask the groups to write on newsprint:
a. Do you think the objectives of the scheme will be met? Why/Why not?
b. What might be other effects of the scheme (positive and negative)?
(30 mins)

2 After each group has completed the two questions in Part 1, hand them Part 2. (**Handout 61**) This lists the results of the scheme, social and economic, for the women and their families. Ask each group to write on newsprint:
a. What are the similarities/differences of your answers to Part 1 in relation to the actual effects of the project?
b. What other information would you need?
c. Re-design the project to take account of gender needs.

(30-40 mins)

3 Ask each group to put their newsprints on the wall for others to read, and in turn share answers.

4 Lead a large group discussion on the case study. *(30 mins)*

Materials

Handouts: Case-study Parts 1 and 2 (**Handouts 60** and **61**
Newsprints, and marker pens.

Facilitator's Notes

1 It is crucial not to give out Part 2 until Part 1 is completed, as it contains the 'answers' to the questions in Part 1.

2 It may be useful to accompany this exercise with a showing of the video The Lost Harvest. *This is about a similar rice-irrigation scheme in Gambia and its effects on women. (See Resources Section)*

3 Facilitators should work through this case study themselves before using it with a group. In the discussion, the following points often emerge:

a. Surprise that the project is seen as successful in its own terms.

b. Implicit assumptions on which the project was based were incorrect (e.g. that increase in household income implies increase in household welfare).

c. Encouragement that participants can spot many, but not all, of the likely problems; not all of which are listed in Part 2.

4 This case study can be done independently of, or be used in addition to, the Harvard and Moser methods of analysis.

5 If time is short or participants are not directly involved in project work, Question c. on re-designing the programme may be omitted. In any case, many people find that they would prefer to go back to the beginning and consult with both men and women, rather than simply 'add-in gender' to the existing project.

Mwea case study: A rice irrigation settlement scheme in Kenya

Part 1: The setting up of the scheme

The Mwea rice-irrigation settlement scheme in Kenya is one where very poor landless peasants of the Kikuyu and Embu tribes have been settled, and taught to grow rice as a cash crop.

The scheme covers over 30 villages with between 400 and 700 people living in each. 'Mwea' is one of four administrative divisions in the larger scheme.

Objectives of the scheme: To raise household income and hence household welfare by the introduction of a monocrop of irrigated rice.

Expectations: the household will adopt rice as a staple-food crop and as a cash crop, the sale of which will provide cash to purchase all other household needs.

The pre-existing farming system

The off-scheme farming system of the Kikuyu and Embu people was characterised by relatively independent spheres of responsibility for men and women. Men and women had their own plots of land. Men generally grew maize and coffee as cash crops; women grew subsistence crops of maize and beans to meet the household's consumption requirements.

In the production process, labour was not completely segregated and women performed about half of their agricultural work on men's crops. Women's labour input on men's crops would vary according to whether men were physically present on the farm (in some cases men engaged in outside work or business or lived away from home). Women would increase their labour input when men were present (whether or not men were working on the crop). But even when men were present, women had considerable freedom in organising the work they performed on men's crops.

Women controlled the production of their plots and used it to provide for the household's subsistence needs; any surplus produce from these plots was sold and the income retained by women for their own use. Men controlled the income from cash crops and this was not usually shared at all with women. In most cases, women were unaware of whether the household's monetary income would be adequate to supply the household's needs. Indeed, a woman would consider herself a failure if she had to ask her husband to provide food which she would ordinarily have grown herself.

Other information

Many men are polygamous. Harvest time is busy. Families have to hire help, or get help from relatives, which will be reciprocated. Additional helpers have to be cooked for.

Implementation of the scheme

Families were allocated plots of good, irrigated land to grow rice through the male head of the family. There was some land available for gardens around the outside of the main farm land. These were divided into equal-sized plots.

Families were settled onto the scheme. Each was provided with a new two-roomed basic house.

Questions

1 Do you think the objectives of the scheme will be met? Why/why not?

2 What might be other effects of the scheme (positive and negative)?

Case study: A rice irrigation settlement scheme in Kenya

Part 2: The results of the scheme

The scheme has been regarded as a model of development. It has achieved its objectives. It has been very successful in getting people to grow rice productively as a cash crop, and household incomes have risen. But it is evident that these higher incomes have not necessarily been translated into improvements in the whole family's welfare, certainly in respect of nutrition.

Moving to the scheme meant that women worked longer and harder, because they also work in the rice fields which their husbands lease in the scheme. Some men work in their fields themselves, but women work more hours than men do in the rice fields. Many men work off the settlement, in nearby towns, and where this happens women have to take on work which men normally do. This flexibility in the division of labour does not work both ways; men would not take bananas to market, carry water, weed, or cook. These are regarded as female tasks.

Although women do most of the work, the procedures of the scheme treat the male head of the household as if he was the main decision-maker and worker. Women receive no payment at all. Women remained in control of the production of their own plots and had access to the proportion of the harvested paddy which was allocated by the scheme for 'home consumption'. Adults in Mwea disliked rice as a food. The rice to which women had access for 'home consumption' was therefore used as gifts to relatives, as a black-market currency to pay casual labour, or in the last resort to feed children and outside workers. So in some cases this was a possible source of small amounts of income for women. Men remained in control of the cash income from the rice crop which increased in the scheme due to successful yields being obtained. It is not clear how men used their higher incomes.

Fuelwood, which women would have collected in the off-scheme environment, had to be bought within the scheme, further necessitating cash incomes for women. Moreover, prices of almost all commodities were higher in the scheme than outside it, so reducing the purchasing power of any income women did obtain. Women at Mwea do most of the farm work in the cultivation of rice, as well as cultivating maize and beans for family consumption on their own domestic plots. The demands of these two conflicted at certain times of the year, especially at harvest time.

Women do not complain of the long hours of work. In fact the women who are most dissatisfied are those who do not have their own subsistence plots. Generally women felt that this was the biggest difficulty facing them on the scheme.

Where women do not have land on which to grow maize and beans, they have to ask their husbands for money to buy them. Women are accustomed to being the providers of food. They feel uncomfortable asking their husbands, or relying on their 'generosity' in order to fulfil food requirements. It implies they are not good housewives. It also makes them dependent in a new way. Also, evidence of deteriorating nutritional standards of children of families in the scheme suggests that subsistence requirements were not always being met.

For those women who have been allocated plots there are problems too. Some women with large families found the standard-size plot too small for their needs. Most of the plots are too far from their houses for women to be able to return home during the day to feed small children and to start the lengthy cooking process. This is another example of competing demands on women's time and energy in their responsibilities at home, as mothers, and for agricultural work.

There are other aspects about life on the settlement which make it difficult and unpleasant for women. The two-roomed houses have not been provided with outside hearths for cooking or with chimneys in the dwellings themselves. Cooking indoors, with no chimney, soots up the room and makes cooking unpleasant. It also makes the room unusable for sleeping. So, the whole family sleeps in the second room in many households. This is not only uncomfortable, it deprives people of privacy. Adults feel it is improper to have their children sleeping in the same room, and if a man has two wives it is considered indecent.

Cooking is particularly a problem at harvest time. In addition to working on their husbands' and others' fields, women have to cook for additional helpers (hired or reciprocated labour). If a woman does not have enough cooking pots and other utensils, she may have to go through the lengthy cooking procedure twice every day.

Many women involved in the scheme experience a high degree of stress. They say they are not happy there. Men find it difficult to get wives who will live there. And it is said that every year numbers of women leave, deserting their husbands.

Questions

1 Compare your answers to questions 4 and 5 of Part 1 with the actual effects of the scheme. What are the similarities/differences?

2 What other information would you have needed in order to anticipate the effects?

3 How would you re-design the programme to take account of gender needs?

Time: 40 mins

Mini-case studies

Objectives

1 To examine a number of short case studies of women's development projects and identify strengths and weaknesses.

Method

1 Ask participants to form groups of four.

2 Hand out the case studies (**Handout 62**) and ask participants to go through each of them, asking the following questions:
a. How does this project affect the workload or status of women?
b. How, if at all, could this project be sustained?
c. How, if at all, does this project contribute to the equality of women?
(20 mins)

3 Ask each small group to feed back to the whole group.
(20 mins)

Materials

Handout 62
Paper and pens

Mini-case studies

Case study: Education

An evening literacy-project for women ran for six months very successfully. Women studied basic literature and numeracy materials for two hours each evening. The emphasis of the materials was centred on health, agriculture and the status of women. After six months the project ceased and classes were set up in another district, again for six months.

A year later evaluators of the project found that the women had lost their literacy skills through lack of use and their status had remained unchanged within the community.

Case study: Environment

Women were selected to be the focus of a forestry project involving the planting of sapling trees in nurseries. They were asked to form village management-committees, and female extension workers came every month to talk with and train women in nursery and forestry techniques.

A few months after the initial meeting the government enforced a law that the nearest forests, which were situated two hours' walk away, uphill, were to become part of a national park and it would therefore be illegal to gather firewood within the park boundaries.

The women felt helpless and had no obvious means available to them to protest against the environmental policy of the government. The female forestry-extension workers, who were non-local, attempted to organise a campaign among the women to protest.

The men in the community were outraged that their women should adopt such a public role and refused to allow their women to attend future meetings with the forestry extension-workers. The women were then compelled to walk greater distances to gather firewood and fodder.

Case study: Relief

The workload of women in a refugee camp meant that only men were able to give their views on the running of the camp to the organisers. Although many separated or widowed women were heads of their family units in the camp, traditionally they were not expected to take part in community-council meetings.

The organisers of the refugee camp attempted to set up mixed committee meetings with 50 per cent representation from men and women but found women were extremely reluctant to come forward.

Case study: Income generation

A project funded by a large international development agency had been set up to target the status of women. Through credit provision, a Women's Development Officer organised with the male bank manager and male Local Development Officer opportunities for women to borrow money for income generating activities. According to the prescribed annual plan the Women's Development officer had to build a child-care centre.

Women in the community were expected to knit numerous garments to sell but there was not a suitable market in the immediate proximity and spare cash in an area of subsistence farming was lacking.

The building of a child-care centre involved carrying local construction materials for many miles, and although women were in favour of the concept of childcare, neither they or the men were willing to spend time building.

The Women's Development Officer predicted failure and felt pressurised by her head office superiors who would enquire why money had not been spent as anticipated. She also felt pressurised by the bank manager who had seen little if any returns on his loans. The Local Development Officer was not particularly supportive. He was of the opinion the women are traditionally agriculturalists and therefore finance is wasted if women are involved in development.

Time: 1½ hrs

Women in a Sudanese camp

Objectives

1 To enable participants to discern and discuss gender issues in an emergency situation, as described in the report of an NGO worker.

(5 mins)

Method

1 Introduce the case study by explaining that it comes from a real-life situation, as described in the report of an NGO worker.

2 Explain that you will be working in small groups, so that everyone can contribute. The case study comes in three parts — the groups will discuss one part at a time. It is not a test but they may, if they wish, see it as a kind of mystery tour.

(5 mins)

3 If there are technical experts in the group e.g. water engineers, stress that the case study is intended to help us to look at gender issues in emergency situations — to look at technical issues as they affect women and men.

(5 mins)

4 Divide the participants into groups of five or six and hand out Part 1 (**Handout 63**) and ask them to discuss the two questions at the end of the sheet. Allow about ten minutes (judging the time by observation of the groups) *(10 mins)*

6 Then hand out Part 2 (**Handout 64**) and ask them to discuss again. *(15-20 mins)*

7 Then hand out Part 3 (**Handout 65**)— this can be handed out to the groups or alternatively you could bring everyone back to the main group before handing out Part 3 and then take the questions as a kind of brainstorm.

(15-20 mins)

8 Lead a general discussion in the main group, taking account of points which should be raised as listed in the *Facilitator's Notes*.

(15 mins)

Materials

Case study and Handouts

Facilitator's Notes:

1 Some of the things that you will be hoping to hear from the group are:

a. They had not expected it to be possible for the group of women to speak to an expatriate male.
b. The group of women was large enough to give them confidence/too large.
c. The sensitive issue of distribution mechanisms (through men) only came out at the end when most women had dispersed.
d. The issue of the food ration was known to the NGO worker — why had nothing been done about it.
e. Although the women see the food as the cause of their diarrhoea it is likely that it is a sanitation problem — both groups are 'right'.
f. Are there things the women hint at (menstruation, harassment)?
g. It is unusual for people to want straight lines of shelter.
h. The needs of children had been overlooked.
i. People were setting up their own ways of regulating problems (by going through the chief structure for maintenance of latrines).

2 You will want to draw some broad conclusions:

a. We should always test our assumptions.
b. Agendas may conflict — between aid workers and affected people, and between women and men.
c. There is a tendency to underestimate women.

3 It is also possible to run this as an activity where the women and men are divided into same-sex groups and are brought together for the discussion of Part 3. If you do this the women will feel much freer to talk about such issues as sexual harassment and violence. Observe whether these issues come up in the men's group.

4 This case study can also be used as a role play. The interpreter may play a key role as a gatekeeper — an important point to note when talking of how to listen to women.

5 This case study has been used with UK groups, with British water engineers and at a workshop in Ethiopia. It stimulated plenty of discussion each time. A difficulty can arise if there is a participant who knows the area concerned and becomes the 'expert' in the group.

Handout 63 *Activity 59*

Case study: Meeting with women in a camp for the displaced, Sudan

Part 1

(This is an extract from a report by an NGO worker in Southern Sudan, where the NGO supports people who have been displaced by the civil war. They are housed in camps where they are largely dependent on NGOs for a daily food ration, and for health and sanitation services. The NGO was concerned about poor sanitation and consequent health risks. The NGO worker decided to convene two separate meetings — one for men and one for women — to find out their views. This is an extract from the account of his meeting with the women.)

On Friday 11 October 1991 the meeting with the women was held. About 80 women crammed into the feeding centre; all types were there, including traditional birth attendants and community health workers, but the majority were probably mothers who would normally have been attending the feeding centre with their children. The only men present were John and myself. Maria translated for me.

The objectives of the meeting were:

1 To learn about women's views on the desirability of pit latrines.

2 To learn about the women's views about the problems over the use of the latrines.

3 To learn about women's views on the maintenance and cleaning of latrines.

4 From what we learned to put together a syllabus for a series of health education workshops on 'Pit latrine use and maintenance'.

The structure of the meeting was kept relatively loose as I wanted this discussion open enough to allow the women to discuss their own concerns as much as my NGO's concerns.

Discuss:

1 What communications problems do you think there might be?
2 What do you think would be the concerns of women in a camp like this (or a refugee camp)?

Meeting with women in a camp for the displaced, Sudan

Part 2 (NGO worker report, continued)

A problem which emerged, however, was that the women's primary concerns are not necessarily connected with the pit latrines at all. Again and again the discussion returned to:

a. The size of the general ration (too small)
b. The content of the ration: it is now not so good as it was. Where is the groundnut paste/salt/beans/soap/cooking oil/milk powder which — they claimed — they used to receive from the NGO in the good old days?
c. Stomach problems caused by the current distribution of Thai dura, which when cooked produces nearly black porridge; women spend much time washing the dura, ridding it of its unpalatable taste.

At one point I asked what the above three points had to do with sanitation and pit latrines. It was stressed vehemently by various women that stomach problems are caused by the poor quality of the food and by the lack of a balanced diet.

Regarding the pit latrines:

1 Women thought on the whole pit latrines are 'a good thing'.
2 They are not currently effective as a sanitation measure as there are not enough of them to reduce the need to use open spaces.
3 Men's and women's latrines should be physically separated by as large a distance as possible. The women stressed that even if it meant a five- minute walk they would still rather walk the distance in order to use a special women's latrine.
4 Children are scared of the pits; they are also scared of the adults (particularly of the men) they might find using the latrines. Women-only latrines would allow the women to spend time in the latrine to teach the children how to use it.
5 There is a problem of overcrowding in the camp. Major objections to overcrowding stem from the fact that men can hear the women's stomach problems (referring to diarrhoea, as was translated to me, but might refer to menstruation).

6 The women expressed a preference for a camp with straight lines, row upon row, rather than the current higgledy-piggledy layout.
7 It was repeatedly stressed that for maintenance and cleaning of the latrines they should be allocated to chiefs, for the use and responsibility of a tribal group only. This repeats what the men said.

Discuss:

What had you predicted and what surprised you about the women's responses?

Meeting with women in a camp for the displaced, Sudan

Part 3

The NGO worker concluded his report of the meeting with the following comments:

We definitely have some pointers for the future. This is the separation of latrines by chief and sex. There is no guarantee that it is feasible to pursue this yet, but it looks as though this is the direction we should go in.

After the meeting with the women was over I chatted with one or two traditional birth attendants and community health workers. Two points emerged:

1 I was surprised to be informed that this was the first-ever meeting between an NGO expatriate representative and a group made up specifically of women only. The women were actually very appreciative of this. During the meeting itself women expressed keenness that similar, further meetings take place along the same lines.

2 The old issue of distributing through men was raised (men not distributing the full ration, selling the remainder to get drunk, and so on). While recognising the dangers of interfering with the status quo I wonder whether there is a tendency to underestimate the women. I replied that my NGO would be happy to distribute through women but that those women interested should organise themselves. I said that widows and women-headed families might be a starting point. If approached by the women with a plan then we can see how to go about implementing it.

Discuss

What are the significant issues/lessons to be learned for work in similar circumstances elsewhere?

C.8 Gender and global issues

This section applies some of the analytical frameworks learned in the previous section to a selection of issues of global concern. We have chosen four sets of issues to illustrate the use of gender analysis.

Gender and conflict: in 1993 Oxfam ran a workshop in Thailand with the AGRA-East (Action for Gender Relations in Asia network for East Asia) on Gender and Conflict: we present a number of activities from that workshop. Armed conflict is, increasingly, having a devastating impact on the lives of women and men in the countries and regions in which Oxfam and other NGOs work. The gender dimensions of conflict are examined in detail in the report of the above workshop (available from Oxfam): in this section we can do no more than offer an introduction to the topic and to the way that gender analysis can illuminate the effects of conflict on women and men.

Gender and the environment: within the context of the search for sustainable development, environmental issues are of central concern to Oxfam's development programme, but we have not run a gender workshop on this topic: we have instead borrowed and adapted two activities from *Gender and Environment:Lessons from Social Forestry and Natural Resource Management*, published by Aga Khan Foundation Canada, and hope to expand our experience of this area of gender analysis. To quote from a paper given by Nanneke Redclift in 1991 to the ODA/NAWO review:

> *We cannot create sustainability on the basis of existing gender inequities, because to do so is once again to subsume women's interests under the wider notion of general and, in this case, even global well-being.*

Gender and economic crisis: a group of activities address the effects of economic crisis from a gender perspective, at the macro-level of Structural Adjustment Policies, and the micro- level of women's daily experience. The micro-level activities can be used with grassroots groups or with NGO groups to examine the kinds of problems that women workers face.

Gender and culture: this is a topic of crucial importance. Religion, as one of the foundation stones of culture in most parts of the world, is also the seat of the most entrenched beliefs and practices relating to the roles of women and men. We present some activities based on texts from the Christian Bible, which have been used primarily with Christian groups. As long as they are balanced with activities from other religions, they can be used in any group looking at the influence of religious tradition in the construction of cultural gender roles. The two activities which use Biblical texts were developed in the African context, for use with Christian women's groups. They could be adapted by replacing the excerpts from the Bible withother religious texts. 'Creation Story' is suitable for use with mixed-sex groups, while the **Activity 73** Chains tht bind us is more suitable for groups of women only.

C.8 Activities

1 Gender and conflict

2 Gender and environment

3 Gender and economic crisis

4 Gender and culture

Time: 2-2½ hrs

The impact of conflict

Objectives

1 To consider ways in which social processes are affected by armed conflict.

2 To explore gender issues in situations of armed conflict.

Method

1 Before the session, prepare flipcharts or OHP transparencies with the texts (or notes from them) on **Handouts 68** Identifying Women's Needs in Conflict, and **69** Women's Issues in the Context of Conflict).

2 Introduce the two case studies, highlighting briefly the impact of conflict on four levels: personal, family, community, state

.(10 mins)

3 Give each participant a copy of both case studies (**Handout 66** and **67)** and ask them to read them through carefully, taking account of the main points at the end of the case studies.

(20-30 mins)

4 Go through the points and issues in **Handouts 68** and **69** using the OHP transparencies or flipcharts you have prepared.

(15-20 mins)

5 Ask the participants to form small groups of three or four, and given each person a copy of the two Handouts. Ask the groups to discuss first one case study, and then the other, in relation to the issues in the Handouts. They should identify women's needs and issues for each case study

.(30-60 mins)

6 Convene the whole group again, and go through any questions raised by the small groups. *(15-20 mins)*

Materials

Flipchart, OHP transparencies, pens
Case Studies and **Handouts 66, 67, 8 and 69**

Facilitator's Notes

1 This is a long session and participants are asked to absorb and think about a lot of information. You may want to have a 10-minute break, for tea or an energising game, between steps 4 and 5.

2 These case studies can also be used for learning the Capacities and Vulnerabilities framework of analysis (CVA), ***Activity 62****.*

3 These case studies were presented in a workshop on conflict by the person who wrote them and knew the situations, and who could therefore respond to questions. We include them here to be used as an introduction to gender and conflict, and as examples of case studies. However, if you are able to, it is better to write up cases yourself about situations you know well, or ask participants to do so. (See also Facilitator's Notes for the CVA ***Activity, 62****, and* ***Handout 59*** *Designing case studies,* ***Activity 56****).. If you or participants write up case studies, make sure they bring out the points you need for the activity i.e. the impact of conflict at the different levels of personal, family, community and State, and that all information takes both women and men into account.*

Uganda case study

Background

Uganda suffered a series of brutal and destructive civil wars and despotic regimes from the late 1960s till the mid-1980s. It is well endowed with agricultural resources, though these were all but destroyed during the war years when people fled from their lands and when huge numbers of animals were killed.

The present government has installed a system of popular representation and overseen a substantial return to production. Insurgency and insecurity continued to exist until recently in the north, but the situation now appears to have stabilised. The country's struggle to regain economic viability puts enormous strain on the small rural producers who form the majority of the population, caught between their own subsistence needs and the needs of the country to collect taxes and to produce for export.

Changes in gender relations

Until about 20 years ago, gender relations among many Ugandan population groups were characterised by a clear division between men's and women's tasks and between the resources each needed to perform them. Broadly speaking, men took responsibility for livestock, over which they had total control, and for the cultivation of cash crops, the income from which was used to underwrite the family's expenses such as taxes, school fees, clothes and basic household supplies. Women helped their husbands on the family farms, following a fairly strict division of labour in which the heaviest tasks were reserved for men. Women also kept fields of their own with which they provided for the family's subsistence needs; they alone worked on these fields and controlled the consumption of the produce, which was never sold and to which men had no access.

This division was backed up by a framework of marriage dominated by the husband's authority but within which wives had certain defined rights, upheld by the clan and the community. From the legal point of view marriage was indissoluble, except by the repayment by the wife's family of the bridewealth that had been paid by the husband. Until this happened, the husband and his clan had total control over the wife's productive and reproductive capacity i.e. neither her produce nor her belongings nor her children were her own, and the burden of supporting her and her children economically fell on her husband and his family. Many Ugandan communities practised the 'inheritance' of widows by the surviving brother of a deceased husband; a widow who refused this arrangement would not only have to fend for herself but would be entirely dispossessed by her husband's family, and stripped of all except — and sometimes including — the clothes she stood up in.

Since then, various factors have impacted on gender relations to create an arrangement in which women have the greater share of responsibility and work, yet still the same limited control over resources, and few enabling rights. These factors include the war, male labour migration (leading to women being obliged to take over many previously male functions), and the increasing pressures to find cash which have resulted in even women's food crops being sold. Loss of oxen through war also adds to the family's agricultural labour burden.

Saved from soldier but not from husband

The personal status of women has in certain respects changed for the better. The ending of the war and the disbanding of armed camps has lowered the risks of violence and rape from soldiers; economic opportunities for women have opened up and there is an increased recognition of the importance of their role. However, there are numerous exceptions to this and levels of domestic and other forms of violence against women are still high. Abused women have few refuges: the common understanding among both women and men is that violence is part of marriage and women have no choice but to tolerate it. Likewise women who have been raped, especially if they become pregnant, may not be able to count on the sympathy of their families.

An increased imbalance between men and women

Within the family, the division of labour has changed from being a relatively clear one to being blurred. Women may have to clear land or perform other traditionally male agricultural tasks in men's absence, while men have moved into women's activities wherever there is a profit to be made by doing so. Women have also tended to lose access to their own subsistence land because of the need to concentrate family labour on cash crops, a factor which has sometimes had alarming consequences for food security and for the environment.

Whereas previously it was regarded as a husband's responsibility to pay children's school fees and provide basic household necessities, these are now regarded as women's responsibility. The need to find cash for family expenses imposes an additional labour burden on women, who habitually work without rest from dawn to night, while their husbands are free for the latter part of the day to engage in leisure pursuits. Women often provide their husbands with spending money, which they may use to buy beer, (often coming home drunk and beating their wives) or save so as to marry additional wives. This labour burden is a critical constraint to women's full participation in the lives of their families as well as their communities. However, it is important to point out that there are increasing numbers of men who recognise this problem, many of whom seek to share the burden of domestic work with their wives in spite of often being ridiculed for doing so.

The imbalance between women's and men's work is one of several factors which have led to increased fragility of marriage, and unhappiness in marriage figures very highly in women's accounts of their problems. Fear of violence and of rejection by husbands is a major cultural undercurrent in the songs and poems sung by women. Women married to violent or indolent husbands may decide to continue in unhappy marriages because they seek the respectability that married status brings or because they are offered no sympathy or help from their own families.

Communities have been changed

In the past, irresponsible behaviour on the part of men, women and young people was censured by the community. Now community pressures have all but disappeared and this has had both welcome and unwelcome effects. On the one hand, brutal punishments such as those meted out in cases of unmarried pregnancy (to the girl and to the boy if he could be identified) are no longer practised. On the other hand, the moral education of children is increasingly neglected as fathers spend more and more time in the bars and mothers are more and more overloaded with work. One consequence of this is the perpetuation of dysfunctional attitudes towards the opposite sex. Similarly, violent or unreasonable husbands are no longer held up to criticism.

In some areas of the country, especially in the north where camps of armed soldiers of various armies have been in existence, there is a growing problem of 'camp followers' — women who have no means of support other than to attach themselves to garrisons, providing sexual favours for the armed forces. Many of these women have been rejected by their communities after being raped — sometimes by the soldiers themselves — or have been repudiated by their husbands, and have been unable to rely on the support of their families.

A positive outcome of the present development outlook of the country is the widespread acceptance of women's role in community affairs. Women are influential in local government and there are a large number of women's groups of different sorts which play important community roles. Women are widely represented in community-based (mixed) groups.

No consideration of gender relations in Uganda can be complete without mentioning AIDS, which is now affecting every village and every section of the community. As is well-known now, women are affected by AIDS not only through their own sexual relations but also as mothers and grandmothers of AIDS patients. There is little doubt that the disruption of the war and the post-war years, and the continued presence of camps of armed forces in someparts of the country, have contributed substantially to the spread of the disease.

The role of the State

The present Ugandan government has put much weight behind its policy of encouraging the participation of women in all areas of national life. A Women's Ministry has been set up to review projects and ensure that women's needs are taken care of. A minimum number of women is required in local government councils at all levels, in addition to the inclusion of specific women's representatives. A constitutional commission is reviewing, amongst other things, women's legal rights, and these rights should be enshrined in the new constitution.

The implementation of such positive policies is beset by many constraints, not least the lack of funds from which all government initiatives suffer, and the even greater lack of resources allocated specifically to women's activities. Moreover, the Women in Development policy as spelt out by the government has been criticised for being focused on encouraging women into ever-more-intensive income-generation, thus increasing their burden of work without making changes in their position in society or in their control of resources.

Main points

1 The division of labour has become much more flexible following the war. This has come about through necessity and has resulted in a huge burden of work for women.

2 Women, whether in marriage or single heads of families, have had to take responsibility for managing and providing for their families. The ending of the war has not resulted in this burden being lifted.

3 Violence against women is still common, and is a function of the levels of violence in society as a whole and of the lack of respect for women in general.

4 Government policies and pronouncements have had a very positive effect in enabling women to take wider public and family roles. However, since they have been focused on increasing women's productivity, they have not tended to amount to much more than an increasing imposition of work on women.

Somalia case study

Background

The Somali nation is spread through five countries of the Horn of Africa, divided by boundaries imposed by colonial divisions. Somalis are predominantly pastoral people, living in a desert environment which is very prone to drought, though towards the south of Somalia higher rainfall permits a variety of different livelihoods including agro-pastoralism and settled agriculture.

The clan system forms the basis of society and its breakdown has been one of the main factors in the current civil war. A clan is a group of people descended from a common ancestor and claiming priority access to a certain piece of land and its resources (such as water and grazing). Clans are divided into sub-clans and even smaller divisions. Although each clan has its own territory, in practice before the war people were scattered throughout the country, often living in peace as minorities within the territory of another clan. The clan system was held together by a number of factors that created checks and balances, preventing any one clan or individual from acquiring inordinate power. These factors included the sharing of natural resources, intermarriage, and trade links.

The breakdown of the clan system was brought about through colonial interference and through 20 years of manipulation by the previous government, headed by ex-president Siyad Barre. The current civil war began in 1988 in the north of the country and worked its way south, breaking out in the capital, Mogadishu, at the beginning of 1990. The north-west (the ex-British colony) later declared itself the independent state of Somaliland.

One of the main effects of the war was to cause the movement of people back to their clan territories, the only places where they could feel safe. In some cases, people had to move several times, as the fortunes of the different armed forces changed. Another change was that central and local government collapsed, and with it all service and supply systems. Even for those people who were not obliged to move, production (agricultural and livestock) soon broke down through lack of supplies and through insecurity — animals and crops were looted, and people lost the confidence they needed to carry on producing. All this led eventually to widespread famine, which earned Somalia world-wide publicity, and which still continues, albeit on a reduced scale.

Some systems have survived, however. The clan elders, a traditional male authority structure which had been almost suppressed during Siyad Barre's regime, took over the responsibilities of local government in many areas. Petty trade, mostly carried out by women, continued as long as there was anything to be sold. Men also continued to operate big business, now controlling the profitable trade in arms, food and drugs.

Trapped in their own homes

Traditionally conflict between clans was regulated by certain 'rules of engagement' which ensured that friction was kept within limits and the vulnerable did not suffer. Fighting was carried out only by men; a code of honour ensured that the women and children of any clan were protected. During the present conflict there have been many examples of this code being followed, but equally there have been examples where women and children living as minorities within the territory of an opposing clan have been massacred, and it seems that this code has at least in part been abandoned.

Loss of mobility is a major constraint on women's ability to fulfil their family responsibilities in the present circumstances. Fear of rape or shooting prevents women from leaving their homes. People who stand in food queues (mostly women and older men) run a strong risk of being caught in the cross-fire if gunmen attack the food as it arrives. Lack of clothes is another reason why women may confine themselves to their houses. Women who need to work on their farms or sell goods in the market-place prefer to go out only at midday when the danger is less. Lack of services and supplies also means that women have further than usual to go for water, for example. In one town, a dozen women have been killed by crocodiles while fetching water from the river, because there was no fuel to operate water pumps.

Impoverished by aid

Owing to the absence of men, women have taken on responsibilities for maintaining and providing for the family. This is nothing new for Somali women, many of whose menfolk have worked away from home (in the Gulf states, for example) for decades. But in the present circumstances, when food, money and other basic necessities have been difficult to come by, providing for a family has been exceptionally difficult. Almost the only avenue open to women is petty commerce, and this has been limited by the lack of produce to sell and by the lack of money circulating in the economy. In addition, food aid has brought its own problems. In some places, farmers who have a marketable surplus have been unable to get a price for their produce which covers the production costs, since food aid has depressed prices. Food aid has put many women retailers out of business, especially in the major cities where food distributions are relatively regular. At the same time, people just a few kilometres away are dying of starvation because they are not on the main routes for relief convoys.

The conflict between different clans has had a very divisive effect on the whole Somali community, breaking up friendships and families even among those who have sought refuge outside Somalia. Owing to the general preference for marrying outside the clan, there are many families in which husband and wife are from opposing clans. Many such marriages have been unable to withstand the pressures this has created. When marriages break up, women are affected differently from men since they run the risk of being separated or alienated from their children, who belong to the clan of their father, as well as from their husband.

More work, no voice

Despite the increased responsibility women have had to shoulder as family providers, they have not always found it easy to gain access to the resources they need to meet this responsibility. Councils of elders consist exclusively of men, and there is no place for women in the taking of major community decisions. Men have tended to resist suggestions that women should join committees or take part in decision making about resources. Though the elders have generally taken seriously their responsibility to protect and defend the interests of those in their care, there are nevertheless many women who for one reason or another cannot claim the protection of a well-placed elder. Some observers have remarked that women heads of households report the number of their dependents honestly, while men tend to inflate the numbers to receive more than their fair share of rations; and generally women have difficulty in pushing for their own and their families' interests.

The existence of elders' councils and other male-dominated committees in many localities poses a dilemma for agencies trying to assist the Somali community to recover from the present crisis: on the one hand, the elders have proved to be instrumental in ensuring the survival of many communities and must be supported if genuine recovery is to take place; on the other, a way must be found for the elders to take greater account of women's vital contribution and need for access to mainstream resources.

Women's behaviour has been under stricter control since the coming of foreign troops to Somalia to oversee relief distribution. One woman who was suspected of being over-friendly with French soldiers was stripped, beaten and imprisoned, to be rescued eventually by a women's organisation. A representative of the organisation was reported as saying that the incident 'highlights the powerlessness of women and lack of respect for them in this society'.

When the State is back, how will it respond to women?

In the absence of a national government one cannot talk of the State in Somalia. In future however, the apparatus of the state will reappear. It is difficult to predict whether the war will have had a lasting effect on social attitudes towards women. Pessimists point out that the previous government had generally positive policies towards women's rights and had introduced legal changes (in women's status in marriage and divorce, for example) which were generally advantageous towards women; many of these policies may in future be discredited by association. However, the present situation contains some positive signs, such as the emergence of genuine women's organisations for mutual support.

Main points

1 The situation of women in Somalia highlights the vital needs that women have in conflict situations: particularly for personal protection and for safe access to the means to continue economic activity, whether it be agriculture, animal rearing or commerce.

2 In a situation of such severity, male attitudes towards women may harden and it may become even more difficult than usual for women to be accepted as partners in economic activities and in community councils.

3 Opportunities exist in even the most desperate situations. Community mechanisms can be very resilient and building on them offers the best hope of guaranteeing people's survival both in the short and long term.

(Source: Judy El-Bushra, ACORD, 1993.)

Identifying women's needs in conflict

1 Women's role in the survival of their families and communities is critical. Efforts to support women may be important for their own sake, but in conflict situations they are essential.

2 Women's ability to survive and support others must be seen holistically, addressing issues of personal psychology, protection of and by women, economic resources and activities, community support, and national and international issues of governance, representation and human rights.

3 Women's capacity to extend their economic performance depends not only on access to the means of production, but also to community fora in which their needs can be addressed, as equal and active community members.

4 Women's health issues have to be seen in a total context of collapse of services and support systems as well as of the range and depth of suffering women experience in conflict. Women's health in conflict covers issues of psychological and social adjustment, personal integrity, injury and disability as well as physical and reproductive health.

5 Conflict dramatically increases levels of violence against women, whether from the actual fighting or not. Personal violence is a major threat to women's well-being and hence to the integrity of communities. Violence against women must be addressed at different levels — locally, nationally, and internationally, and further research should be promoted into the factors which enhance it.

6 Trauma is a largely unrecognised outcome of conflict for men, women and children. It needs to be researched and measures taken to help people recover from it at both personal and community levels. Men and women react to psychological stress differently, with women's needs for supportive social networks frustrated by the lack of privacy and opportunities to have intimate conversations with friends and kin.. Meeting men's needs in overcoming trauma may be of direct benefit to women if they lead to more egalitarian relationships.

7 Women's principal focus of identity tends to be the family. It is at the family level

that conflict can cause women much distress and at the same time it is the family that may offer the most solace and security. Demographic imbalance — more women than men, more female-headed households — limits women's marriage prospects.

8 Women's 'invisibility' and the highly personal nature of some of their problems means that identifying their needs cannot be done by superficial methods of assessment.

9 It is essential to recognise the positive outcomes of conflict as well as the negative ones. Women already do so through their efforts to protect, mediate and promote peace, and through their emerging organisations. New roles and new opportunities may emerge for women in times of conflict: men also have to adjust in various ways, and new arrangements and new attitudes can be judiciously nurtured by NGOs with an appropriate strategic vision.

Handout 69 *Activity 60*

Women's issues in the context of conflict

1 Women-headed households:

temporary, in the context of displacement until reunited with spouse in original place of residence; or

permanent, in the context of death of spouse, or resettlement in a far away place without the spouse who may have decided to stay behind in the conflict area or join the armed forces.

Specific problems:

1 Increased burdens as women are left alone to care for children and the aged.
2 Issue of survival/increased marginalisation in a society where the sexual division of labour determines allocation of resources, rights and opportunities (statistics from Third World countries show that women-headed households tend to be the poorest).
3 More vulnerable to sexual abuse (though women who have their spouses around have also been raped, some in front of their defenceless and fearful spouses).
4 Mental stress/psychological impact of war and its consequences; women have to attend to the needs of family members who have been scarred by war even while they suffer severe stress themselves, and the damage and vulnerability caused by conflict.

2 Sexual abuse and harassment, in the context of the following:

within area/community of conflict, during operations (civilians caught in the war, local or international);
under interrogation/detention by military;
when seeking welfare assistance (e.g. evacuation, food, water, health services).

Forms of sexual abuse/specific problems:

1 Rape: military/political rape (repeated rape by one man/multiple rape).
2 Sexual harassment: threat of sexual abuse; humiliation through verbal vulgarities and abuse by men; vulnerability to touching of sensitive/privateparts by men.
3 Sexual slavery: in the context of forced, regular sexual favours through the mistress system.

4 Sexual commodification: military prostitution, as an established institution/ culture of patriarchy.

3 Severe condition of reproduction-related responsibilities among women civilians caught in the midst of military operations/total war tactics and strategies:

Specific problems: (outside of sexual abuse and harassment, and as women-headed households)

1 As food producers, procurers and preparers: increased hardship due to food blockades, no man's land (limited mobility), food quotas, economic constriction, devastation of livestock/crops;

2 As household health managers: increased hardship due to bombings and strafing resulting in deaths in the household, deaths of infants and children due to malnutrition and outbreak of epidemics, cutting-off of institutional support, limited mobility;

3 As child-carers: unimagined hardship due to all of the above, as managers of children during evacuations, bombing, etc.
As pregnant and lactating mothers: malnutrition, physical and emotional stress.

4 Women's health: (there is a need to separate this as an issue since most often, it is only the health of children and mothers which is addressed in the context of relief assistance during armed conflicts and in evacuation centres)

Specific health problems:

1 Malnutrition among women.

2 Maternal health;

3 Psychological/emotional stress or instabilities resulting from war and its consequences (death, dislocation, rape, etc.).

4 Physical disabilities/illnesses arising from war that make it difficult for women to carry out critical reproductive roles.

5 Sexually transmitted diseases and/or viral/bacterial infection: may be due to rape, inadequate/poor sanitation; often overlooked by women themselves; if unattended, may lead to more serious reproduction-related illnesses such as cancer.

(Source: Gigi Francisco, Women's Resource and Research Centre, April 1991)

Time: 1 hr

Drawing lessons from case studies

Objectives

1 To draw lessons from the case studies in **Activity 60**.

2 To provide a framework to look at gender in conflict.

Method

1 Explain the activity and distribute the coloured cards (1 set, or 1 card per person; in a large group, each person has one card; in a smaller group, each person could have a set of four). Explain that each colour represents a different level: personal, family, community, State.

(5 mins)

2 Ask each participant to write on their card one lesson they have learnt about the impact of conflict, at the level their card represents.

3 Ask the participants to bring the cards and stick them to the board. Ask two participants to help out in organising the cards by common issue at each level.

(20-30 mins)

4 Read out the cards and using the lessons learned, present the broad outline of the way conflict affects gender at all levels.

(20-30 mins)

Materials

32 cards (4 colours)
Blutak or Sellotape

Facilitator's Notes

1 As the previous activity (60) presents a considerable amount of information, it is important to come back to the issues after a break, to give participants a chance to absorb and process the information. Using cards helps to make it more graphic and direct.

2 Use bright, distinct colours for cards to make the levels clear.

Time: 1½-2 hrs

Capacities and vulnerabilities analysis

Objectives

1 To provide participants with a tool to analyse people's needs in times of crisis.

2 To look at ways of identifying women's and men's strengths and weaknesses during crisis.

3 To look at agency interventions in emergencies.

Method

1 Present the Capacities and Vulnerabilities Analysis framework to participants, based on **Handout 70**,allowing time for questions, and using flipcharts or OHP to show charts. *(30 mins)*

2 Ask the participants to form groups of three or four, and give each participant a copy of the El Salvador case study **Handout 72**,to read through. *(10 mins)*

3 When they have read the case study, give each group two copies of the matrix on **Handout 71** and ask them to fill out one chart for the situation of the refugees before they fled; and when that is completed, to fill in the second chart for the situation of the refugees during their time in the camp. *(30 mins)*

4 In the large group, ask each group to report back briefly on their analysis. Ask the to identify any difficulties. Was there sufficient information? *(20-30 mins)*

5 Sum up the session, highlighting:
a Gender relations change in conflict situations.
b Despite negative impact, conflict opens up opportunities for change.

c In most situations, people have resources/capacities for survival.

d Women's capacities have been ignored far too often; this leads to discrimination and can make a project inefficient.

e Disaster-preparedness requires a gradual understanding of capacities and vulnerabilities to be able to respond without undermining men and women.

Materials

Flipchart, pens, **Handouts 70, 71, and 72.**

Facilitator's Notes

1 This framework could also be used with other case studies in this section — for example the Uganda and Somalia cases in Activity 60. These two case studies provide a picture of situations rather than specific interventions. If you use CVA with one of them, you could adapt the activity by asking the participants to fill out the chart, and then respond to the question: What could your agency do to reduce vulnerabilities and increase capacities in this situation?

2 Before teaching this method, it would be advisable to look at the original book, if possible: ***Rising from the Ashes; Development Strategies in Times of Disaster****, by Mary B. Anderson and Peter J. Woodrow, published by UNESCO and Westview Press, 1989.*

3 Make sure you don't allow participants to make any assumptions and guesses where the information is insufficient — challenge these if they appear.

4 Please bear in mind that this framework, like the Harvard frameworks, requires detailed information of the kind it is difficult to provide in a Manual like this. Ideally, CVA should be used with a situation with which the facilitator or participant is very familiar. They should present the case study, and be able to answer questions which participants ask in order to fill out the matrix. CVA should always be applied first to a situation, and can then be applied to the intervention to assess whether capacities and vulnerabilities were identified by the project and appropriately addressed.

Capacities and vulnerabilities analysis (CVA)

'Development is a process by which vulnerabilities are reduced and capacities are increased.'

The Capacities and Vulnerabilities Analysis was developed by the Harvard International Relief and Development Project by Mary B. Anderson and Peter J. Woodrow. It is outlined in *Rising From the Ashes: Development Strategies in Times of Disaster*, by Mary B. Anderson and Peter J. Woodrow published by UNESCO and Westview Press Inc. It is a tool intended to help predict the outcome of interventions as well as assess them by mapping out the strengths and weaknesses of people in an emergency.

CVA is based on the central idea that people's existing strengths, or capacities, and weaknesses, or vulnerabilities, determine the way they respond to crisis. The aim of interventions in emergencies should be to increase, in the long term, people's capacities and reduce their vulnerabilities. This is a developmental approach to relief in emergencies.

- **Capacities**: are the existing strengths in individuals and social groups. They are related to people's material and physical resources, their social resources and their beliefs and attitudes. They are built over time and determine people's ability to cope with crisis and recover from it.

- **Vulnerabilities:** are the long-term factors which weaken the ability of people to cope with sudden onset or drawn-out emergencies. They also make people more susceptible to disasters. Like capacities, they are also categorised in CVA into material/physical, social/organisational and attitudinal/motivational.

It is important to distinguish **vulnerabilities** from **needs**. **Needs** are immediate requirements for survival or recovery from crisis. They are often addressed by short-term, practical interventions (such as relief food). Vulnerabilities require the long-term strategic solutions which are part of development work.

Capacities, vulnerabilities and needs are differentiated by gender — as they are by other factors, such as race, caste, class, ethnicity and age. Women and men experience crisis differently, according to their gender roles. They have different needs and interests. Women, by virtue of their lower economic, social, and political status, tend to be more vulnerable to crisis. They may also be more open to change, and gender roles can change rapidly as a result of emergencies. CVA enables these forms of social differentiation to be taken into account and mapped out on the matrix. (See **Handout 39**)

The CVA framework distinguishes three categories of capacities and vulnerabilities. These are:

- **Physical or Material**: these include features of the land, climate and environment where people live, or lived before the event; their health, skills, housing, technologies, water and food supply; their access to capital and other assets. All of these will be different for women and for men. While women and men suffer material deprivation during crisis, they always have some resources left, such as recoverable goods or skills. These are capacities upon which agencies can build.

- **Social or Organisational**: this category refers to the social fabric of a population or group, and includes structures like families and kinship groups such as clans, social and political organisations, and systems for distributing goods and services. Gender analysis in this category is crucial, for women's roles in these different forms of organisation differ widely. Decision-making in social groups may exclude women, or women may have well-developed exchange systems of labour and goods. Divisions on the basis of gender, race, ethnicity or class can weaken the social fabric of a group, increasing its vulnerability.

- **Motivation and Attitudes**: these include cultural and psychological factors which may be based on religion, on the people's history of crisis, on their expectation of emergency relief. When people feel victimised and dependent, they may become fatalistic and passive, and suffer a decrease in their capacities to cope with the situation, and to recover from it. Their vulnerabilities can be increased by inappropriate relief aid, which does not build on their own abilities, develop confidence, or provide people with opportunities for change.

CVA is a flexible tool:

- The matrix model can be adapted to take into account all forms of social differentiation, such as gender, class, caste, age, race, ethnicity and so on.

- By applying it over time, it can be used to assess change, particularly those in gender relations as a result of the emergency, and of agency interventions.

- There is constant interaction between the six boxes in the basic matrix. Vulnerabilities and capacities are related to each other, and changes in one affect the others. For example, increasing people's social organisation may reduce their vulnerability to material loss, and increase group confidence. This helps to predict and assess the impact of relief and development work.

- CVA can be used at different levels — from community, to national, regional and even international levels, thus enabling links between the different levels to be assessed.

(Adapted from *Rising from the Ashes: Development Strategies in Times of Disaster*, by Anderson and Woodrow, Westview Press, 1989)

Handout 71 *Activity 62*

Capacities and vulnerabilities analysis matrix

	Vulnerabilities	Capacities
Physical/material What productive resources, skills, and hazzards exist?		
Social/organisational What are the relationships and organisation among people?		
Motivational/attitudinal How does the community view its ability to create change		

Source: *Rising from the Ashes* Andersen & Woodrow, Westview Press, 1989

Gender disaggregation

	Vulnerabilities: Women	Vulnerabilities: Men	Capacities: Women	Capacities: Men
Physical/material				
Social/organisational				
Motivational/attitudinal				

Disaggregation by economic class

	Vulnerabilities: rich	**Vulnerabilities**: middle	**Vulnerabilities**: poor	**Capacities**: rich	**Capacities**: middle	**Capacities**: poor
Physical/material						
Social/organisational						
Motivational/attitudinal						

El Salvador refugees

Background

El Salvador is the smallest Central American republic, a densely populated and mountainous country, most of whose citizens depend on subsistence farming. However, the wealth created by the major export crops — coffee and cotton — was concentrated in the hands of only 14 families. For generations, these same families also dominated the government and the armed forces. El Salvador has suffered military rule for much of the twentieth century.

In the early 1970s, the export market collapsed, leaving 40 per cent of the rural population both landless and jobless. Peasant families could not survive on the maize and beans they produced on their poor land. Throughout El Salvador, poor men and women formed organisations to press for fairer distribution of the country's resources. Their peaceful demands for political and economic change were met, however, with brutal repression. Political and religious leaders, including the Archbishop of San Salvador, were assassinated by right-wing death squads. By 1980, a cruel counter-insurgency war had been unleashed, which was to cost the lives of more than 70,000 civilians by the end of the decade.

More than one in four Salvadorans became displaced within their own country, or fled elsewhere. Over a period of six months, some 9,000 refugees from the remote department of Morazan fled to Colomoncagua — 5km across the Honduran border — where they survived for nine years in an enclosed camp, under military surveillance. The escape was fraught with danger, as the groups of refugees had to walk across rough terrain, avoiding military ambush and eating what they could find on the way. Some people died en route; women talked about having had to smother their small babies, to stop the sound of crying.

Almost 6,000 of the refugees in Colomoncagua were under the age of 15 when they arrived. Most of the adults were women who were pregnant or with sole responsibility for their children: hardly any families arrived intact. Of the men, most were considerably older (average age 52) — younger men had either been killed, or joined the guerrilla opposition, or remained in El Salvador as civilians, in hiding. There were a small number of elderly women and men, some of whom had lost their entire families.

Deprivation and repression

Morazan is one of the poorest and most neglected parts of El Salvador. There were few schools, clinics or roads, and no sources of employment, apart from farming. One in four households owned no land at all, and about the same proportion were women-maintained. Thus most men, and many women, had to work as agricultural wage labourers in order to survive. Though earnings were below the minimum wage, one man in three would migrate to Honduras during the coffee-picking season, leaving their families to maintain any subsistence farming plot or kitchen garden. However, only one woman in ten had ever left her home area before becoming a refugee. For most rural women, daily life consisted of keeping the household together: getting up at 4 a.m. to grind maize for tortillas, preparing food, caring for their children and families, washing and mending clothes, agricultural work and managing small livestock (poultry, goats, ducks). Only about 15 per cent of households had access to piped water, and under one per cent had electricity.

There were even fewer educational opportunities for children growing up in rural Morazan than in El Salvador as a whole, where only about 25 per cent of children would complete primary school. A boy might have a two in three chance of going to school for a few years. Half as many girls would attend. Only about 15 per cent of adults could read or write, or do simple arithmetic, when they fled the violence: 35 per cent of men and 40 per cent of women had never set foot in a classroom.

Outside the handful of market towns, *campesinos* in Morazan lived in hamlets made up of just a few scattered houses and would rarely have time or opportunity to socialise. As in most rural areas of Latin America, the Catholic church was often the most important focus of getting together to discuss common concerns. The church had become a stimulus to social action in some areas, for example by promoting interest in local development initiatives, such as agricultural cooperatives and primary health care programmes. Amongst a sample of 126 refugees (60 men and 66 women), 28 (10 men and 18 women) had been involved in some kind of social activity: four men and four women were members of agricultural cooperatives, three women belong to church-run mothers' clubs, three men and three women were on school and road committees, one woman had joined a macrame class, another had attended talks on agriculture, and one man had been in a credit bank.

A small number of these people had been Delegates of the Word, or community lay-preachers — 20 per cent of the men and 16 per cent of the women had held some kind of religious office. Outside the church, about 30 per cent of the men had served in local government, usually in some kind of military or police function; this compares with only 3 per cent of women who had been involved in similar activities. However, it was people like these who were most viciously persecuted by the Salvadoran military — accused of being subversive and savagely murdered. By the early 1980s, the military regarded Morazan as a 'free fire zone', saying that anyone found living there was *ipso facto* a guerrilla sympathiser, and should be killed. Large areas of the department were strafed and bombed. In one village alone, the army slaughtered over 1,000 women, men, children and babies — first shooting them, then cutting off their heads and setting fire to their bodies and belongings.

Only one woman survived, having witnessed the massacre of her entire family, as well as all her friends and neighbours. She began a long and terrifying trek across the border, to the relative safety of Honduras. Many thousands of others did the same. Once there, the refugees nominated representatives to take charge of coordinating essential activities. This was not a simple task for people who had never before lived in such a large settlement, or faced such complex civic responsibilities.

Life in the refugee camps

The circumstances of their arrival in Honduras had a profound effect on the way the refugees were to organise their lives. They had no reason to trust anyone but themselves. In adversity, they looked to each other for support. They wanted to return to El Salvador as soon as it was safe to do so, and saw their unwelcome exile as an opportunity to learn new skills.

Most of the international NGOs which worked with them were development agencies, who constantly stressed the need to address the longer-term dimensions of humanitarian relief. It was clear that the refugees wanted to keep their enforced dependence to the very minimum. Within a few months of their arrival, six of the older men with some experience in tailoring were busy altering the second-hand clothes donated to the refugee community. Soon, with the help of a couple of sewing machines and material provided by a local church organisation, the work was expanded to include shirts, trousers and dresses. Nine years later, every single item of clothing — including underwear, hats and shoes — was manufactured within the camps, in collective workshops which boasted 150 machines and 240 trainees, virtually all of them women and children or youngsters (male and female).

These achievements were replicated across a whole range of traditional activities: hammock-making, pottery, tinsmithing, embroidery, blacksmithing, knitting, musical instrument making, carpentry and shoe-making. The approach was to find an experienced artisan (usually male, since — with the exception of embroidery and knitting — these were male skills) from among the older refugees and establish a training programme to share traditional skills, and to learn new ones. The make-up of the population of Colomoncagua meant that the vast majority of the trainees were necessarily women, children or adolescents. Aid agencies brought in artisans and skilled workers from Europe and elsewhere to upgrade existing methods and modify them for application on a semi-industrial scale.

Participation in the workshops was organised on a rota basis, so that trainees had the chance to acquire a range of work experiences: as they mastered one skill, they would have the opportunity to move on to another workshop. Almost two-thirds of the refugees — 59 per cent of the women and 63 per cent of the men — learned two or more practical skills during their nine-year exile. The most common skills acquired by the men were: housing construction, vegetable gardening, administration, literacy, car mechanics, tailoring, carpentry, tin-smithing, shoe-making, animal raising, pastoral work, health care, teaching, hammock-making and nutrition. In addition, many men learned the traditionally female skills of: child care and discipline, day care for children and grinding maize. The range of skills acquired by women were very similar (including car mechanics), almost all of which were traditionally male areas of work. However, the women also stressed that the organisational skills they had acquired in running collective kitchens had profoundly changed their lives and opportunities. The system was designed to rationalise the amount of time (and fuel) used in cooking for a large population, thus releasing the majority of women to participate fully in the workshop training programmes and other social activities.

Fluid internal and external communication was a key element in uniting the refugee community. A clandestine newsletter was set up to document what was going on in El Salvador as well as in the other refugee camps in Honduras. Local and international radio and press were routinely monitored, to maintain a community bulletin-board. Contact with the outside world was seen to be vital in increasing the negotiating strength of the refugees. A donation of filming equipment became an opportunity for them to learn how to make documentary videos. As a peasant farmer, the man who became the coordinator of these productions had never even seen a tape recorder before leaving El Salvador.

Most of the women in the camps were solely responsible for maintaining their family group. Many had either been widowed, or their husbands had joined the guerrilla opposition forces. Many women were looking after orphans, in addition to their own children. Initially, a Committee of Mothers came together to use the teaching of the Bible to help them reflect on their bereavement. Their meetings also became a space within which they could, for the first time in their lives, share their experiences as women. They began to ask themselves why, for example, a midwife would be paid half as much again for delivering a boy as a girl. As more women came to join them, the Committees established day-care centres for small children — so that their mothers could get involved in other activities — and also set up embroidery workshops, which gave them an outlet for their feelings. In the early days, their artwork depicted the violence they had fled — bombings, massacres and destruction. In time, they depicted also the life of the camps, full of busy activity and creativity.

Building a future

These achievements were possible only because of the investment in education. This gave people access not just to new skills but also to greater confidence, ability to express themselves, and organisational capacity. In 1981, there was not one refugee teacher or health worker. By 1990, the returnees included 407 teachers and 358 health workers, 'to contribute to a new El Salvador', as their flyers said. On the eve of their departure, there were 6,057 students of both sexes and 299 refugee instructors in self-run formal education programmes. Illiteracy had dropped considerably, though it remained greater amongst women (25 per cent) than amongst men (12 per cent). This probably reflects higher initial levels of female illiteracy, as well as the greater household burdens and deeply-held assumptions about the aptitude of women to study.

What is remarkable is the way in which desperately poor and marginalised Salvadorans of all ages developed the vision and the abilities to take control over their lives and their futures — and refused, ever, to become victims. They have taken all of these skills and experiences, as well as confidence, back with them, to build a new country from the ruins.

Time: 1 hr

A Time-line

Objectives

1 To understand changes in programme approaches from an historical perspective.

2 To be able to look at the different factors which were decisive in integrating gender into the approach.

Method

Preparation: Ask at least one participant to prepare a case study (see Facilitator's notes).

1 Explain that the session presents a tool to understand changes and trends in programme development. Give each person a copy of the Timeline chart (**Handout 74**) to study. meanwhile, draw this chart on a flipchart. *(5 mins)*

2 Ask a participant to present his or her case study, or to tread out the case study in **Handout 73**. Give out **Handout 73** if using that case study.ation

3 Ask participants for the critical events, responses, and influencing factors, and fill these in on the timeline chart on the flipchart. Invite participants to ask questions about policy development and the constraints and opportunities faced in introducing gender. *(40 mins)*

4 Sum up the session by:
  a. Drawing conclusions which may be of general use.
  b. Highlighting the kind of sources and information which are useful in this exercise. *(5-10 mins)*

Materials

Handouts74, 75 and **73** ,
Flipchart Pens

Facilitator's Notes

1 This method enables a broader, more dynamic analysis of the programme, not just individual projects.

2 A timeline requires a detailed case study, prepared in advance by one of the participants or facilitating team, who will be able to answer questions. It can help if others also know the programme concerned.

*3 The case study should contain relevant background information, relevant dates, responses and facors affecting responses, and gender issues. See **Handout 59** Designing case studies (**Activity 56**).*

Case study

The evolution of Oxfam's gender strategy in response to conflict in Lebanon

Oxfam's role in Lebanon has evolved in response to the general situation in the country, and in particular to the way the Lebanese NGOs which Oxfam supports have developed their own response to the unfolding war. Factors internal to Oxfam have also played a significant part in determining its policies and actions in Lebanon. This evolution can be seen by looking at four periods of significance in the progress of the war:

1 The Israeli invasion, which took place progressively over 1981/3.

2 Israeli withdrawal, which precipitated the 'camps war' and others over the period 1985/7, giving rise to massive displacement of populations.

3 The height of the Lebanese civil war (1989/90) in which almost the whole country was affected by intense and devastating fighting with huge numbers of casualties.

4 The period following the 1990 peace treaty in which security was restored and political and economic reform has been under discussion.

The first of these periods saw the establishment of an Oxfam office in the country channelling relief goods through local NGOs and UNRWA (United Nations Relief and Works Agency for Palestinian refugees in the Near East). It is hard to tell how far Oxfam was attuned to gender issues at this time since little documentation survives, but gender was not generally seen as an issue then, either within Oxfam or among the partner NGOs. Some women's groups did exist, often affiliated to political parties — and the majority of NGO field staff were women; however, decision-making was largely in the hands of men. The priority of the NGOs was the struggle to survive under occupation.

During the second period Oxfam began to focus on a number of 'progressive' NGOs, supporting the work they were doing in the fields of relief and rehabilitation together with primary health care. NGOs — and especially secular ones — were going through a period of religious and political persecution, and Oxfam's aim was to help them to survive. A substantial number of projects supported dealt with women, and employment of a part-time gender project officer was contemplated. The emergency had given rise to an increasing number of female-headed households and many NGOs were starting to work with women on, for example, childcare and income-generation projects. Though staff in the Oxfam office recognised the need to look at women in development (WID) issues, they did not have the skills to deal with them and were in any case swamped by the pressures of the emergency situation.

The third period (civil war) could be characterised as 'business as usual' for Oxfam, which continued to support NGOs and their work in relief at community level. However, staff in the Oxfam office began to think about carrying out a review of the programme's basic assumptions. As far as gender was concerned, WID was definitely recognised as an issue by this time: partner NGOs recognised women as a main target group in this conflict situation, and Oxfam made deliberate attempts to involve women in project-related discussions. However, women's issues were addressed basically at the individual project level, and nothing like a gender analysis had appeared at this stage.

During the latest stage, internal factors had a greater bearing on developments. Oxfam's strategic planning process was in place, and within the Lebanon, Oxfam began discussions with partners on thinking afresh about their and Oxfam's strategies, and identifying for the first time a coherent shape and direction for the Lebanon programme. Gender and the environment emerged as main themes in the future programme, helped both by incorporating gender into the strategic planning process, and also by the NGOs' awareness of the word — an awareness sparked off in part by the new-found habit of donor agencies to link gender to funding.

The present situation is that political and economic reform and the optimism of the Middle East peace process is coinciding with Oxfam's first year of strategic planning. Gender training and a new gender analysis within the country's own context are in process, and gender will be promoted within a joint review with partners. The atmosphere within Oxfam is now conducive to gender work and there is a consensus on gender within the Lebanon office. The peace process provides some space to discuss gender issues, even though it may ultimately not succeed. Lebanese NGOs are having to consider their position on gender issues very carefully, partly because of the increasing conditionality of donor agencies who believe the Lebanon is no longer an emergency situation, and partly because they — like Oxfam — will soon be having to take religious fundamentalism into account more seriously than they have before.

Main points

1 In the Lebanon, the growth of local NGOs has been closely linked to the course of the war and the emergency needs of the people.

2 Oxfam's view of its role has been oriented towards developing solidarity with its partners and helping to ensure their survival through very difficult times, and this gives Oxfam the credibility to raise new issues such as gender in a positive environment.

3 Gender awareness in Oxfam and its partners has been stimulated by the needs of the situation in the Lebanon, and also encouraged by institutional factors within Oxfam.

4 In order to promote discussion of gender issues among its partners, Oxfam recognises the need first to equip its own staff with appropriate skills.

Handout 74 — Activity 63

Time Line

Dates					
Critical Events (These can be external such as changes in government, laws, disasters, conferences, or internal such as new staff, workshops etc.)					
Your team's responses					
The gender element in responses					
Internal factors affecting your response					
External factors					

Handout 75 *Activity 63*

A note on the use of time-lines

A time-line is a way of charting the evolution of trends, showing how past events led to the present situation and illustrating recurring themes.

A time-line is constructed by looking back over a given period and 'mapping' critical events. This provides the opportunity to discuss with people who were there at the time:

what really happened and why;

what were the factors contributing to the events;

whether core trends can be observed and what they are;

which of these core trends may be expected to continue into the future.

A time-line is best constructed by a group of people, including both those with direct knowledge of the events concerned, and those without that knowledge who can ask questions. It may be a useful tool for conducting participatory research at grassroots level, especially since it makes use of and validates the knowledge and experience of older people. It may also be used as a planning tool within agencies, helping them to assess what conditions are necessary for the achievement of goals, and illustrating areas of 'core competence' which the agency has.

Time: 1 hr

Debate on gender in situations of conflict

Objectives

1 To initiate the debate on incorporating a gender perspective in interventions during situations of conflict.

Method

1 Explain that this is a role-play of a panel discussion in a television studio where a journalist is interviewing two members of two international NGOs: Voice for All and Save the World. Choose actors to be the journalist, NGO workers, camera person, make-up person. The rest of the group are the studio audience.

2 The journalist interviews members of the panel: introduces members and gives the background of the organisations.

(10 mins)

3 Each NGO presents an opposing view: Voice for All believes that it is necessary to integrate gender in conflict response. Save the World is totally opposed to integrating the gender perspective .

(15 mins)

4 The journalist opens the debate. A maximum of three questions are asked of each NGO worker by the studio audience.

5 The camera follows the debate. The audience can try and interrupt, clap or boo.

(30 mins)

6 The jurnalist closes the debate, highlighting the main issues.. *(5 mins)*

Materials

Paper	Props
Camera	Microphones
Make-up person	Camera operator

Facilitator's Notes

1 This session is suitable only for groups with a fairly sophisticated understanding of and familiarity with television. When it was used in a conflict workshop in 1992, it generated a very lively and funny debate. Presenters were selected for their acting skills. However, all the participants in the workshop were urban-based development professionals familiar with TV culture. With other groups, you may find a different form of the role-play would be more suitable — such as a village meeting, an NGO country or local office, etc.

2 If you have a video camera available, you could video this debate and use it as a training tool in a subsequent session or workshop.

Time: 1-1½ hrs

Gender and environment myths

Objectives

1 To discuss a variety of myths and stereotypes frequently encountered in relation to gender and environmental issues.

2 To raise awareness of the power and effects of myths and stereotypes in decision making.

Method

1 Preparation: take a few key points from **Handout76 Gender and Natural Resource Management**, and list them on flipchart or acetate for an overhead projector. Present the myths and discussion points outlined in *Facilitator's Notes*.

2 Make a short presentation, allowing time for a brief discussion in the whole group. *(10-15 mins)*

3 Divide participants into small groups of five or six people and ask them to work on the following questions:
- a What assumptions/myths about gender and the environment do you know of?
- b Why have these myths developed?
- c Can or should these myths and stereotypes be changed?
- d How do they influence your work? *(30 mins)*

4 Ask each group to feed back to the plenary on their discussions.

5 Note down on flipchart some of the assumptions and myths participants have identified, and what suggestions came up about how they influenced participants' work, and how this could be tackled.

6 Give out **Handout 76**.

Materials

Flipchart, pens, **Handout 76**

Facilitator's Notes

1 There are a number of myths regarding the participation of women in agroforestry, cited in ***Agroforestry: Four Myths and a Case Study****, by Fortmann and Rocheleau:*

- *Women are housewives and are not heavily involved in agricultural production.*
- *Women are not significantly involved in tree production and use.*
- *Every woman has a husband or is part of a male-headed household.*
- *Women are not influential or active in public affairs.*

2 Gender myths include: (see also Activity 35 Myths and Effects, and use some of the myths already identified by the group instead of, or as well as, these listed below)

- *Women are submissive and men are aggressive.*
- *Men are ruled by the mind and women by the heart.*
- *Women cannot get along together while men are by nature team players.*
- *Women are better at fine, meticulous work because they are patient and their hands are smaller.*

3 Myths related to natural resources include:

- *Trees use light better than bushes because they are taller.*
- *Cattle should not be kept in semi-arid scrub lands because they contribute to deforestation.*
- *Trees should never be cut.*

4 Discussion points:

a. Why is it important to question commonly held myths or stereotypes in the environmental arena?

b. What is the relative influence of myths and stereotypes on various groups (women, men, local decision-makers), and on state policy, and project initiatives and implementation?

c. What are the values and roles of myths in social processes? Can you use old and new myths to accomplish your development goals? What are the ethics of manipulating myths from the 'outside'?

5 This activity has been adapted from the ***Gender and Environment: Lessons from Social Forestry and Natural Resource Management,*** *published by Aga Khan Foundation Canada, referred to in the Introduction to this section, with some suggestions from Irene Guijt, of IIED.*

6 The activity works well if visual images can be used. It has been used with the video ***Questions of Difference*** *(see Resources Section), showing the section 'Images and Realities' to the group. If this video is not available, other visual images could be used showing women and men interacting with their environment. These images would have to be selected to demonstrate some common myths or wrong assumptions.*

Gender and natural resource management: an introduction

How we manage our global natural resources — soil, water, air, flora and fauna — has become an issue of unprecedented concern. The goals of natural resource management — *productivity and efficiency, distribution and equity, and conservation and environmental quality* — often raise more questions than solutions. Although progress toward these goals may be at times uncertain and inconsistent, the transition from advocacy to action has already begun to take place.

The interest in the environment has not always included a concern for the role of women. However, because of pioneering accounts of the role of women in agriculture dating from the 1960s and 1970s, the importance of women in rural wage, proprietary, and household sectors has received increasing attention. The stereotype of 'invisible' women in rural economies is slowly declining in influence, as is the myth of an earth with perpetually renewable resources.

Deforestation has received the widest notoriety as a symptom of environmental degradation. One of its most forceful illustrations has been the social, economic, and environmental costs of fuelwood scarcity to women and their families. Time allocation studies of women's work have illuminated with frightening clarity the hours and days spent collecting combustible material for the preparation of cooked food.

Other productive activities for the household are equally affected by decreases in natural resource availability. The capability of land to support grazing and fodder production for household livestock has declined, especially in areas of sparse or sporadic rainfall. Access to and control over water for household use remains problematic in many regions. Loss of forest habitat that supplied supplementary foods, fibres, medicines, and other goods has adversely affected not only household maintenance requirements but small-scale rural and household industries.

It seems that the least powerful sectors of society suffer first from loss of access to natural resources: women with their primary responsibilities for household maintenance and wide-ranging productive work; forest-dwelling peoples dependent on forest habitat for sustenance and trade goods; landless people dependent on wage labour and common property for their livelihoods. Ultimately, however, the effects of mismanagement of natural resources also reach the powerful.

Our focus is on gender and environment, with primary examples drawn from social forestry and natural resource management. There is no intention to imply that only women can undertake new and constructive steps toward the wise stewardship of natural resources. However, programmatic attempts to integrate women into active responsibility for natural resource management are a recent phenomenon. They require increased awareness of gender differences and disparities, new sets of social and technical skills, and a decided revision of the traditional worldview that only men manage resources outside the household.

Gender and natural resource management

The natural resource management components of development programmes have expanded rapidly in the last two decades, responding to regional fuel, fodder, and water scarcities, soil degradation, and to decline in forest cover. Women are frequently identified as direct participants and beneficiaries of natural resource development programmes, and yet there has been inconsistent success in ensuring that women benefit in this way.

Many of the constraints to women's participation and benefit have been identified. These include:

- lack of access to technical education and training, credit, extension information, material inputs, markets, and funding;
- lack of input into planning and decision-making processes;
- lack of ownership and tenure rights to land, trees, water, and other natural resources;
- inequitable distribution of goods and services supplied from natural resources;
- differing perceptions between women and men, and between agencies and participants, about types and allocations of resource use.

The institutional response

Spurred by household studies and gender analysis, international programmes for women, and the rising influence of political and professional women, governments and development organisations have, at a minimum, absorbed the words enabling recognition of women's roles in the process of rural development. One result has been the creation of 'women in development' (WID) divisions in many aid organisations. Their goal has been primarily to improve women's lives through such activities as income-generation, literacy and education projects, provision of support for credit and cooperative schemes. In addition to programming specifically for women's projects, the WID divisions of some development organisations have undertaken the 'conscientisation' of their own colleagues. And in certain organisations, the groundwork has been laid for regulations that would require a gender or women's component to every project.

On a more extensive scale, governments, supranational and national donor agencies, NGOs, and Private Voluntary Organisations (PVOs) have designed natural resource management programmes and projects. Many of these focus on forest conservation and social forestry, soil conservation and improvement, water capture and distribution, and watershed management. Although, in most cases, the long-term development goal remains increased productivity, both distributional equity and resource stewardship have attained some importance.

Experience has shown that no single sector can be successfully isolated in any development project. Focus cannot be placed only on a farmer's field; both inputs and outputs inevitably yield unexpected results felt economically, socially, and environmentally. There is an increasing consciousness that management of natural resources takes place in an ecosystem context, in which the consequences may not be measurable or even discernable during a normal project cycle. In the same manner, interventions designed to improve the status of women take place in the context of a human ecology — in their household relationships, their community relationships, and their relationships with the environment around them.

The creative tension between 'women in development' and 'gender' approaches

Inevitably within any discussion of women's issues in rural development, there are creative tensions between the necessity to *focus* on women and the equal necessity to recognise their integration into the system in which they live. As we train ourselves to look at women — women as beneficiaries, women as participants, women as trainers, women as disenfranchised, women as losers, women as winners — we must equally train ourselves to look at women and men at various ages and stages, and at the differing perceptions of reality that we may encounter among them.

We frequently encounter these tensions, both theoretically and in practical project implementation. The availability of considerable funding for both women's programmes and gender analysis studies adds to the tension, but also provides room for reconciliation. When either a gender or a women's component is overlaid on a natural resource development project, it can be significant. When a gender approach is fully integrated into natural resource management development projects, its potential is much greater.

(Source: Adapted from: 'Gender and Natural Resource Management: An Introduction' by Sarah Warren in **Gender and Environment: Lessons from Social Forestry and Natural Resource Management**, Aga Khan Foundation Canada; Toronto, 1992.).

Time: 45 mins-1½ hrs

Downstream effects

Objectives

1 To practise using an ecosystems approach in development and policy design and planning.

2 To analyse the results of interventions (outputs) in order to become aware of the consequences of any action.

3 To look at the potential for chain reactions as a result of any intervention.

4 To relate 'Downstream Effects' to women's practical and strategic gender needs.

Method

Part 1

1 Divide participants into groups of four or five people, and give each group **Handout 77** Impacts of interventions.

2 Ask them to analyse at least three of the five hypothetical situations presented, predicting:

a. two to three positive medium- and long-term impacts on women and men;
b. two to three negative medium- and long-term impacts on women and men.

(45 mins)

3 Ask each group to select one member to report back on their work, which should be presented on the flipchart in the form of a matrix for the large group discussion.

(5-7 mins per presentation)

Part 2

1 Give each group the two mini case studies in **Handout 78** Downstream effects and ask them to relate the discussion questions on the Handout to each case, and

to the first part of the activity. How could the outcomes of these project interventions have been predicted?

(35 mins)

Materials

Flipchart, **Handouts 77 and 78**.

Facilitator's Notes

1 Not all of the hypothetical situations tie both gender and natural resources management together in obvious ways. Encourage participants to look for relationships and identify the gender dimensions of impacts. Youcould extend this activity to include more hypothetical situations suggested by participants, or make up your own before the beginning of the workshop. Work out some positive and negative effects for each one yourself, before the workshop, on women, on men, and on both.

2 In the general discussion at the end of the first part, ask participants if they find the 'ecosystem' approach to programming useful.

3 This activity should be done after Gender and environment myths ***Activity 65*** *Participants should have read the* ***Handout 76*** *related to this activity. It can also only be done after participants have worked through the activities on gender roles and needs in* ***Sections C.6 and C.7****.*

(Source: Adapted from ***Gender and Environment: Lessons from Social Forestry and Natural Resource Management****, op.cit.)*

Impacts of interventions

Although the law of physics 'For every action there is an equal and opposite reaction' may appear irrelevant to social science, there is merit in reminding ourselves of it. Well-intentioned development interventions have often backfired. Regardless of the balance between success and lack thereof, unpredicted secondary and tertiary effects of interventions form the backbone of evaluation literature.

One of the goals of an ecosystems approach is to attempt to predict and weigh the outputs that derive from inputs into a system. For each of the interventions summarised below, predict two to three *positive* long-term impacts and two to three *negative* long-term impacts. Pay careful attention to both biophysical and social, economic, political and cultural results, and to different effects on women and on men.

- A major donor institution establishes a special division that will identify and support appropriate 'women in development' projects in five countries. One of the first activities of the division is to organise a symposium, inviting representatives from each of the five countries.

- Foreign producers of DDT are prohibited from selling DDT in a less-developed country. There is no production capacity in the country, but $5 million is available for alternative malaria-control measures. Barefoot health workers are given a mandate to improve household control measures in the hinterlands.

- For the seventh year, women's groups protest against groundwater pollution arising from an industrial point source. Following publicity related to violence during the last protest season, numerous small grants have been awarded to the best-known protest group.

- A South-east Asian country bans the export of teak harvested from its own forests. It bans all logging in its own forests, and expands a programme of enrichment planting in already-logged forests. It intends, however, to remain a trade centre for timber shipments.

- Private foreign investors, under protest from environmentalists, withdraw plans for construction of a highway connecting the Amazon basin with the Pacific Ocean.

(Source: Adapted from: *Gender and Environment: Lessons from Social Forestry and Natural Resources Management*, op.cit).

Handout 78 *Activity 66*

Downstream effects

The following two mini-cases illustrate real situations in Southern India. They relate 'downstream effects' to an analysis of the practical needs and strategic interests of women. Although the information may seem sketchy, it is surprising how much you can extrapolate, using your own experiences.

Toymakers project

The State Handicrafts Corporation planned to expand the sale of its handicrafts to a European catalogue market. A tribal group used a simple foot-powered lathe system to make small toys. The corporation gave the group a loan to electrify their lathe, and it hired a foreign toy designer to teach the toymakers about new designs and colours.

Most of the toymakers were young women. They purchased special wood, which was the only local wood suitable for turning on a lathe, from the Forest Department. However, as the group's wood needs increased, the Forest Department was unable to meet them consistently because this wood had been over-harvested from the natural forest.

Discussion questions:

a. Does this activity address women's practical needs, strategic interests, or both? Does it have the potential to do so?

b. What changes might be made to this activity to help it to address women's strategic needs?

c. Do any of the myths that you have recently explored relate to this situation?

Tendu leaves project

In a remote village in Kerala, women collected *tendu* leaves (*Diospyros melanozylon* which are used to wrap local cigarettes called *bidi*) from the natural forest and dried them around their household cooking fires. They sold the dried leaves to middlemen to supplement household income.

Personnel from a local rural development project suggested that fuelwood would be saved if a charcoal-fired drying centre was constructed in the village. They proposed that the women form a cooperative and bring their leaves to the drying centre.

However, over the years one man gained control of the cooperative and interceded with middlemen, so the women were forced to sell their undried leaves to this man. They had to collect more *tendu* leaves and made less money than they had before project personnel intervened.

An energy audit of the project found that 50 per cent more fuel wood was being used than prior to the project.

Discussion questions:

a. Does this activity address women's practical needs, strategic needs, or both? Does it have the potential to do so?

b. What changes might be made to this activity to help it to address women's strategic needs?

c. Do any of the myths that you have recently explored relate to this situation?

(Source: Adapted from: *Gender and Environment: Lessons from Social Forestry and Natural Resource Management*, op.cit).

Time: 1 hr

Drawing livelihoods

Objectives

1 To draw the links between the activities of women and men and their use of natural resources.

2 To identify the ways in which natural resource use is differentiated by gender.

Method

1 Ask the participants to form the same sub-groups they were in for the 24-hour day **Activity36**.

2 Give each group some flipchart and pens, ask them to use their 24-hour day charts and identify those of the activities they had noted down which require some form of natural resource.

3 Ask participants to reflect on all the different components related to the tasks (e.g. fetching water requires a water source, a jar which might be made of clay) and draw them on the flipchart. Participants should identify clearly which resources are used by women, by men, and by both.

4 Ask participants to identify which resources were important to women's and men's different roles — reproductive, productive, and community.

(45 mins)

5 Put the flipcharts up on the wall, and draw out the main points in the plenary.

(15 mins)

Materials

Flipchart, pens, participants' 24-hour day charts.

Facilitator's Notes

*1 This activity should be done after participants have learned the 24-hour day, and the Analysing roles and needs (**Activities 36 and 37**). Ideally, it should follow immediately after them.*

2 This activity was used successfully in a workshop in Burkina Faso on PRA, Gender and the Environment, on the first day.

(Source: Irene Guijt, IIED.)

Time: 1–1½ hours

Structural adjustment

Part 1
Objectives

1 To understand Structural Adjustment Programmes.

2 To identify the impact of SAPs on gender roles.

Method

1 Explain the history of Structural Adjustment Programmes (SAPs), using a prepared flipchart adapted for the country or regional experience of participants (see **Handout 79**).

(10-15 mins)

2 Brainstorm the main elements of SAPs. Write the list on flipchart.

(10-15 mins)

3 Divide the group into the same small groups as for the '24 hour day' activity (**Activity 36**), to consider the following questions.

a. How will, or how has, SAP affected the life of the particular man and woman studied in the 24-hour day exercise? Consider particularly

i. Government cutbacks in health

ii. Government cutbacks in education.

iii. Government cutbacks in support to small producers.

b. What are the implications of these effects on our projects?

(20-30 mins)

4 Ask each group to report back, and lead a general discussion about the implications. *(20-30 mins)*

5 Give out handouts at the end of the session.

Materials

Prepared flipchart, flipcharts and marker pens
Handouts 79 and 80

Facilitator's Notes

1 This activity should be done after ***Activity 37 Analysing Roles and Needs*** *in* ***Section C.3****). Add any particular facts about Structural Adjustment Programmes in a relevant country to the information on* ***Handout 79****, to write on the flipchart for the first part.*

2 Add on any of the main elements of SAPs which may be omitted in the group brainstorm. Draw particular attention to the reduction of government spending byreducing and eliminating subsidies; reducing wages and salaries; increasing and introducing user fees for basic services such as health.

Part 2: Structural adjustment and gender needs

Objective

1 To identify the impact of SAPs on gender needs.

Method

1 Put up the flipcharts of the history and the main elements of SAPs and also the flipcharts of examples of practical and strategic gender needs (**Activity 38.**).

2 In small groups discuss the likely changes to practical and strategic gender needs as a result of SAPs.

3 Each group reports back in turn, one change at a time, and the facilitator writes answers on a flipchart, only adding new ideas, until all changes are listed.

4 Discuss in a large group the implications for your organisation.

Materials

Previously prepared flipcharts.

Facilitator's Notes

1 ***Activity 38*** *on gender needs must be done before this, but it need not be immediately before. Re-read the notes for the activity as they apply here also.*

2 This activity raises political issues. You need to guard against despondency that we can't do anything. You need to be aware that debt and SAPs are a problem for everyone, not just women, but to make the point clearly that, when talking about debt and SAPs, gender analysis is vital in order to understand the way in which women and men are affected differently. This is often particularly evident at the household and productive level, and is invisible unless drawn out by gender analysis.

Debt and structural adjustment:

After decades of fairly steady progress during which mortality rates fell and life expectancy rose, the 1980s saw a major tragic reversal in the human condition. The main cause of the reversal was not a sudden deterioration in the internal policies of developing countries but in the external conditions they faced, due to adverse changes in the world economy.

In most parts of the world, the 1950s and 1960s, and to some extent the 1970s, had been a time of fairly steady progress in terms of economic growth and trade liberalisation. But in the early 1970s the rise in oil prices forced many countries to borrow heavily in order to meet the big additional costs which resulted; those who could switched to private borrowing and more or less managed to maintain economic growth. And at the end of the 1970s came a further series of shocks.

First, in 1978-79, was a new rise in oil prices, which precipitated a major world recession from which the industrialised countries have still not fully recovered; their growth rates were only half or two-thirds those of the 1970s, and this in turn depressed markets in the Third World. The second major shock was the unprecedented fall in commodity prices, which has still not been reversed. In 1988 alone, Africa lost something in the region of $19 billion. And the third shock was rising protectionism in the industrialised countries; Third World countries had to pay higher prices for imports while receiving lower prices for exports. The fall in their purchasing power meant that they could import much less than before.

Not only could they no longer earn what they needed, they could no longer borrow it either, for interest rates rose to enormous heights in the early 1980s — to 18-20 per cent. In addition, private lending simply disappeared in the 1980s, and development aid stagnated. A net positive inflow of $38 billion to the capital account of developing countries in 1979 was transformed by 1986 into a net negative outflow of $50 billion — a huge deterioration. Hence the 'debt crisis'.

Developing countries were forced to go to the only lender who would still lend to them: the International Monetary Fund (IMF), whose programmes called for severe cutbacks in government expenditure, in employment, in credit creation and, wherever possible, in subsidies. As a result, the incomes of the poor were squeezed, prices rocketed, and basic health and education services were often reduced by the government.

Statistics show that real wages during the 1980s fell by 40 per cent in Mexico; in Ghana they were just a quarter of the level of 1974. Unemployment was over 25 per cent in Jamaica and during the 1980s it rose from 10 per cent to 16 per cent in Chile and from 5 per cent to 11 per cent in Peru. In Latin America the proportion of the labour force in the informal sector increased by some 10 per cent, but here, too, incomes were depressed. Food prices rose steeply. In Ghana even households with two wage-earners had only enough money to purchase 30 per cent of an adequate diet; government expenditure on education in 1982 was only 30 per cent of what had been in 1974 in real terms, and on health only 23 per cent. In Jamaica there was a fall of 40 per cent per head in social service expenditure in the 1980s.

In 1989 the international community was increasingly concerned with the social effects of adjustment programmes, and the attention of governments and international institutions now focuses on the need to minimise the costs of adjustment to the poorer groups and to have adjustment with growth. It is important in this respect to study the specific effect of the crisis upon women.

(Source: Jeanne Vickers, *Women and The World Economic Crisis*, Zed Books, London 1991 .)

Handout 80 *Activity 68*

The impact of structural adjustment on women

Recent research indicates that in Africa, the Caribbean and Latin America, the instruments of most stabilisation packages have direct and indirect negative consequences for women. For example, currency devaluation in food importing countries results in rapidly rising food prices. Women are responsible for family food budgets and the increased prices but without any compensatory income. The consequent reduced food intake and malnutrition are measurably greater in the case of girls and women of all ages. This is the case also for pregnant and breast-feeding women. The increased time spent on producing, buying, preparing food brings stress, exhaustion and ill-health for women as family managers. This in turn reduces their effectiveness as carers. The removal of subsidies on food, transport, energy and fuel have similar effects.

Public expenditure cuts in housing, transport, childcare, health and education have well-documented immediate effects and serious long-term implications for future development. Women, who comprise a large number of the lowest-paid public sector employees ,are the first to lose their jobs and meagre salaries on which so many family members depend. The burden of coping with these cuts in social programmes is transferred to women's time and personal resources. Rarely mentioned effects of public expenditure cuts are higher rates of women's morbidity and mortality. The effects on birth rates of the reduction or loss of family planning services has yet to be documented. The cuts greatly diminish women's reproductive rights at a time when they are least able to cope.

Adjustment — which encourages the production of goods for export and a one-sided liberalisation of trade and tariffs — has serious implications for women. Export promotion diverts investment away from the production of goods — particularly food, shelter, clothing and transport — for local consumption. Food production on small holdings, largely managed by women, has already suffered from chronic under-investment resulting in poverty, malnutrition and the destruction of national food security in many countries previously self-sufficient, especially in Africa, south of the Sahara.

Research shows that export-oriented production in weak economies rarely transfers technology or skills, creates secure employment, or generates long-term indigenous industry. Furthermore, women's incomes are reduced when food crop production is replaced by cash crops. Liberalisation of trade and tariffs, especially by the least-developed countries, without any reciprocal measures from the United States, Japan or Europe, results in depressed local production and rising unemployment in many cases, especially amongst women. The reduction in purchasing power is differentiated very clearly by gender.

Conclusion

The concept of structural adjustment is based on women's capacity to cope, ,to continue to carry out their economic and social responsibilities in increasingly adverse conditions, and to deny their own needs and interests for the survival of their families and communities. In shor,t structural adjustment relies on women providing those services previously provided by the State.

(Source:The National Women's Organisation (NAWO): Women's Strategies to deal with SAPs)

Time: 1 hr 20 mins

The debt web

Objectives

1 To enable participants to understand the links in the international economic system between Third World Debt and women's lives.

2 To enable participants to work out those links for themselves.

Method

1 Prepare a presentation on the human cost of the Debt Crisis, using **Handouts 79** and **80** from the Structural Adjustment **Activity 68** and **Handouts 82** and **83.**. Bring in your own information and examples also.
(20 minutes)

2 Distribute the Debt Web (**Handout 81**) and ask the participants to form small groups of four or five in order to make their own web. Explain they should start their web by drawing two circles on different parts of a sheet of flipchart, writing 'Third World Debt' in one, and an economic issue of central concern to them in another.
(10 minutes)

3 Ask the groups to think of statements and questions that come to mind when they look at the two phrases on their sheet, and organise them into a web linking the two.
(30 minutes)

4 Ask the groups to pin their Debt Webs on the wall, and lead a discussion in whole group highlighting some of the main points arising from the activity.*(20 minutes*)

Materials

Handout 81, Flipchart, Pens

A debt web

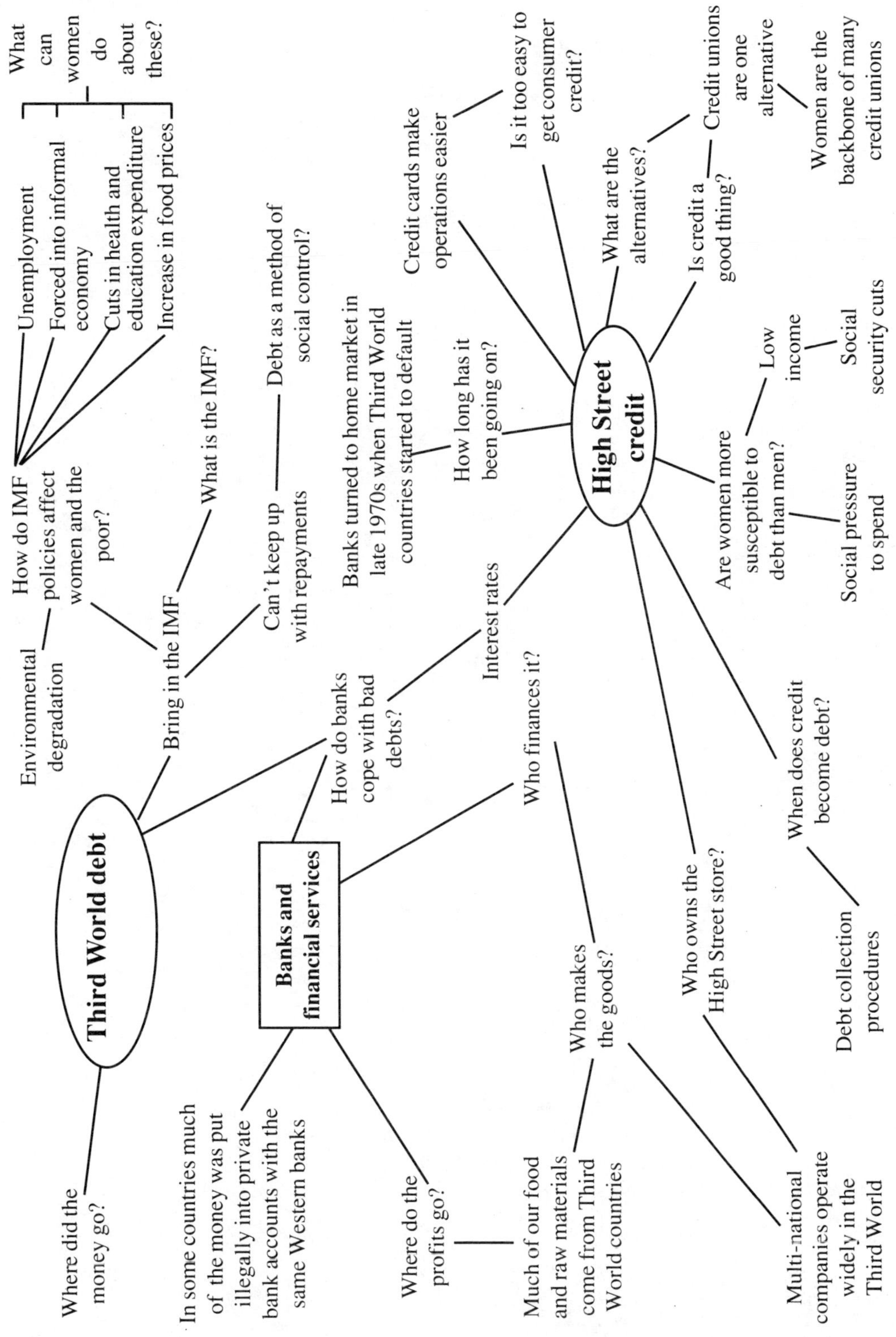
Third World debt
Banks and financial services
High Street credit
Where did the money go?
In some countries much of the money was put illegally into private bank accounts with the same Western banks
Where do the profits go?
Much of our food and raw materials come from Third World countries
Multi-national companies operate widely in the Third World
Who makes the goods?
Who owns the High Street store?
Debt collection procedures
When does credit become debt?
Who finances it?
How do banks cope with bad debts?
Interest rates
Bring in the IMF
Environmental degradation
How do IMF policies affect women and the poor?
Unemployment
Forced into informal economy
Cuts in health and education expenditure
Increase in food prices
What can women do about these?
What is the IMF?
Can't keep up with repayments
Debt as a method of social control?
Banks turned to home market in late 1970s when Third World countries started to default
How long has it been going on?
Credit cards make operations easier
Is it too easy to get consumer credit?
What are the alternatives?
Credit unions are one alternative
Women are the backbone of many credit unions
Is credit a good thing?
Low income
Social security cuts
Are women more susceptible to debt than men?
Social pressure to spend

Time: 1 hr 10 mins

The Shamba and Mama Florence

Objectives

1 To demonstrate some of the effects of the debt crisis on poor women's lives.

2 To enable participants to understand the links between the international economic system and Third World women's lives.

Method

1 Prepare two participants beforehand to role-play the story on **Handout 82.**

2 Ask the two volunteers to perform the role play. Ask the group to listen to and watch what is happening. *(10 mins)*

3 After the role play ask participants to work in twos to discuss the following questions for discussion.
a. What issues were raised in the role play?
b. What similarities can be drawn from the role play from your experiences?
(15 mins)

4 Give participants **Handout 83** Mama Florence.

5 Ask them to form groups of three, read **Handout 83** and discuss again the two questions in 3 above, applied to the story in the handout.
(20 mins)

6 In the big group brainstorm the issues that the role play and story highlight. Write these issues on a flipchart.. Bring out the key points that the Handout raises
- Origins of the crisis
- In comes the IMF
- Human cost

(15 mins)

8 Give participants **Handout 84,** and ask them to read it through.

(5 mins)

9 In the large group, lead a discussion on:

a. What are some strategies people can use to overcome some of the effects of the debt crisis and SAPs?

b. What can women do?

c. What can men do

(15 mins)

Materials

Handout 82, 83 and 84
Flipchart, felt pens

Facilitator's Notes

1 This activity helps to relate SAPs to people's lives. The Shamba story and the Mama Florence story reflect the effect of SAPs on poor women. In an Economic Literacy workshop for Oxfam women partners in Tanzania and Kenya, women began to make links between the lack of drugs in hospitals, the imposition of charges for education, and the lack of support for the cultivation of food crops.

Handout 82 *Activity 70*

The Shamba

Two women are digging at a communal plot together. The first woman is complaining that the better part of her 'shamba' (field) is full of cotton plants which the government has insisted should be planted for export to help pay the foreign debt. She mentions that the government has to earn foreign exchange (dollars) to pay the debt and to buy goods like machinery. The second woman does not understand what the debt is, what dollars are nor what kind of machinery the government needs to buy. The first woman tries to explain.

In their discussion the second woman mentions a man who has stopped growing cotton in order to plant flowers. They find it extraordinary that someone should use their land to plant flowers.

The first woman then remembers their mutual friend who has been selling 'mandaazi' (doughnuts) very successfully, making 300 shillings in a day. Now she makes less than 80 shillings a day because a bakery has opened nearby and people have stopped buying her mandaazi. The second woman says that it not surprising because the loaves from the bakery are sweeter.

Mama Florence

Florence lives in a poor quarter of Lusaka, Zambia's capital. Prior to the debt crisis, this young woman might have been regarded as one of the better-off in Zambia. But for five years, prices of basic foodstuffs have been rising rapidly and it is more and more difficult to survive on the salary of her husband, a junior clerk in a government office. Often the family have to survive on just one meal a day and they can only afford the luxury of meat on pay day.

Florence's children are becoming more and more sickly: the youngest has developed an acute respiratory infection. The doctor prescribed a course of medicine but the clinic had run out of the drug because the government could only afford enough foreign exchange to import one-seventh of the country's requirements of essential drugs. Florence managed to buy the medicine at a high black-market price — and the family's food allowance for the week went at a stroke. She had to borrow.

A week later, her husband came home with news that, due to the IMF austerity programme, introduced to rescue the economy, the price of maize-meal, the staple food, was going to double. Florence says, 'Suddenly it occurred to me that we just wouldn't survive — we would all go hungry!'

The price rise prompted thousands of the urban poor to take to the streets and riot, and the food subsidy was restored after a few days. Even so, the incident shows just how close to breaking point successive price rises can push a family which was formerly reasonably well off.

Origins of the crisis

In the mid 1970s, the big commercial banks in the United States, Europe and Japan were flooded with dollar deposits — the so-called 'petro-dollars' — made by the oil-exporting countries. The banks began to encourage the bigger and apparently more stable countries in the developing world to borrow heavily on seemingly attractive terms. The poorer countries of Africa borrowed from Western Governments, and the World Bank.

By the late 1970s, the industrialised world was tipping into recession causing the world price of the commodities exported by Third World countries — tin, copper, sugar, coffee, tea — to nosedive. Soaring interest rates raised the annual debt burden on Third World countries six-fold. In 1982, Mexico became the first country to demand a longer period to repay its debts. The banks agreed, but insisted that debtor countries should first reach agreement with the International Monetary Fund on an adjustment programme.

In comes the IMF

IMF adjustment programmes force debtor countries to follow a three-point programme: to control inflation, to boost exports and reduce imports.

Control inflation: Make borrowing more expensive, cut public expenditure, raise the cost of public services, abolish subsidies, for example on basic foodstuffs, and hold back or reduce real wages.

Boost exports: Usually near impossible, with the world economy in recession, and Third World countries in competition with each other.

Reduce imports: Many Third World countries are heavily dependent on imported goods, particularly machinery and equipment. As imports are cut, local economies are thrown into complete disarray.

Meanwhile, the Western banks turned to lending at home, enjoying the consumer-credit boom of the 1980s.

Women pay the price of coping

The human cost of repaying debts to Western banks and financial institutions is devastating, and most particularly to women.

As traditional guarantors of family survival, it is they who are most burdened by making ends meet, who eat last, who are the first to be squeezed out of schooling and jobs, and who pick up the emotional and physical price of coping.

Some of these costs are:

Food and the environment: In rural Africa — as in many other parts of the world — it is women who are primarily the farmers producing food for the family. Their governments' need to earn more and more foreign exchange has led many to hunger and desperation. While forests are destroyed for their exportable timber, and more and more fertile land is given over to cash crops — tea, coffee, sugar cane, tobacco — peasant farmers are forced on to marginal lands. This in its turn leads to more soil degradation, the burning of forests and woodland, and hunger.

Employment: In the drive for exports, and the consequent loss of investment in local industries and public spending, millions have lost their jobs. As family incomes decline and prices rise, women must work longer hours inside and outside the home. In all Third World countries, there has been a dramatic rise in the 'informal' sector as women, men and children try to scratch a living by street-selling, making things in their home, prostitution and begging. In some cases, pressure to expand exports has actually increased the number of jobs available to women, but under extremely exploitative conditions, as in the assembly plants in South-East Asia and along the US-Mexico border.

Health: Government cuts in non-profitable sectors such as health provision hits the poor first, and leaves women to pick up the pieces. As subsidies are lifted from basic foodstuffs and taxes imposed, malnutrition is measurably greater among girls and women. The increased time spent on producing, buying and preparing food leads to exhaustion and stress for women. In Bolivia, which used to have an adequate health service, two-thirds of infant deaths are from malnutrition and other preventable causes, and preventable diseases such as TB are more and more prevalent; the price of imported medicines has rocketed and is well out of reach of most people.

The human cost

'I feel my children are going to face a difficult, anguished future. We have put their generation in a cul-de-sac. Their future is black. It's hard for us — it will be harder, blacker, more blighted for them. But they will have to learn that, however hard and bleak their path, they must keep going; because this country mustn't die just for a debt.'
Mexican mother and teacher

'We in the North don't need the Third World's pound of flesh; in fact most of us would be a great deal better off if the South bought our products rather than devote every last penny to interest payments.'
Susan George

'You know there is a limit to the cow, the cow has so much milk. And you can't go on milking the blood. At present they're really milking blood from the South. These countries can't pay it, so they'll collapse.'
Julius Nyerere, ex-President of Tanzania

'The debt crisis should not be discussed too politely. For polite discussions can imply a tacit acceptance of the unacceptable. And what has happened to large areas of the developing world in the 1980s is truly unacceptable.'
UNICEF

(Source: Scottish Education and Development (SEAD))

Case Study: Bolivia

Since 1985, the Bolivian government has rigorously implemented IMF adjustment policies. In the first months, bread prices rose four-fold, and a litre of petrol went up seven times. The consequences of being a 'model debtor' has made Bolivia the poorest country in Latin America on the evidence of infant mortality and malnutrition statistics. Free-market policies combined with the collapse in tin prices have closed most of the country's mines. Many thousands of redundant miners and their families have been 'relocated' from their government-owned homes to be settled as farmers and foresters in sub-tropical, uncultivated areas — without training or capital. Thousands of mining families and peasants seek survival as street traders, domestics, casual labourers, in illegal smuggling, or in growing and selling coca and cocaine. The latter generates more income than legal exports.

For mining families who choose to stay on in the mines, life — never easy — has become very hard. But women have found a communal way of coping through Housewives Committees and communal kitchens, leading to new and imaginative solutions. Zenobia is a miner's wife still living in Siglo XX, a large government-owned mine from which most of the work-force has been made redundant. She has been a member of the Housewives' Committee for nine years:

'We women were raised with the idea that women were made to cook and take care of the kids — that we shouldn't be allowed to get involved in politics. But necessity has made us change our minds. What motivates us to take action as housewives is the situation of need here in the mining centres. We are always dealing with problems like lack of food, medicines and education for our children. For us, the important thing is the participation of men and women together. Only that way will we be able to see better days and see more happiness for everyone. If women continue to worry about the house and remain ignorant about the things that affect our lives, we'll never have citizens who'll be able to lead our country.

'We've gone through years of having nothing to cook. We have had to learn how to cook potato peelings and bean husks, as there have been times when the company store has been empty 'We have always been dependent on the company store for food — the value is deducted from our pay packets. We have to take whatever is on offer — however expensive or unsuitable. What good is tinned pineapple when your children need meat? We can't budget our husband's pay as it almost all goes to pay off our debt to the company store.

'But we've learnt to do other things — like how to run our own food store, how to build greenhouses and grow vegetables. We started the PAM project — the Programa de Ahastecimiento Minero (Miners' Food Programme) — in 1986. Now we run our own store as an alternative to the company's. We started by doing a survey to see what foods people needed to feel their family for a month. Now we sell families a monthly 'shopping basket'. Whatever we can, we buy from local sources and sell at cost price, so the food from PAM is cheaper than that from either the company store or local traders.'We encourage people buying from the store to be part of the project. We ask them regularly what their needs are, what they would like us to order. We make sure our supplies are delivered regularly to avoid panic buying, and we are very strict about quality.'

Eliana, also from Siglo XX Housewives' Committee, describes another part of PAM::'As well as distributing dry foods, the PAM has helped us to build greenhouses so we can grow vegetables to help improve our families' diet, and to earn some money. The project is run through the Housewives' Committee.'The *carpas* (greenhouses) are made from adobe bricks and plastic sheeting. By April 1988 six had been built in Catavi (a neighbouring mine) and eleven in Siglo XX, and some were into their second harvest.

'Before a carpa is built, a site is chosen and the soil tested to make sure it is suitable. Then women, men and children all work together, preparing the ground, and building the carpa. Working and eating together from the soup kitchens run while building is in progress has helped people to get to know each other better and helps to strengthen the community. Each carpa is about 30 square metres in area. Families work together in growing vegetables. Lettuces, radishes, onions, turnips, tomatoes, beetroot and spinach are the most popular crops.

'Each of the groups elects a delegate to take part in planning meetings. Planning what crop to grow in each carpa is essential to make sure that a wide range of food is available . Yields so far have been high. The sun shines all day and creates almost jungle conditions inside, and in the closed atmosphere a good temperature is maintained even at night when the temperature outside drops. 25 per cent of each crop is distributed free to the families involved. 75 per cent is sold at cost price. Each group sets aside money for seed and fertiliser and to replace the plastic when necessary. They are also paying 75 per cent of the value of the carpa back to the project — then they'll own the carpa — and the money is used for building another carpa. As a first stage, forty carpas are planned, which will involve 280 families.

'Everybody is very enthusiastic about this part of the project. We can't just sit back and wait for help, we've got to contribute as well. The project is going well because it's our own work, because the people of this district want it to.'

Time: 1 hr

A cautionary tale

Objectives

1 To become aware of some of the complex cultural issues involved in trying to work with women.

2 To consider how development and relief agencies should deal with cultural barriers to working with women.

Method

1 Explain the objectives of the activity. *(5 minutes)*

2 Divide the participants into groups of four or five and give each group Handout 85 (Part 1 of the case study). Ask them to read through the case and discuss the question on the handout. *(20 minutes)*

3 Hand out Part 2 of the Case Study (**Handout 86**) to each group. Ask them to read it.

4 Bring the group together again and discuss the following questions:
   a. Are there any ways in which this situation might have been predicted or avoided?
   b. What cultural issues does it raise for the implementing agency? *(20-30 mins)*

Materials

Handouts 85 and 86
Pens

Facilitator's Notes

1 This is a particularly useful exercise for people working in an unfamiliar cultural situation, where they may be tempted to make assumptions based on their own cultural values. It shows the danger of introducing inappropriate views of gender equity It also shows clearly that good intentions are not enough!

2 It is interesting to compare the situation described in ***Handout 46 (Activity 48****). The problems were similar, and were eventually resolved, after some difficulties. In this case, the approach was culturally-sensitive, and the women concerned were consulted and involved in the decisions that were made as the situation changed.*

Case study: Working with women — a cautionary tale

Part 1: The Tale

Introduction
This case study involves Afghan refugees living in a refugee camp in the North-west Frontier Province of Pakistan.

This camp is one of the oldest and largest settlements of refugees in the Province, with a total population in the region of 20,000. Numerous organisations have established a range of programmes in the camp, including health, education, water and sanitation, income generation, and shelter.

Programmes involving women were centred mainly around health (mother and child and basic health education) but also involved some income-generating projects.

The widows' project

The organisation involved in this case study had established projects in the camp and felt that they should be doing more for women.

A large proportion of women living in the camp were widows. These women ranged in age from teenagers to quite elderly women; some with and some without children. The organisation targeted this group of women for a specific project because it was felt that they suffered especially from isolation in the camp. They had no male relatives and, therefore, no form of access to the external environment beyond their homes.

The aim of the project was to establish a widows' centre where these women could bring their children and escape from the home for a short time. The centre would run health education programmes, and a children's playground would also be set up in the centre.

The project had been running for a couple of months when the organisation received a strong letter from one section of the camp community. The letter stated that women had been seen washing, and playing on swings, and that men, both Afghan and expatriate, had been seen entering the centre. The letter stated that the centre should be closed down.

The director of the organisation consulted colleagues and it was felt that no action need be taken since other members of the community had not expressed similar feelings.

Discussion question:

You are the director of the organisation involved. What action would you take on receipt of the letter and why?

Part 2: The Outcome

The organisation received a total of three letters over a period of about six weeks. All were of similar strength and content. The organisation maintained its original stance and ignored the letters.

A short while later during Friday prayers in the camp, the mullah condemned the women's centre and the organisation involved. Feelings were such that after the prayers, approximately 5,000 refugees marched on the centre, threatened the guard and destroyed the building and its contents. The refugees did not stop at this. The organisation also had a concrete-making factory and vehicle workshop established in the camp, employing some 350 refugees. The workshop ran training courses in mechanics.

The factory and workshop were destroyed, 15 vehicles vandalised and workshop equipment destroyed. The total damage was estimated at $5 million.

Two weeks later the organisation's concrete factory in Afghanistan was destroyed.

The director was held up by a road block in Pakistan and fired upon. Fortunately he was not injured.

A short time later the organisation completely withdrew from any involvement with Afghan refugee projects in Pakistan.

Part 2: The Outcome

Time: 1 ½ hrs

Creation story

Objectives

1 To examine the Judeo-Christian creation myth in relation to women's subordination.

2 To think about myths from other cultures and identify the parallels with the Christian creation myth.

Method

1 Ask participants to read individually the following texts from the Bible:
Genesis 1: 1-2-4
Genesis 2: 5-3: 24 *(15 mins)*

2 Ask two people to read the texts to the group. *(5 mins)*

3 In small groups of three ask each person to share creation stories from other cultures, that have been handed down from generation to generation. *(15 mins)*

4 In the large group, ask people to share those stories, briefly, and draw out the parallels.

(10 mins)

5 Give participants **Handout 87** Biblical background notes.

6 Go through the hand-out with the group asking different people to read in turns.
(10 mins)

7 Discuss the following questions:
a. What purpose do myths serve?
b. How do people use the biblical creation stories to reinforce the domination of men and subordination of women?
c. How could you now respond to a statement such as 'Women are inferior to men;

we learn this from the creation story in the Book of Genesis'?

d. Identify traditional myths that reinforce the low status of women in society. Share these in small groups.
e. What can you do about myths and stories, both biblical and from other traditions,that serve to ridicule, insult or subordinate women?

(30 mins)

Materials

Bibles
Handout 87
Flipchart
Pens

Facilitators's Notes

*1 Most people know of a variety of creation stories and myths, and in this activity a wide variety of myths can be considered. Some may have come up in the Myths and Effects Activity 35in **Section C.4** — and if so, they could be brought in here too.*

2 You could adapt the activity to use other sacred texts if appropriate.

Biblical background notes

1 **Biblical myths:** Myths are made up stories or fiction, told to explain certain realities or truths of life that are otherwise difficult to understand. There are many such myths in the Bible, but among the best known are the creation stories in Genesis. These creation myths were invented to explain this notion of a Creator, the origins of the universe, the relationship between creation and its Creator, and lastly, our human condition that includes such things as temptation, sin, suffering and death.

Most biblical scholars and theologians today tell us that these creation stories are actually theological statements rather than scientific or historical truths about creation. They do not teach scientific facts; they are not history.

2 **Two creation accounts in Genesis:** These stories come from different Semitic traditions. Not all Christians understand these stories as myths. Some still believe them to be historical facts or true accounts of how God created the world. But believing this can present some very real problems for such people since there are actually two separate creation accounts in Genesis, each contradicting the other. Which account do we accept as 'historical' truth? And which to reject?

a. Genesis 1:1-2:4: In this account, God worked six days to create the world and rested on the seventh. The earth, day and night, the seas, plants and animals were all formed first before God created the 'crown of all creation', human beings. And all of God's creation was good. Woman and man were created as equals together in this story (Gen 1:27). There is no mention here of woman being formed from man's rib; no story of domination and subordination. In this account, our first parents are unidentified and unnamed. There is no story of temptation, sin, punishment, suffering or death.

b. Genesis 2:5-3:24: This is a very different story in which man was formed from the soil of the earth. Once man was formed, then God created plants, rivers, animals, and last of all, woman. This story continues with an account that attempts to explain in symbolic language such things as temptation, sin, suffering and death.

Points to ponder

Neither creation account in Genesis was intended to teach that woman is inferior to man. Yet the Genesis 2-3 story is often used to 'justify' this false interpretation.

We need to understand that Semitic peoples made frequent use of symbolic language in their speech and stories. And these symbolic references are scattered all through the Scriptures. We find them especially in the Genesis creation accounts where we read of woman being formed from 'man's rib'. The rib is a symbolic reference to woman being close to man, of the same kind and same flesh, not different like the animals. The talking snake symbolises temptation, the garden represents life in its fullness, harmony and peace, etc.

Recent studies of the original Hebrew words and texts of the Genesis 2-3 creation story have produced some surprising discoveries. One of the chief discoveries involves the mistranslation of certain Hebrew words. A more accurate translation reads:

Then the Lord God took some soil from the ground and formed earth creature out of it ... (Gen 2:7)

'Earth creature' is a Hebrew word which has no sex or gender meaning. Yet this word has been incorrectly translated 'man' for centuries. The Hebrew words for male and female were not used in the original text until after God removed the rib from 'earth creature'. Only then did the biblical author use words to distinguish the sexes. In other words, in this creation account, there was no 'male' until the 'female' had arrived. The two genders were created together, just as in the Genesis 1 story.

(Source: *Choose Life! A Life Experience and Scripture-based Resource Book for Christian Women's Groups*. Jacqueline Dorr, Nairobi 1991.)

Time: 1½ hrs

Chains that bind us

Objectives

1 To help participants to look at religious rituals and practices that control women.

2 To relate those rituals and practices to our everyday reality.

3 To identify which of those rituals and practices need to be changed.

4 To have a symbolic healing session for women. (Part 2)

Method

Part 1

1 Give to the group the picture 'our experience' (**Handout 88).**

(5 minutes)

2 Brainstorm in the group the answers to the following questions:
 a. How do you personally feel about such traditional practices that control and manipulate women?
 b. What are some other traditional customs among your people that discriminate against women and girls, and are harmful to them?
 c. Are any of these traditions in the process of changing? If so which ones? Why are they changing?

(30 minutes)

Part 2

1 Ask the group to stand in a circle, each person bent over double while one member reads again the story of the Sabbath healing (Luke 13:10-17). (See **Handout 89.)** Tell the women to remain in this bent-over position until they are 'healed'.

A minute or two after the reader finishes reading the story, she then hands a flower (or other healing symbol) to one person in the circle. On receiving the flower, that person stands upright: she is now 'healed'. She in turn then gives the flower to another woman in the circle, who once 'healed', passes on the same flower to someone else, and so on until all in the circle are standing straight and 'healed' once more. Then divide the women into small groups and ask them to sit and discuss the following questions:

(10 mins)

a. What did it feel like to be bent over double?
b. What do you think it would be like to be forced into this position for 18 years? How do you think this woman in the Gospel story responded when she was finally released?
c. Most of us are not physically bent over to the extent this woman was but we are bound down or chained to certain customs and traditions that control us socially, intellectually, and personally.

2 Give all the participants **Handout 89** and ask them to think about a particular tradition which damages women. They should prepare a short presentation to make to the whole group (not more than 3-5 mins). *(15 mins)*

3 Reconvene the group, and ask each small group to present their discussion to the whole group. *(25-30 mins)*

4 Traditional practices that harm women may come up in the brainstorm, such as female genital mutilation, preferential feeding of boys, child marriage, dowry, sati and so on. Include these in a discussion of what is good, and what is harmful, in traditional practices.

Facilitator's Notes

1 Part 1 of this activity is appropriate for groups of diverse cultures. It is designed for women, but depending on your group, could be used with men and women.

2 Part 2 is more meaningful for Christian groups with the text we include. By replacing this text with verses from other sacred texts, you could adapt it.

Our experience

Tradition has always said women must obey and submit to their husbands and in-laws!
In my tradition the elders say it is useless to educate girls because once they marry, they no longer belong to the family!
My parents forced me to marry an old man because he offered the biggest dowry. I had no choice in the matter at all!
When my husband died, my inlaws forced me to marry his brother so that I could raise children in my husbands name!

Biblical background notes

1 **Jeremiah 6:16** The prophet Jeremiah invites us to stand at the crossroads and look carefully in all directions, down every winding path and roadway. Search out the ways and study all the ancient traditions — and then choose the best from among them. If you do this, he says *'you will live in peace'*.

2 **Mart 2:23-28** When Jesus was harshly criticised for breaking with tradition in this story, he reminded his enemies that even their ancestor-hero, King David, broke traditional law when it failed to serve him in time of need. Jesus is telling us too that laws are made to protect, to enrich and to better our lives, and if they do not do this, then get rid of them. Laws must be our servants, never our masters.

The Sabbath was made for the good of the people:
People were not made for the Sabbath.

3 **Mart 7:1-23** The Jewish people had many laws controlling ritual practices, as for example, the washing of hands. This custom was a ceremony that had nothing to do with cleanliness for health reasons. Ritual or ceremonial washing symbolised an inner cleansing of the spirit, a washing clean of sin, a determination to change and become totally converted. And here, Jesus told the Pharisees that they were hypocrites, more concerned with the strict observance of the law itself than with any spiritual meaning or inner cleansing. Blind obedience to ancient traditional laws that have long since lost their significance and value is a useless exercise.

4 **Luke 13:10-17** In this story we read of a woman who had been bent double for 18 long years. It is one of the Sabbath healings for which Jesus was criticised. The Jews had many laws that regulated Sabbath observances and Jesus was accused by a synagogue official of breaking the Sabbath by 'working', eg healing. Once again he responded by accusing his enemies of hypocrisy, suggesting that anyone would do as much — or more — to help their animals on the Sabbath day. So why deny this same assistance to a suffering human being? His response made his enemies ashamed of themselves. Jesus completely rejected any law or tradition that treated people harshly and unjustly.

Whenever and wherever tradition or law denied life, freedom, hope and justice to others, Jesus deliberately broke with these same traditions. We need to keep reminding ourselves that he came to set us free from all that binds and imprisons us:

I have come that you may have life:
Life in all its fullness (John 10:10)

Points to ponder

1 **Certainly, much of cultural tradition is sacred,** essential and good, and its positive values must continue to be respected and retained at all cost. But we are not speaking here of those godly and nourishing traditions that bring life to a society. Rather, we are referring to those negative practices and customs (found in all ethnic groupings) that hold woman enslaved, that prevent her from developing into a full human person intellectually, psychologically, socially, spiritually, politically, economically. Unfortunately, there are still many such traditions present today that cripple women and prevent them from walking upright with dignity and a true sense of self-worth.

2 **In patriarchal societies**, law and traditions benefit men. They are the ones holding the reins of power and authority. In order to retain this power, men often feel they must oppress and control women, and they accomplish this largely through laws and traditions that dominate women. Men are quite happy with this arrangement, so if women desire change, then women themselves must work together to bring this about.

3 Change can only come then, through women joining together to study these issues of domination and discrimination. They need to ask themselves, 'which customs or practices in our communities oppress women?' 'What traditional values do we went to keep?' 'Which ones do we want to change or abandon altogether because they are oppressive?' Discrimination and oppression of all kinds are forms of injustice and therefore sinful.

(Source: *Choose Life!: A Life Experience and Scripture-based Resource Book for Christian Women's Groups*. Jacqueline Dorr, Nairobi 1991)

C.9 Working with women and men

This section is designed to help participants to work with women and men on gender issues in their own organisations or in popular or 'grassroots' organisations. The frameworks of analysis we presented in the previous section may identify the need to question and alter the nature of development or relief interventions. In many Oxfam-run workshops, facilitators have been asked by the participants to give guidelines on how to go about implementing the insights of gender analysis. How do we introduce gender-awareness into our own work, and the work of others?

1 Listening

The first group of activities focuses on listening, and gathering information. It is not enough to know what questions to ask; it is necessary to know how to listen, particularly how to listen to women. Listening well, and hearing what people really say, not what you expect them to say, is a skill which needs practice and awareness. Women are often constrained by many political and cultural factors in their ability to communicate their real needs and interests, and to give information about themselves. Working in a gender-sensitive way, in the practical sense, means knowing how to listen to and find out about women as well as men. A number of activities in this section focus on listening and gathering information.

2 Working with women and men

This groups of activities looks at some of the dangers of not listening to and talking to women, at the dangers of excluding women from effective participation, and at practical ways of introducing gender issues to counterpart agencies.

C.9 Activities

Time: 40 mins

Distortion of message

Objectives

1 To show the importance of good listening.

2 To show how easy it is for messages to be distorted.

Method

1 Ask for five volunteers, who then leave the room with one facilitator. The facilitator explains that they will be asked to listen to and repeat a story which they will hear. They wait outside until they are called in one by one, in turn. *(20 mins)*

2 The facilitator enters with the first volunteer and they sit facing each other in chairs in the centre of the group. The facilitator reads the story once only to the volunteer. The volunteer cannot ask any questions and must not see the paper. The rest of the group remains silent.

3 Then the second volunteer is called in and the first volunteer has to repeat the story as she/he remembers it to the second volunteer. The same rules apply. The volunteers remain in the room after they have had their turn speaking.

4 This is then repeated until finally the fifth volunteer repeats the story to the facilitator. The facilitator then reads out the original story.

5 Then, in the large group, ask what was learned in that exercise. *(20 mins)*

Materials

A story relevant to the local situation, not more than one page long.

Facilitator's Notes

1 Choose a realistic story, not too long, but with some lists of names and things to remember.

2 Points to emerge from the discussion:

a. It is very easy for a message to be distorted.
b. It is hard to remember something one does not understand.
c. Sometimes the meaning gets lost or changes — it may even have the opposite meaning from the original.
d. Listeners' own assumptions may affect what they hear.
e. It is easier to remember information accurately if one can see it written down or ask questions.

Time: 35 mins

Listening skills

Objectives

1 To experience the effects of not being listened to.

2 To identify listening skills.

3 To practise listening skills.

4 To relate these to gender work.

Method

1 Ask the group to form pairs and share experiences of not being listened to.
(5 mins)

2 In the large group, drawing from experiences just discussed, brainstorm 'what makes a good listener'.
(15 mins)

3 Ask the pairs to reform and practise good listening, based on the list of skills identified. One person talks and the other listens actively for five minutes, then they swap around for five minutes. Finally they discuss the experience together for five minutes.
(15 mins)

4 In the large group, ask participants to share their experiences of being listened to, and of listening; and how these are related to working with women.

5 Give out **Handout 90** Good and bad listening.

Materials

Handout 90

Facilitator's Notes

1 One problem often identified by women is that of not being listened to, or taken account of. The problem often identified by men (or women) in their work with women is of not knowing what the women want because women's views are not expressed. Learning to listen can be the first step for a programme worker trying to work with women. Listening is not just a passive process, but needs working at in order to encourage, accept, appreciate and understand what another person is saying. This is particularly important when that other person is somewhat fearful or reluctant to speak, or if she feels that certain things will not be understood (as may often be the case with uneducated women). If people often have the experience of not being listened to, they may find it difficult to express themselves freely when first asked, but will often respond to good listening.

Good and bad listening

Some examples of blocks to good listening include:
a. 'On-off listening' when the listener 'switches off' at times.
b. 'Red flag listening' when certain words trigger a response that causes us to stop listening.
c. 'Open-ears, closed mind listening' when we quickly decide we know what is to be said.
d. 'Glassy-eyed listening' when we appear to listen while daydreaming.
e. 'Too-deep-for-me listening' when we stop listening because we don't understand.
f. 'Don't-rock-the-boat listening' when we don't listen to something that may challenge our opinions.

They also identify some 'do's and don'ts' in listening. In listening we should **try to do** the following:
a. Show interest.
b. Be understanding of the other person.
c. Express sympathy.
d. Single out the problem if there is one.
e. Listen for causes of the problem.
f. Help the speaker associate the problem with the cause.
g. Encourage the speaker to develop competence and motivation to solve his or her own problems.
h. Cultivate the ability to be silent when silence is needed.

In listening, do **not do** the following:
a. Argue.
b. Interrupt.
c. Pass judgment too quickly or in advance.
d. Give advice unless it is requested by the other.
e. Jump to conclusions.
f. Let the speaker's *emotions react too directly on your own.*
(Source: Training for Transformation)

Good and bad listening

Time: 2 hrs

Listening to women

Objectives

1 To practise listening skills in a real-life situation.

2 To listen to what women say.

Method

1 Explain the exercise and divide the participants into small groups (no more than four people per group). Their task is to find a group of women and simply listen to what they have to say.

(10 mins)

2 Each group goes to listen to some women. If necessary they explain that they are participants on a course on women and development and they are learning how to listen to women.

(30 mins)

3 Back in the large group, each group reports in turn:
a. Which group did you visit?
b. What did they talk about?
c. What did you hear?
d. How did you find doing the task? (Easy/difficult..)
e. What was the reaction of the group?

(30mins-1hr)

4 Lead a group discussion on the differences or similarities between the experience of the groups, and what is to be learned from the exercise.

(30 mins)

Facilitator's Notes

1 Some people can feel uneasy about visiting a group of strange women without the visit being arranged, and without an introduction. They could choose to go on a pre-arranged visit. Others felt that the facilitators might have told the women what to say — they were able to choose their own group of women to listen to.

2 It can be difficult for men to accept that they are just going to listen, and not to tell the women anything. However, when we did this activity, explaining that they are 'students' on a training course seems to have been accepted as a reason, and the women did talk to all the groups.

3 Some groups found it impossible to do this activity without asking questions or having a dialogue. It may be beneficial for the facilitators to accompany the groups on their visits to ensure that good listening skills are being used.

4 This activity can be done either with preparation or not. In our case one group had been informed of the visit previously, another one was an Oxfam project partner; the remaining two were found by the group themselves. The groups visited should be women only.

Time: 1¼ hrs

Did you know she knows a lot?

Objectives

1 To discuss how women's knowledge is ignored.

2 To raise awareness of the importance of gathering data and perspectives from women for development planning.

Method

1 Explain the aims of the session to the participants. Hand out the chart (**Handout 91**).

(5 mins)

2 Ask the participants to think about a woman they know (in their family or in a community where they work) and fill up the chart provided (**Handout 91**What does she know about...).

(15 mins)

3 Participants share with the group information from the chart. Write down key words from the debriefing on flipchart.

(35 mins)

4 Wrap up the session highlighting the following:

a. Listening to women is essential for gender sensitive planning.

b. Because of their multiple roles (community/social, productive and reproductive) women can provide important information for planning.

c. Because of their caring role and social networks women are better placed than men to provide information about household issues.

d. Because of women's subordinate position they may have a different perspective in relation to use and allocation of, and control over, resources at community and family level. Development workers need to understand these differences.

e. Women's work is still largely invisible. We must consult them to ensure that their contribution to household economy as well as workloads are fully incorporated into planning.

(10 mins)

Materials

Handout 91(one per person), flipchart and pens

Facilitator's Notes

This activity could be used in a field visit, and combined with the previous one, ***Activity 76*** *Listening to Women.*

Handout 91 *Activity 77*

What does she know about ...
Herself

i.______________________________

ii______________________________

iii.______________________________

Her children's needs

i.______________________________

ii.______________________________

iii______________________________

The economy of the household

i.______________________________

ii.______________________________

iii. ______________________________

Her work in agriculture or other activities

i. ______________________________

ii. ______________________________

iii. ______________________________

Her neighbours' needs

i. ______________________________

ii.______________________________

iii.______________________________

The problems of her community

i. ______________________________

ii. ______________________________

iii.______________________________

The problems of other women

i.______________________________

ii.______________________________

iii.______________________________

Time: 3–4 hrs

Working to include women

Objectives

1 To explore ways of working to include women.

Method

Part 1: Preparation

1 Give each participant a copy of **Handout 92** and go through it with them.

(5-10 mins)

2 After outlining the role-play divide the participants into three groups:

i. The NGO assessment team (all male).

ii. The community group, comprising elders (all male) and equal numbers of women and men.

iii. A group of more or less equal numbers of women and men should make up the 'observers' of the role play.

One person should be nominated timekeeper and 'run around' link between the groups.

(5 mins)

3 Ask the three groups to go into separate rooms to discuss the briefing and to identify issues to be discussed in the role play.

4 Explain that the meeting was to be held at the temporary camp before the return of the community to their home village.

5 In addition to the general briefing given above, give each group of participants (separately) additional information relevant to their roles.

i. NGO assessment team:

a. Their task is to identify the community's needs and the priority of those needs.

b. The NGO has no food resources available, but this may be available from the government relief agency of WFP (World Food Programme).

c. The NGO is not involved in the health/nutrition sector in general.

d. The NGO has worked in the region for some years, but in other districts with other ethnic groups.
e. Stress to the NGO team that the objective of the role play is 'to explore ways of working with women' and not to get too caught up in the issues of types of assistance, etc.

ii. The community group:
a. The local wells at the home village are owned by a rival ethnic group. The community group uses the ponds whenever possible or walks 10km to a well put in by the government for public use.
b. The clinic in the home village never opened as there were no staff assigned, so the community uses the health centre 5km away. The community's TBA is trained and the trained CHA (Community Health Agent) is very active. Health is therefore not a major issue for the return home.
c. The community traditionally lives in stone houses and will rebuild them over time, therefore shelter is not an issue upon return to the home village.
d. The women in the community group have heard from their husbands about the forthcoming meeting with a visiting NGO team but they have not been invited to the meeting as in their culture meetings are for elders and the men of the community.

6 Ask the community group to split into their sub-groupings along gender/leadership lines and to look at the following questions:
a. What needs do the elders see as a priority for NGO assistance?
b. What needs do the men see for NGO assistance?
c. What needs do the women see as a priority for NGO assistance?

7 Tell the elders and men to come together just before the role play starts and share their basic priorities and needs. The women are not consulted and told not to be present at the meeting (physically out of the room).

8 Observers: the observers should sit in with the community group during the preparation period and hear the additional information given. Stress that the task of the observers during the role play is to assess the role of the NGO assessment team in 'exploring ways of working with women'.

Part 2: Role play of meeting between the NGO team and the community

9 Bring all the groups together for the meeting — excluding the women, who have to stay out of the room.

10 After the meeting convene the whole group, and ask the observers to report back on how they felt the NGO team had performed in terms of exploring ways of working with women.

11 Make notes on flipchart of the main issues and allow time for a general discussion.

Materials

Flipchart and pens. **Handout 92**

Facilitator's Notes

1 When this role play was performed in Ethiopia a number of strategies were tried by the NGO team:

- *They raised questions related to areas of women's activity, such as water availability and collection and infant mortality—however the elders spoke 'for' the women.*

- *The teams brought up the possible needs of particular groups such as widows and women who maintain their households alone. The elders said there were such women in the community and allowed some of the women to be called to the meeting to speak to the team.*

- *To facilitate this, one of the NGO team was changed to a woman. This made access to women by the NGO team more acceptable to the men and the elders.*

- *They suggested to the community that the team split up, so that one group would remain talking to the woman, and the other would move around the camp looking at conditions and thus taking the opportunity to talk to the woman.*

2 There were some interesting comments from the participants after the role play.

Elders: one noted that he had realised the power implicit in his role and enjoyed dominating the meeting with the NGO team. Another felt that the elders had been too obstructive to the NGO team and in his experience the elders would not have been so dismissive of the suggestion that women attend the meeting to discuss the issues which concern them like water and health.

Men: a general comment from the players was that although the elders were speaking on behalf of the community about going home, there was dissent among the men because at least two had decided to stay in the camp.

The men had found it interesting that the elders were not prepared to allow for this. Some of the men had also felt that the women should have been invited to the meeting when the NGO team had asked about the issues of water and health but could not speak over the elders to the NGO team.

Women: the players (who were in fact all women) commented that their exclusion from the meeting was 'typical', and even when they eventually attended (as widows and heads of households) they were talked over by the elders, and their spokesperson didn't say all she wanted to but was continually cut off.

NGO team: All the members found the session hard work. A couple of the members admitted that they kept forgetting that the objective of the role play was to explore ways of working with women and were trying harder to find ways for the NGO team to assist the community.

The NGO team felt that the experience of the role play had helped them to think about their work with communities in a new light.

(Source: Based on a role-play in ***Getting the Community into the Act,*** *by Pat Ellis, published in 1983 by Women and Development Unit, Extra-Mural Department, University of the West Indies.)*

Briefing for role-play

Background:

1 A displaced community group has been living in a camp sited near a town for six months.
2 The group was displaced by ethnic conflict in their home area.
3 They had no harvest last year because of drought.
4 They are traditionally rural and rely on agriculture for a livelihood.

Situation for role play:

1 Government officials have discussed with the group the possibility of returning to their village, and the group has agreed.
2 The government has asked NGOs working in the region to assist the returning group with basic services and needs.
3 An assessment mission of staff from one NGO has requested a meeting with the community group members to discuss their needs.

Considerations:

Displaced Camp: Monthly food rations;
Water trucked from sources to camp;
PHC, supplementary feeding for women and children provided at camp;
tents (family size) provided.

Home Village: No household food stocks because no harvest last year;
Traditional wells are not functioning and rain-water ponds are dry;
Community buildings (eg clinic, school) and houses were looted and destroyed in ethnic conflict

Note: The timing of the NGO visit to the camp and the planned return of the group to their home village is during the local dry season. The traditional planting season for the staple food crop is six weeks away.

The community group: 1 Traditional leaders (elders) speak to 'outsiders'.
2 Women do not have a public role in the community.

Time: 1½hrs

Working with men and women on gender

Objectives

1 To recognise the particular difficulties and possibilities for both men and women in their work with men and women on gender issues.

2 To come up with strategies for this work.

3 To relate what is learnt about gender to the work in the field.

Method

1 Introduce the aims of the exercise. Divide the group into small groups (five or six people) of men-only and women-only. *(5 mins)*

2 Ask each group briefly to share a few successes and problems in working with women on gender issues, and list these on flipchart. Ask them to write down some ideas for strategies to work with women. *(15-20 mins)*

3 Ask them to do the same for working with men on gender issues. *(15-20 mins)*

4 Ask the small groups to report back in the following order:
a. The first women's group reports strategies for working with women. Then the other women's groups add on any new ideas. After this the men's group(s) report strategies for working with women.(10 mins)
b. The second women's group reports strategies for working with men, then the remaining women's group adds any new ideas. After this, the men's groups report strategies for working with men. *(10 mins)*

5 Guide the whole group to discuss the issues which arise. *(10 mins)*

Materials

Flipchart, paper, pens

Facilitator's Notes

1 This activity and others where the group is split into single- sex groups may cause some division between women and men in the group, thus it should not be done in a group that is already divided. It should be done when a good group feeling has been established. It should be followed by two or three quick exercises to get the group back together again, e.g.

***Listening in pairs**: if there are approximately equal numbers of men and women, make pairs of one man and one woman. Each takes a turn, for five minutes, to talk about their feelings about the activity. The other one listens and tries to understand, and does not interrupt.*

***Numbers**: everyone walks about the room. The facilitator calls any number from two up to the number of people in the group, and participants try to form into groups of that number. For example, if the facilitator calls out 'four', everyone has to rush to form groups of four. The game is ended by calling the number of people in the group and everyone gets into one big group.*

*(Also see **Energisers** section.)*

2 When this activity was used in India, some interesting differences emerged between the men's and the women's groups. The men's group, for example, felt that in any context, gender issues should be raised with the women initially, and only raised with men after the women had gained strength and confidence.

The women's group, by contrast, felt that gender should be raised with all groups, mixed, men's and women's, at every opportunity, and should always be linked with caste and with class.

Both sexes felt it useful to work with gender-aware workers of the opposite sex when raising gender concerns, especially in mixed groups. Participants noted the importance of not giving out stereotyped signals as a man or woman when interacting with the opposite sex. This highlights the importance of gender awareness at the level of personal behaviour for effective gender-sensitive work with development projects and programmes.

Time: 2–3 hrs

Village meeting role play

Objectives

1 To give participants a new tool for using in work with women and men.

2 For people to experience the frustration of being ignored as a woman in decisions that concern them.

3 To enable participants to see how easy it is for women's concerns and other crucial information to be ignored when the agenda and the participants have already been set.

4 To enable participants to relate the role-play to real-life situations and suggest ways of involving women in decision making.

Method

Part 1 Preparation

1 Inform the group you are going to do a role-play and ask for five volunteers.

2 Take the five volunteers out of earshot of the main room. Brief them on their roles and give them their role-card (**Handouts94-98**). Give the 'development worker' a map of the area (**Handout 93**). Ask each person to consider their role on their own for five minutes.

(5 minutes)

Ask the 'government worker' and 'development worker' to discuss together and the three 'headmen' to discuss together.

(5 minutes)

3 Meanwhile hand out the role statements to the remaining group, after dividing it up into three groups of 'women' from three villages (**Handout 99**).

Ask them to read their statements, then discuss in their 'village groups'. It is important to tell them to put away their papers and not reveal their identity until told to do so. *(5 minutes)*

4 Arrange a table with two chairs on one side and three on the other side in the centre of the room.

Part 2 Role Play

5 The three 'headmen' come and sit down.
The 'development worker' and 'government worker' enter and all introduce themselves.
Explain the purpose of the meeting and explain you will stop the role-play at any time by clapping hands.

6 After each participant in the meeting has stated their position, and a discussion or argument has developed, clap your hands then inform them that the audience is in fact the women from the three villages. Then say they can go ahead with their discussion.

7 After a few minutes, if they have made no effort to consult the 'women', clap your hands again and tell them to consult the women from all the villages.

4 If they fail to consult at least one woman from each village, then make sure that they do.

5 After consultation, if they return to their discussion as before, allow the discussion to continue for a few minutes before finally stopping it.
(30-45 minutes)

Part 3 Debrief

6 Women from each 'village' in turn say how they felt at being excluded, not consulted and bound by 'cultural rules'. Allow the expression of frustration and anger. Look at differences in how women interpreted cultural rules.

7 The 'headmen' debrief in turn. Especially on how they felt about consulting 'their' women.

8 The 'government worker' and 'development worker' debrief, especially on consulting women.

9 If it hasn't come out in the role-play, ask why no-one discussed the design of the well. Explain that all the information was present on the role cards. Women describe the water pots they use. Explain (if necessary) that the well might not have been used wherever it had been placed, because of the design of the well and the shape of the water vessels. Point out the difficulty of finding out useful information when the agenda is already set, such as what women use water for, how this affects their livelihoods, etc. *(15-30 minutes)*

Part 4 Relating the role-play to real life

10 In large or small groups, discuss the following questions:

a. Have you ever seen a situations like this is real life?
b. What could be done to overcome it?
(These can be listed on flipchart if appropriate). *(10-15 mins)*

Materials

Map drawn on flipchart (**Handout 93**).

Role-cards for:
Handout 94 Development Worker x 1
Handout 95 Government Worker x 1
Handout 96 Headman from Mwingi x 1
Handout 97 Headman from Ikutha x 1
Handout 98 Headman from Kalongo x 1
Handout 99 Women (as many copies as participants)

Facilitator's Notes

1 The roles of the government worker, the development worker and the headmen are all male, and best played by men. If there aren't enough men in your group, they can be played by women.

2 The women in the role-play should be played by men as well as women — it is a useful learning exercise for men to feel how it is to be ignored.

3 Ask participants to base the way they play their parts on their own experience, to make it more realistic. They should not exaggerate roles.

4 You can change the village names to those which suit your part of the world.

5 It is important to finish the activity on a positive note — on what could be done to improve the situation (Part 4) — or follow it with another activity, such as ***Activity 88, Construct an Image****.*

6 It is very important that the players of the male roles do not know that the 'audience' are in fact the village women, until you tell them.

7 It can take a long time to give the instructions for this activity: do it when you have plenty of time.

Handout 93 Activity 80

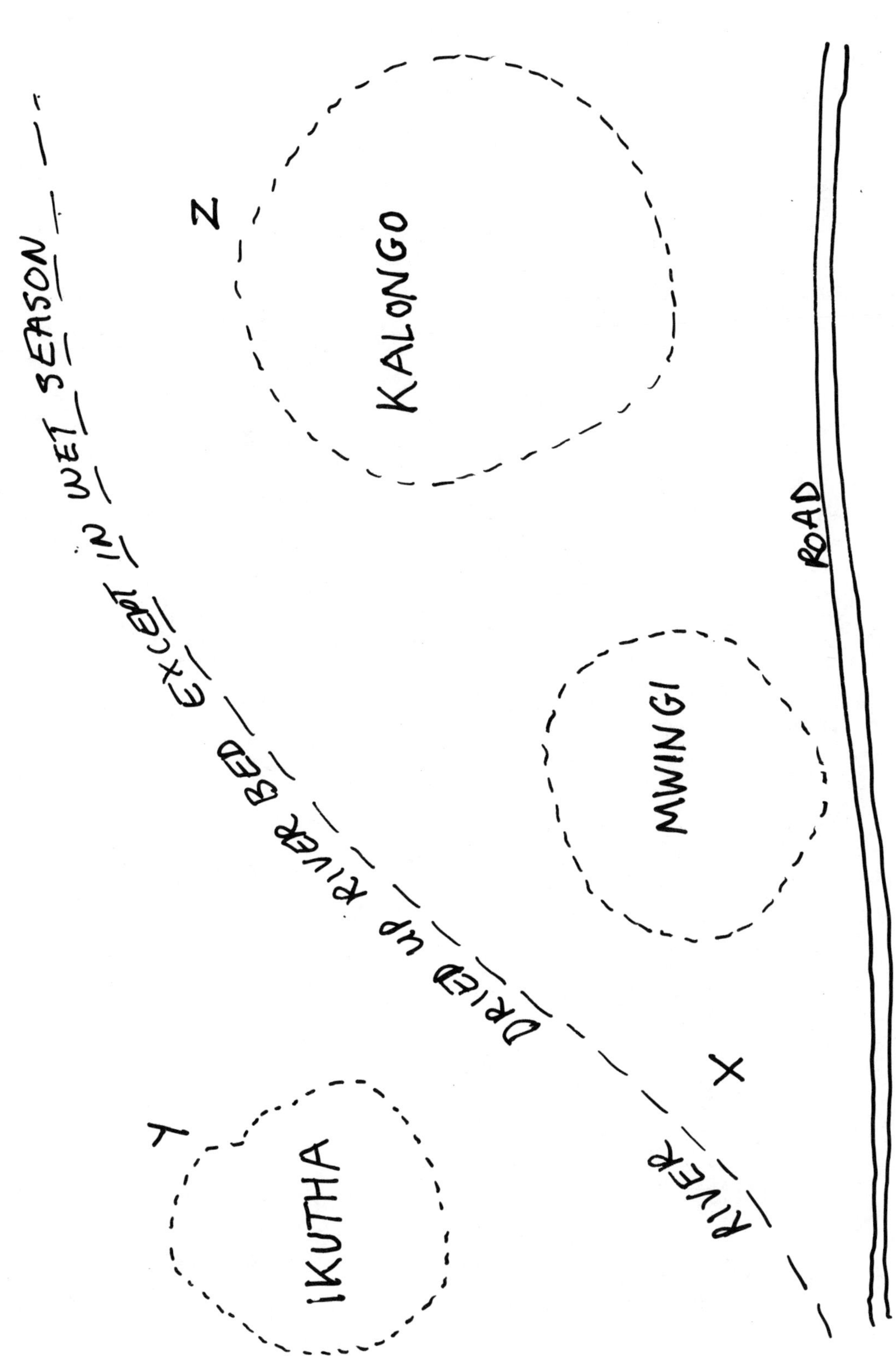

Role: Development worker

1 You are a development worker. There is a lot of sickness in this area, (which comprises three linked villages: Kalongo, Ikutha, Mwingi), much of it caused by contaminated water. Your agency has great expertise in providing water pumps which are hygienic and efficient. The pumps raise large amounts of water quickly and efficiently and have a flat concrete surround.

2 There are only three places where it is technically possible to site the well: X, Y and Z.

3 Your favour X, since it is nearer to the road and it would be easier to bring in supplies.

4 In this area you have to liaise with the government, and you are in contact with their Department of Water Affairs over this matter. Your agency would like to consult with the community. The government department has been very slow, but at last has set up a community meeting to discuss this issue.

Role: Government worker

1 You are the government worker in the Department of Water Affairs. You are happy that a foreign agency is willing to put in a water pump since there is a great need in the area, and the government cannot afford to put pumps everywhere.

2 The foreign agency has said that they want to talk to the community leaders, so eventually you have set up this meeting. However, the government does not want foreign interference in political affairs, and you must make sure that they do not stir up trouble in the village.

3 You know that three possible sites have been mentioned. You believe that it would be more efficient if your department chose the site because you can look at it in the context of planning for the whole country. You favour site Y since it is the furthest from any other supply.

Role: Kalongo village headman

1 You are one of the community leaders (headmen) from village (Kalongo). You have been informed that you will be getting a water pump which will supply the three villages (Kalongo, Mwingi, Ikutha). You are very glad and want the pump sited as near as possible to your village.

2 You think it should be placed at the centre of your village because you have the largest village and therefore the greatest number of people will benefit. Also you have worked hard for your people and want to prove to them that you are a good leader by bringing development to them.

3 You have heard that one of the possible sites is at Z, which is on the outskirts of Kalongo, your village. You don't think that makes sense and you want to ask for it to be put in the centre, which is also near your house.

4 You want to know what the pump will be like and how it will benefit you.

Role: Ikutha village headman

1 You are one of the community leaders (headmen) from village (Ikutha).

2 You have been informed that you will be getting a water pump which will supply the three villages (Kalongo, Ikutha, Mwingi). You are very glad and want the pump sited as near as possible to your village.

3 You think it should be placed at the centre of your village because you have been suffering terribly, especially in those years of little rains. Your village is the furthest from any existing water supply and getting enough water has really been a problem sometimes.

4 The people from Kalongo seem to dominate the group of three villages, and you are not sure if they will allow you free access to their pump if it is situated in their village.

5 You want to know what the pump will be like and how it will benefit you.

Role: Mwingi village headman

1 You are one of the community leaders (headmen) from village (Mwingi).

2 You have been informed that you will be getting a water pump which will supply the three villages (Kalongo, Ikutha, Mwingi).

3 You are very glad and want the pump sited as near as possible to your village.

4 You think it should be placed at the centre of your village because your village is between the other two villages, so that everyone will be able to use it. Also if the water is there you might be able to take the produce there without too much difficulty.

5 You want to know what the pump will be like and how it will benefit you.

Role: Village women

1 You are the women. One of your tasks is to provide water for the family. You collect it from particular places in the river at different times of year. You have to travel many kilometres to get it, particularly when the rains have not been good. You collect it in pots with rounded bases.

2 Some of you come from Kalongo village. This is the biggest village, and is nearest to the river. You have vegetable gardens there beside the river and use the water to irrigate your vegetables. You then use them for family food. Some of you also have fruit trees there. You sell some of the surplus after feeding your family.

3 Some of you come from Ikutha village. You have the biggest problem with water since you are furthest from the river. It takes you three hours to walk to the river in the dry season.

4 Some of you come from Mwingi village. In addition to your other work you sometimes go to town and sell surplus crops or other things in the market. You can only grow vegetables for part of the year, because the rest of the time it is too dry. You have some vegetable gardens near the river. You spend more time in the dry season going to fetch water.

5 It is not considered proper for you to speak to strange men in public, or to contradict your leader or your husband publicly, or to volunteer your opinion.

6 There will be a community meeting for the community leaders to discuss the siting of a new water pump. You can attend if you are not too busy.

Important: In this role-play, do not reveal your identity until asked to do so.

Time: 2 hrs

Working with partners on gender

Objectives

1 To discuss problems faced by NGOs in trying to incorporate a gender perspective into the work of project partners.

2 To look at two different situations:
a. The problems that NGOs working with a gender perspective face.
b. The problems of working through male-dominated institutions.

Method

1 Introduce the activity .*(5 mins)*

2 Present the Burmese case study (male-dominated institutions) (**Handout 100**) using flipchart for the main points. *(30 mins)*

3 Allow for questions and discussion. *(20 mins)*

4 Repeat the process with the Philippines case study (gender perspective of NGOs: **Handout 101**)) *(50 mins)*

5 If there are two facilitators, while case studies are being presented, the other facilitator writes down key issues on flipchart.

6 Sum up the session, addressing the questions:
a. What does the Philippines case tell you about the situation of women in Burma?
b. Are there common strategies that can be identified from these cases?
Summarise the key points. *(15 mins)*

Materials

Flipchart, pens, paper, **Handouts 100 and 101**

Facilitator's Notes

1 If you are doing this as a sole facilitator, prepare flipcharts with the key issues before the session.

2 If participants have knowledge of the areas of these case studies, you could ask them to present the studies.

Case study: Working with partners on gender issues in Burma

Burma's political problems started soon after Independence in 1948 when a series of opposition groups went underground. During successive governments, both democratic and military, a number of uprisings took place, with the largest in 1988 being led by students. Thousands were killed or arrested, while around 10,000 fled to the border areas. After pressure from the international community, the government held elections in 1990 which were considered to have produced a fair result. The main opposition party, the NLD, won 85 per cent of the vote, but the junta refused to hand over power. The current situation is a stalemate; however, the government at present has the upper hand, having acquired international support since announcing the elections, notably from logging and oil companies. It is believed that it may soon be in a position to overcome the opposition groups.

The Burmese Relief Centre

The Burmese Relief Centre was set up in 1988, originally to help students living around the Thai border. It later started extending assistance to refugees from the Keren ethnic group, who had been in exile or semi-exile since soon after Independence. About 70,000 Burmese refugees now live in camps in Thailand. BRC works through the All Burma Students Democratic Front (ABSDF), the Keren National Union (KNU) and through other member organisations of the Democratic Alliance of Burma (DAB). It works both in camps in Thailand and in areas inside Burma controlled by the resistance forces. Most of BRC's assistance is focused on three elements: emergency provision of food, medicine, clothing, etc; medical training; and education.

Specific problems of women

Within these populations, the particular problems women face are the following:

1 Forced labour, either in construction work or as porters for the Burmese army. Women form about 50 per cent of the labour force in construction work and are about 20 per cent of army porters. Survival rates among the latter are extremely low,

with illnesses, including malaria, resulting from lack of care and lack of food. Women porters in particular are often subject to nightly gang-rape by soldiers.

2 Lack of family planning and pre- or post-natal care. Abortion is common and there is much inaccurate knowledge surrounding childbirth.

3 Infant mortality rates are very high, reaching 50 per cent of under-fives in some of the areas controlled or partially controlled by the resistance.

4 Single-parent households.

5 Prostitution. 40,000 Burmese women are estimated to be working in Thai brothels. Many of these are girls who enter domestic or other sorts of menial service and are later sold into prostitution. The prevalence of AIDS is very high among prostitutes in Thailand and the killing of AIDS victims is not uncommon.

BRC is able to address some of women's problems, notably 2 and 3 above, but on too small a scale to solve the problems, being restricted both by lack of funds and staff and by the lack of gender awareness within BRC and its partner organisations.

The students and the Keren refugees present two different communities with different gender profiles. Keren refugee women are highly respected and valued by men. They have equal opportunities and often control the family budget. There is a death sentence in cases of rape. Yet Keren women face many problems which the current political organisations are not dealing with, since there are few women at the higher levels of the organisation. For example, despite women being 52 per cent of the Keren population, there are only 5 women out of 45 in the central committee of the Keren National Union (KNU). Women tend to feel satisfied with their present role and don't want to challenge men.

The Keren Women's Organisation was in fact set up by the president of the KNU, with the intention of bringing women into the political struggle, rather than at the instigation of Keren women themselves. The KWO is thus an arm of the KNU, to whom its policy is subordinated; KNU policy is set up by men and women are not consulted in the process. The KWO is also disadvantaged financially, receiving around 10 per cent of the movement's (diminishing) income while the KNU receives 90 per cent.

The Burman student population, around 2,500 of them living in 22 camps on the Thai-Burma border, have a somewhat different composition, since women form less than 10 per cent of this population. Most students have sought refuge as individuals rather than families, and women have proved reluctant to cut themselves off from their families to the same degree as men. Commitment to the revolutionary struggle is a strong part of the students' motivation, in addition to fear of reprisals from the government.

Women among the students tend to feel they have no significant role in the struggle (there are no women on the central committee) and their morale is low as a result. In addition, they face many health problems and, having no knowledge about or access to contraception, many of them become pregnant. The women students have limited occupational options; those with education may become teachers or nurses, while those without tend to be cooks or cleaners. However, one woman has recently received training in women's development and may soon begin to change things.

For women's needs to be addressed as a higher priority, much groundwork needs to be done in raising gender awareness among all parties, as well as strengthening women's representation within the political structures: for example by strengthening the KWO, by increasing the number of women in the KNU central committee, and by promoting a women's movement within the ABSDF. However, this issue is currently clouded by the serious military situation in which the rebel movements find themselves. Is this the moment to start working for greater gender equality?

On the one hand, women stand to gain considerably from a Keren victory (in terms of freedom from gross abuses such as slave labour and, in the longer term, prostitution). Because of this, maintaining the military integrity of the movement is a priority for women as well as for men.

On the other hand, the refugees' survival depends not only on military strength but also on the strengthening of the community's coping mechanisms, which are in fact being eroded by the inability to address gender issues. It is perhaps exactly at this critical time, when all established patterns of behaviour are threatened with radical change, that gender most needs to be addressed.

Main points

1 In situations where gross discrimination is practised against a particular group, for example on ethnic or political grounds, the goal of gender equality within that group may appear to some to be subordinate to the needs of the political and military struggle, which aims to create the conditions for empowerment of the whole community. But can empowerment of the community exclude women?

2 Enabling all sections of the community to contribute to that struggle as fully as possible is also a vital survival strategy for the whole population. Times of crisis provide opportunities for change.

3 Helping resistance organisations to become aware of the gender dimensions to their struggle may be a timely contribution by outside support agencies.

(Source: Shona Kirkwood, Agra-East Conflict Workshop, Thailand, 1993)

Case study: Psychosocial support systems for women in the Philippines

Attending to the psychosocial needs and problems of people — especially women — during armed conflict is a relatively new field of disaster response in the Philippines.

While more and more NGOs are now aware of the great need to address the problem, the majority are still in the process of defining approaches to respond to the psychosocial effects of conflict. Only a few groups have gone beyond the research and conceptualisation stage and have begun to implement direct programmes with psychosocial services. Yet even these advanced groups still have to emerge from the 'infancy stage' of psychosocial work. Currently, each of them still faces problems associated with lack of human resources, lack of funds, and lack of experience.

If psychosocial work in general is as yet an emerging field, then much more so are psychosocial services directed towards the particular circumstances of women in situations of armed conflict. However, a few groups have already begun to establish mechanisms in response to this. These include some women's groups at national level. Already hampered by the problems mentioned above, these women's NGOs also have to contend with a male-oriented and male-dominated culture which tends to refuse to acknowledge women's needs and concerns. Nevertheless, despite major obstacles, hopes are high among these women's NGOs that co-ordinated efforts to raise the key issues in this field of disaster response will lead to a higher level of effectiveness in the future.

Psychosocial effects of armed conflict on women in the Philippines

The most obvious effect of armed confrontation between government troops and rebels is the massive displacements of communities, causing serious economic and psychosocial problems. Women are particularly vulnerable in this situation. Data from NGOs show the extent of armed-conflict-related traumas suffered by women.

- Emotional and mental distress caused by physical and economic displacement, especially in women-headed households.

- Experience of disaster-response NGOs show that women act as both father and mother in most situations of armed conflict. Having to take care of the children, they face the additional burden of ensuring that the family has enough food to eat.
- On top of this; women constitute the majority of volunteers for disaster-response groups. As such, they take part in registering disaster victims, acting as disaster-response committee members, attending training courses and acting as negotiating panel for peace talks with warring groups.
- Women have to do at all this at the same time as trying to cope with the emotional stress of being physically separated from their husbands, who may be in hiding for fear of being suspected as a rebel or may be combatants.
- The fact that women comprise the majority of disaster volunteer workers reflects a gender-bias not only at the community level, but within NGOs as well. Many NGOs believe that women are easier to mobilise for disaster response because:
  i. they are not tied to production work;
  ii. disaster response is a women's job;
  iii. women are more committed to service because of their innate nurturing/maternal spirit.
- The distress of having to face all these is often expressed in psychosomatic illnesses. Women in evacuation centres, for example, usually complain of recurring headaches, or body pains and dizziness without any identified medical cause.
- Torture. Because they are more visible in the community (having to do all the fathering-mothering at the family level and volunteering for community work etc.) women are more vulnerable to extreme human rights abuses than men. Reports of women direct service workers (who compose the majority of the DSWs) being harassed are common. At times, they are even used as human shields as in the case in Masbate and Ifugao, where women direct service workers (DSWs) were made to stay with soldiers in one room for about a week to thwart any attempt by rebels to raid the building.
- Rape and other forms of sexual abuse. Apart from the usual physical torture, women are also vulnerable to rape and other forms of sexual abuse and harassment. Cases of women being raped first (sometimes in front of their husbands) before being killed are not uncommon.
- Cases of 'comfort women' do occur. For example, in the Masbate and Ifugao incidents, the DRWs involved later related (during a training) that the soldiers who stayed with them in the one room made several attempts to rape them. Soldiers did this usually after a drinking spree.
- Rape is said to be mainly perpetrated by government soldiers during a military operation. Past experience with civil war in the Philippines has alsoshown that rape at times is part of the war strategy. During the Muslim war (in the southern part of the Philippines) in the 1970s, warring groups raped the women of their enemies as a way to 'get back' at their foes.

Response

At the community level, there are rarely, if at all, any support systems provided for those suffering from psychosocial effects of conflict. The communities or the NGOs do not only lack the professional capacity to assist, their attention is also focused on the more basic concern of ensuring that the children are safe from physical harm during the emergency.

On the part of the government, most agencies given the task of attending to the displaced communities do not consider assisting psychosocial cases as part of their work. Hence, apart from sometimes bringing a patient directly to the mental hospital, they just ignore the problem.

Even among the NGOs, only a few (less than ten) have set up services at the national level in response to psychosocial effects of armed conflict. These programmes started only a year or two ago.

Of these few NGOs, only about two or three deal specifically with women victims. The rest are not gender-sensitive and have no gender perspective in their programmes. Programmes are then implemented without gender considerations.

Type of psychosocial support services provided

As mentioned, the majority of these groups are new in this line of work, having taken off only in the middle 1980s. Except on gender issues, these groups use similar approaches and methodologies in their work, which include the following:

a. Tension-relaxation training aimed at relieving psychosomatic symptoms of patients.
b. Individual counselling and group counselling to patients.
c. Group dynamics among patients.
d. Individual and group counselling of relatives.
e. Sessions with community members.

All these are aimed at relieving the tension of the patient as well as providing a conducive atmosphere for her/him to get well.

Staff running these programmes are composed mostly of psychologists. Services of psychiatrist-consultants, however, are also tapped for extreme cases. But problems usually occur when psychiatrists come in since most patients oppose the idea of seeing psychiatrists. People associate psychiatry with losing one's mind.

Problems faced by these groups generally focus on the lack of human resources, lack of experience and reference materials to guide them, and financial constraints. Those who do attempt to respond to women's psychosocial problems, however, face additional constraints related to gender, one of which is the lack of gender-sensitive psychiatrists in the country.

Gender-related problems also crop up during therapy/counselling sessions for relatives or community. Men usually view counselling sessions as tasks of women, and so do not attend and actively participate in these activities. Taking care of the patient is also seen as the mother/wife's task.

As mentioned, the few NGOs that work on psychosocial problems resulting from armed conflict are still in their infancy. The following issues are important to raise the level of work:

1 The need to incorporate gender perspectives, issues, and concerns in armed-conflict related disaster response and in other fields of community work. Only a few NGOs are addressing the specific problems of women victims of armed conflict. This is not only true in the psychosocial field but also in relief and rehabilitation. NGOs generally do not make specific provisions for women in relief/rehabilitation work despite the fact that women have expressed particular needs during emergency situations and that displacement increases their burdens.

   This is not to say that most NGOs do not have an awareness of the value of gender in development. However, the majority lack the necessary knowledge and skills to take definite steps in integrating gender into their programmes and services. In this situation, gender training is definitely required.

   Along with gender training, efforts should be made to incorporate gender issues into existing training programmes. This is specially true for current disaster management training programmes which do not recognise women's needs and roles in disaster response, despite the fact that the majority of disaster volunteers and training participants are women.

   Likewise, other fields of community work such as health, organising, socio-economic work, lack a gender perspective.

2 Continuing research and documentation on women in relation to armed conflict. There is currently a dearth of information on the impact of armed conflict on women, including the psychosocial effects of war. Data on this would facilitate essential work such as training curriculum development, programme planning, and even awareness raising.

3 Creating space for sexually-abused women. An atmosphere for the women victims to come out into the open should be encouraged, and people should be informed about the issue to erase stigma and biases. There are now several groups working towards this although they do not specifically deal with those victimised in situations of armed conflict. As a result perhaps of these groups' efforts,

compared with the previous years, more Filipino women have publicly related their traumatic experiences and thus contributed to the public's education on the issue of sexual abuse.

4 Recognition of mental health as an issue and the need to correct misconceptions about mental health. There is a tendency for people, even health workers, to ignore or not to recognise or acknowledge mental health concerns. Community and even health workers tend to look at people's disaster-related problems in terms of physical and economic needs only. Hardly anybody looks into the disaster's effects on the people's mental and/or emotional well-being and people adjudged as having mental problems are stigmatised. For example, one difficulty expressed by psychosocial workers is the patient's reluctance to be referred to psychiatrists. They associate psychiatry with having 'gone crazy'. Even their relatives express negative reactions at the idea for fear of the attached stigma.

Although this trend has started to be overturned now with more people realising the need to look into disaster victims' emotional and mental health, increased efforts have to be made in this respect. There is a great need for NGOs to exert efforts to correct misconceptions and other myths surrounding mental health. People should be brought to recognise the role of psychiatryin mental health.

5 Creating structures for community-based approaches in psychosocial response work. One of the limitations of the current work being done in the country is the NGOs' inability to set up psychosocial support mechanisms at the community level. This should be done to supplement the prevailing clinical approach.

This is not to diminish the importance of the clinical approach. But one limitation of the clinical approach is the reality that there are more patients than there are psychologists to attend to them and that success of treatment could be boosted when there is a mechanism at the community level to do follow up work. Furthermore, the psychosocial impact of any armed hostility may be lessened with the timely pro-active intervention of a community-based structure.

A lot of work remains to be done in the field of providing psychosocial support to women victims of armed conflict in the Philippines. Work has just been started by a few groups who have now raised key issues that if addressed can help improve and order approaches to work.

In our experience, the simple act of consistently asking about the particular needs of women disaster victims led to a partner's initiative to add a session on gender issues in one training programme.

(Source: Arlene C Mahinay, Agra-East Conflict Workshop, Thailand, 1993)

Time: 1 hr

Finding out about women

Objectives

1 To explore practical ways of finding out about women.

2 To enable participants to share ideas and methods for finding out about and from women.

Method

1 Ask the participants, if a mixed group, to split into groups of women only and men only. Explain that the practical questions which arise for women and for men in consulting women are very different.

(5 mins)

2 Ask the groups to make lists on paper of the methods they had used or knew about or could suggest for finding out about women.

(30 mins)

3 Ask each group to report back in turn, one new idea at a time. Write these on flipchart, noting any that are suitable for women or for men.

(10 mins)

4 Draw out of the discussion common perceptions of useful methods, and the differences in the ways women and men seek the views of women.

(15 mins)

Materials

Flipchart, sheets of paper, pens

Facilitator's Notes

You may be asked why the group is divided into single-sex groups. Explain (and discuss) the fact that in many cultures it is not possible or easy for women to talk to men, especially strangers.

Time: 1½ hrs

Positive action

Objectives

1 To identify some positive actions which can be taken to encourage a gender perspective in partner organisations.

Method

1 Explain the aims of the session. *(5 mins)*

2 Divide the group into small groups of four or five and ask each group to make a list of different types of resistance they face in addressing gender issues with partners, and why these occur; and to produce a list of positive actions which could be taken.

(60 mins)

3 Ask each group to stick their list on the wall and read all the lists.

(10 mins)

4 Pick out the main issues. Give out **Handout102** and go through the points with the groups.

(10 mins)

Materials

Flipchart, pens
Handout 102

Ideas for working with project partners in exploring gender in their work

Raising gender issues with partners can either strengthen or weaken partnership. It can strengthen partnership if it is done as part of a long-term strategy of permanent dialogue: it can weaken it if done on an *ad hoc* basis, and can lead to issues about imperialism and cultural inappropriateness being raised.

A long-term strategy for working with project partners should be characterised by:
- open dialogue;
- the ability to listen to critical questions from partners;
- transparency in our approaches to our work;
- recognition that learning is a two-way process;
- time;
- resources;
- clear prioritisation on where to start, who to start with and why.

The following is a list of possible components for such a strategy in relation to work on gender.

1 Joint training workshops on gender involving NGO staff and project partners, using resources from local organisations and the resources available from within the NGO.

2 Strengthening ties with and understanding of women's organisations and movements, since they will have information and insights about the situation of women in the country or region which will help us to develop our own country or regional perspectives and outlook.

3 Strengthening and developing a consistent strategy for networking and information exchange between those working on gender issues and those working on development issues in general, at country level.

4 Commissioning research which documents and synthesises the experiences of men and women in a range of situations; prioritising the contracting of local and regional researchers for this task and investing resources in documentation and distribution.

5 Strengthening the NGO's resource-base of local women consultants, trainers and experts which will enhance the likelihood of culturally-sensitive gender-balanced perspectives being incorporated into planning.

6 Prioritising the integration of gender into technical issues by supporting the training of specialist gender staff to work with or in technicalteams.

7 Inviting the participation of partner groups in agency meetings and workshops.

8 Providing gender-sensitive partners with opportunities to contribute to the design of agency strategies and long-term planning.

9 Encouraging agency staff to develop skills as 'trainers of trainers'; strengthening partners' ability to explore gender issues in their own work; providing resources such as time, training and technical resources to facilitate this.

10 Exploring mechanisms whereby we can establish dialogue with ongoing partners, such that our experience on gender can be incorporated in concrete ways during project design and implementation.

11 Encouraging the development of ties and networking between partners on a regional or cross-regional basis.

12 Aiming through research and practical experience to recover the concept of gender as it is expressed in the societies in which we work, and working through with partners its liberating and oppressing aspects.

13 At grassroots level, seek out individuals holding moral and spiritual authority within the community who share the agency's concern for equity and social justice, and who can become our allies, and strengthening them in their work.

C.10 Communicating gender

It is important to consider the way in which development work is conveyed to others — whether for fund-raising, education or other purposes. NGOs have a responsibility to represent their partners in development fairly and accurately. NGO publications or advertisements may be one of the few places where people in Northern countries gain information about other countries. NGOs' commitment to opposing racism, sexism and all forms of discrimination should be reflected in the materials they produce.

This section is designed for workers in NGOs producing materials for the public. It is based on training done with Northern (European) NGO workers, who in their work communicate about Southern (African, Asian, Latin American, and Middle-Eastern) people. Racism and representation have to be considered at the same time as gender. Communicators should look at the way women of colour are represented in materials, both images and text, and at the way messages are communicated about women of different religious traditions. For example, messages about Muslim or Hindu women may be presented in a way which echoes Western cultural prejudices. If you use these activities for other groups of people, you may need to adapt them.

The activities aim to help participants to:

1. Look at how meanings are constructed through the interplay of words and images.
2. Look at the range of stereotypes of 'Third World' women in a variety of media and how they fit into a broader context of racist/sexist ideology.
3. Explore what is meant by 'positive' and 'negative' images of women in development.
4. Look critically/constructively at their own agency materials, and share policies and experience in producing materials which reflect women's roles: problems, successes, examples.
5. Develop practical ideas for communicating roles of women/women organising for change effectively, looking at the process as well as the actual materials.

These activities shoud be used with participants who have some understanding of gender. We have used themas a one-day course following on from a one-day Gender and Development course. If you are not incorporating these activities into a gender and development workshop, you would have to, at least, start with **Introductions, Expectations** and **Sharing Work Experiences** on gender, as usual, and include one activity, such as What is gender? **Activity 17**, so that people had an agreed understanding of gender. Note that some of the activities in this section require preparation well in advance, to select photos or slides and NGO materials.

The activities in this section were developed by Janet Seed and Focus for Change for Oxfam's Gender and Communications Course.

C.10 Activities

1–1½ hrs

Images

Objectives

1 To look at how images are 'read', and how this is affected by cropping and captioning of images.

2 To explore visual stereotypes of different cultures, races, men and women in the media, and how this wider context affects how NGO materials are 'read'.

3 To examine what we mean by 'positive' and 'negative' images.

4 To explore the issues of power and accountability in relation to visual images.

Method

1 Prepare in advance three sets of slides or photos to correspond with the first three objectives, according to the trainer's notes below. (The fourth objective will be covered in all groups.) If using photos, pin the photos onto three separate boards.

2 Show the first set of slides or photos. *(10 mins)*

3 Lead a discussion on the set of slides or photos, bringing out the points in the trainer's notes and handout. *(10-15 mins)*

4 Repeat stages 2 and 3 for the other two sets of images (total 40-50 mins), (10 mins to view images plus 10 mins discussion per set).

5 Sum up, and give out **Handouts 103** and **104**. *(10-15 mins)*

Materials

Either a set of about 30-40 slides, plus slide projector.
Or a set of about 30-40 pictures, plus three large boards.

These will need to be carefully chosen, well in advance, to represent the points you wish to make. You can collect pictures from development NGO publications or advertisements, travel or tourist brochures, newspapers and magazines. If the training takes place within one NGO, you can use some of the pictures they have in their library. Some ideas for images are in **Handout 105** Samples Images. There are also many training packs which use images (See Resources section).
Handout 104 Afterword
Handout 103 Images
Handout 105 Sample Images

Facilitator's notes

Set 1: choose a picture that has a very different meaning if you cut it in half. Show first one half, then the other, then both; and ask for people's reactions. show a complete picture and a small part of it enlarged, wherethese give different meanings; ask for reactions. (See Handout 105 Sample images.)

Set 2: choose pictures of both black and white men and women from a variety of different sources. Choose images which are 'consumed' in your country but which may be 'produced' in another country. The images chosen should reflect the stereotypes commonly seen: women being passive, dependent, decorative objects, as in advertisements whshowing women cooking in evening dresses; men being strong. Also, show differences between races, such as adverts with white men and computers, not black men or women. In Northern countries, Southern women may be seen as 'exotic', Southern men as dangerous. Also include some of the NGO stereotypes: 'starving, helpless victims of famines'; wide-eyed dirty children with outstretched hands, desperate mothers; and pictures which romanticise or idealise women: rural images with a 'timeless quality, scenic poverty.

Set 3: choose pictures which show people being helpless and being strong, family pictures taken by people living in Southern countries, charity pictures from Northern countries, photos which deliberately use different titles or are constructed in such a way as to challenge our way of viewing them. Include some pictures which challenge sex-role stereotyping: men with babies, women working in traditionally 'male' jobs. Include pictures of women in women's groups. You may have difficulty in finding some of these images. The Oxfam journal Focus on Gender may be a good source. If necessary, take your own photos.

Use the above notes, plus the notes on ***Handout 103****, to guide discussions. Allow people time during the session or later to read the handouts and discuss them. Note that the book 'Our Own Freedom' from which* ***Handout 104*** *comes received some criticism for not naming all the women in the pictuures and not contextualising enough. Nevertheless, we have found the handout valid and useful.*

Images

Set 1: Images are ambiguous. Our own experience and the dominant ideology of society can affect how we 'read' a picture. The photo shows appearances at a particular moment — it doesn't tell us about what happened before or after, relationships or power — or anything happening outside the frame. The same place, people or event can be photographed in many different ways. The photographer chooses what to focus on. How the picture is framed — at the time of taking it and afterwards through cropping – affects how we see it.The title makes a big difference to how we 'see' the picture. General titles such as 'a village in Africa' encourage generalisation and stereotyping. We need people's names, place, context, to understand.

Set 2: These stereotypes have enormous power over us — both as producers of images and how we read them — even when we know them to be untrue. Whatever images NGOs produce, how they are seen is influenced by these other images which may be in the same publications. For example, images may construct:

a sexist context — women are used to sell consumer goods, represented as passive desirable sex objects; the 'norm' is white, young middle-class, slim, rich — others are invisible. Women at work are shown in domestic caring roles. Images of Third World women may romanticise their poverty.

a racist context — the development of photography coincided with the spread of colonialism. It was used to reinforce an ideology of racism which in turn sustained widespread theft of land and resources. Ethnophotography focused on measuring 'Primitive'peoples, portraying them as alien, exotic ('the noble savage'), and inferior. Present-day images of black people continue to stereotype them.

The same process of constructing an ideology of inferiority was used in relation to people with disabilities, and is a common one experienced by many oppressed groups.**Northern NGO images** of people from Southern countries used to,and some still do, show images of passive starving victims, in need of help.

Set 3: Are images of poverty and suffering always to be avoided by NGOs or does this also distort reality? Should we only show Third World poverty with its root causes and links to Northern countries, such as the international trade system, arms trade, debt crisis, or political oppression? If such images are used , do people understand the intended message, or will they be 'pulled' to see only the image of the helpless famine victim? Can 'positive images' of women also become stereotypes and not reflect reality when they are used continuously? NGOs should include images of women in all their roles : home management/child care; community work; productive work; employment; leadership; and in different situations — urban and rural, peace and war.

Power and accountability

We need to consider the 'power triangle' involved in photos -

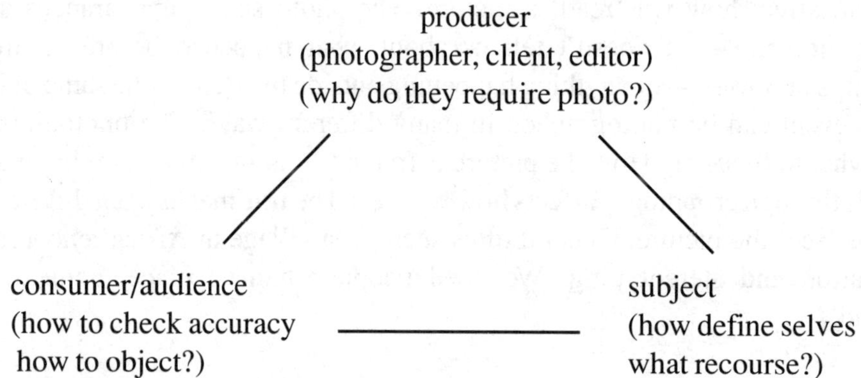

People using images for fund-raising face particular constraints. They may feel it necessary to use dramatic images showing people as victims in order to draw people's attention and thus raise money. What is the long-term impact of this?

Sometimes there are difficulties in obtaining photos that reflect the reality of a group. Some groups do not want to be photographed.How would we feel if we were photographed in this way? (We tend to take pictures of ourselves when we are 'looking nice' and to commemorate happy occasions, holidays, weddings etc.) How much can people be informed about the use the photos of them will have?

How far can 'Southern ' groups be involved in the process of NGO image -making in the 'North', and what would the consequences be of increasing this involvement? It would imply changing the whole process of producing images (see power triangle above) — who takes the photos, what brief they have, who's involved in choosing the images used. Such a process must be part of the long-term policy decisions of the agency.

The EC-NGO liaison committee has produced a Code of Conduct for producing 'Images and Messages related to the Third World' (see **Handout 107**) and a number of Northern NGOs (eg Oxfam, Christian Aid, and SCF) also have their own guidelines. These are discussed after **Activity 86** What do you want to say?

Afterword: from 'Our Own Freedom'

On a photographic trip to West Africa I travelled with one of the few women field staff working for a development agency. Years previously, in a village which was part of a United Nations Women's Project she had asked the women what they thought of the project. Their response was clear. 'Oh them', they said, 'They come to the village, talk to the men and then go away again. They never speak to us.' From that point she determined never to visit a village again without talking to women.

Working with her, taking pictures and listening to women express their point of view was an education for me. This book started then. In villages all over Africa I have sat in circles and listened to women's lives being interpreted by men. Sometimes by foreign development agents, sometimes by local aid workers and sometimes by village men themselves. In Upper Volta though the women did the talking. They spoke about health, about literacy, about farming and everything else that concerned their lives. They spoke from their own everyday experiences. Gradually, I began to realise that I had been as guilty as anyone else in the way I had photographed and selected images of African women for more than thirteen years. I had the Western attitude which devalues women's work and ignores their central contribution to their own economies. I had accepted men's interpretations of African women's work and lives.

Photography has been used to exploit or misrepresent many peoples outside the modern, industrialised economies of the West. The African view is that most photographs are taken of them to ridicule and oversimplify their culture. They know photographers earn large sums of money by presenting them as exotic fodder for colour magazines or as emaciated victims with no autonomy or skills.

(Source: Maggie Murray and Buchi Emecheta, *Our Own Freedom*, Sheba, London, Britain, 1981.)

Sample images

1

2

Set 1: Examples of photos with a different meaning if half is cropped out of the picture.

1 A woman villager from Bubrubi on Lake Victoria, Tanzania, collecting firewood. Geoff Sayer/Oxfam
2 Two English visitors to Calcutta photographing Mr Biswas, Director of the Fellowship of the disabled. . Peter Wiles/ Oxfam

3

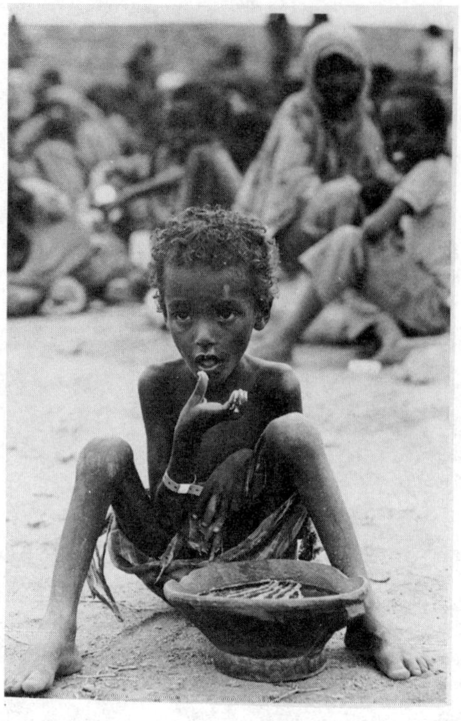

4

5

Set 2: The power of stereotypes: 'exotic' people, helpless victims, and idealised views of rural life..

3 Young tribal women, Hyderabad. Rajendra Shaw/ Oxfam
4 Child in emergency feeding centre, Somalia. Martin Pope/ Oxfam
5 Boatmen on Inle Lake, Burma. Ben Fawcett/Oxfam

6

7

8

Set 3: Pictures which challenge gender stereotypes by showing women in traditional 'male ' (strong, active) gender roles, and men in 'female' (weak, passive) gender roles.

6 Father with his children, Kalsaka village, Burkina faso. Mark Edwards/Oxfam
7 Rajasthani woman, at work carrying sand, on a building site in Delhi. Mike Wells/Oxfam
8 Women soldiers, Honduras. Oxfam.

9

10

11

Set 4: More pictures to make us think

9 A positive image, showing that women can take an equal part in mixed groups. A meeting of an organisation of landless people, Bangladesh. Tanvir/Oxfam

10 The caption for this image, used by the Edinburgh District Council Women's Committee to draw attention to violence against women, is 'By the time they reach 18 one of them will have been subjected to sexual abuse'; this shows how a caption can transform the way an image is perceived.Franki Raffles

11 The caption for this image was 'Refugees receiving kitchen utensils and agricultural tools, Tore, Sudan'. Such a caption reveals a degree of gender-blindness: the fact that there are no women in the photograph is not acknowledged. UNHCR/Miller

Time: 30 mins — 1 hr

Representing community groups we work with

Objectives

1 To help participants to focus in greater depth on how images are read.

2 To help participants to relate the analysis of images to their work.

3 To show how gender is implicit in all images.

Method

1 Choose about 50 photos from various sources. These can be from the same sources as the previous exercise, but they should not be the same photos.

2 Place the photos on tables or on the floor, in the middle of the room, where they can all be seen.

3 Ask participants to walk round and look at all the photos, and to choose one which they feel represents the community groups with which their organisation works. They should also have a second choice, in case two people choose the same one. At this point people should just look at the photos, not pick them up.

(5 -10 mins.)

4 Ask if everyone has made their choice. When they have, ask them to pick it up. If two people choose the same photo, they should negotiate.

5 Divide the group into small groups of four to six. These should be composed of people from different organisations or different parts of the organisation. Ask them to show their photos and discuss:
a. Why they feel the photo is representative.
b. Differences within the group: why there are different perceptions about the people shown in the photos and what they are doing.

(10-15 mins.)

6 Reconvene the large group. Each person holds up their photo with no comment: then lead a general discussion on:

a. Similarities and variation in perception within the group.
b. Is there a gap between the photographer's intention and the effect on the viewer?
c. What is said about women and men, and what or who is left out.
d. What is a good image for the organisation and for the community represented?
e. Is there a tension between images used for fundraising and those used for education?
f. Does the photo fairly represent both women and men in the community?

(15-30 mins)

Materials

50 photos from various sources: development publications or photo library, family snapshots, showing a variety of different situations, types of development projects, men, women, girls, boys and mixed groups.

Facilitator's notes

1 This exercise is very similar to Activities 11 What is development and 12 What is community development, so do not do those activities as well as this one. This is an example of activities where the basic task is the same (choosing a representative picture), but the objectives, and therefore the discussion and outcome are completely different.

2 Points to bring out:
a. It is impossible to represent even one small community group in a single representative image, and certainly impossible to represent the variety of groups and organisations that an agency works with.
b. There are very personal responses to images, for example as to what one sees as positive or strong
c. Every image says something about women and men: what is it, and is it what we want to say?.

Time: 20-30 mins

What do you want to say?

Objectives

1 To arrive at some guidelines for practical work in using images, using learning from previous activities and existing guidelines.

Method

1 Ask the group to brainstorm: 'What do you want to say about women and men in development?'.

2 Highlight key points for producing guidelines, and write them on newsprint.

3 Give out **Handouts 106** and **107** and any other relevant guidelines on images (eg organisational policy on images).

4 Discuss in the large group:
a. How useful are guidelines and checklists?
b. How can they be implemented?
c. What are the barriers within the organisation to implementation?

5 Put up the flipchart with basic communication needs as a reminder. Keep this and the other handouts and the brainstorm on the wall for reference

Materials

Flipchart, pens
Handout 106 Extract from Oxfam draft paper on gender and communications
Flipchart with contents of this Handout written on it.
Flipchart with basic communication needs written on (see *Facilitator's notes*).
Handout 107 (EC-NGO guidelines)
Organisational policy or guidelines on images (if any).

Facilitator's notes

1 Checklists can be difficult to follow, unless people work through them in practice.

2 Guidelines can be contradictory, confusing, and overgeneralised. Yet it is important for people to think about the principles of what they are trying to do in order to move on from critique to production.

3 Remind group of basic communication needs (written on newsprint)
Who is the target audience?
What is its existing viewpoint?
What message do you want to get over?
How to cut through indifference: why should they read it?
Design and image.

Extract from an Oxfam paper on communications

Gender sensitive communications should highlight that:

1 Women in poor and developing countries bear a large part of the burden of poverty and are the key to successful implementation of projects, yet they are rarely consulted in decision making.

2 Many problems faced by women in developing countries originate in industrialised countries.

3 Overcoming discrimination and exploitation is a complex, long-term process, in which poor women are already engaged.

4 The variety of experiences of poor women shape their views of development and determine the strategies they are adopting to overcome poverty and gender inequality.

5 Women in developing countries must have an opportunity to define their needs and priorities, the solution to their problems, and the support they want.

6 Women are not a homogenous group, and their roles and needs vary greatly from one culture or society to another.

7 Women cannot be seen in isolation from men: the nature of gender relations determines what they can do, what supports, and what oppresses them.

EC/NGO Code of Conduct

Images and messages relating to the Third World

1 General objectives of the Code of Conduct

- This Code is both a challenge and a guide for European NGOs. Its aim is to encourage NGOs to examine the material they produce on the Third World and to be especially attentive to images that over-simplify or concentrate on the apocalyptic or idyllic aspects of life.

- It invites NGOs engaged in fundraising activities to re-examine their appeals to the public.

- It serves as a reference for NGOs working to strengthen the solidarity, cohesion and force of the NGO movement.

- It is recommended that the EC Commission take this Code of Conduct into account in its work with European NGOs.

NGOs and fundraising

Several systems of fundraising are used by Northern NGOs. These include large-scale annual appeals, thematic campaigns or emergency aid campaigns. The means applied can involve mailings to regular donors, the production of posters or the holding of sales (books, cards, crafts, background material, etc.).

A lot of images and messages are produced by NGOs during these fundraising activities and the type used are determined by the particular viewpoint of the NGO concerned.

Each NGO must decide on the best system to adopt whilst ensuring that the methods applied and the messages sent out by the NGOs, its partners and its sponsors do not present an image of dependency or 'handouts'.

NGOs should avoid the following:

- images which generalise and mask the diversity of situations;
- idyllic images (which do not reflect reality, albeit unpleasant), or 'adventure' or exotic images;
- images which fuel prejudice;
- images which foster a sense of Northern superiority;
- apocalyptic or pathetic images.

2 Code of Conduct

We, **development NGOs established in the member states of the European Community** representing a variety of humanitarian non-profit-making associations engaged in activities to support the development process in the South and in the North, adopt this Code of Conduct as a guide in our daily work in order to improve the images projected by the North of the South.

This Code calls on European NGOs to:

- **examine** their work and review their working methods so as to put an end to the old notions of 'emotional shock' and disaster relief and to ensure the right kind of development education is undertaken;

- promote greater **unity** among NGOs and other social movements to enable an improved distribution of information;

- undertake to examine the **contents of messages** sent out in disaster appeals t to ensure these do not undermine the work of development eduction which calls for long term response;

- provide **adequate training** for members of staff who are responsible for producing information material and seek specialists to advise them in their work;

- above all, ensure that the **viewpoint of the South** is taken into account when producing images and messages.

If international development co-operation is based on the principles of solidarity and the sharing of resources, then the **participation of our Southern partners** in public awareness raising activities is essential for the correct projection of images and messages. In this day and age we can no longer speak about the Third World and project images thereof without previous consultation.

This is not an easy task as the communications possibilities vary significantly from one developing country to another, and from NGO to NGO. Communication is hindered in some places by the remains of the colonial system or the effects of control of the international communications system: the traditional media either give no coverage of the South or they do so from a Northern perspective.

NGOs should work towards:

- guaranteeing the Third World **right of access** to the major means of communication in the North;

- guaranteeing the **circulation of Southern cultural products** in the North, beyond the traditional market outlets;

- promoting **local and autonomous cultural production**;

- **facilitating further the movement of people** in both directions, to ask Southern visitors for their opinions on Western society and to share their knowledge and experience.

True solidarity is not a one-way process. Is it not arrogant to wish to resolve single-handedly the development problems of the South when our own society is itself suffering from widespread development problems?

3 Recommendation

In the light of the above, European NGOs will undertake to review their development education material and content of the messages produced. Messages should aim to improve the public's understanding of:

- the **realities and complexities** of the countries of the Third World in their historical context;

- the **obstacles** posed to development;

- the **diversity** of situations in these countries;

- the **efforts** being made in the South itself;

- and the **progress** made.

4 Practical guidelines

1 Avoid catastrophic or idyllic images which appeal to charity and lead to a clear conscience rather than a consideration of the root problems.

2 All people must be presented as human beings and sufficient information provided as to their social, cultural and economic environment so that their cultural identity and dignity are preserved. Culture should be presented as an integral part of development in the South.

3 Accounts given by the people concerned should be presented rather than the interpretations of a third party.

4 People's ability to take responsibility for themselves must be highlighted.

5 A message should be formulated in such a way that generalisations are avoided in the minds of the public.

6 The internal and external obstacles to development should be clearly shown.

7 Interdependence and joint responsibility in underdevelopment should be emphasised.

8 The causes of poverty (political, structural or natural) should be apparent in a message in order to enable the public to become aware of the history and real situation in the Third World, and the structural foundations of these countries before colonisation. It is the situation today, coupled with a knowledge of the past, which should be the starting point for examining ways in which extreme poverty and oppression can be eliminated. Power struggles and vested interests should be exposed and oppression and injustice denounced.

9 Messages should avoid all forms of discrimination (racial, sexual, cultural, religious, socio-economic).

10 The image of our Third World partners as dependent, poor and powerless is most often applied to woman who are invariably portrayed as dependent victims, or worse still, simply do not figure in the picture. An improvement in the images used in educational material on the Third World evidently requires a positive change in the images projected of Southern women.

11 Southern partners should be consulted in the formulation of all messages.

12 If an NGO calls on the services of other partners (institutions, organisations or private companies) for a fund raising activity, it shouldensure that the recommendations of this Code are respected by all parties. Reference should be

made to the Code in the sponsoring contract(s) between the NGO and its partner(s).

5 Conclusion

The information in our daily news too often presents the Third World in a way that is incomplete and biased — starving people portrayed as the helpless victims of their own fate. This fatalistic approach can be overcome with the provision of **more realistic and more complete information**, thereby increasing **awareness** of the intrinsic value of all civilisations, of the limitations of our own society and of the need for a more **universal development** which respects justice, peace and the environment. It is the duty of NGOs to provide the public with truthful and objective information which respects not only the human dignity of the people in question but the intelligence of the public at large.

This Code was adopted by the General Assembly of European NGOs meeting in Brussels in April 1989. The Liaison Committee's Development Education Working Group was called upon to formulate a strategy for its implementation and follow-up.

Time: 45 mins — 1 hr

Critique of materials

Objectives

1 To analyse critically materials produced by participants' organisations.

2 To broaden the analysis to include text as well as images.

Method

1 Collect a wide range of materials produced by the organisation(s) to which the participants belong. Lay these on tables or the floor in the centre of the room, and ask each person to choose one at random. If the organisation does not produce many materials, you can hand one advertisement or leaflet to each participant. *(5 mins)*

2 Explain the method of analysis to participants, writing main points re visual, text and total impression on flipchart. Participants then each analyse their document individually.

(10-15 mins)

3 Divide participants into small groups, to collate their information.

(10-20 mins)

4 One representative from each small group reports back on what they have found. Lead a general discussion, writing any key points to emerge on a flipchart.*(20 mins)*

Materials

A variety of materials from different sources: newspaper adverts, 'mail drops', fundraising leaflets, educational materials, press releases, lobbying materials, trading catalogues and other publicity. There should be at least one per participant. These will have to be renewed each time you do this exercise. If you are laying them out, remember to allow time for that — perhaps do it in a break.

One pen per participant. Highlighter pens are particularly good .Flipchart and pen

Facilitator's notes

1 It is better to allow people to pick their own document to analyse from a range, as otherwise they may be suspicious that you have chosen the worst examples. It is particularly useful in a large organisation, which may have different departments producing different materials which may not normally be seen by people in other departments. If you are doing this activity with people from a variety of organisations, you need to stress that people should be analysing the document, not attacking the person or organisation who produced it.

2 Materials should be analysed in the following ways:

***Visual**: number of women, men, boys, girls; white/black people. What are they doing? How are they portrayed? How is photo labelled? Is any one named — who?*

***Text**: mention of women, men, girls, boys (gender-specific); and children, people, community, youth, family (not gender-specific). What are the associations or messages? How accurate?*

***Total impression**: what is the overall impression? Does the text back up or contradict the images e.g. 'children' for a picture of boys; 'community meeting' for a picture of men; 'family' with a picture of women.*

3 If participants work mainly with text rather than images, they may analyse documents only by text, not images.

4 Discussion points :
a. What is the overall impression of women's and men's; girls' and boys' roles from these materials? How accurate is this?
b. How are women and men represented?
c. Where do women get left out, both in text and images? How accurate is this? (e.g. Refugees are mainly women and children — is this reflected in the images and text? In materials on debt, are women mentioned? How? In productive and community roles or only as victims?)
d. What are the differences between materials used for different purposes e.g. fund-raising and education?
e. Should materials consciously seek to redress the balance, in contrast to all the usual stereotyped images available?
f. How would you feel if you were represented by such images?
g. Would you use different images if you knew the subjects would see them?
h. What would be empowering for the women and men represented? Would they feel happy with the materials?
i. What are the successes? What are some of the gaps? What could be done to avoid some of the pitfalls?

Time: 30 mins

Construct an image

Objectives

1 To construct an 'ideal' image, based on previous learning and guidelines.

Method

1 Divide participants into two groups. Each group is asked to represent a particular aspect of Southern women in an image or collage of images. They should make a sketch in as much detail as possible — sex, setting, body language, activities, country , camera angle, etc. They should aim to make a strong impact and make the viewer /think about the issues, disturbs assumptions without using negative images. They should try to be adventurous using ideas in **Activity 84** Images.

Group 1 : Poor women as the largest, most vulnerable sector of the population are particularly affected by natural and human-made disasters.

Group 2: Many problems faced by Southern women originate in the North.

(20 mins)

2 Each group pins up their sketches and both are discussed and compared in the large group.

(10 mins)

Materials

Large sheets of paper/newsprint, pens.

Facilitator's notes

1 Make clear that this is not a test of drawing ability. The roughest of sketches will do, with perhaps some notes at the side; the important thing is the ideas.

2 If you have a very large group, you can divide into more than two groups, giving the extra groups other aspects of women's lives (eg women's multiple roles).

Time: 1-2 hrs

Publicity design

Objectives

1 To develop practical ideas for communicating about development in a gender-sensitive way.

2 To relate what has been learned to individual work experience.

3 To be creative.

Method

Part 1

1 Divide the participants into small groups, based on their job or role in the organisation and the type of communications they usually produce (fundraisers, educators, campaigners, and so on). Explain that each group will design a different formof publicity, based on their job:
a. poster campaign
b. mail shot for fundraising
c. poster or leaflet for use in schools.
d. press release
e. one-minute speech for public meeting or radio programme.

2 Give **Handout 108** COPADEBA Case Study Part 1 (only) to each participant. Tell them to imagine that they have been asked to produce some publicity, based on this project, and this is the only information available to them.

3 Each group considers, and writes up briefly on newsprint:
a. main issues, including a gender perspective
b. what images would they like to use
c. who would like to consult with
d. what further information would they like
e. what process might they go through to try to get some input from the people involved in the project or from that country (At this stage they do not map out the design) *(30 mins)*

4 Groups put up their newsprints on the wall, and read each other's. *(15 mins)*

Part 2

5 Participants return to their small groups. Explain that some more information has now become available, although it might not answer all their questions. Give out Handout 109 COPADEBACase Study Part 2. From all available information, groups now design their piece of publicity. They should draw in the images and write in the text, or at least the captions and the headlines if producing materials. *(20-30 mins)*

6 Groups briefly present their publicity. *(max 5 mins. per group)*

7 Comments and discussion, bringing out points in Facilitator's Notes. *(20-30 mins)*

Materials

Handout 108 COPADEBA Case Study Part 1
Handout 109 COPADEBA Case Study Part 2
Flipchart, paper, pens.

Facilitator's notes

1 This is the only activity which is done in groups responsible for the same function, as it is useful to share ideas. You may need to adapt the case study, or write one based on your organisation's documents, but do not make it too long.

2 You may find some resentment from participants that there is insufficient information or time. However, in most cases, people find this quite realistic! If participants' work experience is very different, you could adapt this exercise: you will need to find this out in advance.

3 After groups have presented their publicity, ask:
a. Was the task difficult? Was it realistic in the amount, and type of information that they usually receive for their work?
b. What similarities and differences were there in the key issues as seen and represented by the different groups?
c. Did you quote Manuel Rodriguez? How do you think he would feel about the publicity?
d. What were the reasons for the choice of photos or other images.

4 Then lead on to wider discussion and draw conclusions and recommendations for the future:
a. What are the practical limitations on producing gender sensitive materials?

b. How did groups tackle the problem of meaningful collaboration with partner groups? How can these problems be overcome?
c. There is a need for clear aims and objectives; this is a long process.
d. What training and guidelines should be given to photographers, fieldworkers, and communications staff? Are existing ones good enough, and are they followed?
e. How can communications be monitored for accuracy, accountability, and power?
f. What changes need to be made in participants' own working practice, their departments, and organisation (eg short and long-term funding, informal creative groups, basic communications courses, more black staff, work with black and women's organisations, consultations, use of local photographers)?
g. There is a need for co-ordination within and between organisations, and the formation of alliances.

COPADEBA case study: Part 1

My name is Manuel Rodriguez. My city is Santo Domingo, the capital of the Dominican Republic.

Like all Third World cities, Santo Domingo suffers from chronic lack of services and resources for the number of inhabitants.

The rural-urban drift has contributed greatly to this situation with rural dwellers escaping in their thousands from the harsh reality of the subsistence farmer in the countryside.

When these people arrive in the big city the promise of opportunity and plenty is a dream unlikely to be realised for the majority. They face homelessness and their children face the prospects of no education and a life on the streets — the lucky ones 'employed' in the legitimate informal sector, with the unlucky ones turning to crime, drugs and prostitution.

It is these marginalised people in their tin shack communities of the city shanty towns that my project was set up in 1979 to assist. The Committee for the Defence of the Communities Rights (COPADEBA) was set up in response to the threat of evictions from land on which they had established themselves on arrival in the city.

That struggle in 1979 was successful and together with these communities we have continued with efforts to improve their living conditions. The struggle for clean water, sanitation, roads, proper houses in these shanty towns has now been usurped by our current dilemma.

In late 1987 a plan was initiated by the government to 'develop' the northern part of the city. This plan was presented to the affected communities when it was already being implemented.

The plan called for the construction of major avenues to surround the city which would effectively mean the need to relocate whole communities with a view to beautifying the city i.e. hiding the ugly face of poverty behind high walls, to welcome the thousands of anticipated visitors in 1992 as part of the 500th Anniversary of Columbus' arrival.

Seven marginalised communities, totalling around 50,000 families are to be uprooted to facilitate this plan. Properties are being rapidly destroyed in most cases without appropriate valuations.

The affected families are to be relocated in a new community about 20km away from the city centre, where the government plans to build houses and sell them to those concerned.

Very little has been said to the communities and many questions are unanswered.

COPADEBA, with church support, is talking to the government and offering alternative proposals to the plan, including the need to look at spending public money more appropriately by improving conditions in the shanty townsrather than building avenues to hide them and as a consequence dislocate some communities from their families, friends and livelihood.

COPADEBA is doing this through the production of popular information (audio-visuals and booklets) to facilitate community knowledge and action.

COPADEBA case study: Part 2

Some further information:

1 The committee is elected at meetings. They are men who can negotiate with the government and come up with plans.

2 Not enough homes are being built to rehouse everyone. The price of the new houses is too high for most people.

3 There are no facilities e.g. market, school or clinic at the new site. Transport is very scarce and expensive.

4 Some men are employed in the formal sector. Others are unemployed.

5 Many women have the sole or main responsibility for looking after their family, who may be with them or at home in the village. Women work in the city: many as domestic workers, others selling in markets or selling tacos illegally on the roadside to passing workers, a few as prostitutes.

6 Many women are very concerned about the implications of this plan and are active against it — distributing materials and demonstrating. There is one woman social worker attached to the committee.

7 Some people are reluctant to challenge tourism as it brings in money.

C.11 Strategies for change

The activities in this section aim to help participants in the workshop to use their acquired awareness and analytical skills to move on to planning practical action. The opening activity summarises the workshop, making clear that the process which it has followed has been a logical one, moving through various awareness-raising stages, to sharpening up existing analytical and data-gathering skills and learning new ones, to formulating plans for action. Before going on to action planning, there are a number of activities (Vision, Sculpture, Setting Priotities) which allow participants to think about far-reaching ideas for change in an imaginative way. This provides a useful basis for planning practical action.

The Action Plans will vary according to the kind of group with whom you are working: a small NGO with a very specific field of activity, such as, for example, a women's legal aid centre, will produce very different plans from those produced by a group from a large international funding agency. When considering the Action Plans, it is important to consider very carefully whether they can be implemented, and how they can be implemented. They should not be so ambitious that they are unrealisable. Some of the activities (**Activity 95** Introducing gender to our Organisations, and **Activity 96** SWOT Analysis) look at the difficulties which might have to be faced in implementing action plans, and ways of overcoming these difficulties.

Follow-up is important. If you are training people from your own organisation, you should consider ways of following up the workshop to assess the impact of the course and the participants' success or failure in implementing their Action Plans. If you are an independent trainer, it would be helpful to consider ways of assisting participants and groups to monitor their own progress. Please refer to the Facilitator's Notes for ideas about follow-up.

C.11 Activities

Time: 30 mins

Preparing for planning

Objectives

1 To summarise the main learning points of the workshop thereby enabling participants to refresh their memories for planning.

Method

1 Preparation: prepare newsprint, or transparencies if you are using an overhead projector, with the key issues and concepts which surfaced in the workshop. Do this before the session.

2 Present these to the group, allowing for discussion and adding to the key points. Make explicit the progression of the workshop through the logical steps of awareness-raising, to analysis, to action.

(30 mins)

Time: 1-2 hrs

Vision

Objectives

1 To enable participants to consider deeper and wider issues around the topic of gender.

2 To help people use their imaginations to visualise the kind of gender-aware social justice they would like to see in society.

Method

1 Explain to the participants that they will be doing creative visualisation, which is a way of allowing ourselves to create a vision from our imaginative powers. This vision can help us to make plans which will lead towards its realisation.

2 Explain that they will be asked to imagine a time in the future when gender relations are the way they would like them to be. The first step is to relax so that their minds are free to imagine.

(10 mins)

3 Ask the group to walk round the room freely mixing. Stay out of the group — you are the guide. After a few minutes, tell participants to stop at a distance from the others and to observe how they feel in themselves. Then ask each person to lie down on the floor or sit in a position they find very relaxing. Help the participants relax by talking gently, slowly and steadily. Use any relaxing technique you know, or read out the text below:

(20 mins)

Read this in a slow, soothing voice, with plenty of pauses:

'Whether you are lying or sitting down, close your eyes now. Breathe in deeply. Take the breath into your abdomen and breathe the tension out of your body with the out-breath. Keep breathing regularly in this way, slowly and deeply.

Now start relaxing each part of your body, letting the tension flow out of each part with each out-breath. Feel the tension coming out of your feet, and move your awareness up to your ankles; let them relax. Then your calves, your knees, your thighs.

Relax the muscles in your back, in your stomach. Let go of any tension in your abdomen. Breathe it out.

Now release tension in your fingers, feel your hands relax, then your wrists, your forearm; feel the elbow joint soften and relax as you continue to breathe slowly. Breathing slowly and deeply, relax your upper arms and your shoulders. Let your shoulders drop and soften, let the tension drain out of them. Let your whole body feel heavy and keep your mind relaxed and clear.

Let your chest area relax as you breathe in and out of it, taking cool air in, and letting the tension flow out with the out-breath. Feel your whole spine relaxed and free of tension.

Move your awareness up into your neck and throat and jaw, and let them relax and feel soft and open. Let go of all the muscles around your mouth, your eyes, your cheeks, your forehead. Be aware of your head, and your scalp, and allow any tension there to flow away.

Let your whole body feel relaxed and comfortable. Now allow your mind to imagine.'

(15-20 mins)

4 Then read, very slowly, with lots of pauses:

'I want you to imagine that you're in an area you know well, your community or where you're working. We're going forward in time, imagine that we're in a time machine and we're speeding up and going forward faster and faster in time, to a time when gender relations are what you want them to be. So think about when that time would be, how long will it take for your area to get to the state where gender relations are what you want them to be? I want you now to imagine that you're landing in this new century or time and observe what is going on....

Just imagine looking all around you, look all around and see what you can see. Look in the fields, what are people doing in the fields? Are there men there, are there women there, what are they doing? Are there boys and girls around? What are they doing?..... What kind of expressions are on their faces? Are they laughing, angry, sad? How do they interact with each other?

As you walk around the village or the town, or wherever it is that you're going back to, imagine what everybody is doing in their daily life. What are men doing and what are women doing? Do they seem happy? Do they seem sad? How are they interacting with each other? What are the children doing?

Now I want you to imagine that you are walking inside a house and as you go in the house, notice what the house looks like and who is in the house? What are they doing? What are the men doing, and what are the women doing? What are the boys doing and what are the girls doing?..... How do they seem to feel about what they are doing? How do you feel about what you see? Feel the positive energy in your vision.

And now I want you to imagine going back in time, we're going to go back in time to just five years from now.

What might be happening in five years that would lead us towards that vision in the future? I want you to imagine, just as we did before....' (Repeat the same sequence as before.)

'And now, I want you to come back to your body as it is now, we're back in today, we're back in this room, in this place and you're sitting on a chair or lying on the floor and now I want you to feel that you're back into your body, your body is starting to feel light again. You're coming back from your vision and you're right here and now and whenever you feel like it, open your eyes and look around you. Look all around you and make sure where you are and who is in the room with you.'

(30 mins)

3 Ask participants to share aspects from their vision in pairs or in their support groups.

(5 mins)

4 Ask the participants how they found the exercise. This is to make sure that nobody found it disturbing or worrying. Then ask participants to share any bit of their vision that they would like to. This can then lead on into thinking about the first steps towards the vision at a personal, organisational, or societal level, and as a first step towards thinking about plans.

(30 mins — depending on time available)

5 Ask participants to sit in a circle and say in turn 'One thing I'm going to do towards my vision'.

Facilitator's notes

1 This activity provides a change in tempo and style from analytical activities, and enables participants to think more freely before they begin to use various analytical techniques to focus on strategies and action plans.

2 This activity can be very relaxing, and plenty of time should be allowed for participants to slow down and allow themselves to visualise and imagine. Some people find this much harder than others. You should be in a comfortable, relaxed position yourself. Pause at the end of each sentence, and read very slowly. Keep a watch on participants. If someone falls asleep, let them sleep!

3 Check whether this is an activity your group will be comfortable with. In some cultures, it may not be appropriate; in others, people may be very familiar with this form of meditative activity.

Time: 40 mins

Sculpture: What needs to change?

Objectives

1 To help the participants to clarify and share what they have learned about gender that is oppressive and needs changing.

2 To start to identify ways of changing oppressive gender roles.

3 To bring the whole group together, have fun and be creative.

Method

1 Introduce the theme of the sculpture: 'Women and Men Worldwide: What needs to change?' Allow participants 5-10 minutes to brainstorm ideas. Write these on a newsprint.

(5-10 mins)

2 Explain how sculpturing works (see *Facilitator's notes*). Ask for a volunteer to be the first sculptor. It needs one courageous person to start the ball rolling! Stress that the sculpture is created by everyone and each person sculpts one idea only.

3 The first volunteer sculptor uses as many people as necessary to make a human sculpture illustrating one idea s/he has about the theme. Then s/he explains what the sculpture represents.

4 Write up the main ideas raised. Continue doing this as new elements are added. Ask everyone what they think about the sculpture. Does anyone want to add another idea? Someone in the actual sculpture can ask for a replacement, step out and become a sculptor. The new sculptor builds onto the existing sculpture, by altering people's positions, adding new people, using props like tables and chairs. S/he explains what new idea this represents.

5 Continue with new sculptors until everyone is happy with the sculpture created. You could take a photograph to keep a record of it. The final sculpture should contain all the ideas the group raised.

(25 mins)

6 Recap the main points made, and use them as a basis for discussion:

How can we contribute to making changes we have seen as necessary?

7 If there is time, you could 'destroy' the original sculpture in ways that show these changes happening — this is an empowering way to finish the session and it is fun!

(15 mins)

Facilitator's notes

1 This is an energising exercise, helpful when people seem tired, muddled or lacking in direction.

2 'Living sculpture' is a method that can be used to express any concept in a visual, physical way, rather than verbally. (it has been used to expressempowerment, machismo, etc.) One person acts as sculptor to arrange the others to represent the concept as a tableau or single image. People then take it in turns to be the sculptor and change the sculpture until it represents all the ideas.

3 It is important to finish the session on a hopeful note: that changes ***are*** *possible.*

4 This activity can be used after discussion about gender roles and needs, or later in the workshop, as a preparation for defining strategies and action plans.

5 A variation of this would be to ask participants to break into small groups, and ask each group to produce a sculpture. Each group then shows their sculpture to the other groups. You can then reconvene the group for discussion, and find ways of combining all the sculptures into a single work of art!

Time: 1 hr

Maseno West: Impact evaluation

Objectives

1 To show the positive impact of gender training at grassroots level.

2 To show the importance of institutional structural and policy support for the success of gender training.

3 To identify possible weaknesses and strategies for further success.

Method

1 Give out copies of **Handout 110** Maseno West Case Study to each participant for them to read.

(10-15 mins)

2 Divide into small groups to discuss and answer the questions. Ask participants to write the answers on a flipchart.

(30 mins)

3 Put up all the flipcharts and ask each group to report back in turn. Ask one group to report on each question, with other groups adding any additional comments.

(30 mins)

4 Do a round asking each person to say 'What I can take from this case study to use in my work'.

(15 mins)

Materials

Flipchart, pens, **Handout 110**

Facilitator's notes

1 The most important things to bring out are the need for gender training to be backed up with policies, structures and practices.

2 One of the possible drawbacks could be said to be that it was originally a 'top-down' approach—depending on one man's enthusiasm and commitment to justice.

3 The possibilities for the future include:

a. Introducing a legal rights component to workshops — including property rights, custody of children and writing of wills. (This is already happening in the project)

b. Women-only workshops; support and discussion groups to focus on women-specific issues such as sexuality, sexual harassment, domestic violence, contraception and women's health.

Maseno West gender training for the area community development programme of Kenya

Maseno CPK (Church of the Province of Kenya), is a new diocese located in the Western Provinces of Kenya. Much of the area is drought-prone and there is little local industry. A significant proportion of the male population live and work in the cities, leaving women and families to survive on subsistence farming and the little money sent by the men. Even among the men who remain, post-colonial and cultural patterns of behaviour dictate that they take little responsibility for the bulk of agricultural and domestic labour but continue to exercise control and authority over their families and property. As a consequence, women in the area tend to be overburdened with work and have limited cash to meet household expenses.

The project

In 1990, the diocese appointed a new development coordinator who had experience of working in community mobilisation and in awakening awareness of gender and development issues. He approached Oxfam with a proposal to support a gender and development training component in the diocesan community programme. The proposal's emphasis was on women's over-work, the absence of men from the rural areas and traditional myths about men and women. The development coordinator's strong stand was that the key to tackle poverty was a change of attitudes and behaviour among men in the community.

The programme objectives were:

1 To explore ways of involving all community members (both men and women in various development activities.

2 To enable community members to examine and change their attitudes towards the different roles of men and women so that they can work together to plan and implement projects.

3 To address the role of male responsibility in the development process, in order to reduce women's work burdens.

These objectives were to be achieved through gender-in-development training workshops for staff, clergy and community.

Training model

The Maseno West's gender-in-development training takes the form of three-day residential workshops. The topics covered include:

a. The role of women and men in the Bible.
b. Assumptions about women and men in the culture.
c. An analysis of the present roles of men and women and what they do daily.
d. The nature of development and factors which retard development.
e. Participatory leadership.
f. Action for development.

The Bible is used as the entry point for addressing the nature of present-day gender relations. The characters and histories of Old Testament figures suchas Sarah, Deborah, Ruth, and Abraham, form the basis for debate and discussion. A composite of these biblical figures are developed by the participants as role models for their own lives. The other activities of the workshop such as the 24-hour day and planning for development are all integrated into the biblical model.

In addition to the gender-in-development workshops, gender-awareness training forms part of other workshops and training.

Oxfam's involvement

Oxfam Kenya had been committed to gender work and running gender training courses with partners for many years. The Maseno CPK development coordinator attended one of these courses. After this he submitted the project proposal for gender training in the diocese. Oxfam met with the diocese to discuss gender issues and agree programme objectives. The programme began in 1991 and had continued for two years when the evaluation took place.

The diocese

The influence of the new development coordinator plus constant meetings with Oxfam changed the attitudes and structures of the diocese, for example:

1 Policy changes to allow women to seek leadership positions e.g. of the four senior coordinators, three are now women.

2 Diocesan structures: the Synod has placed a quota of at least five women in the Synod.

3 A women's desk has been set up in the district. In contrast to the Mother's Union, this has no marital or religious conditions of membership.

The evaluation

Two consultants were asked to undertake an evaluation to measure the impact of the project.

Positive impact

1 All men interviewed are now engaged in agricultural work they had not undertaken before the training. The tasks included, cleaning, planting weeding, harvesting, tending livestock, and milking cows. Most of the above had been regarded as women's and children's work, with the exception of land clearing. Certain tasks have myths associated with them; for example, in that area there is a belief, that if a man milks a cow he will fall sick and die. The man who related this myth continued to milk, despite the horror of the neighbours.

2 Men were undertaking household chores normally carried out by women.

3 Many men talked of how they now sit down and discuss financial decisions together with their wives.

4 There is now a new respect for the women and what they are engaged in, as partners in development projects and as providers.

5 Technical experts and resource persons included women, and self-confidence of women has grown.

6 Increased male responsibility for the reproductive role in the family gave children confidence with their fathers, which led to closer and more enjoyable relationships. One result of this was an increased awareness of children's health and well-being. The men now take their children to the health clinics.

7 Some men had been ridiculed by neighbours and family as a result of taking on traditionally women's chores. They were mocked for allowing their wives to 'rule over them' and 'sit on them'.

Areas of concern

The project has kept to its objectives and been consistent in stressing both in workshops and in follow-up the need for development activities where women and men share both the work and the benefits of development projects. This is one of the project's strengths.

For women, however, there are many gender issues of importance which cannot be addressed within this development model. The CCS team is aware of this limitation, particularly of the lack of activities that can address women's strategic gender needs. The present training model concentrates on gender relations between couples and nuclear families. It does not address women's capacity and rights to live independently and unmarried if they choose. One young woman said that the workshop made her realise her need for a husband; she had thought she could live alone, but now she thought she needed a husband to help her with 'all the work'.

Questions

1 What helped to contribute to the success of the project?

2 What are the possible drawbacks and difficulties?

3 What could be done in future to help to take the gender work further in this project?

Time: 1 hr

Setting priorities

Objectives

1 To start focusing on strategies.

2 To provide space for women and men to express what they think the priorities are for gender-focused responses.

Method

1 Display the cards with the statements on the floor and explain the session. (See **Handout 111**)

(5 mins)

2 Divide the participants into three mixed groups and ask them to prioritise and to arrange the cards: those with which they most agree on the top and those with which they least agree at the bottom; with the rest in the middle, thus forming a diamond.

(45 mins)

3 Compare the priorities of the three groups and discuss similarities and differences with the whole group.

(10 mins)

Materials

Cards cut from **Handout 111**.

Facilitator's notes

1 You could also use, in conjunction with this activity, or just before or after it, ***Activity 92*** *Sculpture: What Needs to Change.*

2 The statements are samples, adapted from a training workshop on conflict — you can adapt these further or use your own, more appropriate to your needs and the experience of the participants in your workshop.

Priorities Statements: Diamond activity

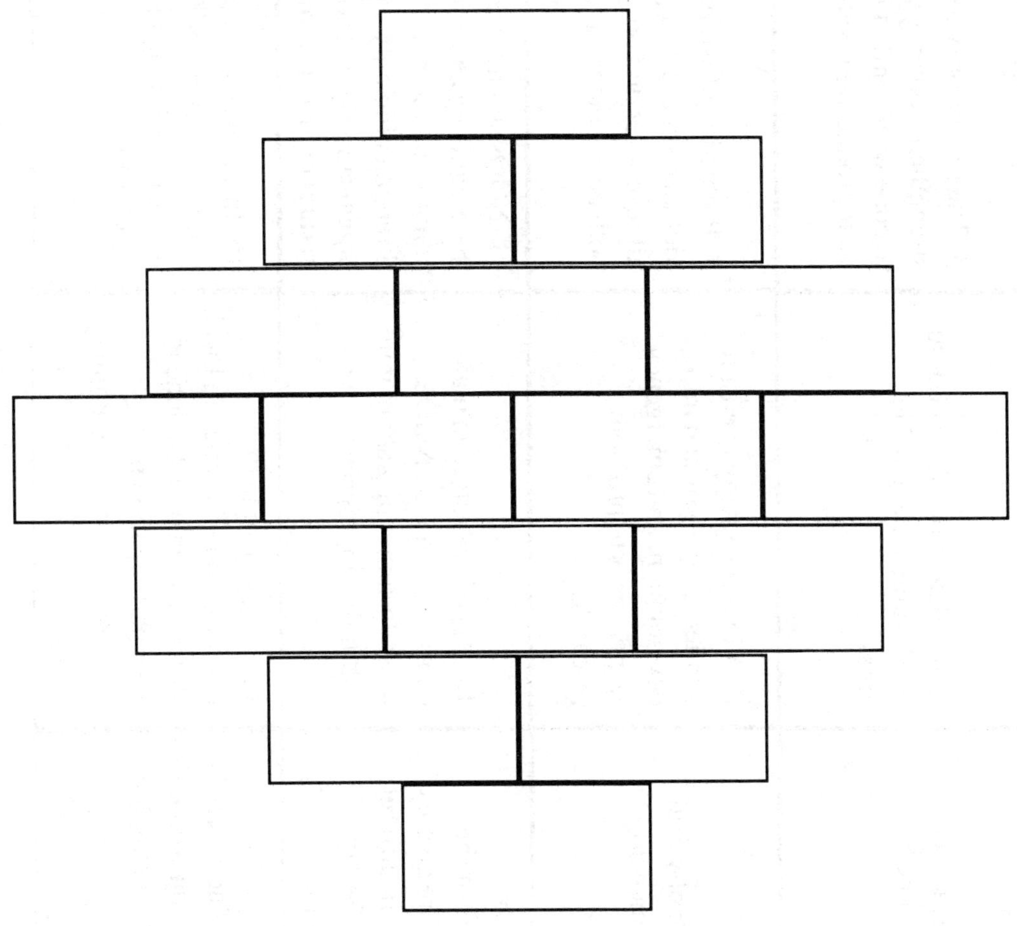

1 In times of acute crisis everyone has the same basic needs	2 It is dangerous for NGOs to send women into conflict areas.	3 The first priority to strengthen women's capacities to cope with conflict is to meet their productive needs.	4 The first priority to strengthen women's capacities in times of conflict is to look at their organisational involvement.
5 Women tolerate physical stress better than men do.	6 A major strategy to ensure gender is incorporated into development and emergency responses is to promote research.	7 Protection of women against violence should be a priority in all responses and programmes, both development and relief.	8 Health interventions should prioritise women's health.
9 Women are the best informed members of the community: they are aware of existing resources in different households and different household members.	10 Rape is a feature in many conflict situations. NGOS must do something about it in culturally appropriate ways.	11 NGOs should strengthen the organising capacities of all community members. Strengthening only women's organisations creates divisions in rural or urban communities.	12 In situations of acute crisis, existing community structures tend to be male dominated. NGOs are not in a position to question these structures.
13 In situations of acute crisis you can only work on women's basic needs, not their strategic interests.	14 Strengthening the participation of women in local structures can only be done if their participation is acceptable to other community members.	15 In situations of conflict a priority intervention for NGOs is to work with men to adjust to new realities.	16 Societies where gender relations are more egalitarian are better able to adjust to changing gender patterns in recovery phases.

Time: 40 mins

Introducing gender to our organisations

Objectives

1 To help people to find ways of introducing gender into their organisation.

2 To give people the chance to act out ways of dealing with a new or difficult situation and possible hostility.

Method

1 Tell the group the purpose of the role play, what you are going to do, and what it should show. (For example, dealing with hostility from people in their organisations when they return from a workshop on gender.)

2 Stress that people should feel free to use the activity as a way of trying out their own strategies.

There are two options:

i. Demonstrate the role play with other people from the group. You could choose to do it in a way that would not work well on purpose. You could then invite people to come up and try out their own strategies.

ii. Leave out the demonstration and invite people from the large circle to come up and try out their strategies.

3 Let the participants try out their strategies. Give support for people taking risks. *(15 mins)*

4 After 20 minutes ask people to come out of their roles and return to the large circle.

5 Ask the group which strategies worked the most effectively.

6 Ask them what were the characteristics of the effective strategies. Write these up on flipchart

7 This was used at a workshop after one participant talked about the hostility she expected from her male comrades when she went back to her organisation after the gender workshop. She was asked to take on the role of one of the men and say the kind of things she would expect him to say. She stood in the middle and greeted various women who took it in turns to role play her returning to her organisation.

Facilitator's notes

1 This activity has been used in South Africa in a popular education workshop. We have adapted it a little for use in this Manual.

2 This is a fairly open activity and participants can adapt it to suit their own situations.

(Source: ***On our Feet: Taking Steps to Challenge Women's Oppression****, CACE, UWC, South Africa.)*

Time: 2 hrs

SWOT Analysis

Objectives

1 To identify the strengths, weaknesses, opportunities and threats participants face in promoting gender-sensitive work.

2 To prepare for the identification of strategies for gender-sensitive work.

Method

1 Explain the SWOT analysis, based on **Handout 112**. *(5 mins)*

2 Pose the guide question: What are the strengths, weaknesses, opportunities, and threats that you have in relation to promoting a gender-sensitive approach in your work?

3 Divide the participants into small groups, by country or organisation if appropriate (preferably no more than four groups), and ask each group to discuss their ideas and experiences, writing down main points on paper.

4 If the groups need help in their discussion, offer guidance at this point.

5 Give each group a copy of **Handout 112** and of the SWOT chart (**Handout 113**), and ask them to fill it out drawn on prepared newsprint. *(1 hr)*

6 When each group has filled up their chart, put up each newsprint for discussion.

7 Lead an analytical discussion of the charts, comparing and categorising the items on them *.(30 mins)*

Materials

Flipchart, paper, pens
Handout 112 and 113

Facilitator's notes

1 The small groups will need guidance in brainstorming ideas — don't allow lengthy discussions to develop, but encourage participants to write their ideas down as they come.

2 This activity can lead into ***Activity 97 Recommendations for Integrating Gender*** *or to* ***Activity 98 Goals and Action Plans****.*

Handout 112 *Activity 96*

SWOT Analysis

1 The SWOT analysis is designed to help people to identify the internal strengths and weaknesses of their organisation or group, in relation to the opportunities and threats presented in the external environment.

Guide questions for this are:

- What major external opportunities do we have?
- What major external threats do we face?
- What are our major internal strengths?
- What are our major internal weaknesses?

2 This is part of a process of strategic planning, one of whose essential components is examining the relationship between internal and external environments. This should give organisations and groups the basis for identifying strategic issues, and to develop strategies.

Handout 113 *Activity 96*

SWOT Analysis Chart

Strengths	**Weaknesses**
Opportunities	**Threats**

Time: 1½ hrs

Recommendations for integrating gender

Objectives

1 To formulate recommendations for integrating gender into the organisation's programmes.

Method

1 Explain the session, going through the differences between aims and objectives, and explaining the importance of tying recommendations clearly to aims and objectives. Use SMART to explain how to set objectives. (See Facilitator's notes)

(15-20 mins)

2 Divide the participants into four thematic groups:

- assessment/monitoring
- management, staff development issues
- work with NGOs
- priority interventions and ways of working with women.

Ask each group to suggest one aim and not more than three objectives. They should produce two recommendations to achieve each objective.

(15 mins)

3 Ask each group to put up their newsprints on the wall and to select a presenter to present them to the whole group.

(40 mins)

4 Summarise the discussion, picking out highlights and filling in gaps.

(10 mins)

Materials

flipcharts, pens

Facilitator's notes

1 This activity should directly follow the SWOT Analysis (Activity 96) so that recommendations for action arise from the factors identified in that session. The participants should have their SWOT charts, and if you managed successfully to categorise the items, refer back to the discussion and points recorded on the newsprint.

2 It may be useful to remind participants to be clear about their aims as they do this activity — they should have these aims in mind in order to set out their objectives. They need to identify their aims and objectives clearly in order to come up with recommendations for what they want to achieve.

3 Remind them of the difference between aims (overriding, general, guiding, long-term, open) and objectives, which should be specific, measurable, achievable, relevant and timebound. The acronym SMART helps people to remember these criteria.

Time: 1 ½hrs

Action plans

Objectives

1 To enable the participants to identify their aims and define their objectives.

2 To enable the participants to draw up Action Plans, individually or in appropriate groups.

Method

1 Divide the participants into groups according to their organisations or countries as appropriate. Otherwise, suggest they form small groups of three or four people, and work out their goals and plans individually, but in discussion with others in their group. Ask each team to discuss and list on newsprint:

a. What are your aims and objectives?

b. What are (i) the obstacles (ii) the positive forces that will hinder or help you to achieve them?

(If you have done the SWOT analysis, participants can refer back to this.)

c. What can be done to decrease the obstacles and increase the positive forces? Consider these in terms of strategies you can adopt.

(1 hr)

2 Ask the participants to formulate their Action Plans. These should outline the action they will take to achieve their aims and objectives. They should list the actions, and clarify who will take it, and set a time for it. Emphasise that the Action Plans should be realistic and include how and when they will be implemented. They should be drawn out on newprints.

3 Remind the group that their objectives should be SMART (specific, measurable, achievable, relevant and timebound). See also **Activity 96** SWOT Analysis.

4 Ask each group of participants to share their Action Plans in the plenary, putting them up on the wall.

(30 mins–1 hr)

Materials

flipcharts, pens

Facilitator's notes

*1 This is similar to **Activities 96** SWOT Analysis and **97**Recommendations. You could adapt the SWOT activity by adding the Action Plan (Steps 2-4) to it.*

2 The obstacles and positive forces and the elements that will help or hinder can be represented graphically in a 'force-field analysis':

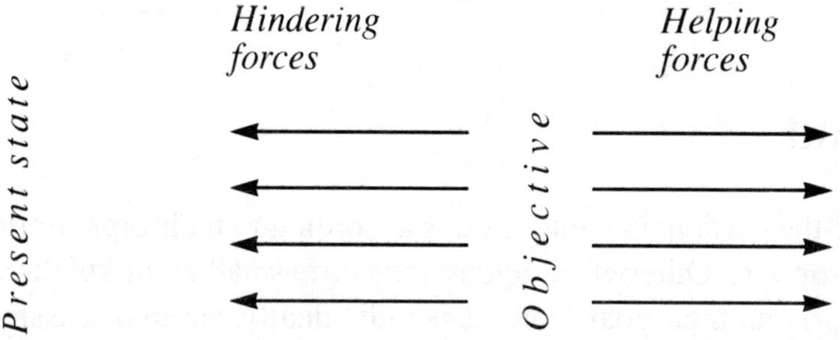

This highlights the need to work on boosting helping forces as well as decreasing hindering forces. It also helps to clarify which forces are worth putting energy into, in order to try and change.

3 It is important that each participant should have a copy of their Action Plan, so that they can show it to their manager or team, develop it further, and act upon it.

4 There is a tendency for Action Plans to be filed and forgotten after the excitement of training has been overtaken by the pressing problems back in the 'real world', outside the training centre. Encourage people to list specific objectives that they will be able to implement.

C.12 Evaluations

This section brings the workshop or training course to a close. It includes activities designed to evaluate the workshop, on the spot, and to finish the event in a positive and entertaining way. This is particularly useful when the workshop has been a long and intense one.

The 'on-the-spot' evaluation is more of a spontaneous reaction to the workshop than an evaluation as such: a true evaluation would have to measure the results of the workshop against the original objectives, and set criteria for the measurement of these. The value of the 'on-the-spot' responses lies in their immediacy and in the information they yield for you, the facilitators and planners, for the purposes of future training courses. This kind of activity gives you some indications of aspects of the training methods and content you may need to change, to reinforce or to even to remove. Of course, it is important to assess all the responses in the context of the culture and experience of the participants, and taking into account the way the dynamic of the group evolved throughout the workshop.

The sample evaluation form we have enclosed is one used frequently by Oxfam for gender workshops, and is only given as a guide. You would need to adapt it to suit your particular needs. Please refer also to **Section B: Trainer's Guidelines** for further discussion of evaluation.

It is always a good idea to end the workshop on an 'upbeat' note: the **Activity 100** Creative Evaluation is designed to provide entertainment and fun as well as the opportunity for participants to act out their responses rather than verbalise them, on a group rather than an individual level.

C.12 Activities

Time: 30 mins

Individual responses

Objectives

1 To evaluate the workshop and collect information for future workshops.

Method

1 Hand out the evaluation forms, ask all the participants to complete them and hand them in. (This is to make sure that you get all evaluation sheets in.)

(15 mins)

2 Ask all the participants to go round saying one word, phrase or sentence (depending on time available) to summarise the workshop.

Materials

Evaluation forms (**Handout 114**)

Facilitator's Notes

*1 We have provided a sample form in **Handout 114**, as a guide to the kinds of questions it is useful to ask. Please adapt this for your particular group, according to the nature of the group, the kind of workshop and what you want to find out.*

2 Remember an important aspect of this is to obtain reactions and ideas which may help you to improve your training methods and course content.

Sample evaluation form

Please write your comments below to assist us in finding out how useful the workshop has been, and how we might carry the issue forward. Thank you.

1 What did you find most useful about the workshop?

2 What did you find least helpful about the workshop?

3 Was the content of the workshop (please tick the appropriate word/s)

❏ Not useful ❏ About right ❏ Very useful

Comments:

4 Was the style of the workshop (please tick the appropriate word/s)

❏ Unhelpful ❏ About right ❏ Useful

5 What do you think you have learned in the workshop?

6 How will you use what you have learned, in your job?

7 What might stop you using what you have learned?(Include your own attitudes and fears.)

8 How would you like to see this taken forward?

9 Any other comments.

Questionnaire no:
Sheet 2

		Not at all				Completely
S.1	I find it easy to listen to others.	1	2	3	4	5
S.2	I find it easy to express my feelings to others.	1	2	3	4	5
S.3	I can analyse an organisational structure for gender imbalance.	1	2	3	4	5
S.4	I can analyse projects using the Moser Gender Planning Method.	1	2	3	4	5
S.5	I can analyse projects using the Harvard Case Study Method.	1	2	3	4	5
S.6	I know one way of collecting gender-sensitive data in a village.	1	2	3	4	5
S.7	I can explain what gender is to others.	1	2	3	4	5
	Total S					

		Not at all				Completely
B.1	I feel totally confident in groups.	1	2	3	4	5
B.2	I participate actively in a group.	1	2	3	4	5
B.3	If I hear someone making a discriminatory comment, I challenge them.	1	2	3	4	5
B.4	I feel confident to raise gender issues with men.	1	2	3	4	5
B.5	I feel confident to raise gender issues with women.	1	2	3	4	5
B.6	I have a strategy for incorporating gender into policy and practice.	1	2	3	4	5
B.7	I will get support to carry out my gender work effectively.	1	2	3	4	5
	Total B					
	Grand Total (A+K+S+B)					

Resources

This section offers a guide to some of the publications on gender and development, for general reading and reference, and to materials and manuals on gender training. There is a vast literature on gender and development, which we have not attempted to give an account of here; the titles we list are those referred to in the Manual and additional publications we feel are particularly useful.

The majority of the training manuals we refer to are written in English. Some have been translated into other languages. Oxfam has also produced a number of gender training workshop reports (many of which have been drawn upon for this Manual) and these are a source of ideas and material. They are available from Oxfam, and some of them have been translated into French or Spanish.

Contents

1 Background reading

Anderson M.B. and Woodrow P J (1989), *Rising from the Ashes: Development Strategies in Times of Disaster*, Paris: Westview Press, UNESCO.

Ashworth, Georgina (1993) *Changing the discourse: A Guide to Women and Human Rights*, Change, London.

Bakker, Isabella, editor (1994) *The Strategic Silence. Gender and Economic policy* Zed Books and the North South Institute.

Bareham J. (1991) *Womanwise: A popular guide and directory to women and development in the Third World*. Scottish Education and Action for Development. Edinburgh.

Brazeau, A (July, 1990), *Gender Sensitive Development Planning in the Refugee Context*: Geneva, UNHCR.

Bunch, Charlotte and Roxanne Carillo (1990) *Feminists Perspectives on WID, in Persistent Inequalities*, New York and Oxford: Oxford University Press

Buvinic, M.(1984) *Projects for Women in the Third World: Explaining their misbehaviour,* International Centre for Research on Women.

Bystydzienski, Jill, editor (1992) *Women Transforming Politics: worldwide strategies for empowerment*, Indiana University Press, 1992.

Enloe, Cynthia (1989) *Bananas, Beaches and Bases: Making Feminist Sense of International Politics*, London: Pandora Press.

Feldstein, Hilary Sims and Susan V. Poats (1989) *Working Together: Gender Analysis in Agriculture* (Volume 1: Case Studies & Volume 2: Teaching Notes). West Hartford, CN: Kumarian Press.

Freire, Paulo (1973) *Pedagogy of the Oppressed*, Penguin Books, Middlesex, England.

Gallagher, Margaret and Quindoza-Santiago, Lilia (editors) (1994) *Women Empowering Communication: a resource book on women and the globalisation of media.*

Isis (1986) *Powerful Images: a Women's Guide to Audiovisual Resources*, Isis International.

ISIS (1990) *Directory of Third World Women's Publications*, ISIS International.

ISIS (reprinted 1991) *Women in Development : a resource guide for organization and action,* ISIS/Intermediate Technology Publications.

Kabeer, Naila (1994) *Reversed Realities: Gender Hierarchies in Development Thought,* Verso, London & New York.

Longwe, S (1992) 'Towards Better North-South Communication on Women's Development: Avoiding the Roadblocks of Patriarchal Resistance' mimeo.

Longwe, S (1989) 'Supporting Women's Development in the Third World: Distinguishing between Intervention and Interference'. Paper presented to FINNIDA in Helsinki.

MacDonald, Mandy (1994) *Gender Planning in Development Agencies: Meeting the Challenge,* Oxfam UK, Oxford.

Moser, Caroline (1989) 'Gender planning in the Third World: meeting practical and strategic gender needs', *World Development,* 17,11,

Moser, Caroline (1993) *Gender Planning and Development* Routledge.

Mosse, J (1993) *Half the World, Half a Chance*, Oxfam, Oxford.

Oakley, A (1982 reprint) *Sex, Gender and Society*, Pitman Press, Bath.

Ostergaard, L (ed)(1992) *Gender and Development, a Practical Guide*, Routledge

Radcliffe S. with Townsend J. (1988) *Gender in the Third World. A Geographical Bibliography of Recent Work*, IDS, Development Bibliography Series 2.

Riano, Pilar, editor (1994) *Women in Grassroots Communication:Effecting Global Change*, Sage Publications.

Rogers, Barbara (1980) *The Domestication of Women: Discrimination in Developing Countries*, London, Tavistock Publications.

Rowbotham, Sheila and Mitter, Swasti (editors)(1994) *Dignity and Daily Bread: new forms of economic organising among poor women in the Third World and the First*, Routledge.

Schuler, M. Ed. (1992) *Freedom from Violence: Women's Strategies from Around the World*, UNIFEM WIDBOOKS, New York.

Sen, G & Grown, C (1988) *Development Crises and Alternative Visions: Third World women's perspectives*, Earthscan, London.

Townsend J. (1988) *Women in Developing Countries — A select annotated bibliography for Development Organisations*, IDS Development Bibliography Series 1.

United Nations (1991) *The World's Women 1970-1990: Trends and Statistics*. United Nations, New York.

UN Publications, (1993) *Methods of Measuring Women's Economic Activity*.

Wallace T. with March C (eds.) (1991) *Changing Perceptions: Readings on Gender and Development,* Oxfam.

Waring, Marilyn (1988) *If Women Counted: A New Feminist Economics*, New York: Harper Collins.

Young, Kate (ed.) (1988) *Women and Economic Development: Local, Regional and National Planning Strategies.*

Young, Kate et al (eds) (1984) *Of Marriage and the Market: Women's Subordination in International Perspective*, London, CSE Books.

Young, Kate (1993) *Planning development with women. Making a world of difference*, Macmillan, London.

Zed Books and the UN/NGO group on Women and Development: *Women and World Development Series* (They are available free of charge to developing countries from the NGLS, United Nations, Palais des Nations, CH-1211 Geneva, Switzerland.)

Vickers, Jeanne (1991) *Women and the world economic crisis.*
Forbes Martin, Susan (1992) *Refugee Women*
Smyke, Patricia (1991) *Women and Health*
Tomasevski, Katarina (1993) *Women and Human Rights*
Bullock, Susan (1994) *Women and Work*
Rodda, Annabel (1991) *Women and the Environment*

Journals:

Oxfam, *Focus on Gender*: journal with a different focus each issue giving perspectives on gender and development; three issues per year. Case studies, practical debate, and images based on Oxfam's field experience.

Tribune Magazine: Ideas and graphics for training activities on a variety of topics such as gender and debt, health, water, etc. Particularly useful for training with grass roots women. Available in English, Spanish and French and is free to people in Asia, Africa, Latin America, Middle East, South Pacific and Caribbean. Available from International Women's Tribune Centre (see organisations list).

2 Training Resources

Anderson M.B. and Woodrow P J (1989), *Rising from the Ashes: Development Strategies in Times of Disaster*, Westview Press, UNESCO, Paris. Full details and case studies of CVA method (Capabilities and Vulnerabilities Analysis.) used in dealing with emergencies. This method begins from a basis of gender awareness and is an extremely useful tool.

Houston, Gaie *Little Red Book of Groups and how to lead them better* Rochester Foundation. Provides help and exercises on how to lead a small informal group and cope with or change what is happening. Covers clear communication, understanding group dynamics, and how to empower all the members.

Crone, Catherine and Carman St John Hunter (1980), *From the field — tested partipatory activities for trainers*, World Education, New York. Developed for trainers by trainers to use in the field, it includes five areas of activities: becoming a learning group, discovering needs, choosing and using methods, evaluation, and planning and field testing participatory learning activities. The activities are learner-centred and involve techniques of doing, analysing, and reflecting. Step-by-step instructions suggesting time, material and setting are provided. Also contains comments on trainers' experiences of using activities with particular groups. Available from: World Education, 210 Lincoln Street, Boston, MA 02111, USA

Daswani, M et al. (eds.) (1989), *Participatory Training for Women*, Explores the various dimensions involved in training poor illiterate and semi-literate women at the grassroots level. Includes case studies of participatory training programmes for women pavement dwellers, community health workers, rural women, a women's awareness camp, women activists, and trainers; and reflections on women's learning processes, pre-training preparation, training methodology, support systems for women learners during training, and trainer roles, and training for empowerment. Available from Society for Participatory Research in Asia, 45, Sainik Farm, Khanpur, New Delhi — 110062.

Hope, Ann & Sally Timmel (1984), *Training for Transformation: A Handbook for Community Workers*, Volumes 1,2,& 3, Mambo Press. Designed for community workers, educators, and development practitioners. Book 1: critical awareness theory; tools to help people shape their own lives; putting it into practice. Book 2: skills for participatory education, group leadership, and goal achievement. Book 3: long-term planning and building solidarity in people's movements. Sections on basic participatory learning techniques, listening surveys, making and using codes, and working with groups. Includes activities, charts, graphics and resources. There is little reference to gender. Available from: Mambo Press, P.O. Box 779, Gweru, Zimbabwe

Srinivasan, Lyra (1990) *Tools for community participation — a manual for training trainers in participatory techniques*, PROWESS/UNDP Technical Series. An approach to participatory training that has been successfully used by United Nations Development Programme in the water supply and sanitation sector. Section 1: principles of community participation in development, planning and designing of training workshops, and evaluation and follow-up techniques. Section 2: participatory training activities including many interesting and unusual methods, described step-by-step. Includes photographs, charts and simple drawings. A short video is available as a complement to the manual. Available from: Women, Ink.777, United Nations Plaza, 3rd Floor, New York, NY 10017, USA

Svendsen, D.S. & Wijetetilleke (1983), *Navamaga: Training Activities for Group Building Health and Income Generation*, Washington, D.C, OEF International. Includes over 60 innovative training activities for rural communities, on identifying needs and developing small-scale health and income-generating projects. Though designed for use with literate groups, the interactive nature of the activities and illustrations make it adaptable for non-literate groups. Available from: Women, Ink.777, United Nations Plaza, 3rd Floor, New York, NY 10017, USA.

Vella, J (1989), *Learning to teach: Training of trainers for Community Development*, Washington, D.C., OEF International. Based on the principle of educating through the eyes of the learner. Clearly-defined tasks for each activity conclude with a "proof of learning" summary. Numerous illustrations, photographs, and charts. Recommended for anyone new to participative training or running a training of trainers session. Available from: Women, Ink.777, United Nations Plaza, 3rd Floor, New York, NY 10017, USA.

Fearnley C, Seed V, Peck C and Hyanus M (1990) *Missing Links: Development — Racism, Power and Responsibility*, Training for Awareness, Analysis Action. RVA, London (Amwell St London). A training pack which looks at issues of power in development work, with a main focus on racism. Some activities would be useful for gender training because of the similarities between anti-racism and gender training, and because in most NGOs racism needs to be considered as well as sexism.

Meachim Sally, Richards Dave, Williams Ohnkeni (1992) *Focus for Change: Class, gender and race inequality in the media, in an international context*, Reading International Support Centre, 103 London Street, Reading, Berks RG1 4QA5. Tel 0734 586692 Fax 0734 594357. Teaching pack for UK groups about inequality in the world. It links participants' own experience with wider political/economic structures and looks at the interlinking of oppressions — mainly class, race and gender. Information on training in sensitive subjects, and a source of images, and activities on communications and the media.

3 Gender and Development Training Resources

Canadian Council for International Co-operation (1991), *Two Halves Make a Whole: Balancing Gender Relations in Development*. In five sections including a general discussion of gender and development, gender and development training, case studies, and evolution of theories and practice. Training material includes activities adapted from Harvard and Moser methods and sample formats for workshops. Contains case study presentations of the integration of gender into institutional programmes.

CACE, Centre for Adult and Continuing Education, University of the Western Cape (1993) *Gender, Development and Power: some issues and methods for gender trainers*, Private Bag X17, Belville 7535, Cape Town, South Africa, tel (021) 959 2798/9, fax (021) 959 2481. Report on a workshop held in the Western Cape. Describes some 'gender training nightmares', and examines different aspects of power and types of resistance.

Mackenzie, Liz *On our feet: taking steps to challenge women's oppression: A handbook on gender and popular education workshops*, Centre for Adult and Continuing Education, University of the Western Cape, Private Bag X17, Belville 7535, Cape Town, South Africa, tel (021) 959 2798/9, fax (021) 959 2481. Three sections: Getting a foothold (a background on gender and popular education); Stepping out (how to organise and run a workshop to challenge gender oppression); and Up and Running (a selection of workshop exercises).

Coady International Institute, *A Handbook for Social/Gender Analysis*, Ottawa: Social and Human Resources Development Division, Canadian International Development Agency, 1989. Public Affairs, CIDA, 200 Promenade du Portage, Hull, Quebec, K1A 0G4. Designed as part of a training programme for CIDA staff to improve skills in development planning. Includes a section on rapid appraisal techniques.

Commonwealth Secretariat (1992), *Entrepreneurial Skills for Young Women : A Manual for Trainers*, London: Women and Development Programme, Commonwealth Secretariat, Marlborough House, Pall Mall, London SW1Y 5HX, UK. Contains many clearly designed activities for developing entrepreneurial skills among women in the informal sector (both literate and illiterate). Three sections: gender training, achievement motivation training, and starting and running a business.

Commonwealth Secretariat (1984): *Tutors Manual on Training Skills for Women*, Commonwealth Secretariat, Marlborough House, London SW1Y 5HX. A manual to focus trainers' awareness of and ability to analyse their own strengths and weaknesses, and to build their competence. Contains a range of materials which have been tested in workshops.

El Bushra, Judy & Eugenia Piza-Lopez (1993) *Development inconflict: the gender dimension—Report of an OXFAM AGRA East workshop held in Pattaya, Thailand 1-4 February 1993*, Oxfam UK/I, ACORD. Contains case studies and workshop methodologies. Includes participatory activities on issues such as: the impact of conflict on gender relations, survival strategies, psycho-social effects of conflict; and the use of tools like the Harvard Framework, Capabilities and Vulnerabilities Analysis, and Timelines.

African Women Development and Communication Network (FEMNET) (1993): *Gender and Development: A FEMNET Manual for Trainers*. FEMNET Kenya, Raja & Sons Building Westland, PO Box 54562, Nairobi, Kenya. The FEMNET Team's methodology is based on the Harvard method of gender analysis. Other tools of gender analysis are also used in the case study work, and there are a number of long and short case studies.

Guijit, Irene (1994) *Questions of Difference: PRA, Gender and Environment*, International Institute of Environment and Development (IIED), Reading, UK. An audio-visual training package of film sequences and case studies from Brazil, Pakistan and Burkina Faso, with supporting documentation and slides. It can be used for half-day to three-day training modules. Available in French, Portuguese and English from IIED.

Institute of Development Studies, Sussex University (1992) *Gender and World Development*. A training pack for the use of tutors in development training. It consists of subject modules on Socio-Economic statistics, Employment, Health, Housing, Urban Transport, Household Resource Management and Planning in Agricultural Production, and accompanying tutor's notes. Available from Publications Office, IDS, Sussex University, Brighton, East Sussex BN1 9RE, UK, Fax 0273 691647

Kindervatter, Suzanne (1987) *Women working together for personal, economic and community development: A handbook of activities for women's learning and action groups*, OEF International, Washington, DC. Guidelines to address the needs of low-income women, and 18 participatory training activities, on themes of group formation, goal setting, business skills, community organising, and women's rights. Line drawings, posters, stories, role plays and other interactive techniques to build self-esteem and confidence. Many activities can be used with illiterate groups. Available from: Women, Ink. 777 United Nations Plaza, 3rd Floor, New York, NY 10017, USA

Kraus-Harper, Uschi and Harper, Malcolm (1991) *Getting down to Business: a training manual for businesswomen*, Intermediate Technology Publications, Myson House, Railway Terrace Rugby CV21 3HT. Designed to assist trainers to organize and conduct more effective courses for women in business.

May, Nicky (1991) *No short cuts: a starter resource book for women's groups field workers*, Change, London. Four main sections: field worker support for women's groups; women's group organisation; women's group activities; and resources. Includes ideas for choosing viable projects, practical advice for obtaining funding, managing the project, and lists resources ona variety of activities from handcrafts to health, plus a list of research and resource centres.

Overholt C, Anderson M.B., Cloud K. & Austin J.E. (1985) *Gender Roles in Development Projects: A Case Book*, Kumarian Press, West Hartford, USA. Provides background reading in technical areas concerning women and development and introduces an overall framework for project analysis, and case studies as a vehicle for group discussion. The case studies are from seven developing countries, each a different type of project. The Harvard method of analysis develops problem-solving and decision-making skills and is based on participants taking an active part in the learning process.

Parker, A. Rani (1993) *Another Point of View: A Manual on Gender Analysis Training for Grassroots Workers*, UNIFEM. A training technique to provide a tool for designing and implementing gender-sensitive programmes with particular relevance for community-based development workers. Provides a step-by-step guide for a two-day workshop for community development practitioners or trainers. Focuses on drawing out local gender perceptions and expectations, to enhance the transformative possibilities of programmes.

Piza-Lopez, Eugenia & Candida March (1990) *Gender Considerations in Economic Enterprises — AGRA East Meeting 20-23 November 1990*, Philippines, Gender & Development Unit, Oxfam. Covers the main aspects of incorporating gender analysis and building gender awareness into income-generation projects. Includes papers on methodology, the adoption of a holistic approach, and project design, followed by case study experiences from the Philippines, Java, Kenya and Vietnam. Contains guidelines on developing an agenda, the design and implementation of projects, and evaluation of economic enterprises for women.

Sandler, J and Sandhu, R (1986) *The Tech and Tools book: a guide to the technologies women are using worldwide*, Intermediate Technology Publishing, UK. A research manual of appropriate technologies used throughout the world in women's projects. Includes sections on support systems, credit training and technology transfer.

Seed, Jan (1989) *East Africa Gender Training Workshop, Arusha, Tanzania 21st-23rd June 1989, Report*, Gender and Development Unit, Oxfam. Describes the range of activities and exercises undertaken, and the responses of participants. The activities cover values or attitudes towards women and men, reality of women's and men's lives, analysis of projects for how they involve women and men (Moser method), and strategies for changing the involvement of women and men.

Thomas-Slayter B, Lee Esser A, Dale Shields M, *Tools for Gender Analysis: A Guide to Field Methods for Bringing Gender into Sustainable Resource Management*. Focuses on the use of gender analysis to increase the effectiveness of development programmes in general, and projects for sustainable resource management in particular. Produced by the ECOGEN (Ecology, Community Organisation, and Gender) research project carried out in three North American universities, and presents a number of participatory appraisal tools for analysing gender relations and resource use at the community or village level.

Varghese, Shiney & Jan Seed (1991) *Training of Gender Trainers Workshop, Vishwa Yuvak Kenra, New Delhi, India 24 February — 3* March, Gender and Development Unit, Oxfam. Provides materials and content for the training of gender trainers. In two main sections: understanding gender (exercises and reflections on gender roles, policy approaches); and gender training skills (planning strategies, group dynamics, evaluation and follow up).

Warren S T (1992) Gender and Environment: Lessons from Social Forestry and Natural Resource Management. A Sourcebook. Aga Khan Foundation, Canada. The material in the Sourcebook came out of a workshop held in 1990, and is organised into five sections:

background articles on issues of gender, environment, and natural resources, including discussion questions;

a set of cases from the field with discussion questions, related to exercises in the book;

exercises related to the cases and background articles;

a glossary of relevant terms;

a bibliography of published resources and easily accessible material.

Whyld J, Pickershill D and Jackson D (eds) (1990) *Update on anti-sexist work with boys and young men*, Whyld Publishing Co-op, Moorland House, Caister, Lincs LN7 6SF. A compilation of reports on different kinds of work on sexism with young men and boys, mostly in the UK. Gives reading lists on anti-sexist work with boys, teaching materials on gender, sexuality and sexism, and materials on masculinity and the men's movement.

Plus packs and Audiovisual Aids

Birmingham Development Education Centre (1989) *Working Now*. Black and white photos of women and men in non-stereotyped work. Activities designed for primary schools in UK but can be adapted.

Intermediate Technology (1994) *Do it herself An international study of Women's technical knowledge and innovation*. The exhibition explores the 'unsung' innovations that women throughout the world have devised. Based on 22 case studies from 17 countries, consists of 16 laminated panels and a book of activities. The panels include: Involving women, defining technology, sharing knowledge, developing policy, recognizing wisdom, planning action, beginning locally. Activities include: Women's and men's work and how this effects technical innovation; Why is women's knowledge often ignored? Why does it matter? The book also has the text of the exhibition, details on the photographers, and a list of further resources. For further information/ possibility of borrowing or hiring the exhibition contact the British Council of Intermediate Technology office nearest to you. Intermediate technology offices: Bangladesh: GPO Box 3881, Dhaka 1000; Kenya: PO Box 39493, Nairobi; Peru: Casilla Postal 18-0620, Lima 18; Sri Lanka: 33 1/1 Queens Road, Colombo 3; Sudan: PO Box 4172, Khartoum; UK: Myson House, Railway Terrace, Rugby CV21 3HT; Zimbabwe: PO Box 1744 Harare. (Summaries of case studies used in *Do it herself* are in the *Appropriate Technology Journal*, vol 20 no. 2 September 1993, IT publications.)

Institute of Social Studies Trust *Critical Voices for ICPD*. An accessible, short, hard-hitting document of the responses of rural Indian women to the population problem in the form of quotations and suggestions. Institute of Social Studies Trust, Kamala Devi Bhavan, 5, Deen Dayal Upadhyay Marg, New Delhi — 110 002, tel 3312861, fax 00 11 3323850

International Labour Standards and Women Workers: information kit — a multi-media information kit on women workers' rights, to promote awareness and improve the economic and social status of women. International Labour Office (ILO), 1993.

Oxfam (1992) *How does the world look to you?* Activity Pack on use and interpretation of images. Oxfam, Oxford.

Oxfam Education Catalogue lists all of Oxfam's current education resources including videos. Available from Oxfam.

Returned Volunteer Action (1985). *Manomiya*, London, RVA. Board Game where players discover for themselves that some farmers are women, and the way the odds are stacked against them.

4 Videos

(Below is a selection of videos which we have found useful in gender training. It is by no means a comprehensive list.)

Action Aid (1990) *Kale Nyabo.* (25 minutes) Presents the many roles that women farmers in Central Uganda undertake to support themselves and their families. Designed to encourage student discussion. Available from ActionAid (UK) Hamlyn House, Archway, London, N19 5PG tel 071 281 4101

Anderson, Alexandra and Cottinger, Anne (1985). *Hell to Pay.*(52 minutes) Exposes the devastating effects of the foreign debt in Bolivia through the testimony of women. Available from Cinenova (distributors of films and videos directed by women) 113 Rona Road, London E2 OHU, tel 081 981 6828, fax 081 983 4441. A catalogue is available on request.

Deschamps, Lorette/Cine Sita Studio D (1986) *No Longer Silent.* (56 minutes) Looks at the various forms of discrimination faced by women in India and the struggle of some Indian women to bring about change. Covers issues such as the dowry system, the apparent bias of the legal system and the practice of aborting female foetuses identified by amniocentesis. Available from Cinenova.

Homoet, Jet and Wilkie, Simon (1993) *That Fire Within.* (62 minutes) Film about the positive achievements of women in Namibia, their roles, strategies for survival

and their families. National Film and TV School, Beaconsfield Studios, Station Road, Beaconsfield, Buckinghamshire, HP9 1LG, UK. Tel 0494 671234 fax 0494 674 042.
Intermediate Technology/The International Broadcasting Trust (1991) *Pain, passion and profit* (50 minutes) Anita Roddick (Body Shop) looks at two women running businesses to support their families and communities: Tipaga Niadiow in Ghana, processing Shea butter and Florida Ogada, in Kenya, producing clay stoves. The film looks at the problems womens face in setting up businesses. It highlights how development aid has often hindered the efforts of women in business and how few development agencies recognise the wealth of knowledge held by women, or the important role women's businesses play in the survival of communities. The video is accompanied by an information poster. Concord Films Council, 201 Felixstowe Road, Ipswich IP3 9BJ. tel 0473 726012, fax 0473 274531. Also available from IBT as a package *Women mean business* designed for young people, and suitable for business studies GCSE, the pack has the video divided into 7 sections, teachers' notes and students' activity sheets. Contact IBT, 2 Ferdinand Place, London, NW1 tel 071 482 2847 fax 071 284 3374.

International Crops Research Institute for the Semi-Arid Tropics and Television Trust for the Environment (1993) *Participatory Research With Women Farmers.* (22 minutes) Designed as an educational tool, looks at ways of involving farming communities in the production of pest-resistant cultivars for the complex, risk-prone agriculture of the semi-arid tropics. Available free to organizations in the developing countries from TVE postbox 7, 3700 AA Zeist, The Netherlands; tel (31) 3404 20499;fax (31) 3404 22484; e-mail GEONET Geo2:TVE-NL.

Jackson, Judy (1991) *Portraits of change.* (50 minutes) Stories of two women, Regina Gordhilo, from Brazil and Neila Sancho from the Philippines, who are negotiating changes in their societies and struggling against injustice and oppression. Regina became an activist when her son was killed by the police. She went on to become the first woman leader of the Rio Council and to defend the people of the shanty towns. Neila is co-founder of Gabriela, an organisation of women who help women set up income generating projects, child care facilities and campaign for human rights, against poverty and oppression. Available, with accompanying booklet giving the background of the women and an overview of women and development worldwide, from Concord Films Council.

Masri, Mai and Chamoun, Jean (1986) *Women of South Lebanon 'Zahrat El Kindoul'*. (71 minutes) The Women of south Lebanon speaking about their lives under occupation. Available from Cinenova.

Miller, Julia/IBT (1985) *Seeds of Resistance* (50 minutes). Focusing on women in La Paz Bolivia and rural Zimbabwe organising for greater economic power and to achieve equal rights, provides background to the study of the relationship between the struggle for women's rights and issues in development. Concord Film Council.

Miller, Juliet (1985) *The Impossible Decade.* (50 minutes) Commissioned by the UN this film assesses what actually happened to women during the decade for women. Interviewing women from all over the world, covers issues such as training, women's participation in development, and equality in the family. Available from Cinenova.

New Internationalist (1986) *Man-Made Famine* (65 minutes video full version, 33 minutes interviews only) Analysis and interviews with three African women farmers showing that ignoring their needs causes famine. Available from Concord Films Council.

OMA (mass organisation of Angolan women) *Angola is our Country* Examines the contribution of women to the reconstruction of Angola. Interviews with textile workers, displaced peasants in a resettlement programme organised by OMA and activists from OMA. Available from Team Video Productions, Canalot 222 Kensal Road, London W10 5BN tel 081 960 5536.

Open University (1992) *Gender Matters* (22 minutes) Part of the Developing World Series. Looks at the role of women in solving Developing World problems. Video U208/02V for course U208, Third World Development. Available to preview or buy from Open University Educational Enterprises Limited, 12 Cofferidge Close, Stony Stratford, Milton Keynes MK11 1BY.

Oxfam (1991) *Framing the Famine* (30 minutes). Looks at how the image of famine-torn Africa is constructed by TV news and charity advertisements. No particular mention of gender issues. Available from Oxfam.

Oxfam (1991) *Banking on Women* (25 minutes) Report on a credit scheme organised by women in a village in India. The scheme is run and funded entirely by its women members. Available from Oxfam.

Raghavan, Rajiv Vijay (1988) *Women's Rights in India (*27 minutes*)* Part of the People Matter: Six documentaries on Human Rights series. The film covers all aspects of Women's rights in India including reproductive rights and family planning policy. Available from the Avise Foundation , Rooseveltlaan 197. 1079 AP, Amsterdam the Netherlands. Tel (31) 20422788 Tlx 11063 Avise NL.

Sistren Theatre Collective (1985) *Sweet Sugar Rage* (42 minutes) Shows work of Sistren Theatre Collective to raise awareness about the issues effecting Caribbean Women. Sistren is an independent popular theatre company developed by working-class women in Kingston, Jamaica which uses drama in education as a means of problem-solving at a community level. Available from Cinenova.

Sweeney, Ann-Marie/ TV Viva Brazil/Piupa Production UK (1992) *Amazon Sisters* (52 minutes) Inspiring account by women from Amazon region fighting for social/political justice, defending their environment against 'Development' programmes. Available from Oxford Film and Video Makers, The Stables , North Place, Oxford OX3 9HY.

Trinh T Minh-ha (1982) *Reassemblage* (40 minutes) Challenges the stereotypes of women in Senegal. Available from Cinenova.

Trinh T Minh-ha (1989) *Surname Viet Given Name Nam* (108 minutes) Film on the repression of Women in Vietnamese society. It focuses on aspects of Vietnamese culture as seen through the history of women's resistance in Vietnam, the oral tradition, images promoted by the media and the lives and visions of vietnamese women. Available from Cinenova.

War on Want/Cinestra Pictures (1987) *Women for a Change* Highlighting the British Government's aid policies and practices in relation to women in Africa, Asia and Latin America, the film aims to raise public awareness of how the needs of women are not seen as priority by the aid planners. It then shows women organising themselves and campaigning to create better lives. Available from Cinenova.

Vera Productions (1988) *International Women's Day* (13 minutes) Explores the history of the day and shows highlights from activities organised by women. Available from Cinenova.

5 Organisations and Networks

Abantu for Development (People for Development), an NGO aiming to contribute to the capacity of African women to be articulate and be involved in the decisions that affect their lives. Trains in skills for policy and analysis in economics, media, the environment, and heath, advises, contributes to formal and informal training and education methodology from an African perspective. Promotes information and training links with centres between continents. Produces a monthly newsletter for members, focusing on development education. 8 Wisden House, Meadow Road, London SW8, UK, tel: (071) 498 9324, fax: (071) 735 6682.

Alt-WID (Alternative to Women in Development Project), initiated by Center of Concern Washington, D.C., to bring a gender, race and class critique to the development process both in developing countries and within the US. Contact Center of Concern, 3700 13th Street, N.E. Washington, D.C. 20017, US, tel: (202) 635 2757, fax: (202) 832 9494.

Asia and Pacific Women's Resource Collection Network : Training and research institution of the UN Economic and Social Commission for Asia and the Pacific. Aims to ensure the full participation of women in the economic and social development of their communities. Produces the APCWD Women's Resource

Book in collaboration with the International Women's Tribune Centre in New York. Asian and Pacific Development Centre, Pesiaran Duta, PO BOX 2224, Kuala Lumpur, Malaysia.

Association of African Women for Research and Development/Association De Femmes Africains pour la Recherche Sur le Developpment (AAWORD/AFARD) a pan-African NGO, founded in 1977, organising different research working groups which memberscan join in accordance with their areas of specialisation and research interests. Aims to create networks among African women researchers and those concerned by problems of development in Africa. Holds seminars, publishes materials including *Echo*, a quarterly bilingual newsletter, also available to the public, and the *AAWORD Journal* — a bi-annual, academic research forum. B.P. 3304, Dakar, Senegal. tel: 23 02 11, telex: 3339 CODES SG.

AWID (Association for Women in Development) aims to create and sustain an international dialogue on ways of achieving a full partnership of women and men in the creation of a better world. Publishes a Membership Directory listing individuals and organisations by subject interest as well as alphabetically. Office of Women's Programmes, 1060 Litton Reaves Hall, Virginia Tech, Blacksburg, VA 24061-0334, tel: 703 231 3765, fax: 703 231 6741.

Centre for Women's Global Leadership at Douglass College, Rutgers University, USA. Founded in 1989, the Centre's goals include developing ways of bring women's perspectives and strategies into greater visibility in public policy deliberations nationally and internationally and to build international linkages among women in local leadership that enhance their effectiveness and increase their global consciousness. Runs an annual Women's Global Leadership Institute with a thematic focus, held in June, bringing together participants to compare, contrast, and learn from each other as well as consider common strategies for the future. Contact the Director, Douglass College, 27 Clifton Avenue, New Brunswick, New Jersey, 08903, USA. Tel: (908) 8782, fax (908) 932-1180.

CHANGE, formed in 1979 to conduct research and publish reports on the condition and status of women worldwide, making links between the 'First', 'Second' and 'Third' worlds to challenge double standards and patronising attitudes. Aims to educate and alert public opinion to gender inequality and encourage international exchange of information on strategies to overcome disadvantage, discrimination and subordination. Campaigns, provides consultants, and publishes news bulletin, practical and issue-based books and country reports. PO Box 824, London SE24 9JS, UK, tel/fax: (071) 277 6187. For French speakers, there is a francophone CHANGE called Femmes et Changement, at BP 418, F-75527, Paris, France.

CIPAF (El Centro de Investigacion para la Accion Femenina), Dominican Republic, promotes solidarity around feminist issues relating to development. Carries out research, education through conferences, meetings and published materials including videos, seeks to change policy of popular organisations, promoting women's issues, and fosters networking with other organisations around the world. Apartado Postal 1744, Santo Domingo, Republica Dominica, tel. 532-4443.

DAWN (Development Alternatives with Women for a New Era), launched in 1984 to reflect the growing awareness of women of the need for alternatives to the dominant model of development with its adverse consequences for the vast majority of women, and for the environment. Analyses development processes and strategies,conducts research/analysis, training, advocacy, international relations, and communications activities. Publishes books and other material including *DAWN Informs*, a triennial newsletter. c/o Women and Development Unit (WAND), University of the West Indies, School of Continuing Studies, Pinelands, St Michael, Barbados, tel: 809 426 9288, fax: 809 426 3006.

FIRE (Feminist International Radio Endeavour) is a women's radio project founded in 1991, broadcasting a two-hour daily programme (one hour each in Spanish and English) on the shortwave station Radio for Peace International (RFPI) in Costa Rica, and is heard in over 100 countries around the world. FIRE enables women's voices, in all their diversity, be heard by the international community, crossing barriers of nationality, culture, race, geography and language. Live broadcasts from women's events, training, distribution of programmes on cassette, strengthening and supporting women's networks, constructing a feminist radio communications proposal. Broadcasts each day at 0000, 0800, and 1600 UCT (Universal Co-ordinated Time) in Spanish, and 0100, 0900, and 1700 UCT, in English. Frequencies: 41 meters: 7.735 MHz AM 2100-0800, 31 meters: 9.375 Mhz USB 24 hours, 19 meters: 15.030 Mhz AM 24 hours, 13 meters: 21.465 Mhz, USB 1200-0400. Send your tapes on all issues for broadcast, labelled clearly, including your name and contact details. FIRE, Radio for Peace International, APDO 88, Santa Ana, Costa Rica, tel: (506) 249 1821, fax: (506) 249 1095, e-mail: rfpicr@nicaro.apc.org

Institute for Women, Law and Development is an international network of organisations committed to the defence and promotion of women's rights on a global basis. Education, training, advocacy, networking, research, documentation. Links individuals from activist groups, research institutions, advocacy and human rights organisations throughout the world. 733 15th Street, N.W. Suite 700, Washington D.C. 20005. Tel: (1-202) 393 3663, fax: (1-202) 393 3664.

International Association for Feminist Economics (IAFFE) is a non-profit organisation advancing feminist enquiry of economic issues and educating economists on feminist points of view on the economy, fostering dialogue and resource-sharing among feminist economists throughout the world, joining with other feminist associations in educating economists, decision-makers, public officials, and the general public on feminist points of view on economic issues.

Organises annual conference, sessions at national and international meetings of economists, publishes newsletter, uses electronic mail (e-mail) network, compiles bibliographies and list of working papers, issues policy statements for public distribution. Contact Jean Shackelford, Department of Economics, Bucknell University, Lewisburg PA 17837, USA, tel. 717-524-1476, fax: 413 545 2921. To subscribe to e-mail network, send a message on e-mail to listserv@bucknell.edu, stating: subscribe femecon-l <your name>

International Women's Health Coalition, 24 East 21 Street, New York, NY 10010, tel. (212 979 8500, telex: 424 064 WOM HC.

ISIS International: Women's International Information and Communication Service. A decentralised global women's network which is coordinated by international teams: information and communication service, facilitates global communication, gathers and distributes internationally materials and information by women and women's groups. Promotes networking and solidarity . Focuses on exchanging ideas and experiences from a holistic feminist perspective which examines the patriarchal as well as political, economic and social aspects of issues with which women are concerned. Resource centre with wealth of materials covering wide range of areas. Produces several journals including Women's World, Women's International Bulletin and Women in Action. Over 50,000 contacts in 150 countries, sending material to ISIS's Information and Documentation Centre. Contact: ISIS Internacional, Casilia 2067, Correo Centra, Santiago, Chile, tel. (56-2) 633 45 82, fax (56-2) 638 31 42, e-mail: Isis@ax.apc.org.; ISIS International Quezon City Main, 1100 Philippines, tel (632) 9957512/993202, fax (632) 997512 office hours only, commercial fax Attn. ISISINTMNL (632) 8150756/8179742/9212690, e-mail: Isis@phil.gn.apc.org.

The International Women's Tribune Centre (IWTC) A non-governmental, non-profit international organisation supporting associations in the Third World encouraging active participation of women in the development process. Responds to requests for information on development projects, UN activities and future plans. Resource centre on women and development. Can assist project activities and supply information on fundraising. Publishes a quarterly IWTC Newsletter. IWTC, 777 UN Plaza, New York 10017 USA Tel 212 687 8633 Fax 212 661 2704

National Women's Network for International Solidarity in UK for women concerned with international issues. Facilitate information exchange between groups and individuals, feminist solidarity for women and women's organisations in Uk and abroad, campaigning for change in the policies of governments, aid agencies, and other institutions. Publishes monthly newsletter and Members' Register. Box 110, 190 Upper Street, London N1 1RQ, UK.

Oxfam Gender Information Network Directory is a network begun by Oxfam in 1994. Open to all gender and development practitioners interested in linking, sharing information on best practice, etc. The network includes Oxfam staff working in the UK/Ireland and in the field, Oxfam's existing partners, Southern and Northern organisations working on gender and/or with a feminist agenda. Write for a questionnaire to Sue Smith, Gender Team, Oxfam, 274 Banbury Road, Oxford OX2 7DZ.

Vrouwenberaad Ontwikkelingssamenwerking a network of professional women in Women in Development (WID) in the Netherlands, started in 1978. Organise special issue meetings, promote action research, publish position papers, advise Dutch development agencies on empowerment of women, participate in international discussions e.g. with WIDE, liaise with political parties and action groups in Netherlands. PO Box 77, 2340 Oegstgeest, The Netherlands, tel. (0) 71 159159.

Women, Ink. a project of the International Women's Tribune Centre (IWTC) to distribute material on women and development. Publishes catalogue of published material concerning women's development and empowerment internationally. 777 United Nations Plaza, Third Floor, New York, NY 10017, USA, tel. (1-212) 687 8633, fax (1-212) 661 2704.

WIDE (Women in Development Europe) is a network of women development workers and researchers, set up in 1985 after the end of the last UN Women's Decade. WIDE members share knowledge, insights and research into WID issues. The network seeks to raise awareness in European NGOs, and lobbies at international institutions and fora in support of women in the South. WIDE aims to consult the agents of change and development working in the South about their priorities in relation to women's development. Each country is encouraged to form a national WIDE group if there is not an existing women in development network in place. WIDE issues a bimonthly newsletter. Squaire Ambiorix 10, 1040 Brussels, Belgium, tel: 32 2 732 44 10, fax: 32 2 732 19 34.

Women in Law and Development in Africa (WILDAF) is a new regional network dedicated to promoting and strengthening action-strategies that link law and development to empower women and improve women's status in Africa. Facilitates communication among network members; promotes effective ways of using law as an organising and educational tool at the local national and regional levels; provides assistance in the form of training and advice to local groups in designing and improving legal programmes and strategies; coordinates the exchange of information on legal issues. Regional coordinator: Florence Butegwa, 2nd Floor, Lenbern House, Union Avenue/ L Takawira St, Harare, Zimbabwe. Tel 263 4 752105 Fax 263 4 731901/2.

Women Living Under Muslim Laws International Solidarity Network. Exchange of information through documentation centre and Dossiers, networking in order to respond to urgent appeals and situations of emergency, comparative Exchange

Programme on status of Muslim women in different countries, educational and training workshop, searches for relevant research work for dissemination. Boite Postal 23, 34790 Grabels, Montpellier, France, Tel 010 33 67 45 43 29 Fax 010 33 67 45 25 47.

Women's Exchange Programme International acts as an intermediary and offers services such as advice, fund-raising, training and organisation for international cross-cultural exchange programmes, to women's groups, organisations, networks, companies and (semi) governmental bodies in order to stimulate and support international women's networking. Mathenesserlaan 177 PO Box 25096, 3001 HB Rotterdam, Netherlands

Women's Global Network on Reproductive Rights. An autonomous network of groups and individuals who are working for and support reproductive rights for women, eg those campaigning for better reproductive laws and policies, those providing reproductive health information and counselling, those in self-help health groups. The Network builds links and exchanges between new and existing groups, initiates meetings on women's health and reproductive rights, organises and participates in international actions and campaigns, responds to requests for information, provides practical support, publishes a newsletter four times a year. NZ Voorburgwal 32, 1012 RZ Amsterdam, The Netherlands Tel (31 20) 20 96 72

Women's World Banking. A global non-profit network established in 1979 to advance and promote the full economic participation of women. Clients are women entrepreneurs at micro-level in industry, agriculture and commerce. Over 50 affiliates in over 40 countries share know-how in building financial and business services for clients. New York office used as centre for service and communications, providing institutional and financial services to affiliates. 8 West 40th Street New York, NY 10018, USA, tel. (212) 768-8513, fax: (212) 768 8519.

World University Service. Networking and lobbying for change is an increasingly important part of the work of WUS, which is committed to promoting education as a basic human rights and improving access to education across the developing world. WUS (UK): 20 Compton Terrace, London W1 2UN, UK, tel. (071) 226 6747

[illegible] Stage of [illegible] in Different [illegible] Educational and [illegible] [illegible] [illegible]
[illegible] 23, [illegible] [illegible] 1
of 15 [illegible]

Women's Exchange Program [illegible]

Women's [illegible]

Women's [illegible]

[illegible]

[illegible]

Index